SHOOTING

How to become an expert marksman with rifle, shotgun, handgun, muzzleloader and bow

Edward A. Matunas

• • •

Drawings by Dana Rasmussen

Published by Outdoor Life Books

Distributed to the trade by Stackpole Books

Copyright © 1986 by Edward A. Matunas

Published by
  Outdoor Life Books
  Times Mirror Magazines, Inc.
  380 Madison Avenue
  New York, NY 10017

Distributed to the trade by
  Stackpole Books
  Cameron and Kelker Streets
  Harrisburg, PA 17105

Library of Congress Cataloging-in-Publication Data

Matunas, Edward.
    Shooting: how to become an expert marksman with
rifle, shotgun, handgun, muzzleloader, and bow.

    Includes index.
    1. Shooting.   I. Title.
SK37.M37 1986   799.3   85-32098
ISBN 0-943822-63-7

*This book is dedicated to the memory
of my father, Edward J. Matunas*

Acknowledgments

A great many people helped to make this book possible. To all those who have given me their assistance during the past thirty-seven years I express my sincere thanks. Special thanks go to Dick Dietz, Chub Eastman, Pat Weisman, and the National Shooting Sports Foundation.

E.A.M.

Contents

Preface   *vii*

PART I — Shooting the Rifle

1. Aiming the Rifle   *3*
2. Making the Shot   *25*
3. Basic Shooting Positions   *31*
4. Shooting the Hunting Rifle   *36*
5. Target Shooting   *51*
6. Selecting a Rifle   *71*
7. Tuning Your Rifle for Maximum Accuracy   *89*
8. Accessories for Rifle Shooting   *97*
9. Basic Ballistics for the Rifleman   *109*

PART II — Shooting the Shotgun

10. Selecting a Shotgun   *131*
11. Skeet: Best Way to Learn Shotgunning   *145*
12. Shooting the Shotgun in the Field   *159*
13. Trap Shooting   *168*
14. Crazy Quail and Other Shotgun Games   *176*
15. Shotgun Accessories That Make Sense   *181*
16. Basic Ballistics for Shotgunners   *187*

PART III — Shooting the Handgun

17. Selecting a Handgun   *205*
18. Handgun Sights   *219*
19. Tuning the Handgun for Accuracy   *228*
20. Basic Ballistics for Handgunners   *234*
21. Useful Handgun Accessories   *245*
22. Single-Action Shooting   *254*

23. Double-Action Shooting   *265*
24. Silhouette Shooting with a Handgun   *275*
25. Shooting the Hunting Handgun   *292*
26. Handgun Holsters   *299*

PART IV — Archery
27. Selecting a Bow   *309*
28. Tuning a Bow for Accuracy   *319*
29. Selecting Arrows   *329*
30. Important Archery Accessories   *335*
31. Target Shooting   *346*
32. Shooting the Hunting Bow   *353*

PART V — Muzzleloading
33. Selecting a Muzzleloader   *361*
34. Loading the Muzzleloader   *370*
35. Shooting the Muzzleloader   *390*

PART VI — Maintaining Equipment, Skills and Safety
36. Maintaining Accuracy   *399*
37. Practice Means Reloading   *407*
38. Exercises to Increase Shooting Skills   *425*
39. Safety with Firearms and Ammunition   *428*
    Index   *435*

Preface

"Shooting" can have many different meanings. To some, "let's go shooting" means rounding up some tin cans and a supply of 22 ammo, and heading for an empty lot. To others, it might mean a trip to the range to determine the worth of a certain rifle and/or lot of ammunition. Shooting can mean hitting steel targets on a silhouette range or shattering clay targets on a trap or skeet field. Shooting also means putting an arrow into the gold, pouring powder and shot down the barrel of a muzzleloader, or bringing a quarry to bag.

Despite these differences, all shooters have a common goal: to hit the target. It doesn't matter whether the range is 25 or 600 yards or whether the target is paper, steel or clay, or a bird or animal. Every shooter would like to become a proficient marksman in the shortest possible time. Unfortunately, it takes many shooters a lifetime to develop only a modicum of proficiency. They fail to enjoy shooting fully because it is hitting that makes it fun. However, hitting need not be difficult if you understand and practice the basic principles of shooting.

This book will show you just how easy shooting is if you obey these principles. After reading the parts that cover your favorite shooting sports, return to those pages from time to time to refresh your memory. This will help you maintain your skills and develop the greatest proficiency in the shortest time.

Edward A. Matunas

SHOOTING THE RIFLE

PART I

This diagram shows the principle of aiming a rifle. The shooter's eye, the rear sight, and the front sight are aligned on the target. But the sights are adjusted to raise the muzzle above the line of sight, thus compensating for the force of gravity on the bullet as it travels toward the target.

AIMING THE RIFLE 1

Aiming a rifle—that is, the proper aligning of sights on a target—is the most important step to successful shooting. Naturally, you must provide the rifle with the necessary support to keep it steady while you align the sights and during the time you squeeze the trigger. But without proper sight alignment you will be unable to hit your target.

The actual aiming of a rifle brings the bore of the gun into correct alignment to deliver the bullet to the exact spot you wish to hit. To accomplish this, you use sights. Properly adjusted sights point the muzzle at the correct elevation to compensate for the drop of the bullet. As many shooters realize, a bullet begins to fall the moment it leaves the muzzle. The accompanying drawing will help explain the relationship between the bore line, the sight line and the bullet's actual path of flight. The shooter's eye and the sights will, if connected by a straight line, lead directly to the target. The bore line, however, will point upward at some angle determined by the velocity and shape of the projectile as well as by the distance to the target.

Aligning the Sights   If the bullet is to strike the intended mark, you must align the sights with extreme exactness. Even the smallest error can effect a substantial change in where the bullet strikes. When using nonoptical sights, an error of 0.001″ in sight alignment can, depending upon the exact distance between the front and rear sight, cause a bullet to strike 1 inch from the intended mark. Research has shown that casual shooters using open sights commonly misalign them—enough to cause aiming errors of 2 to 6 inches at 100 yards, from shot to shot. This error in sight alignment is what often causes us to miss our targets.

Shooters vary in their ability to align sights, especially the nonoptical type. This is in part because visual acuity varies from person to person. It is also in part the result of the amount of practice the individual has had in sight alignment. The more often a shooter aligns sights, the more adept he will become at performing the task with a high degree of precision. An inexperienced shooter might fail to place the front bead in the bottom of the sight notch. This "coarse bead" will cause shots to go high of the intended mark. Placing the bead too low in the rear sight, drawing a "fine bead," will cause the shot to go low. Left and right orientation of the bead must also be correct, or else the shot will go to one side or the other.

The Master Eye   It's important, if you shoot with both eyes open, that you sight with your master eye. In that it is beneficial to keep both eyes open in order to maintain some depth perception, it is important to determine which is your master eye. This is true even if you partially close one eye or squint somewhat. It is easy to determine which is your master eye. Simply look at an object—say, a clock on the wall—at least 15 feet away. Then point at it with an index finger. Your arm should be fully extended when pointing, and your pointing finger should be held at eye level and midway between both eyes. Now close one eye. If your finger does not appear to move in relationship to the target, the open eye is your master eye and should be used for sighting. If your finger "moves" notably when you close one eye, then the eye that is open is not your master eye, and it should not be used for aiming. If you completely close one eye when shooting, it matters not which eye is used to align your sights.

Fortunately, most persons who shoot right-handed have the right eye as a master, and those who shoot left-handed have a left master eye. The few who find that the master eye is on the side opposite their shooting shoulder will be forced either to learn to shoot with the gun on the shoulder of the side of the master eye or to close the master eye completely when shooting.

Adjusting the Sights   If sights are to serve their function properly, they must be adjusted so that, when aligned, the line of sight and the bullet's line of flight intersect at some given range. Commonly, a rimfire rifle might be so sighted that line of sight and the bullet's path intersect at 50 yards. With a big-game rifle, the shooter often adjusts his sights so that sight line and bullet line intersect at 200 yards. But a new rifle taken from the box seldom shoots to the same point at which the sights align. Because each of us sees somewhat differently, our rifle sights must be adjusted for our individual eyes.

To adjust sights properly, you should fire a few shots at a target at a comparatively short range, perhaps 25 yards. The purpose of starting at short range is to ensure that your first shots will strike somewhere on the target. If you fired at a longer range and completely missed the target, you would not have any idea in which direction to move your sights in order to correct them. Typically, a gun might shoot high or low, thus indicating a need for a vertical (elevation) adjustment. Simultaneously, the gun may also prove to be shooting left or right of where the sights were aligned. To correct for this, move your sights horizontally (windage). The proper method of sight adjustment is to move the rear sight in the *same* direction you wish to move your point of impact. If your first shots are low and right, move your point of impact high and left. Thus, you would raise the rear sight notch and move it to the left. Front sights are moved in a direction opposite that to which you wish to move the point of impact. However, it is seldom necessary to move a front sight—most rifles' sights are designed to accomplish the necessary adjustments with the use of only the rear sight.

It is extremely important to adjust your sights with a great deal of exactness.

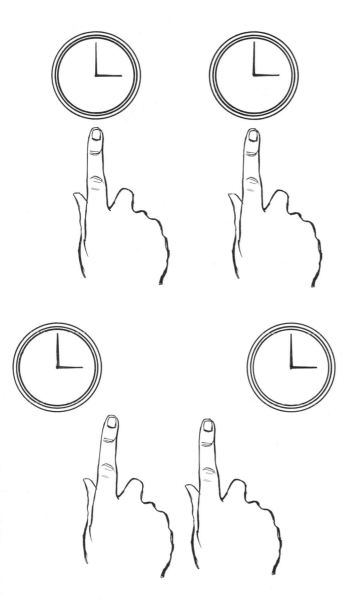

To determine your master eye, point at a clock on a wall and close one eye at a time. The finger and image will stay aligned when only the master eye is open, but will move to the left or right when the master eye is closed.

Sights should be adjusted while shooting from a benchrest, which offers a rock-solid position. The forearm should be hand held, but the back of the hand should be supported by a sandbag or rolled-up coat. Every effort should be made to ensure that the gun is motionless and the sights perfectly aligned when the trigger is squeezed. If your gun is not properly sighted in, you will be unable to score hits with it later on.

After sighting in at 25 yards, move the target to a full 100 yards' distance and repeat your firing. Centerfire rifles are often best adjusted so that the point of the bullet's impact at this range is about 2 inches higher than your aiming point.

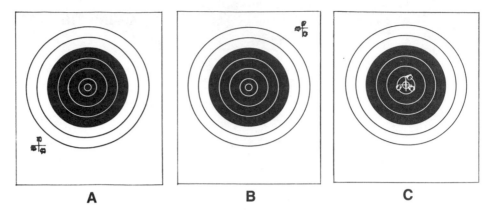

A   B   C

Adjusting sights: If your first shots are low and left (A), move rear sight up and right. Fire several more rounds. If they are slightly high and right (B), lower the sight slightly and move it to the left. Repeat until the shots are striking the aiming point. Preliminary shooting should be done at short range.

A typical benchrest for sighting in a rifle. Shooter is equipped with sandbags for supporting the fore-end and stock, and a spotting scope for determining hits.

Sighting in his rifle at the bench, this shooter shows good form. The rifle is rested on the front sandbag, the shooter's left hand is "steering" the rear bag—everything is perfect for optimum results.

After firing his first group, shooter adjusts his scope. Rifles are generally sighted in at 25 yards, then at 100 yards.

Depending upon your caliber and the bullet being used, this will result in your rifle hitting the point of aim at about 200 yards. Regardless of what you may have been told, you cannot sight in at a short range. Differences in velocities, bullet shape and other factors make it essential that you do your final sight adjustments at 100 yards. Some shooters even go to longer ranges for final adjustments, but rimfire shooters can sight in so as to have the line of sight and bullet impact coincide at 50 yards.

When adjusting sights, fire in groups of three shots and consider the center area of the shots as your point of impact. Allow your barrel to cool completely between groups, as bullets fired from a warm barrel may not group in the same place as shots from a cold barrel.

The use of an aperture sight (often called a peep sight) differs little from the use of a standard open sight. The bead is easily centered in the aperture, but the alignment of the bead on the target remains most critical. With a scope, the center of the aiming reticule is placed on the target. (More on these sights in a short while.)

Sight alignment demands the maximum in precision. If you need glasses, be sure to have your shooting glasses (always worn for eye safety) ground to your prescription. Because sight alignment is critical to shooting, it is important to understand the shortcomings and the advantages of the various types of sights.

Types of Sights

Open Sights   Rifle sights come in a great profusion of types and value. The most common is the open sight. Most factory rifles come equipped with either open "iron" sights or no sights at all. Factories furnish open sights not because they are the most efficient but, rather, because they are the least expensive.

Open sights were devised shortly after the invention of firearms. Ancient matchlock rifles often can be found with some form of iron sight, even though crude and nonadjustable. Improved iron sights came about with the advent of rifled barrels. Today, almost all rifle iron sights are adjustable for windage and elevation.

Iron sights with easy-to-make adjustments do away with one of the biggest drawbacks of open sights. But some iron sights are extremely difficult to adjust accurately for exact point of impact desired. Driving a sight to the left or right in its dovetail with a hammer and punch does not allow for very precise increments of windage adjustment. Some iron sights have elevation slides that are moved into position by loosening screws. These are supposedly a great improvement over the crude stepped-ladder slides often used. However, screw adjustments are not without fault. They are difficult to loosen without losing the original setting, and the position to which you move the sight may well be altered notably when you tighten the screws.

On the best iron sights windage is controlled by a threaded sight blade and a windage screw. A turn of the windage screw provides a very positive and constant amount of movement. It is relatively easy to repeat a given amount of

Best open sights are easily adjustable. On this sight on a Remington rifle, windage and elevation adjustments are controlled by two screws.

The open sight on this rifle is adjusted for windage with a hammer and punch and for elevation with a stepped "ladder." Such adjustments are hard to make when sighting in.

movement with such an arrangement. Elevation is changed by loosening a single screw that holds a sliding sight base to a tapered ramp. The ramp and base are marked clearly to indicate relative position to one another. All this allows for comparatively easy adjustment.

The correct fit of front sight bead to rear sight notch is important when open sights are used. If the front bead, or blade, is too small, it will be difficult to center it in the rear sight notch. If it is too large, it may more than fill up the rear sight notch, making it impossible to shoot accurately.

The open-style sight is extremely rugged. The difficulty of sighting in each year is a bit of a burden, but once adjusted, open sights hold well, requiring a very severe knock to move them from the chosen adjustment. But difficulties in adjustment are only a small part of the problems with iron sights.

A major disadvantage of iron sights is that they hide a great deal of the target from view. The longer the range, the more they hide. Thus, iron sights are at their best for short-range shooting—50 yards or less—at large targets. In poor light, iron sights are extremely difficult to see and use. Light falling on the front bead from varying angles will cause you to see false front-sight centers, resulting in inaccuracy.

As light hits a front sight from directly overhead or slightly to the rear, the brightened portion of the bead will be its center. Under such conditions, you will center the bead in the rear notch correctly. But light striking the bead from one side will illuminate that side while leaving the other side darker. The illuminated side will then look like the center of the bead. Thus, you may well end up aligning the edge of the bead in your rear sight. The result will be a shot that goes to the side of your intended point of impact.

During the middle of a bright day, you will tend to draw a fine bead with open sights. Under poor light conditions (early morning, late evening, overcast days), you will not be able to see the relationship of front and rear sight as sharply, and you will inadvertently draw a coarse bead. Obviously, then, change in light and the resulting fine to coarse variations in alignment can make notable changes in the point of impact of a bullet fired from your rifle.

A lot of game has been taken with iron sights. But most of it has been at comparatively short ranges—a good deal of it at less than 100 yards.

Aperture Sights   The easy-to-use aperture sight does away with many of the problems of open sights. The aperture itself does not hide any portion of the target; the only portion obscured is that covered by the front bead. The exact amount of obscured target will vary with the size of the front sight and the distance to the target. At the practical ranges for an aperture sight (to about 200 yards), no notable change in hunting accuracy will be caused by increasing the size of the aperture through which you look. Therefore, most savvy hunters will remove the screw-in disk from their peep sights in order to obtain the maximum field of view and light.

When you use open sights, you must align your eye with the rear sight, then align the front sight with the rear sight, and finally align both sights on the target. This is a relatively slow procedure. To complicate things further, the human eye

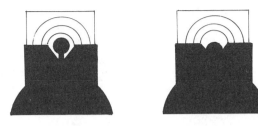

Two correct sight pictures with open sights: left, front bead covering point of impact; right, top edge of bead covering point of impact.

Drawing a coarse or too fine a bead in an open sight affects vertical accuracy. Left: Coarse bead; front sight too high in rear sight notch; shot goes high. Center: Fine bead; front bead properly positioned in rear sight notch. Right: Too fine a bead; front bead too low in rear sight notch; shot goes low.

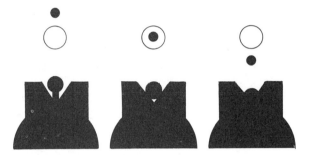

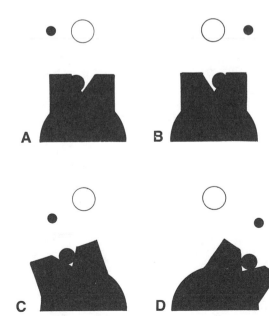

Incorrect sight pictures affect horizontal accuracy. A Bead to the left; shot goes to left.

B Bead to right; shot goes to right.

C Gun canted to left; shot goes low and left.

D Gun canted to right; shot goes low and right.

is unable to focus simultaneously on a rear sight, a front sight and a distant target. Thus, something will appear as a blur in the sight picture. Young eyes may see a sight picture with the rear sight blurred, the front sight only slightly hazy and the target in focus. But older eyes may leave both sights as impossible-to-see blurs when the target is in focus. Obviously, open sights are slow and optically difficult to use. An aperture, or peep, sight eliminates two of these problems.

Because one simply looks through the aperture of a peep sight, with the eye automatically centering on the strongest point of light (the center of the aperture), there is no need to be able to see the rear sight. In fact, most shooters who use aperture sights tend not to be conscious of the rear sight; they simply look through it as they might look through an open window. The aperture sight thus does away with the need to see the rear sight or to align the front sight with it. Because your eye automatically centers itself in the center of the aperture, you can simply look at the front bead to align it and the rear sight properly. Naturally, a bead could be positioned other than in the middle of the aperture. But if you allow your instinctive visual system to work, you will find that no conscious effort is involved in correct alignment. Thus, an aperture sight becomes easy and quick to use. Simply put the front bead *on* the target to align sights properly.

Less-expensive peep sights use a sliding bar to adjust elevation and windage. Better sights have coin- or screwdriver-operated knobs that adjust in positive "click" increments. On such sights, one can feel and hear a precise amount of elevation or windage adjustment. This makes sighting in quick and easy, with only a minimum amount of ammunition being expended. The best peep sights do not have any knobs that can be inadvertently moved, but incorporate locks for adjustments. With such sights, neither curious hands nor field abuse will result in the sight setting accidentally being moved. In my opinion, the best of all hunting peep sights is the Williams Foolproof. Once sighted in, it will stay that way until you deliberately unlock and move the adjustment screws.

For target shooting, where frequent adjustment of the rear sight is normal, large, easy-to-use, finger-adjusted, target-style knobs are preferred. However, remember that it does not take much to move such knobs. Therefore, you must handle the gun carefully and visually verify sight setting before beginning to shoot.

Correct sight pictures with aperture sights. Left: Bead on point of impact. Right: Top edge of post at point of impact.

This Ruger Mini-14 has an easily adjustable aperture sight.

Finest of all aperture sights is the Williams Foolproof. It is easy to adjust and locks into place to prevent accidental misalignment.

Good peep sights are as rugged as open sights, quicker to use and more accurate. Peep sights are ideal when the ranges are relatively short and the target is comparatively large. Peeps are a good selection when you know the gun will see a significant amount of abuse. But for most shooting or hunting, nothing can equal a good telescopic sight.

Telescopic Sights   Let me say that I firmly believe that a good peep sight is to be preferred over a cheap scope. An inexpensive scope, with poor optical qualities, is of no benefit. One must be able to see clearly under a wide range of light conditions if a scope is to prove practical. Thus, the optics of a scope and its ability to transmit light are the critical factors in determining whether the telescope is to prove a practical advantage over an aperture sight.

Additionally, a scope must be impervious to weather. If water or moisture seeps inside of a scope, it will soon be rendered useless. A fogged lens or a lens with large water deposits on the inside is not very useful for sighting. Finally, a scope and its mount must be rugged enough to withstand normal use and recoil. If the scope's adjustment tends to change with recoil or a normal amount of hard rifle usage, it will prove useless despite any optical qualities it might possess.

A good telescope sight, mounted in a set of solid rings and bases, is essential to bring out the best in any rifle.

Naturally, a scope should be able to withstand the occasional hard knock to which a rifle may be subjected.

In that the scope mount is a critical part of maintaining a scope's alignment, a very sturdy mount should be used. Fortunately, rugged mounts are the rule rather than the exception. This was not always the case, but gimmick mounts and flimsy construction are for the most part things of the past.

The weakest links in scope mount bases and rings are the screws used to hold everything together. Savvy shooters will frequently coat all screws with a few drops of a suitable grade of thread-locking substance. Such coating, when dry, will keep screws from backing out due to recoil or vibrations, yet allow for the removal of the screws if necessary.

I do not recommend the use of iodine or other rusting substances to "rust" screws into place. If the scope base or scope ever needs to be removed, it may be impossible to do so without damaging the mounting system beyond repair.

There was a time when easily removed mounts were quite popular. But as scope design improved and scopes became more rugged, the need to remove a scope in the field virtually disappeared. Also, the shooter who, in the past, removed a scope for close-in shooting has found that the improvement in scopes now provides a field of view large enough for very short-range shooting, even at fast-moving game.

Today's scopes are rugged, dependable and optically superior to the products of years ago. There is seldom a reason ever to remove one from a rifle. I have accidentally dropped scope-equipped rifles without causing any damage that rendered the scope unfit for continued service.

I hunt in rain that often doesn't quit for days and in snow, fog and extreme cold. None of these factors has affected my scopes. But a shooter who wants to be able to hunt in almost any weather must equip the scope with a good set of lens caps to keep the rain and snow off the outside of the lenses. If a shot is taken with reasonable promptness after the caps are removed, it is unlikely that enough snow or rain could get on lenses to interfere with the shooter's aiming a well-placed shot.

Despite what nonusers think, scopes are quick to use. Simply look through a scope, place the reticule on the target and shoot. Nothing could be faster. Both target and sighting reticule remain sharp because they are both on the same optical plane.

Large fields of view, standard with most of today's low-powered scopes, do away with the old complaint of it being difficult to locate moving game. Some of the older low-powered scopes had fields of view as small as 20 feet or less at 100 yards. At 25 yards, this meant a field of view of perhaps only 5 feet. Today's scopes routinely offer fields of view (at 100 yards) of 40 feet, 50 feet or even more.

Make no mistake, the magnification of a scope is one of its most important features. It is for this reason that fixed 2½- or 3-power scopes are considerably less popular than 4-power scopes. Most 4s offer a sufficiently large field of view with ample light transmission and magnification for almost any big-game application.

The inexpensive Weaver Top Mount, shown here on a Remington 700 Classic, is rugged and adaptable to almost every rifle.

The Burris Top Mount, shown here with all of its various ring and base configurations, is typical of today's higher quality mounts.

When mounting a scope, careful consideration must be given to bolt handle clearance around the eyepiece.

The two-piece Leupold mount allows a wide range of windage adjustment, independent of internal scope adjustments.

Variable-Power Telescopic Sights   Variable-power scopes are becoming quite popular for a number of reasons. At low-power settings, they usually afford sufficient light transmission for early-morning and late-evening hunting, along with ample fields of view. The variable also offers the advantage of being able to be turned up to a high-power setting to give the target a large profile for long-range shooting. However, these scopes sometimes have a bit of an optical problem that causes the point of impact to wander when the power setting is changed. In the best variables, the amount of change is very small and of little consequence when actually hunting.

My favorite big-game scope is a Leupold 1½- to 5-power variable. Set on 1½ power, this scope offers a field of view of 66 feet at 100 yards. Even at 25 yards, this converts to a field of view of 16½ feet. That's more than enough to pick up a fast-moving buck. And when turned to the 5-power setting, I have enough magnification for even the longest shot.

The variable-power scope's most important application is not associated with any one type of hunting. A fixed 4-power is more than adequate for almost any big or small game. For extremely long ranges and when no short-range shooting will be undertaken, the hunter could wisely move up to a fixed 6-to-8-power scope. The smaller field of view obtained with such scopes will not be a handicap if most shooting occurs at 150 yards or more. The additional magnification will enable the shooter to make what might otherwise be a very difficult shot. For hunting in extremely poor light, a fixed-power scope with a very large objective lens and ample magnification (6 to 8 power) is required.

For the two-season hunter or for the hunter who uses his rifle for various

Leupold 1½ to 5X Vari III is a reliable scope for all kinds of hunting except varmint shooting.

Setting can be viewed from top on variable scope. Here the shooter has chosen a setting of about 4.25 power.

types of hunting, the variable can be a real asset. For example, the deer hunter can set a 2-to-7-power variable at the lowest power for hunting in brush. By turning it to a 4 power, he will be able to take the longer shots with ease. Come spring, when it's time for varminting, the rifle can be sighted in with a varmint-weight bullet at the 7-power setting. Likewise, for the infrequent antelope, goat or sheep hunt, the 7-power setting is the right choice. The variable feature is seldom used during a specific hunt. It does, however, allow the same rifle to be used for a wide range of different types of hunting.

When you use a variable, sight in the rifle with the scope set on the maximum power that will be used with the load for which it is being adjusted. This will cause any minor point-of-impact change occurring with a power change to be least notable. The lower power will normally be used at shorter ranges, where minor changes in the bullet's impact will have little noticeable effect.

Variables, by nature, are a good deal more expensive to manufacture than fixed-power scopes of similar quality. For this reason, the budget-minded shooter is best advised to purchase a fixed-power scope. A variable will prove to be far less scope than a fixed-power scope of the same price. It has been my experience that one needs to spend about $125 or more (suggested retail pricing) in today's market to get a good-quality fixed-power scope. Of course, one can spend a great deal more. I have, for example, a Zeiss 6-power scope on a Model Seven in 222 Remington that has a suggested retail price of $340. A good-quality variable will cost perhaps $250 or more at full retail. Price tags of $50 less to maybe $100 more seem to cover most of the good offerings. However, one variable (a Zeiss scope) sells for a suggested retail of $540.

Scopes are expensive, but they can greatly enhance your ability to take game under almost any condition. A good scope is useful when poor light might prevent any possible use of open or even aperture sights. And with a scope you can confidently take shots at ranges that are impossible with iron sights. A 300- to 400-yard shot is no big accomplishment with a good scope. At such a range, the average shooter would be hard pressed to keep his shots anywhere on the game when using iron sights. A good rifleman with a quality scope can often make clean, one-shot kills at ranges where the target is barely visible to the naked eye. And that's the kind of help most hunters can put to very positive use.

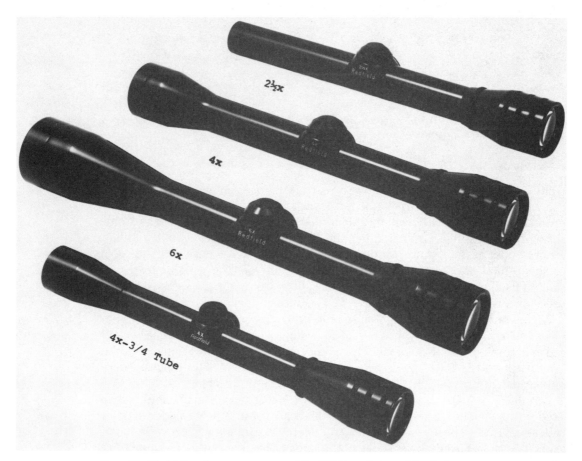

Four Redfield fixed-power scopes. The 2¹/₂X makes an ideal short-range scope; the 4X is for all-round hunting; the 6X for long-range hunting. The 4X-³/₄ tube is suited for 22 rimfire rifles.

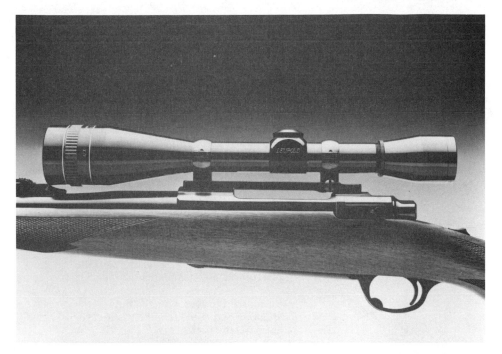

Adjustable objective lens scopes such as this Leupold 12X are ideal for the precise focus required for extremely accurate shooting. This scope can be parallax-free at any range from about 35 yards to infinity simply by rotating the front lens.

Reticules   There is a wide range of reticules offered in scopes. The most universal is the standard duplex crosshair. For the average hunter, this style of reticule will always prove best. Post and crosshair, dots, very thin crosswires or range-finding reticules are best left to such time when the shooter has gained a great deal of experience. When a shooter knows he requires a reticule different from a duplex or perhaps standard crosshair, he will also know exactly which reticule he needs.

The experienced varmint hunter may decide that a very fine crosshair or dot will serve him best, while the hunter who never leaves the brush may opt for a coarse dot or a heavy post and crosswire. But these reticules can prove to have serious drawbacks under less than optimum conditions. The fine crosswire or dot will not be visible in poor light, and the coarse dot or post will obscure distant targets. Most shooters do their best, under a wide variety of conditions, when they select either a duplex crosshair or a standard crosshair of moderate thickness.

When selecting the power of a scope, do consider the requirements for a large field of view and for light-gathering ability. The higher powers generally afford less light transmission unless a very large objective lens is used. In general, the accompanying table will give most shooters the optimum power for the types of hunting indicated.

SCOPE POWER-SELECTION GUIDE

Scope Power	Suggested Applications
2½ or 3X	Big-game hunting to a maximum of 150 or perhaps 200 yards.
4X	The best all-around power. Practical for use on big game from the shortest to longest ranges. A good power for a 22 used for everything from plinking to varmint hunting at maximum ranges.
6X	Suitable for long-range big-game hunting. Ideal for shots from 150 to perhaps 400 yards. Should not be used in heavy brush or for timber shooting, as the small field of view will make it difficult to pick up moving game at short ranges.
8 to 12X	Best suited to long-range varmint shooting and some target shooting, such as steel silhouettes.
15X or more	Best suited to benchrest shooting. High magnification makes off-hand shooting almost impossible, as all body movement is greatly magnified. Small field of view and low levels of light transmission make for difficult shooting when light is poor.
1.5 to 5X variables	Ideal variable range for big-game hunting from shortest to longest practical ranges. Also, the ideal power range for a 22 rimfire. Lowest power provides a very large field of view, while highest power is ample for difficult shots.
2 to 7 (or 8) X variables	Best suited to the one-gun hunter. Lower powers can be used for big-game hunting, higher powers for varminting.
3 to 9X or more variables	Usually more scope than required, but still quite popular with many hunters.

Scopes for Rimfires   The only application that justifies the purchase of an inexpensive scope is the 22 rimfire used only for plinking and occasional hunting. But such scopes are not for poor light conditions, nor should they be used in wet weather. They will, however, add pleasure to a session at the range, when plinking at tin cans or when taking an occasional rabbit, squirrel, woodchuck, or crow.

Types of scope reticules.

Proper sight picture with a crosshair reticule.

When the rimfire shooter requires an all-weather scope or demands the best possible optics for maximum accuracy, he should select one of the high-quality scopes designed for centerfire applications. Nothing more than a 6-power will usually be required because of the limited range of the rimfire cartridge. And often less power is better, especially for shots at moving game.

Some shooters insist upon backup sights to prevent the possibility of being put out of business by a damaged scope. This seldom happens with today's scopes. But a set of iron sights, properly sighted in, does add a lot of confidence for many shooters who wouldn't think of going afield without a scope. Scopes are the best possible sights for any application except one in which severe abuse will be a factor. And at today's prices, few shooters subject any rifle to severe abuse. The modern shooter decides not between an ancient sight form or a modern optical one. His decision is geared to what power scope will serve his needs best.

Regardless of the sight you decide to use, you must put your maximum effort into precise alignment for each shot. A misalignment only a few thousandths of an inch on an open or peep sight will mean several inches of miss. Optical sights will, of course, need to have the reticule aligned as exactly. However, because you place only a single reticule on a target in the same focal plane as the reticule, optical-sight alignment is notably easier to accomplish.

Sight alignment is always achieved independent of the target—that is, the eye and the front and rear sight are brought into proper alignment before addressing the sights to the target. Concentrate on making the sight alignment correct. When this has been accomplished, move your upper torso, arms, hands and rifle sights as a single unit, bringing the sights to bear on the target. If you fail to move your upper torso, arms, and rifle sights as a single unit, you will invariably cause some misalignment to occur in the sights before they are brought to bear on the target. Because this step is vital to proper sighting, discussion of it will be repeated at various points in this text. Obviously, the problem is not as great with optical sights. However, for each and every shot, your eye should be placed in nearly as identical a position as possible with respect to its position behind the scope.

MAKING THE SHOT

2

There are a number of important aspects to making a successful shot in addition to the key task of sight alignment. You must know when and how to squeeze the trigger properly, how to afford the maximum support for your rifle so as to keep the sights in alignment during the squeezing of the trigger and how to hold into the wind. You will also need to know how high or low to hold at long and short ranges. The proper control of breathing, the necessary follow-through and the ability to handle recoil and muzzle blast are also important.

Achieving Accuracy in Shooting

The essentials of a good shot can be broken into two main categories: art and science. Mastering the science of shooting simply is the willingness to commit to memory the wind drift and trajectories of your favorite cartridge or cartridges. It also involves learning the advantages of different bullet shapes and cartridges. But all this will be discussed later, in the ballistics chapter. For now, let's discuss the art of shooting, which includes all those factors not related to the bullet's actual flight after it leaves the muzzle.

Sight Alignment   As stated earlier, the first step is proper sight alignment. You must strive to see the sights exactly the same each time and make every effort to align them precisely without regard for the target. Having done this, you move rifle and sights into positive alignment with the target and begin your trigger squeeze. But the sights won't stay still. They bob and weave about the target, and the harder you try to hold them steady, the worse things become. What to do? Begin with learning to breathe correctly.

Breath Control   No one can shoot well when his chest is heaving up and down after a hard climb or run. You must be able to control your breathing so that you will not be winded from exertion when you make your shot. Obviously, the better physical condition you are in, the wider the range of circumstances under which you will be able to control your breathing. An athlete who has just walked comfortably to the top of a hill will find his breathing normal, and he will be ready to take a shot. The fellow who spends 50 weeks a year sitting at a desk may find his breathing (perhaps gasping is a better word) labored when he reaches the top of the same hill. He will be unable to control his breathing and will have to wait to take the shot. Seeing that the intended target is about to depart for another county might lead this individual to try the shot anyway, but invariably it will be poorly placed or perhaps a complete miss.

The first step in controlled breathing is not to allow yourself to become so winded that you cannot quickly bring your breathing back to normal. Overexertion to get into position for a shot is wasted effort, as you will be in no condition to make the shot when you arrive. Each shooter must pace himself to his own physical condition.

Breathing while shooting must be done correctly. One procedure that works well is to take a deep breath and then exhale it very slowly. Take another deep breath as you bring the rifle to your shoulder; exhale half of it, and hold your breath. Now is the time to align the sights, bring them to bear on the target and begin your trigger squeeze. You will find that when your breathing is under control, the rest of your muscles will be cooperative. If you can control your breathing, your legs and arms will not be so fatigued as to tremble under the effort of the shot. If you are breathing correctly, the second step to making a good shot will have been accomplished. If not, you will be well on your way to a poorly made shot.

Your own physical condition is the key to determining the extent of the exertion you can enter into just prior to taking a shot. I once ran several miles in order to cut off a caribou and be in position for a shot. By pacing myself and resting before going the last 50 yards, I was able to get my breathing under control quickly enough to make a good shot. Yet, on another hunt I had to pass up a shot at a good whitetail buck because my heart was going like a trip hammer after a relatively short climb. I simply hadn't taken into consideration my low level of stamina after having had almost no sleep the previous night. Breathing is vital to being rock-steady as you hold your rifle during trigger squeeze.

Trigger Squeeze   The actual squeezing of the trigger must also be undertaken properly. If you simply grab your rifle and then yank or jerk on the trigger, it will be almost impossible to obtain any degree of proficient marksmanship. You must place only the pad of the first joint of your index finger on the trigger. To do so, you must grasp the pistol-grip section of the stock in such a manner that when the index finger is extended, the pad of its first joint falls comfortably onto the trigger, with no other finger contact with the rifle. Practice this grip until you hold the rifle in the same manner each time you pick it up. When you actually make the shot, squeezing the trigger should be a slow and deliberate effort. Squeeze the trigger only while the sights are in positive alignment. When the sights wobble from alignment, stop your squeeze but maintain all the pressure you previously applied to the trigger. When the sights are again in alignment, apply additional pressure to the trigger. A well-placed shot must be made within the time frame of being able to do so comfortably within the half-breath you are holding.

WRONG

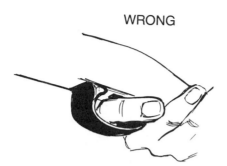

Wrong way to grip the trigger. Too much finger wrapped around the trigger will result in poor trigger control and a jerky pull.

RIGHT

Right way to grip the trigger. Only the first pad of the index finger should rest on the trigger. With this grip, it is possible to squeeze the trigger smoothly.

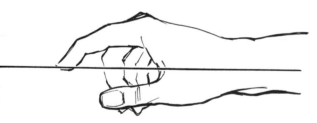

When the trigger finger is properly positioned, the ball of the finger will fall into alignment with the wrist.

At first, you may need to take another breath before you can get off the shot. In this case, stop the entire process and begin anew: Hold your breath, align the sights first with one another and then on the target and, of course, begin a new trigger squeeze. This procedure should be practiced repeatedly until you can accomplish it easily within one held breath. Such practice is best done without the use of ammunition; dry firing, it is called.

The actual moment of discharge should never be anticipated. The gun's firing should always come somewhat as a surprise. If you anticipate the actual firing, invariably you will yank or jerk the trigger, thus causing accuracy-destroying rifle movement. You must accomplish the shot with an absolute minimum of gun movement if you are to hit your target. Therefore, you must make every effort to achieve a smooth and steady trigger squeeze and avoid any movement, voluntary or involuntary, when firing the rifle.

Involuntary movement can often occur at the moment the gun discharges or, if you anticipate the firing, a split second before the gun goes off. Such movement is called a flinch. Any flinching will destroy the alignment of your sights, and the shot will be a poor one. Reactions to the recoil or the muzzle blast are the most common causes of shooter flinch. To prevent any possibility of such a condition, you must learn the need to follow through on each shot.

Follow-through   Expressed simply, follow-through means maintaining your sight alignment and a positive nonmovement until the bullet is well on its way downrange. Follow-through can also be described as a total lack of shooter reaction to the actual firing of the rifle. If you find the recoil of a particular rifle painful or even just objectionable, it will be difficult if not impossible to avoid an involuntary flinch. A soft recoil pad can often make the difference between a fair shooter and a good one because it will remove the pain of shooting and hence help get rid of an involuntary flinch. Too, the use of a lighter recoiling cartridge is sometimes necessary for some shooters to become proficient.

Practice can help you overcome a recoil flinch. However, that practice must be done in building-up stages. If a 30-06 causes you to flinch, there is little point in further shooting with that cartridge. Start with a lighter cartridge and work up in increments until you can handle the recoil of the heavier round. Then practice frequently enough to maintain your proficiency. It's no surprise that many of the best marksmen started with extensive rimfire shooting, moving then to varmint cartridges such as the 222 Remington and then perhaps to a 243 or 257 before graduating to the 270 or 30-06 cartridges.

Noise, too, can cause involuntary flinching. For this reason it pays to wear a good set of earmuffs for all practice shooting sessions. Too, the earmuffs will prevent you from incurring a hearing loss during your practice sessions.

When you can "ride out" your shot, so that even after the recoil has moved your sights off the target they will still be in proper alignment with one another, you will be well on your way to having mastered the required follow-through.

Summary   When will you know that you have made significant progress in mastering the essentials of making a good shot? When your shots are no longer randomly dispersed on the target and when they begin to form small, tight groups, you will know that things are beginning to come together. Because the essentials of making each shot count are so vital to successful marksmanship, they will be discussed at other points in the text.

On the range, a good set of ear muffs
will help prevent involuntary flinching
from the painful effects of muzzle blast
on your ear drums. Shooting glasses
should always be worn for safety.

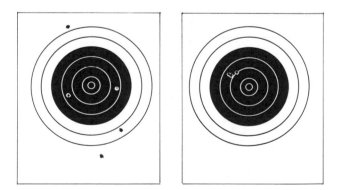

Target at left with scattered shots indicates shooter has not mastered the fundamentals. Target at right with tight group indicates that the shooter is fairly proficient.

In the prone position, the shooter addresses the target at about a 45-degree angle. The right leg may be pulled up slightly, as shown, or extended. The front elbow should be directly below the barrel; the rear elbow placed comfortably to the side.

BASIC SHOOTING POSITIONS 3

Whether your goal is to be an accomplished target marksman or a proficient field shot, you will need to have a good understanding of the basic shooting positions. Marksmanship does not refer only to a rifleman standing up and hitting his mark. It should equally mean using the best possible position to assure maximum support and steadiness for the rifle under a wide range of conditions. Any position should be favored to the extent that it affords the most stable shooting position for the circumstances of a particular shot. In the field, the offhand position is the last possible choice. Prone, sitting and kneeling all offer a better shooting platform, with prone being the steadiest. Target shooting, in various types of match shooting, involves proficiency in at least one or perhaps all four basic shooting positions.

There are, of course, a great many variations to the prone, sitting, kneeling and offhand positions. The major variation is whether or not a sling is employed. But each shooter may choose some slight variations of legs, arms or torso to afford maximum comfort and steadiness as dictated by physical size and shape as well as the fit of the rifle being used.

One can shoot with or without a sling. But in that the sling adds a great deal of stability to the rifle, I will discuss the basic positions in conjunction with a sling. (Proper sling adjustment is covered in Chapter 4.)

Prone Position   In the prone position, a shooter generally lies down at a 45-degree angle to the target. The butt of the rifle should just be able to be placed on the shoulder. If it goes easily to the shoulder, the sling may well be too loose to provide maximum support. The elbow of the left arm should always be directly under the barrel and fore-end. If it is moved even slightly to one side, your arm will tire more quickly in its attempt to be a unipod to support the rifle. Keep the right elbow on the ground, considerably away from the rifle. Exact positioning of this elbow will be determined by the individual shooter's comfort and steadiness. It pays to try some variations to determine where this elbow should be placed for maximum stability. The hand supporting the fore-end should not grasp it; rather, let the fore-end settle into the hand, and then simply bring the fingers into contact with the stock. If the sling is properly adjusted, it will force the fore-end tightly against the hand, thus securely holding the rifle in position. Exact placement of the feet can vary widely. The secret of success is comfort without movement. Of course, there are many fine points, but the foregoing will get you started. You can then refine your position to one that is ideal for you.

Sitting Position   Only after the prone position has been mastered is it time to move on to the sitting position. Many shooters prefer a toes-in-the-air, heels-into-the-ground posture for shots taken while sitting. I prefer to place my feet flat to the ground, a position that prevents some trembling. The sitting position can be quickly mastered if the shooter has previously become adept at the prone position.

I found it to be a great help when I stopped resting my elbows on my knees and went to laying the lower portion of my upper arms against the upper portion

In the sitting position, the shooter places the lower part of his upper arm on his upper shins. Keeping the feet flat on the ground helps reduce wobble.

of my lower legs. Not until I began using this position did my sitting performance start to improve. This is as rock-steady a position as can be used while sitting. Master the sitting position before attempting the far more difficult kneeling position.

Kneeling Position   Many shooters sit on the side of their foot rather than on their heel when shooting from the kneeling position. Either posture seems to be satisfactory. Because of the arthritis in my ankles and feet, I have found the kneeling position quite uncomfortable. And the results of my shooting from this posture have reflected this discomfort.

It takes a great deal of practice to eliminate the body movement that is present in the kneeling position. However, you must eliminate as much of this movement as possible, or you will never become highly proficient. The kneeling position requires experimenting to find what best suits your physical requirements. How-

The best kneeling position is to sit on the foot. It is far more comfortable than sitting on the heel of a severely arched foot.

ever, remember that the forward elbow should be directly beneath the barrel and that the lower portion of the upper arm is best supported when rested on the upper shin.

Offhand Shooting Offhand shooting demands a great deal of strength and stamina if you are to be effective. Always bear in mind that you are trying to create a motionless gun support with your body. This position requires more practice than the other three positions combined. In the beginning, vary your position slightly until you find the steadiest and most comfortable one. Then make every effort to repeat the chosen position exactly for each shot. Feet, legs, hips, torso, shoulders, arms, head and neck must be brought into exactly the same position each time. Eventually, with sufficient training, your body will be able to lock up to a very high level of steadiness when you assume the practiced position.

For effective offhand shooting, the front elbow should be directly below the barrel, the rear elbow nearly horizontal to the shoulder. If you find your trigger finger going deeply into the trigger guard, raise your rear elbow until the trigger finger is positioned correctly. If you find you are straining to reach the trigger, drop the rear elbow somewhat. By raising or lowering the rear elbow, you can compensate for a stock that is somewhat too long or too short. A change in its

In the correct offhand position, the forward elbow is directly beneath the barrel and the other elbow about horizontal. Raise the rear elbow if your gun is too short and lower it if the gun is too long.

position will either push your trigger finger forward or pull it rearward.

One rule to keep in mind is that sheer force is not the way to approach rifle holding. That muscles need strength is true, but without the proper position of the limbs you will not be successful. For this reason, it is vital to have a good coach in the early stages of shooting. Only by having someone carefully watch your position and suggest changes can you correct all the faults. And the elimination of faults is at the root of good shooting form.

It is my belief that every rifleman should learn how to shoot small-bore position matches even if they have little interest in the sport. The knowledge and skill gained will be useful and beneficial for all other forms of rifle shooting. And only with small-bore shooting can most shooters afford the large amounts of ammo required to gain real proficiency from the various basic positions.

In the field, it is always prudent to use whatever artificial support is available. A rolled-up coat placed over a log or rock can afford support for the back of the hand holding the forearm. The top of a fencepost, a tree limb and a host of other natural aids can be employed to gain steadiness. However, always remember never to brace the barrel or fore-end directly against anything except your hand. All the support you can find should be for the back of your hand, arms or torso. Resting any rifle directly against any object will notably change the bullet's point of impact.

4 SHOOTING THE HUNTING RIFLE

Hunting rifles can take a great many configurations. A rifle for squirrels may be a bolt-action sporter in 22 rimfire, with a good scope, capable of 1 inch or less groups at 50 yards. Or the hunting rifle may be a pump, lever or semiautomatic 22 with accuracy just passable for rabbits and plinking. A hunting rifle can also be a short, lightweight, highly accurate centerfire, such as a Remington bolt-action Model Seven, or it can be more traditional in weight and length, as is the Remington bolt-action Model 700 Classic. A hunting rifle can also be a lever-action 30-30 or 300 Savage or a pump or semiautomatic. All these and a great many others are carried afield each autumn by hunters throughout the country.

The level of performance obtained with rifles varies from very impressive to less than sporting. Shooters who try shots beyond the range capabilities of their equipment or their own personal abilities should not be allowed to hunt, in my opinion.

With rimfire rifles, only the bolt action will prove suitable for shots at 50 yards or more with but rare exceptions. Centerfire rifles of the lever, pump and semiautomatic types are sometimes acceptable for 200-yard shooting. However, some of these types are barely adequate for 100 yards, though on occasion one will be accurate enough to allow shots to 250 yards to be taken in a sporting manner. Chapter 6, Selecting a Rifle, will outline the steps in assuring that a specific hunting need will be served by the rifle selected. This chapter will explain shooting techniques that can turn a poor rifleman into a passable one, a passable rifleman into a good one. And while it becomes more difficult to enhance skills as one gains proficiency, it is possible that even a good rifleman can learn a few tricks that might turn him into a superb shot.

The fine points of shooting apply equally whether one is trying for a head shot on a squirrel at 50 yards with a 22 or for a heart shot on an antelope at 300 yards. Both shots demand equal accuracy and a great deal of competence. The 1-inch target offered by a partially obscured squirrel's head at 50 yards corresponds to the 6-inch vital area on the antelope at 300 yards. Both shots demand 2-minute-of-angle accuracy, and both demand something better than an offhand, no-support attempt at getting lucky.

Hunting rifles are available in a wide variety of calibers and styles to meet the hunter's preferences and needs. These are some of the author's favorites (from left): Remington Model Seven in 7mm-08; Remington Model 700 Classic in 300 H & H Magnum; Ruger No. 1 Single Shot in 30-06 Springfield; Winchester Model 70 Featherweight in 270 Winchester.

Importance of Accurate Shooting Shooting the hunting rifle demands skills that are in some ways greater than those necessary for benchrest or target shooting. After all, a poor shot in any target sport may simply eliminate you from being among those with the better scores. But a poor hunting shot can mean a missed animal, if you are lucky. All too often, the results of poor hunting shots are poorly hit animals, which are then subjected to undue pain and torment. If the animal is lucky, the hunter may get a second or third shot that will dispatch it from long-term suffering. But if the animal's luck continues to be poor, it may escape, even if only temporarily, to continue its suffering. No hunter worthy of the name should ever take a shot that could result in his quarry incurring anything but a swift and, as near as possible, painless death. The nobility of the quarry never diminishes, but the stature of the reckless shooter can become quite small indeed if he stoops to banging away at game that he cannot, in good conscience, expect to kill cleanly with the first shot.

It is vital when shooting the hunting rifle to remember one's own limitations. A lost opportunity is no shame. Passing up shots that you can't expect to make will make you a better sportsman and perhaps even prompt you to do a bit more practice in order to increase your proficiency.

Practice   I still remember my first larger-than-deer big-game hunt, a trip to Labrador for caribou. Having done my homework, I knew I might be called upon to take a very long shot, and I wanted to ensure success. At the time, I was working on a Lyman handbook, and my office and ballistics lab were on the corner of a 200-yard rifle range. I made it a practice at the end of each day to take my caribou rifle and 10 rounds of ammo out to the firing line. I fired a 5-shot group from the prone position, using a military sling, then duplicated the effort from an offhand position. When I started my practice sessions, the best I could do from the prone position was a 6-inch group; from offhand, I could not consistently keep my shots on a 12-inch target. Needless to say, I wasn't impressed with my ability. But before a month had elapsed, I was holding my prone groups to about 2½ inches and the offhand groups under 6 inches. When the time came to depart for the hunt, I was confident of my ability and knew what I could expect to accomplish in the field with my chosen rifle and ammo.

The most important lesson I have learned over the years, with respect to my ability with a rifle, is that it takes constant practice to maintain one's marksmanship. I now make a strong effort to practice field-position shooting at least twice a month, shooting 30 rounds during each session. If circumstances prevent me from getting to the range for a full month, I can usually detect a falloff in proficiency in the following shooting session.

The need for constant practice with a hunting rifle cannot be overstressed. But not everyone has the opportunity to fire five or ten rounds through his favorite hunting rifle each day. Yet some sort of regimen is required if you are going to be proficient in the field. At an absolute minimum, you should get to the range once every three or four weeks and fire no less than four five-shot groups from the offhand position. Additionally, at least one five-shot group should be fired from each position—sitting, kneeling and prone. Your offhand targets should be fired at 50, 100, 150 and 200 yards, ideally, while the sitting, kneeling and prone targets should all be fired at 200 yards. And all should be fired with the aid of a sling. Finally, fire five rounds at 100 yards, offhand, without the aid of a sling.

It is a wise move to save your targets, marking the date and position used. You will be amazed at the increase in proficiency over perhaps as few as five or six sessions of practice. But more importantly, you will begin to understand your own capabilities and will learn to respect the limiting factors when hunting.

Some shooters never gain sufficient proficiency to take a shot past 200 yards. But knowing this will keep them from inflicting lingering pain on any of their quarry.

Supporting the Rifle   You must realize the importance of using whatever means practical for improving the steadiness of your aim. This means never taking a shot without the aid of a sling whenever its use is possible. It also means never shooting offhand when you can kneel or sit, always remembering that your best shot can be made from a prone position. If you practice as suggested, these points will become obvious.

When seeking to steady your rifle for the best possible shot, don't hesitate to use any sort of rest you can find in the field. Leaning your forearm-holding hand against a tree or resting it on a fencepost will greatly enhance your ability to hit the desired mark. Draping yourself over a boulder, with your elbows firmly supported, will enable you to make clean kills at amazing ranges. A rolled-up coat used to steady your rifle can bring benchrest-like accuracy to your field shooting. Regardless of what form of support you use, just remember to insulate the rifle from the support with your hand. Resting the rifle directly against any solid support will result in the bullet's point of impact shifting a notable amount. Under such circumstances, any gain in steadiness may be more than offset by the change in point of impact.

Even the most unlikely part of the landscape can often be used for a solid support. I have, on several occasions, even used densely limbed bushes for support, by first laying my jacket over them. While the amount of support afforded was not as great as it would be from other more solid rests, it was indeed a better position to shoot from than no rest at all.

When using a rest, be sure to insulate the rifle from the support with your hand. In top drawing, shooter uses a rock under his upper arm to gain steadiness. Drawing below shows how even a rolled-up jacket can serve as a rest.

Not every hunting shot can be taken with the aid of a rest. A good rifleman should be capable of standing on his feet and hitting the mark to at least 200 yards. But do not settle for anything less than the most certain shot you can manage. Despite the ridiculous regulation of at least one state in which I have hunted—that all shots be taken from an offhand or unsupported firearm position—supporting the shooting hand is a sign of good sportsmanship. After all is said and done, the first shot should produce a clean kill, and anything you can do to ensure that end will make you a better sportsman.

Positioning the Feet Learning proficiency with a rifle first demands that you assume the proper foot position. Especially if the shot is to be made from the offhand position, it is important to assume the correct foot position before the rifle is brought to the shoulder. Any attempt to mount the rifle prior to or during the positioning of the feet will result in an awkward stance that could detract from the stability of the shooting platform you are attempting to create. It may be helpful to look upon your body as a tank and its gun turret. Everything from the waist down is your mobility to get to the location of the shooting. But once into that position, all movement should be limited to the portions of your body above the waist. Without a stable base, the movable turret of your body will not be able to perform as you hope.

The positioning of the feet is made with respect to the target's location. Regardless of how you are standing when the target is sighted, take the time to ensure that your left foot (assuming you are shooting right-handed) is placed forward, with your left toes pointing directly at, or as much as 45 degrees to the right of, the target. The exact position of your left toes will depend upon the fit of the rifle you are using and, to some extent, on your own shooting style. If your rifle fits well with the clothes you are wearing, you will probably find that the best toe direction is somewhere between 25 and 30 degrees to the right of the target. With a stock that is somewhat short, you will find that less of an angle will help compensate for lack of trigger pull length, while with a stock that

When feet are positioned correctly, a line drawn across the toes will point directly at the target. Also, your weight will be evenly distributed between both feet, turning your body into a stable bipod.

is too long for the clothes being worn, a greater angle will feel best. Under no circumstances should your left toes be pointed in any direction other than from 0 to 45 degrees to the right of the target.

Your right foot should be placed just far enough behind your left foot so as to ensure an equal distribution of your weight on both feet. The toes of the right foot should be pointing approximately 45 degrees to the right of the direction assumed by your left toes. By so placing your feet, you will ensure that your weight is distributed and balanced evenly over both feet, thus providing you with a stable bipod from which to shoot. If you place the greatest portion of your weight on one foot or the other, you will in effect turn your body's bipod into a unipod and thereby reduce the stability of your shooting platform.

Practice getting your feet into position naturally, until it occurs without conscious effort. If you happen to have your right foot forward when your target is sighted, take the step to position your left foot as described *before* you mount your gun and *before* you *actually* decide between taking the shot as is or using your sling and some sort of rest. By positioning your feet automatically, you will be able to make the shot from the most stable of offhand positions and in the shortest time, should a fast shot be called for by circumstances.

If you need to turn, whether a slight amount or a full 180 degrees, it should be accomplished simultaneously with the positioning of the left foot. It is best not to move the right foot under most circumstances but, rather, to position it by pivoting on the toes. This will keep body motion to a minimum. The shooting stance for your feet should be practiced extensively with rifle in hand, under varying terrain conditions.

Practice assuming the correct stance until you can do it without thinking. If you make a conscious effort never to begin to bring the rifle to your shoulder until your feet are positioned correctly, you will eliminate the chance of taking a shot from a poorly balanced or awkward position. Establishing the proper support for your shooting turret is the first step in mastering marksmanship.

Mounting the Gun   Once you have established the proper stance, you can mount your gun. If you are going to use the hasty-sling position, you can bring your rifle rapidly to your shoulder. If you have decided there is sufficient time to use a military-sling position, then slip into the sling as outlined above.

As you bring the rifle to your shoulder, get both your left and right arms into very exact, steady positions. Your arms are the connection between rifle and "turret," and unless they offer the most rigid support possible, your rifle barrel will wave about, making positive alignment of sights very difficult. When sights wander excessively on and off the target, the shooter will frequently try to yank the trigger at a moment when the sights appear to be properly aligned. Such jerking of the trigger often results in a complete miss or, worse, a poorly placed shot.

The proper position for the left elbow is directly below the rifle, not at some point to the left of the barrel. For most shooters, maximum stability occurs when the elbow-to-wrist position of the left arm creates a 15- to 45-degree angle to the barrel. The only way to determine what is best for you is to pick up the rifle

Good offhand shooting form: one elbow below the gun, the other held high.

and try to hold the sights or reticule steady on some distant target for 10 seconds. With at least a three-minute rest between each attempt, vary the position of your forearm 5 or 10 degrees. Those with limited experience will be likely to find that the position of the elbow changes with extensive practice. Once you learn which position is best for you, make certain your elbow is where it belongs each time you mount the rifle. Be certain you grasp the fore-end far enough toward the muzzle so that your elbow positions well in front of the trigger guard. Grasping the fore-end too far back will not afford as rigid a support for your rifle.

The position of your right elbow is vital to the proper placement of your trigger finger. If your elbow is too low, you will tend to put too much finger around the trigger, thus preventing your squeezing it directly rearward with the pad of the finger's first joint. The proper right elbow placement ranges from being horizontal with the rifle's barrel to perhaps 20 or 30 degrees above the horizontal position.

If the stock is too long, even the horizontal position might prove uncomfortable, and the shooter may be forced to drop the right elbow slightly below the horizontal. Of course, it would be better to have the stock fitted properly rather than to assume a less-than-ideal shooting position.

Slightly short stocks can often be accommodated for offhand shooting simply by raising the right elbow a bit higher than normal. As the elbow is raised, the trigger finger will be pulled farther away from the trigger. You should, by trial and error, decide exactly what elbow position will place the pad of the first joint of your trigger finger on the front face of the trigger. You will need to change the position of your elbow whenever you increase or decrease the amount of clothing between your shoulder and the rifle butt.

Trigger Control   Simply knowing the correct position for offhand shooting will not make you a marksman. The position must be practiced until it can be assumed without thought. And it must be combined with proper trigger control. I have not yet met a rifleman able to hold his sights motionless on his intended quarry. Therefore, proper trigger control is required to ensure that the rifle will discharge at one of the exact split seconds when the sights are correctly aligned on the target.

As explained in Chapter 2, proper trigger control first requires that you breathe normally. If you are winded from a long climb or hard stalk, you need to regain control of your breathing before attempting a shot. No one can make consistently good shots if his chest is heaving up and down with labored breathing. Obviously, being in good shape will allow you to have the best possible control of your breathing under the widest range of conditions.

With your breathing under control, mount the rifle as you take in a deep breath. Then exhale about half the air from your lungs and stop breathing. Align the sights on the target and begin to squeeze the trigger. Apply trigger pressure only when the sights are just about perfectly aligned. This means that as the sights come into alignment, you apply a bit of trigger pressure. The instant the sights begin to drift off the target, stop applying any additional pressure. (Do, however, maintain any pressure already applied.) You may have to start and stop applying pressure several times before the rifle fires. But if your trigger breaks clean and without the necessity of undue weight being applied, you can easily get off the shot before you come close to needing another breath. Naturally, the task is not as easy as it sounds. But, as with any sport, practice will make you quite proficient.

Remember, the shot must be squeezed off. The trigger should release the sear without your being able to anticipate the exact moment of firing. If you can anticipate firing, then invariably you will be guilty of at least a slight trace of involuntary flinch, resulting in a less-than-perfectly placed shot. Any attempt to yank or jerk the trigger will result in the same involuntary flinch, in addition to gun movement directly attributable to the violence of the attack on the trigger. A trigger should be caressed, so to speak, rather than poked at in a random manner.

Controlling Your Body   It is important to remember that after the rifle has been mounted, any body movement required to compensate for a change in the target's position must be made from the waist. If you twist your legs, you will weaken the stability of your shooting position by introducing unnoticed strain on various muscles. Make all movements from the waist—be they left or right, up or down, any combination thereof. This simple step can turn you into a rather effective rifleman. Do not make the mistake of trying to reposition your feet once you have mounted the rifle. If such repositioning becomes necessary because of an extreme change in the target's position, then slightly drop the rifle from your shoulder before moving your feet, and do not bring it back to the shooting position until you have assumed the correct stance.

Remember that for right-handed shooters, the right hand does not support the rifle in any manner. The rifle is held in position by the left hand and by the friction between butt plate and shoulder, created by the rearward pressure of the left hand pulling the rifle against the shoulder. The importance of a nonslip butt plate is obvious. A smooth, curved butt plate is the worst possible choice. A flat rubber butt plate or recoil pad are the best selections. A flat rubber surface will tend to remain where placed rather than slide about on the shoulder. The right hand should merely be positioned around the pistol grip so as to be comfortable with the trigger finger in proper position. The right hand's sole function is to provide correct trigger squeeze. In practical application, especially with slippery metal or plastic butt plates, you may be forced to use the right hand to prevent the rifle from slipping downward from the shoulder. However, if more than a minimum amount of control is required, you will adversely affect your accuracy potential.

Moving Targets

All of the foregoing applies to motionless targets. But what about moving targets, such as a running deer or antelope? Well, first, let me state that I believe most hunters should not fire at running game. Running animals offer extremely difficult targets. A hunter must not only lead the target to compensate for its forward motion, but also, in many instances, must time the shot for the up-and-down motion of perhaps a bounding deer.

With a lot of practice, one can learn to hit moving targets consistently. But how does the average hunter get that practice? How many shots can be taken at running deer in a season's hunting? Hundreds of shots need to be taken to gain any level of proficiency. And what about all those shots that will not hit the intended targets as hoped for while one is learning to shoot running game? There will be some missed animals, causing little, if any, harm except perhaps to the hunter's ego. But there will be a lot of wounded and crippled animals. It is my honest belief that in the interest of good hunting ethics, most hunters should consider running game nonsporting targets.

There are some ways to gain experience. For instance, one can practice on running targets at a range. Some range facilities do have running boar and running deer targets. When range proficiency has shown that you are up to hitting the vital organs of a moving target, then you can justifiably take shots at moving game. However, keep in mind that an animal target moving across flat terrain is far easier to hit than game that may also be leaping up and down. A caribou or antelope going hell-bent-for-high-water is an easier target than a startled whitetail deer whose initial getaway will often be characterized by an up-and-down bounding.

Many ethical hunters refrain from shots at any running animals, based not only on a high probability of a poorly placed shot resulting in undue suffering, but also on the fact that they were unsuccessful in their efforts to get within range of the game without spooking it. These hunters should be applauded for their sportsmanship. But for those who would like to learn how to hit running game, trying to hit moving targets at a local range is the proper way to begin. When a reasonable level of proficiency has been acquired at the range, one can graduate to running rabbits and a 22 rimfire rifle. Rabbits are relatively easy to incapacitate with almost any kind of hit. Therefore, even if only wounded, the animal will usually be motionless enough to afford a simple follow-up shot to prevent any undue suffering.

It is easy to speak out against the inexperienced shooter attempting to hit moving game. It is far more difficult to refrain from trying a shot at the only buck seen after ten days of hard hunting. It is even more difficult when the quarry being hunted is one of the larger game animals.

I acquired my own ability to hit running game when my hunting ethics were considerably different from what they are now. In my early years of hunting, the shot and the resulting meat supply were the important part of the hunt. Today, I find that being part of the quarry's environment and merely sighting the quarry on its home turf are the main points to my hunting. The shot and resultant meat supply or trophy are now only a small portion of the satisfaction gained from hunting. But every hunter must satisfy his own needs and conscience. What is best for me may not be your cup of tea. With this in mind, some discussion on how to hit moving targets follows.

Leading   The first consideration in hitting a moving target is, of course, leading the animal. When a target is moving, it will not be in the same position when your bullet arrives as it was when you pulled the trigger. The intended target keeps moving forward during the time it takes the bullet to reach it. If circumstances are such that the animal moved 2 feet during this time, you will have had to aim at a point 2 feet in front of the target in order to hit the intended mark.

However, it is almost impossible to hold at a stationary point in front of a moving animal and fire the rifle at exactly the right moment. What you must do is lead the animal by the correct amount and then maintain that lead by swinging with the animal as you squeeze the trigger. Good shotgun shots quickly learn that a sustained lead is far superior to a snap shot, one directed from a motionless gun at a point ahead of the moving target. The number of hits made by snap shooting is only a small percentage of those made when employing a sustained lead.

However, the most efficient method of shotgun leading, in which the gun is started behind the target and is swung through the game at a faster rate than the game's forward motion, then fired when the correct lead is obtained, does not work well with a rifle. The rifle shooter must be more precise in his lead, since he does not have the 3-foot-diameter shot pattern to compensate for aiming error. His single bullet must be placed exactly into a vital zone perhaps no bigger than 6 inches in diameter. And the rifle hunter must accomplish this task at ranges that may be as much as three to ten times longer than that of his shotgunning counterpart. The preciseness of a sustained lead is a must when shooting moving game with a rifle.

How much lead is required depends entirely upon the speed of the bullet, the speed of the game and the angle the game is moving at in relationship to the hunter. For example, a deer running 90 degrees to the hunter at 30 feet per second will traverse 3 feet during the time it takes a 270 cartridge, with a 130-grain bullet started at 3,000 feet per second, to travel 100 yards. Therefore, you will need to lead that deer by the same 3 feet if it is 100 yards away. If the deer were traveling at a 45-degree angle to the hunter, the horizontal distance traveled in relationship to the hunter would be only 2 feet, although the deer's actual forward gain would be the original 3 feet.

The accompanying tables list the average speed of running big game, the time of flight of some popular big-game loads and the resultant lead required for game traveling at right angle to the hunter and at a 45-degree angle to the hunter. Obviously, game moving straight at the hunter or straight away from him needs no horizontal lead, although some compensation for a vertical lead might be required under extreme circumstances. But one must keep in mind that angles encountered in the field and individual animal speeds can vary. For instance, we have listed the average speed of a running elk as 35 feet per second. However, running elk have been reasonably well documented to travel as slow as 25 feet per second or as fast as 40 feet per second. And what appears to one hunter as a running elk may appear to another as an elk merely engaged in a fast trot.

The point is that the tables presented are mathematically correct for the circumstances shown and the use of a sustained lead. Under field conditions, notable changes in lead will be required. If the game is traveling half the listed speed, a lead reduction of 50 percent will be required; if the game is traveling 50 percent faster than listed, a 50-percent increase in lead distance will be necessary. For the serious mathematician, the 45-degree angle leads do not take into consideration the increasing or decreasing distance the game will be from the hunter as it moves along its course of travel. Such calculations, which can be solved with the use of calculus, are meaningless because the differences are measured in fractions of an inch to at most several inches. Under most hunting conditions, a shot placed within 6 inches of the intended mark will get the job done satisfactorily.

One needs to refrain from generalized leads. A statement such as "Try a lead of 3½ feet at 150 yards and 7 feet at 200 yards" has little relationship to mathematical fact. And one cannot afford to "try" a lead. If you use the accompanying tables to determine leads, you will be off to a good start. You can make simple interpolations for angles not specified or for animals running at greater or lesser speeds than the average speed listed.

When all is said and done, the ability to lead game properly in the field is as much art as science. The ability to determine speed of game, angle of flight and the amount of lead required cannot depend upon mental mathematics when in the field. The animal would be long gone before you finished your calculations. The art of "knowing" how much lead is something that must be acquired. This brings us back to "running" targets at the range and practice on rabbits, be they jacks or cottontails.

I cannot repeat enough that game speed can vary substantially. An antelope pursued by a car can reach speeds in excess of 50 miles per hour for short distances. However, the presence of a hunter or even the report of a rifle is seldom enough to drive game to run at the greatest possible speed. Only extreme fright will push animals to their maximum speeds. Most running game animals are simply putting a little distance between the hunter and themselves; they are not really frightened but, rather, are exercising caution.

Keep in mind also that terrain plays an important part in speed. A goat seldom has the opportunity to get going fast simply because of the nearly unbelievable angle of his home turf. It's hard to travel with a meaningful horizontal speed when going nearly straight up over terrain where it is nearly impossible to find footing.

Know your quarry's average likely speed and the leads necessary for your cartridge and bullet at 100, 200 and perhaps 300 yards, for an animal traveling at 90 degrees to you. If the game appears to be going slower or faster than average, adjust your lead accordingly. And if the game is traveling at less than a 90-degree angle, decrease your lead accordingly. With sufficient time and practice, you can attain a high level of proficiency.

Keep in mind that on the tables for 45-degree angles, the lead is expressed in the horizontal distance as perceived by your eye. In reality, the game will still travel the same distance as in the 90-degree-angle table, but with respect to horizontal distance, the lead will appear to be the amount shown.

On game that is bounding up and down, the shot must be timed to coincide with the animal being level with your swing. In my opinion, the best place to do this is when the animal is solidly on the ground between leaps. If you are swinging well, allow the animal to hit the ground and flex his muscles in preparation for the next leap. Your shot must be timed to reach the target before it again leaves the ground. Because of the complex nature of such shooting, I would never attempt such a shot beyond 75 yards. There simply is too much risk of wounding an animal under such shooting conditions. Keep in mind that a bounding animal is not moving when all four legs are on the ground. You need to swing with the animal to keep your crosshair on him as he bounds, but the shot will be at a stationary target, requiring no lead if it is timed properly.

Ballistics Shooting the hunting rifle in the field, of course, entails a knowledge of the range limitations imposed by your rifle and of cartridge accuracy capabilities. Certainly, with most lever-action, pump and semiautomatic centerfire rifles, 200–250 yards is the maximum range. For an accurate bolt-action rifle with suitable scope, shots to 400 yards may be within the boundaries of good sportsmanship, depending upon the rifleman's individual capabilities. But whenever the ranges become so long, the rifleman must make allowances for the bullet's drop from the line of sight. If a rifle is sighted in for a bullet point of impact to be 2 inches high at 100 yards, the hunter need not be concerned with his bullet's trajectory until it has fallen more than 3 inches below the line of sight. This information can be gained from Chapter 9, which covers basic rifle ballistics. It should be committed to memory or put into a small chart that can be taped to the rifle's scope.

Hitting moving game is not an easy task, though it is not impossible. One should gain a great deal of practice at the range and on rabbits before graduating to big game. The unquestioned best practice possible is the shooting of jackrabbits in open country with a centerfire varmint load. Such cartridges will literally explode a jack and will nearly eliminate the possibility of poor hits resulting in cripples. Regrettably, not every rifleman has the opportunity to afford himself such practice.

Positions in the Field As previously noted, in the field there are better shooting positions than offhand. When time allows, a kneeling, sitting or prone position will afford more support and better accuracy. However, these positions make it very difficult if not impossible to swing with moving game. You can't swing from the waist in the kneeling position because your left elbow is being braced by your knee. In the sitting position, both elbows are being supported by your knees; in the prone position, both elbows are placed solidly against the ground. When attempting shots at running game from the prone position, most shooters resort to point shooting—simply picking out a spot in front of the target and shooting at it. This method results in a high percentage of misses. Thus, moving game paradoxically means offhand shooting. The limitations of most riflemen's abilities means that any offhand shooting should be restricted to a maximum of 200 yards. Thus, the responsible rifleman will confine any shots at moving game to 200 yards or less.

The toughest big-game shot I ever attempted was at a small antelope, which later proved to be 390 paces away. I made the one-shot kill with a 270 while draped over a 5-ton boulder. I couldn't have been more steady if I had been shooting from a benchrest. Yet, I've seen standing hunters shoot at running caribou and antelope at twice that distance. Apparently, they feel that a lucky bullet might stop an animal long enough for them to move in for a killing shot. Even a mortally wounded animal can travel faster and farther than most hunters suspect. And bullets seldom, if ever, expand past 500 yards.

The variations in kneeling, sitting, and prone positions are as great as the variations in field terrain. It would be impossible to detail all the many variations of these positions. The important point to remember is to assume the most stable position possible. In all positions, the basics of offhand shooting always apply. One simply supports one or both elbows to increase the steadiness of the rifle's support. And, as discussed earlier, the use of a sling is always recommended regardless of the position from which you shoot.

Shooting a hunting rifle is a lot of fun. It is the most fun when you can hit your target. To ensure hits, I strongly suggest that you get in as much practice as possible. Summertime varminting is a great method to learn proficiency. And if you can't get in enough centerfire practice, extensive 22 rimfire shooting is a superb way to sharpen your skills. Regardless of the exact nature of practice available, your skills will be enhanced by any shooting you engage in. Field shooting is difficult only for those who refuse to practice.

APPROXIMATE GAME SPEEDS
(in feet per second)

Animal	Traveling at 90° to hunter	Apparent speed of animal traveling at 45° to hunter
Goat	20	15
Sheep	20	15
Bear	20	15
Deer	30	20
Caribou	30	20
Elk	35	25
Pronghorn	50	35

TIME OF FLIGHT (seconds) FOR POPULAR HUNTING LOADS

Caliber & bullet wt.	100 yds.	200 yds.	300 yds.	400 yds.
30-30; 170 grs.	0.318	0.519	—	—
243; 100 grs.	0.106	0.223	0.352	0.495
270; 130 grs.	0.101	0.211	0.332	0.465
30-06; 180 grs.	0.116	0.242	0.380	0.530
300 Win. Mag.; 180 grs.	0.109	0.228	0.358	0.502

Remington 540-XR position rifle is a highly accurate and moderately priced 22 target gun.

Remington 40-XR is considered by many to be the best possible position rifle for small-bore shooting.

Remington 40-XB Rangemaster is a popular centerfire target rifle.

Remington 40-XC target gun is designed for the National Match Course of fire.

TARGET SHOOTING 5

Small-Bore Shooting

Rimfire rifle shooting began to take a positive direction during the 1920s. The first availability of commercially manufactured target-grade 22 rifles and the introduction of match-grade rimfire ammunition during this period, allowed the sport to begin its real growth. The highly competitive nature of small-bore match shooting quickly forced the accuracy of rifles and ammunition to reach an amazing level. With a good rifle and a compatible lot of ammunition, today's top shooters can consistently obtain 1-inch groups with 10 shots at 100 yards from a prone shooting position. By any standards, this is mighty fine performance for mass-produced ammunition.

Rifles for small-bore target shooting are highly specialized and generally suited for no auxiliary purpose. In fact, the serious competitor may well have a rifle for each of prone, outdoor-position, gallery and international styles of shooting. This is specialization to the extreme. Small-bore rifles capable of winning performances are quite expensive. A beginner may be satisfied with a modestly priced rifle, but very quickly he will want a more sophisticated rifle of a better grade. Eventually, a serious shooter will be satisfied with nothing of less quality than a high-grade rifle and the highest levels of accuracy.

The prone shooter must have X-ring accuracy or 1-inch groups at 100 yards; he will settle for no less. A shot outside of the X ring is almost certain to reduce his chances of winning a match. Any competitive rifle must, therefore, be capable of this level of accuracy. Small-bore target rifles characteristically have long (often 28 inches), heavy-diameter barrels as well as generously proportioned stocks. Weights of 9 to 14 pounds are commonplace for small-bore rifles.

Most American manufacturers have long since given up the production of target-grade rimfire ammunition. The only target-grade ammo being manufactured in the U.S. is CCI's Competition Green Tag. However, several imported brands are available. Ammunition should group 10 shots into 1¼ inches or less at 100 yards to be considered useful for competition.

Accessories   Besides a rifle of top quality and the best possible ammo for it, today's small-bore shooter needs a great many accessories in order to be

Some of the most accurate 22 rimfire ammo in the world: CCI's Green Tag and RWS's R-50 cartridges.

able to compete. Depending upon the discipline of small-bore shooting to be engaged in, the shooter may require a padded shooting jacket, padded rifleman's glove, cuff, hook, sling, cartridge box, telescope, spotting scope, shooting mat, shooting glasses and a great number of other items.

Because of the comparatively long in-barrel time of 22 ammo, the shooter needs to learn and apply techniques that will prevent any gun movement after ignition and during the bullet's passage through the bore. In the long barrels often encountered in small-bore shooting, the bullet actually begins deceleration while it is still in the barrel. The small powder charge of a rimfire cartridge is completely burned well before the bullet exits. Expanding gases lose their ability to impart additional velocity in about 23 or 24 inches of barrel. Accordingly, a 28-inch barrel, a length frequently used, means less muzzle velocity than, say, a 22-inch barrel. Small-bore shooting thus requires shooting skills not necessarily employed in centerfire shooting.

Perhaps small-bore target shooters are too fixed in their ways, as it might well be that a gain in performance could be achieved with a shorter but stiffer barrel. Benchrest shooters learned long ago that a barrel 20 inches or even shorter can offer some definite advantages. I suspect a 22-inch rimfire barrel might prove to be ideal for small-bore shooting.

Small-bore shooting is an extremely difficult and demanding sport. It takes a great deal of practice to gain even a modicum of proficiency. And it takes an inquisitive nature to keep up the constant search for ammo lots that will perform at the desired levels in a specific rifle.

Benchrest shooters, who think they are involved in shooting's most difficult sport with respect to precision, haven't tried small-bore shooting. True, it's not easy to shoot a ¼-inch group from a bench with carefully loaded ammo, even though the gun is rock-steady. But it is far more difficult to shoot a 1-inch group at 100 yards, using factory-loaded ammunition, while lying on your belly and supporting the rifle only with your elbows, arms and hands.

Once prone shooters have mastered the fundamentals of position, breathing, trigger squeeze and follow-through, they tend to rely a great deal on their equipment to provide the necessary precision. Position shooters, who shoot at 50 yards, will find a superbly accurate barrel important. But their ability to supply a rigid shooting platform for the offhand, kneeling and sitting positions becomes the greater part of performance. The position shooter also shoots prone, of course, but only for 25 percent of his shots.

Position-shooting rifles demand stock configurations notably different from those used for 100-yard prone shooting. Length of pull is generally shorter and most frequently combined with an adjustable butt plate that can be moved vertically on the stock. It usually has a hook that is replaceable with a prone position plate. Extremely deep fore-ends are required in order to achieve a competitive score in the kneeling position.

With time, patience, enough money and a strong desire to get the job done, most serious small-bore shooters can learn which equipment will provide the maximum in precision and also fit personal shooting habits and preferences. But the real challenge of any small-bore shooting comes in acquiring the ability to hold the rifle steady. Without this ability, it is impossible to become an accomplished shot. Perhaps the best way to accomplish the task is to begin in the prone position.

Practice   Your initial effort should not be geared to shooting out the X ring but rather to shooting small groups. Once small groups are within your capabilities, it's no real feat to adjust sights so that the group centers itself in the X ring. To begin properly, the sling must be adjusted to provide the maximum possible support. And any attempt to shoot groups without a well-designed and padded rifleman's coat and glove will result in only mediocre performance.

After finding the steadiest position, usually best accomplished with the aid of a coach, you need to learn to align the sights correctly without regard for the target. This means looking through the blurred rear sight aperture while aligning the very top edge of the front sight post at the strongest point of light in the rear aperture, which will thus center and align the front sight. If an aperture front sight is used instead of a post, you must learn to center the strong point of light in the center of the front aperture. Alignment can best be learned by itself—that is, without any target.

You must repeat the exercise of sight alignment over and over until it can be done precisely the same every time. Yet, make no effort to commit the alignment of sights to rote. It needs to be thought about each and every time in order to achieve the precise alignment required. When sight alignment is mastered, practice bringing the rifle into position to put the properly aligned sights on the target.

Beginning shooters often make the mistake of first seeing the target and then attempting to align the sights on it. The proper procedure is first to align the sights, then to move the rifle so that the previously aligned sights can be placed on the bull's-eye correctly. This step alone will bring the novice a long way toward becoming an accomplished shot.

When the rifle is moved to bring the two aligned sights onto the target, the sights must be exactly positioned for each shot. Practice, practice and more practice is required. Fortunately, the cost of rimfire ammo is not so great as to prevent most shooters from practicing as required.

To obtain the most uniform aperture sight picture possible, you will require a stock that fits well, and you must position your head on the stock exactly the same for each shot. This is an essential part of the overall precision necessary to become competitive.

Big-Bore Shooting

There is a wide variation in big-bore target shooting formats. Civilian and military-style shooting often involve standing slow-fire and rapid-fire shooting at 200 yards; rapid fire with standing and prone positions at 300 yards; and prone slow-fire shooting at 600 yards. When facilities allow, shooting may be conducted at ranges of 800 or even 1,000 yards. Such shooting is done with highly accurate rifles of traditional target configuration.

Then there is silhouette shooting, conducted at ranges of 200, 300, 385 and 500 meters. All silhouette shooting is done using hunting-style rifles without the aid of slings or other artificial support. Besides hitting the steel target, you must knock it over. Thus, this is no game for light-caliber cartridges. There are no bull's-eyes; the only points scored are for targets knocked over, with the location of the hit on the target having no weight in the scoring.

The governing body for almost all target shooting is the NRA, and a shooter who is seriously interested in any of the many forms of small- or big-bore target shooting would be well advised to join this organization and to take advantage of the many aids it offers.

Big-bore target shooting requires a great deal of highly accurate ammunition. For most shooters, this means reloading. Ammunition designed for hunting simply will not prove accurate enough for serious target shooting. The major ammo companies gave up long ago on trying to load and sell centerfire rifle cartridges capable of match accuracy. Even their finest efforts—and, indeed, some ammo produced was very accurate—were easily bested by reloaders. Thus, for the most part, a serious big-bore target shooter must first become a skilled reloader if he is to be successful.

Recoil Big-bore shooters tend to wiggle and squirm into what many small-bore shooters would term unorthodox positions. However, the major differences,

Walking the line at a big-bore match.

for big-bore target shooters, are the ranges at which they shoot and the recoil they endure. The big-bore shooter must learn to read the wind and any mirage over a much longer piece of landscape. It is not unusual to have the wind trucking in opposite directions over different points in a 600-yard range. Also, the big-bore shooter must learn to control the fatiguing effects of recoil. While surprising to some, constant practice is one of the best methods for building tolerance to recoil.

The effect of recoil is, of course, cumulative. A shooter firing 40 rounds in a day will not be as fatigued by recoil as one who fires 50, 100, or even more rounds. Despite this, repeated exposure to recoil will allow a tolerance to develop that can be acquired in no other manner.

Techniques Big-bore shooting techniques do parallel those of small bore in many, if not all, of the basics. There are many classifications of high-power target shooting, including service rifle matches (semiautomatics), match rifles (where the bolt gun is most often used), long-range (where bull barrel rifles are often encountered) and a number of international-type competitions.

The big-bore shooter who has first mastered the skills of small-bore shooting will be in the best position to make a good showing early on in his centerfire efforts.

Silhouette Shooting

Silhouette shooting is a target sport that originated in Mexico. The targets are not paper bull's-eyes, as in most rifle shooting games, but rather they are steel silhouettes cut in the outline of targets the Mexican hunter might encounter in the field: prairie chicken, javelina, wild turkey and ram. These silhouettes are placed at varying ranges, depending upon whether a rimfire rifle or a centerfire rifle will be used. Too, the targets vary considerably in size; smaller ones for rimfire ranges and large, heavy ones for centerfire distances.

Silhouette ranges need not be flat and level; in fact, they are often laid out on rolling terrain. It is necessary that the targets be the prescribed distance from the shooter, but the course between the two can and often is quite varied. Targets are fired at in groups of five, with a total of ten targets at each range; that's forty targets in all.

As in any shooting sport, only accurate rifles will prove highly competitive.

The ram with a white bull's-eye superimposed to indicate the best aiming point.

The turkey silhouette.

The javelina or pig silhouette.

The chicken target with a white bull's-eye card placed over it to show the aiming point.

But the average bolt-action hunting rifle combined with accurate ammo will prove sufficient for very competitive shooting. In fact, silhouette shooting is designed specifically for hunting rifles.

Of all the forms of target shooting, silhouette shooting is perhaps the most fun. While punching holes in paper does appeal to a great number of capable riflemen, other shooters simply do not enjoy such shooting, regardless of the challenge. Many of those who do not find any appeal in paper targets can get a great deal of enjoyment from shooting steel targets. I heard one shooter describe the clang of the bullet's impact and the target's falling as "pretty near the most fun a grown man can have when it's not hunting season."

Silhouette shooting is not easy. Twenty-two rimfire silhouette targets are set up, with the chickens at 40 meters, pigs at 60 meters, turkeys at 77 meters and rams at 100 meters. That's a long way off to be shooting at what amounts to a very tiny target. If one were to superimpose a bull's-eye on each of the targets, these would measure only about 1$\frac{1}{10}$ inches on the chickens, 1$\frac{3}{4}$ inches on the pigs, 1$\frac{9}{10}$ inches on the turkeys and 2$\frac{1}{4}$ inches on the rams.

All rifle silhouette shooting is done from the offhand position without the aid of a sling. In fact, no artificial shooting aid of any type is permitted. The shooter simply has to stand up and have at it. With a maximum score of 40 knockdowns possible, it may be surprising to see the apparent low scores of most shooters—until the game is actually tried. The low scores suddenly become very difficult to attain. Targets must be actually knocked over to be scored as hits. Turning a target about on its stand is frustratingly scored as a miss. And there is a time limit that breaks down to 30 seconds per shot.

Big-bore silhouette shooting is conducted at very long ranges, especially when one considers that only the offhand shooting position is used. The chickens are fired upon at 200 meters, the pigs at 300 meters, the turkeys at 385 meters and the sheep at 500 meters. Even when the ranges are reduced to yards rather than meters (to facilitate the use of existing ranges in the U.S.), a great deal of satisfaction comes when a turkey is knocked over or a ram falls to the ground. If bull's-eyes were placed over each of the centerfire targets, they would measure only 6 inches, 9$\frac{1}{4}$ inches, 10$\frac{1}{2}$ inches and 12 inches, respectively, for the chicken, pig, turkey and ram. It's easy to miss such marks, and the extra area supplied by the body does not make it notably simpler.

Classes of Shooter   Shooter classifications run from B to triple A and are based on scores as follows:

HIGH-POWER RIFLES

23–40	AAA
17–22	AA
11–16	A
0–10	B

SMALL-BORE RIFLES

25–40	AAA
20–24	AA
15–19	A
0–14	B

It takes a great deal of capability to reach the triple-A classification. Shooters who attain this level of proficiency can justifiably call themselves skilled riflemen.

Twenty-two rimfire silhouette rifle shooting is quite similar to the big-bore event. True, the targets are set at only a fifth of the distance, but equally true is the fact that the targets are one-fifth the scale of their centerfire cousins. And the rimfire game has the distinct advantage of allowing all shooters the opportunity to participate. Not every shooter enjoys the recoil of forty rounds with a cartridge heavy enough to knock over the rams. Because rimfire ammunition is comparatively inexpensive, almost everyone can afford the cartridges necessary for practice sessions as well as for serious competition.

Shooting silhouettes with the rimfire (or a centerfire cartridge) can do a great deal to improve your ability in the game field. And you can take along the family, since silhouette shooting does have a great deal of spectator appeal.

Rifles and Ammunition Most hunting rifles, with sling removed, will meet the regulations for silhouette shooting. To qualify, a centerfire rifle must be of 6mm or larger caliber and must weigh no more than 10 pounds 2 ounces. Rifles used must not have artificial shooting aids, such as a palm rest or hook butt plate. Any sight, telescopic or metallic, may be used. While there are other dimensional restrictions, most hunting rifles are acceptable. In the light, small-bore rimfire classification, a maximum rifle weight of 7½ pounds is enforced as well as a minimum trigger-pull weight of 2 pounds.

For centerfire shooting, one needs a cartridge capable of knocking over the steel targets at the maximum ranges. Thus, few shooters use 6mm's, since hits on the 500-meter ram with these cartridges do not always result in the target being knocked over. Most shooters select a rifle of .27, 7mm or .30 caliber, with the 308 Winchester cartridge being quite popular.

Because some magnum cartridges are capable of severely damaging the steel targets, many clubs expressly prohibit their use. These heavy calibers offer no advantage in shooting, and their heavy recoil can prove to be a distinct disadvantage because of the shooter fatigue they induce.

A 6-power scope is about the minimum for silhouette shooting, but most shooters seem to do best with scopes of 8, 10 or 12 power. Too much magnification can easily prove a handicap, as the shooter's wobble will be amplified and cause a tendency to yank the trigger as the crosshair wobbles on and off the target. The best scope power, in my opinion, is the minimum that will (1) allow you to see your target clearly at the maximum range, (2) show when your crosshair is where you want it, and (3) have enough power and sharpness to let you see your wobbles without making them appear severe. A high-quality 6-power scope can get the job done, but I prefer the extra magnification of 8 power;

Two popular silhouette rounds are the 22 long rifle and the 7mm-08 Remington.

Federal's special 22 long rifle silhouette ammo.

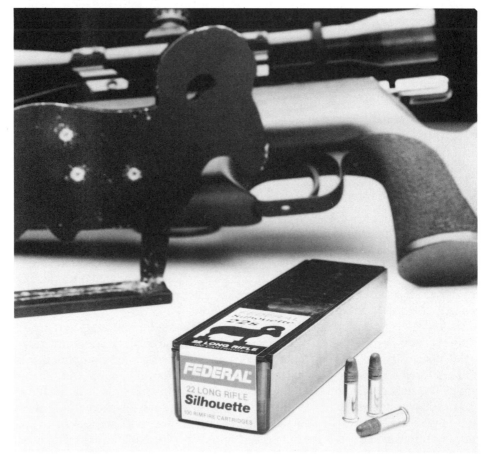

Popular centerfire silhouette cartridges include (left to right): 270 Winchester, 7mm-08 Remington, 280 Remington, 308 Winchester and 30-06 Springfield.

Silhouette scopes often have large knobs for quick and accurate adjustments.

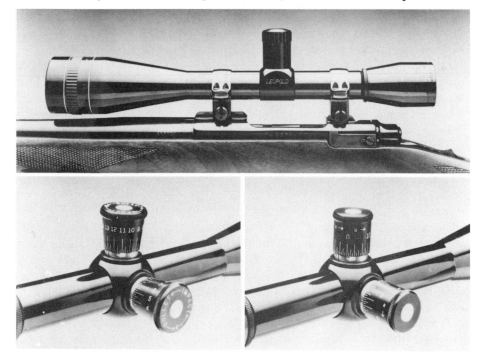

10 power is just a bit more than many can handle from the offhand position.

Cartridge selection varies somewhat, but the 270 Winchester, 7mm-08 Remington, 308 Winchester and 30-06 Springfield are all popular and adequate. Of course, any cartridge developing similar ballistic levels would prove satisfactory for shooting *siluetas metalicas*.

Techniques   Hitting the metallic targets at any range demands maximum concentration and well-developed shooting skills. The basic techniques described earlier in this book are important. You will need to master trigger squeeze, for instance, before you can begin to score well. And proper control of breathing is essential as is sight alignment.

With 30 seconds allowed for each target, there is more than ample time for slow, precise, deliberate rifle remounting, extra breaths during the same shot, repositioning of feet and so on. Each movement needs to be well considered, concise and executed properly the first time. While it may not occur to a beginner, the rifle should be removed from the shoulder between each shot. This allows the muscles to relax for a few seconds, thus preventing undue strain from occurring over the five-shot string. Some ranges require that the shooter fire on the second bank of five targets immediately after firing on the first group. I, for one, prefer this, as it maintains my concentration. Other shooters prefer to rest between banks of targets. If you shoot at more than one facility, you may well have to adapt to both methods.

For shooting silhouettes, I prefer a scope that is fully adjustable for parallax. Fixed-focus scopes are often set to be parallax-free at 100 or 150 yards. For rimfire shooting, there will be some amount of parallax at the 40-, 60- and 77-meter ranges. And in big-bore shooting, all the target ranges will have some amount of parallax present in the crosshair/target relationship.

For those unfamiliar with parallax, it is a phenomenon that allows the crosshair to move visually as the eye is moved up and down, left or right of the centerline of the scope's optical axis. Such movement may only be a fraction of an inch at a specific range with a good scope. A lesser scope may have as much as an inch or more of parallax. While this condition is not critical, I do feel that the presence of any handicap, small or great, detracts from a rifleman's performance.

Scopes with adjustable objective (front) lenses can quickly be set to remove any parallax at a specific range. Such scopes are of significant value for any serious target shooting.

Silhouette shooting cannot be taught well through the written word. You will need to get out and actually shoot the game to begin to become proficient. However, coaching is allowed, and such help can be very beneficial. The coach not only can advise the shooter where each shot strikes, but also can remind the shooter of the fine points in hitting targets. This kind of aid can help a shooter move quickly from a B classification up to AA. Beyond this, a good coach can prove invaluable in helping the AAA shooter realize the maximum number of targets within his capabilities.

Shooters who have difficulty in locating steel targets locally may want to contact the Metallic Silhouette Company, 2222 Peavy Circle, Dallas, TX 75228, or Titan Metallic Silhouettes, 5740 Tichy Blvd., Commerce City, CO 80022, for literature and pricing on their fine line of targets.

One word of caution: Do not mistake your ability to knock over a turkey at 385 meters or a ram at 500 meters to mean you are up to taking such long shots in the hunting field. A gut-shot steel ram will fall over and be scored as a perfect hit. A gut-shot animal is only wounded. But none of this is to suggest that silhouette shooting is not desirable practice for hunting. Indeed, it is actually excellent practice for any offhand field shooting. One simply must remember that when hunting, only shots that will reach vital organs are sporting.

Benchrest Shooting

Benchrest shooting is a sport of accuracy. Everything possible is done to enable the shooter to place five or ten shots into a hole not too much larger than the one at the end of his barrel. Extremely accurate rifles are used. Barrels are often short and of a large diameter to make them as stiff as possible. Actions are usually single-shot bolt models. Stocks are squared off to fit the supporting rests (a benchrest shooter hardly touches his rifle) and may be made of wood or fiberglass. But the sport gets its name from the shooting platform used to support the rifle—the benchrest.

A benchrest is a very sturdy, tablelike affair with its legs usually firmly supported by their extension into concrete footings well below the ground. The idea of a benchrest is to supply a steady, immovable shooting platform. In addition, a support for the forearm of the rifle is used and is adjustable for elevation; it is called a pedestal. Another sandbag is used to support the underside of the buttstock.

Shooters who are not competitive benchrest marksmen often use a benchrest to test the accuracy of a hunting rifle. For competition or accuracy testing, knowing the proper techniques will help in obtaining the smallest groups. Sometimes the tables used for benching a rifle offer less than the firm, steady support required. But for informal purposes, almost any bench can be used.

I've been shooting from a benchrest for perhaps 30 years, yet I have never fired in a benchrest match. My benchrest shooting has always been restricted to testing the worth of a rifle or a new load. And the rifles I have fired from the bench have usually been hunting rifles. Sometimes they were heavy varmint rifles, sometimes light woods carbines; often the rifles used have fit somewhere between these two extremes.

Because my benchrest experience has been informal, I sought out the advice of two serious competitive benchrest shooters for the contents of this chapter. Ed Shilen is world renowned as a benchrest shooter, and Skip Gordon is not exactly an unknown, since he is the originator of the well-known annual Super Shoot Benchrest Competition. The following material is the result of the input of both these fine competitors.

Most rifle enthusiasts will go to the bench at one time or another. They want to develop loads, zero their equipment, familiarize themselves with a new rifle or even enter into informal competition with a friend. (This *can* be dangerous. Owning bragging rights around the club is all well and good, but too much of this kind of activity can lead one into competitive groups shooting on the grand scale—organized benchrest.)

The basic piece of equipment for benchrest shooting is a pedestal. With a sandbag on its platform, it is used to support the rifle's fore-end. At left, the Hart pedestal; at right, the B-square pedestal which folds into a compact unit.

Hunters are interested in determining point of impact, while others may want to find out just how good their rifle can be. The former will perhaps shoot three to five shots at a given target; the latter will probably shoot five- or ten-shot groups. The first is an exercise in accuracy, while the latter shooting is a matter of precision. The big-game hunter really doesn't care if he can place all five shots in one ragged hole; he simply wants to know that his gun is properly sighted in and capable of keeping its shots in the vital areas of his quarry. But the serious varmint shooter may well want all ten shots to group into one very small, ragged hole.

Whatever the individual's objective, there are certain techniques that can be employed that will make a session at the bench more meaningful. The purpose of this section is to offer some suggestions that may be of help to hunter, varmint shooter and aspiring benchrest shooter.

The ideal place for investigating a rifle's potential is a ballistics tunnel. Realistically, however, few shooters have access to such a "condition-free" range. The quotation marks are used advisedly. Each tunnel has its own supply of peculiarities; a tunnel does not guarantee a shooter's being able to place shot after shot into the same hole!

The next best thing to a tunnel is a calm day. Ordinarily, the time to test a rifle is in the early morning or late in the afternoon, when the wind is often quiet. It follows, therefore, that any attempt to evaluate a rifle's performance in bad weather is a total waste of time.

Although it is possible to jerry-build a front rest, such an arrangement will always be a poor substitute for a proper pedestal. The rest must be stable and not given to moving under recoil. The foot screws of the rest should be of hardened steel with sharp points so they can be securely pressed into the bench top. Vertical adjustment of at least 4 inches is a must. The unit should be designed so that final adjustments can be locked into place.

A word of caution: Some rests incorporate a fore-end stop that may create all kinds of problems insofar as repeatability is concerned, if a shooter uses the stop to position his rifle. When so doing, it's imperative to back the fore-end off the stop at least "a hair" before pulling the trigger. The fore-end must not be in contact with the stop when the rifle is fired. In that this step may be forgotten, rests without stops are preferred.

The leather bags attached to the pedestal are designed for benchrest rifles and have a flat surface between the "ears" of approximately 3 inches. They can be adapted for the narrower stocks of field rifles by use of V-shaped wedges. In practice, however, the original conformation is entirely adequate; the shooter need only place the stock off-center so that it rests lightly against one of the "ears." There are two types of rear sandbag, bunny ear and rabbit ear. The former should always be used when the rifle has a cheek piece, in order to prevent canting.

Even during the calm of early morning and late afternoon, there will usually be some air movement. The placing of some simple wind flags will help the shooter. They need not be elaborate, just some stakes with 18- to 24-inch strips of ribbon will suffice. The stakes should be high enough so that the flags are at a height approximating the muzzle-to-target line. On a 100-yard range, the flags might be placed at 25, 50 and 75 yards.

For maximum accuracy, the rifle for benchrest shooting should be set up so the pedestal is lined up with the target and the bore line squared in the bag.

The rifle's fore-end should extend 2 inches beyond the sandbag. Tape serves as a guide to help the shooter position his rifle in the same place for each shot.

The rear bag should be placed midway between the pistol grip and the buttplate.

If the rifle is equipped with low-power hunting optics, a spotting scope is a valuable asset. Practically speaking, a 20X will provide adequate definition of bullet holes and a reading on any mirage condition.

The single most important factor in shooting successfully from the bench is consistency. The rifleman must concentrate on doing everything the same way, shot after shot.

Comfort is essential. The rifle should be in a position that is convenient for the shooter. The height of his chair plays a critical role. If the only support is too low, cushions can be used; if it's too high, however, the shooter will have to contort himself into an unnatural and uncomfortable position. Regrettably, the benches at most shooting ranges are far too low for upright shooting. An adjustable-height stool can play a significant role in allowing the shooter to attain a comfortable position.

Before firing, the shooter should spend some time observing the flags to determine prevailing conditions. If most of the flags are hanging limp, the shooter should be sure not to fire when there's even a slight "twitch" among the ribbons. If there is a breeze, the optimum time to shoot is when all of the flags are reacting identically. The shooter should strive to fire all of his rounds under the same conditions.

Because the individual working with a sporter rifle need not concern himself with time, unlike the competitive benchrest shooter, "holding" for conditions will not be necessary. Wind, variations in wind velocity, and mirage will affect point of impact. The more sophisticated enthusiast should feel free to determine the effect of conditions, but only after he's satisfied with the basic performance of his rifle. With practice, one can learn how to hold for varying wind conditions or changing mirage. However, only a great deal of experience can begin to show you how to accomplish this task.

Targets   Although any kind of target can be used, an official benchrest target is recommended. The 200-yard target sheet has a 2-inch sighting square and a 1-inch ten-ring, both of which are adequate for use with a hunting-type scope of lower magnification. Each sheet contains two targets; by holding on various corners of the sighting squares as well as their centers, a minimum of ten groups can be fired before one has to change targets. (In competition, the upper target is for "record," the lower target for "sighting" and determining the effect of conditions.)

Jackets with nylon shells should not be worn while trying to determine a rifle's potential. This may cause some eyebrows to be raised, but it is passed along in all seriousness. In an informal experiment, shooters without such jackets achieved groups that were appreciably smaller than those of shooters who wore jackets. The slippery surface of nylon-shell jackets evidently affects trigger control by eliminating friction where the shoulder is in contact with the butt.

Equipment   Normally, a sporter rifle isn't subjected to the same rigorous cleaning procedures as its competition cousin. However, a clean barrel will shoot more uniformly. Any rifle shoots more consistently if it's scrubbed and patched after every 15 or 20 rounds, and so it is suggested that cleaning gear be included when the shooter heads to the range for a bench session.

Sporter-weight barrels tend to heat up very quickly. The heat rising from the barrel will distort the sight picture, ultimately to the point where virtually nothing can be seen through the scope. A simple heat shield can be made. A target that is rolled up and taped to the objective lens housing will serve effectively.

Technique   The exact benchrest technique used depends upon the rifle. For instance, many benchrest competitors shoot free recoil—without any contact with the rifle other than the finger on the trigger. For trigger control, they "pinch" it, with the thumb against the trigger guard. But a field rifle with a 3- or 4-pound trigger cannot be pinched successfully. A trigger pull of less than 2 pounds is required to use the "pinch" method of trigger control successfully. Too, there are very few shooters who would obtain any great degree of enjoyment from shooting a 270 or 30-06 free recoil style. To use this method, a rifle needs a minimum of recoil. A 220 Swift is about as heavy as you can go for this style of shooting. Even a 243, when fired unsupported, will slam into the shoulder hard enough to cause discomfort.

Proper form for benchrest shooting. Shooter keeps his elbow flat on the bench to prevent strain on the arm. The thumb rests lightly against the stock and the index finger barely touches the trigger. Ammo is close at hand to avoid unnecessary movement between shots.

View from the shooter's left side. The left hand is used to make small adjustments in the rifle's position. The bag is squeezed to lower the muzzle and twisted to compensate for wind or mirage.

The shooter must adapt his technique to the rifle. The important factors to remember are:

1. Firmly "plant" the pedestal.
2. Make sure pedestal, rear bag and bore are in line with the target.
3. Get comfortable.
4. Watch the conditions.
5. Develop a system so that each shot is fired in the same way under identical conditions.
6. Be patient; there's no hurry.

No one can shoot any better than he can see. Benchrest shooting demands the very finest in optics. Select the brightest, sharpest scope you can afford and select one of ample power. Scopes of 20 to 25 power are good choices for the competitor. But even more important than magnification is the clarity of the optics. You should be able to clearly define a bullet hole with your scope. Power alone will not accomplish this; you need optics that are sharp as well as powerful.

If there is any one secret to successful benchrest shooting, it is learning to do everything in the same way for each and every shot. This "sameness" must take on a clinical approach. Nothing, absolutely nothing, can vary from shot to shot. Even the placement of the feet on the ground must be identical.

Obviously, shooting groups that measure only a few tenths of an inch from the center of the two widest shots demands only the finest possible ammunition. As noted, no one shoots factory loads in serious benchrest shooting. Each competitor carefully handloads his own ammunition in a very exacting manner. (See Chapter 37.)

Benchrest shooting is a challenge, but only those interested in determining the most minute factors that affect a rifle's ability to put all its shots in one hole need seriously consider the sport. It's not a tinkerer's idea of fun. But it is the ultimate challenge in rifle and shooter precision.

SELECTING A RIFLE 6

For a great many people, shooting means using a rifle. This can cover a very broad spectrum. One may wish to plink at tin cans, to be a competitive small-bore target shooter, to compete in high-power matches, to shoot steel silhouette targets, to hunt small game, varmints or big game. Such wide diversification results in a great variety of types of rifles offered to shooters, not to mention the multitude of possible caliber choices. Some rifle models are offered in as many as twelve calibers, ranging from the diminutive 17 Remington varmint round all the way up to the elephant-stopping 458 Winchester Magnum cartridge.

There are few riflemen who are unaware that a 243 Winchester cartridge is less than suitable for elk or that a 300 H & H Magnum is not the ideal woodchuck round. Yet, a great many shooters select cartridges that are less than ideally suited to the intended purpose. If a writer suggests that the 30-30 cartridge is not ideal for deer, a flood of mail from successful hunters who have taken deer every year with this cartridge condemns his "lack of knowledge." The fact remains that this cartridge, designed in the 1880s, is less than ideal for most of today's deer hunting. Because of variations in ranges that can be encountered in any part of the country, most riflemen would be better off with a cartridge that supplies a flat trajectory to 250 yards.

I have hunted extensively for deer in the heavy cover of New York, Connecticut, Vermont, New Hampshire and Maine. Many scribes have written that, in these states, far more deer are taken at ranges well under 100 yards than at ranges exceeding this distance. But the average range at which I have killed over twenty-five deer in the Northeast states is very close to 220 yards, and a few kills have exceeded the 300-yard mark. Why, then, would I or anyone else wish to be handicapped with a 30-30 or similar cartridge that is best suited to 150 yards or less? A very important step in selecting a rifle is obviously the shooter's choice of a cartridge. Equally important is plenty of shooting practice.

22 Rimfire Rifles

A goal of everyone who hunts with a rifle should be a high level of proficiency; marksmanship, it's often called. Therefore, almost every hunter should own a 22 rimfire rifle. The rimfire, because of its low noise level and inexpensive ammunition, allows the shooter to practice a great deal more than he could with the exclusive use of centerfire cartridges.

Ideally, the rimfire rifle selected should be of the same action type as the owner's favored big-game rifle. Also, the sights on the rimfire rifle should duplicate the sights on the big-game rifle. By matching action and sights, the shooter then duplicates, in part, his big-game rifle whenever he uses his rimfire rifle.

Cost and Quality Of course, rimfire rifles are often selected for specific applications. One shooter may demand a highly accurate rifle for suburban varminting or shooting steel silhouettes competitively. For this shooter, a $300 to $600 rifle may not be out of line. The cost of a good scope and mount may well add several hundred dollars to the price of the rifle. My favorite silhouette 22 rimfire rifle is a Remington Model 541-S equipped with a Weaver top mount and a Weaver 6X scope. I also have a Kimber bolt-action 22 rifle with a 1½–5 Leupold variable power scope mounted with Redfield rings. I use this rifle for cold-weather squirrel hunting, as I like its easy-to-release clip and large bolt handle for use when wearing heavy gloves.

But there are also several inexpensive 22s in my rack. I have a Remington Nylon 66 semiautomatic equipped with an inexpensive Bushnell 3–7 Custom variable-power scope. This rifle proves ideal for plinking sessions, canoe trips

For practical purposes, it helps to match your rimfire rifle in action type and size to your centerfire rifle. Shown here are the author's Remington 541-S 22 and his Remington 700 Classic in 270 Winchester.

and as a general knockabout 22. My wife's Ruger 10/22 with its Leupold 2½-power Compact scope is a delight for her. She likes its compact size, ease of loading, light weight and excellent accuracy. It is her only 22 rifle, and she is completely satisfied with it for all of her plinking, informal silhouette shooting and occasional small-game hunting. My 11-year-old son's ultralight and diminutive Chipmunk rifle, with its Bushnell custom 4 power scope, keeps him very happy. My Remington 40X target rifle has zero appeal to any member of the family except me. Thus, it is obvious that a specific shooter's desires or needs can result in drastically different selections of rimfire rifles.

A 22 rifle, whether it is to be used as a means of enjoyment unto itself or solely as an instrument to practice skills to be applied to centerfire shooting, must fit the physical and mental requirements of the shooter. And it must be suitable for its most demanding application.

For instance, a rifle that is difficult to load or operate will seldom see more than limited use during very cold weather, when heavy gloves are a must for comfort. Nor will a 22 rifle capable of only 2-inch groups at 50 yards make much of a gun for shooting at squirrels' heads at 75 yards, despite any merits it may have for plinking at tin cans.

The selection criteria applied to rimfire rifles are very closely aligned to those for centerfire rifles. The latter will, however, require somewhat more deliberation because of the wide variations in caliber choice and accuracy requirements. The first consideration should always be cartridge selection.

Cartridges When the rifle's application is known, cartridge selection is not too difficult. For varminting to about 250 yards, the 222 Remington or 223 Remington cartridges are ideal. For extended range varminting, the 22-250 Remington is hard to beat. If your varminting requires the use of a cartridge suitable to the longest possible ranges, the 243 Winchester, 6mm Remington, 257 Roberts or 25-06 Remington may well prove to be best. If you need a rifle primarily for varmints but suitable for occasional deer hunting, any of the 6mm's or .25-caliber cartridges mentioned are suitable choices.

On the other hand, if you desire a rifle primarily for antelope, deer and black bear hunting but still adaptable to off-season varminting, the 270 Winchester, 308 Winchester or 30-06 Springfield are all ideal choices. When the intended application is only for big game weighing up to 500 pounds, the 270 Winchester, 7mm-08, 280 Remington, 308 Winchester and 30-06 are all excellent choices. For still heavier game, the 30-06 is most adaptable. You could easily justify a 300 H & H Magnum, 300 Winchester Magnum, 8mm Magnum or even the 338 Winchester Magnum for game that weighs from 500 to 1,400 pounds. Of course, there are a number of other suitable cartridges that are useful under specific conditions.

Chapter 9, on rifle ballistics, will help you to determine which cartridges are suitable for your applications. When factory loads are limited to a narrow range of bullet weights, handloading your own ammunition can broaden the applications of a cartridge. For instance, the 7mm-08 is currently available only with 140-grain bullets in factory ammunition. This weight is ideal for game from 100 to 300 pounds. But for off-season varminting, you could load some 115-grain bullets and get double duty from this fine cartridge.

Types of Rifle Actions

Once you have selected the appropriate caliber for your shooting, you need then to decide upon the type of rifle you will use. There are single-shots, lever-action repeaters, pump-action repeaters, semiautomatics and bolt-action rifles from which to choose. It may well be that your selection of cartridges will limit the type of rifle action available. For example, if you decide on an 8mm Remington Magnum, the only gun available is a bolt-action. But if a 308 Winchester is your selection, you can choose from single-shot, lever-action, pump, semiautomatic or bolt-action rifles.

Each action style has its advantages and disadvantages. And action types will have a great bearing on the suitability for specific applications. Therefore, some discussion of the various actions is in order. The basics will apply whether you are considering a rimfire or centerfire rifle.

Semiautomatic The semiautomatic rifle is often more accurate than a great many lever-action rifles. It would indeed take a full-length book to go into all the technicalities of why this is so. For our purposes, suffice it to say that I have tested a great many firearms, and the results usually bear out this point. Exceptions do exist, of course. For instance, if one were to compare specific rifles of the semiautomatic type to specific lever-action rifles, it would be easy to find a semiauto that would be less accurate than a lever-action rifle.

The accuracy of most semiautomatics will allow hunting shots to 225 yards. This is based on the assumption that the maximum hunting range for a rifle is the maximum range at which it can group five consecutive shots into a 6-inch target. Individual rifles that are able to perform well above this level are sometimes encountered. Generally, though, you should select a semiauto only if your needs will not require shooting past 225 yards.

The only real advantage to a semiauto is a reduction in apparent recoil. Semiautomatics spread recoil over a greater period of time, turning what might be a harsh jab from a rifle of another style into a prolonged push. A shooter who is unable to handle the recoil of the 30-06 in a bolt rifle, but who needs the energy level of this cartridge for hunting, may well find a semiauto the answer to his problems. Handicapped shooters also may find that a semiautomatic allows for follow-up shots that would be awkward to accomplish with other rifles.

The semiauto's disadvantages include less accuracy and often additional weight or length compared to other action types. But I think the greatest disadvantage is the rapid availability of follow-up shots. Semiautomatic users sometimes regress to an attitude of not putting their best effort into the first shot. Because it is so easy to make follow-up shots, they feel these will take care of any mistakes. This kind of attitude can result in a lot of misses or poorly placed shots.

Some users of semiautos regress to a point where they feel it is perfectly OK to keep firing shots into the brush where their quarry disappeared. After all, they might just luck out and hit the unseen game! On several occasions, I have been unlucky enough to be in the same woods with some of these so-called hunters. Obviously, the use of a semiautomatic demands very mature gun handling, and not all shooters are able to avoid abusing the rapid-fire capability of these rifles.

SEMIAUTOMATIC CENTERFIRE SPORTING RIFLES.

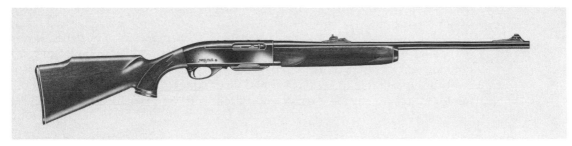

Remington Model Four

Browning BAR

H & K Model 940

Because of the abusive use of semiautos, some jurisdictions have banned their usage.

Most semiauto 22 rifles will prove capable of 2-inch groups at 50 yards. Again, individual exceptions can occur. Thus, the semiauto 22 is suitable only for plinking and for some of the less demanding hunting situations. Semiautos generally are unsuitable to serious varminting or squirrel shooting, where often the hunter's quarry may be partially obscured, with only an inch or so of head showing.

Lever Action   Lever-action rifles span a very wide range of accuracy performance. For instance, I have found that 94 Winchester carbines, on the average, group somewhere between $3\frac{1}{2}$ and 5 inches at 100 yards. Yet, I have shot a few specimens that would group $2\frac{3}{4}$ to 3 inches at this range and a few rarer examples that would do no better than 6 or 7 inches.

Among the best lever-actions I have shot were several Marlin 336s and a number of now-discontinued Winchester 88s, which were fully capable of putting five shots into 2 inches at 100 yards. Despite such rare accuracy, most Marlins were, at best, 150–200-yard rifles because of the limitations imposed by the 35 Remington and 30-30 cartridges for which they were chambered. The Winchester 88s in calibers 243 and 308 were, on the other hand, suitable for 250-yard shooting. Indeed, I witnessed one 265-yard kill on a large white-tailed deer by a woman using a Model 88 Winchester in 243 Winchester. Her ammo was carefully loaded with 100-grain Nosler Parition bullets, and the deer reacted as though it had been hit by lightning. My observations have shown that users of lever-action rifles either curse or praise their choice, with no middle-of-the-road evaluations.

As a whole, I feel that the lever-action's performance shows the widest variation in accuracy. Some models prove barely usable at 100 yards, and others can sometimes cut it to 250 yards. As a group, most lever-actions are only 200-yard rifles when combined with suitable cartridges.

It has been my experience that lever-action rimfires are slightly less accurate than semiautos of the same caliber. I own a number of semiautos that are capable of $1\frac{1}{2}$- to 2-inch groups at 50 yards, but I have never used a lever-action 22 capable of better than 2-inch groups. Most lever rifles seem to group between $2\frac{1}{4}$ and $2\frac{1}{2}$ inches at this range. Such accuracy is suitable for plinking but not much more. While I'm sure exceptions must exist and that there are some individual lever-action 22s capable of noticeably better accuracy, I am equally sure that such rifles are comparatively few in number.

Often cited as an advantage of lever-action rifles is the assumed speed at which a second shot can be taken. However, this advantage does not seem as real in practice as it does in print. Centerfire lever-action rifles offer poor leverage in extracting the fired cartridge, often making it necessary to apply considerable effort in working the action. Many shooters find it easiest to drop the rifle from the shoulder when cranking the lever down and up. But a shooter using a bolt-action rifle need not lower his rifle from the shoulder and can frequently get off well-aimed shots as quickly, if not more quickly, than someone using a lever-

LEVER-ACTION CENTERFIRE RIFLES.

Winchester 94 BigBore XTR

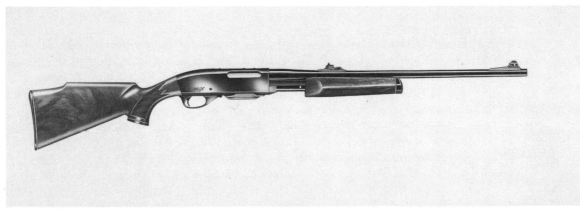

Marlin 336

A typical pump-action rifle: the Remington Model Six.

action. Thus, the imagined speed of a lever-action seems to be more of a wishful excuse to justify their usage. The only genuine advantage to lever-action rifles is that they often cost considerably less than any other type of centerfire rifle.

The disadvantage to the lever is its poorer accuracy compared to bolt, pump or even semiauto rifles. Thus, lever-action rifles are best selected only for short-range use.

Pump Action   Currently, there is only one sporting pump-action rifle being offered, the Remington Model Six (and its lower priced version, Model 7600). My experience with this rifle indicates that it can be considered a 225–250-yard rifle. The action of this rifle is extremely smooth, and it may be a fine choice for the hunter who does most of his shooting with a pump-action shotgun. This pump rifle will often prove accurate enough to be used for off-season varminting at ranges to possibly 150 yards with good handloads.

Pump-action 22s are far more abundant than their centerfire cousins, being offered by such firms as Remington, Browning and Rossi. On the whole, accuracy seems to be in the range of 2 inches or slightly less at 50 yards, making pump 22s suitable for all but the most demanding shooting. Some pump 22s are unsuitable for the mounting of a telescopic or aperture sight. This should be kept in mind when making a selection.

Pump-action rifles are very fast to use. In practice, when well-aimed shots are taken, most users of slide-action rifles can effectively shoot as fast as someone using a semiautomatic. Is such speed required? Probably not, but if fast shooting appeals to you, then a pump might well be your choice.

The disadvantages of a pump are limited accuracy as compared to a bolt and the potential noise that can be made by the fore-end rattling about. However, the latter disadvantage is more of a disadvantage in print than in the field. As with all action types other than a bolt, cartridge extraction and ejection can be difficult, with the occasional fired cartridge that decides to be balky when it's time to rid the chamber of it.

Bolt Action   Bolt-action rifles are always the choice of those who demand the utmost in accuracy. When matched with suitable ammunition, the average centerfire bolt-action rifle will produce five-shot groups of 1½ to 1¾ inches at 100 yards. Models that do no better than 2-inch groups should be considered the poorer examples. One is more likely to find a bolt-action rifle capable of 1¼-inch groups than to find one that will shoot only 2-inch groups. Because of their inherent accuracy, bolt-action rifles as a whole are suitable for use to 300 yards. Carefully tuned, quality bolt rifles can frequently shoot 1-inch or smaller groups at 100 yards. With such rifles, the rifleman has the capabilities of taking game to any range within the ballistics capacity of his cartridge.

The longest shot I have ever taken at a big-game animal was at 460 of my very long paces. I used the 270 Winchester cartridge in a rifle that had been carefully tuned. The shot struck the bottom edge of a big bull caribou's heart and resulted in a clean, one-shot kill. I'm sure the distance was at least 450 yards, and it may have been 20 or 30 yards greater. With any rifle action other than a bolt I would have had to pass up that shot at what turned out to be a fine trophy and a lot of very good meat.

Because a bolt rifle lends itself well to a good trigger design, shooters invariably find that they can shoot their very best with these rifles. The triggers on autos, pumps and lever rifles, on the other hand, frequently need to be heavier and almost always have a certain amount of creep or take-up. Such triggers prevent the shooter from doing his best. Thus, bolt actions are not only more accurate but are often easier to shoot.

At one time, the bolt-action rifle was offered in right-handed forms only. But today's hunter can purchase several models of left-handed bolt-actions; the Remington 700 is perhaps the most popular of these.

Yet, in the field, many lefty shooters use right-handed bolt-action rifles without undue difficulty. They simply support the rifle with the trigger hand's grip on the pistol grip and work the action with the right hand. However, left-handed shooters would be wise to purchase one of the bolt actions made specifically for them.

With the advantages of superior accuracy, better triggers and rugged dependability, one might well question what disadvantages exist with bolt rifles. For sporting purposes, in fact, there simply are none! A combat soldier or police officer may find positive usage for faster firepower, but for sport hunting there is nothing to detract from a bolt-action rifle's performance. Choose some other action type and it may or may not suit all your needs as you use it through the years. But a good bolt rifle will always prove up to the task, whatever it may be.

Of course, if you are a serious target shooter or varmint hunter, you will find that only bolt-action rifles are used in your sport. The single exception is military-type high-power matches, where highly refined and carefully hand-built semi-autos are used. With some military-type semiauto rifles, it is possible to build a rifle that will come close to matching a bolt rifle's accuracy. However, such accuracy is not possible with sporting semiautos.

Rimfire bolt-action rifles are available in a wide price range, and as you might expect, the accuracy levels vary a great deal. The cheapest of the 22 bolt-action rifles may group no better than 2 inches at 50 yards. The best of these rifles will prove capable of half-inch groups with target-grade ammunition. On the average, 1¼- to 1½-inch groups are the norm.

There are still other advantages to bolt rifles. Most allow for easy cleaning of the barrel from the chamber end without disassembly of the rifle. Most other rifle types need to be cleaned from the muzzle end. This means a higher risk of destroying the rifle's potential accuracy by damaging either the crown of the rifle's barrel or the vital last few inches of rifling.

Most bolts can be cleaned thoroughly by simple bolt removal. Other action types often require extensive disassembly. The use of a gunsmith is almost a necessity on more than a few of these.

LIGHTWEIGHT CENTERFIRE BOLT-ACTION RIFLES.

Remington Model Seven

Ruger Mannlicher stocked 77

Ruger 77 Ultralight

STANDARD WEIGHT CENTERFIRE BOLT-ACTION RIFLES.

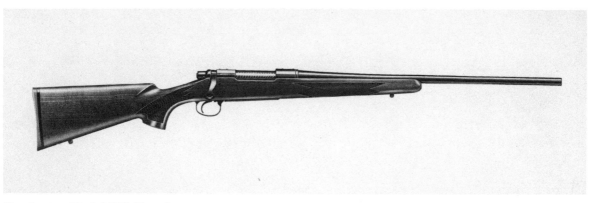

Remington Model 700 Classic

Remington Model 700 ADL

Ruger M-77

HEAVYWEIGHT CENTERFIRE BOLT-ACTION RIFLES.

Remington 700 BDL Varmint Special

Winchester Model 70XTR Sporter Varmint

Ruger 77 Varmint

Making Your Selection

I feel that most shooters are best served with a bolt-action rifle. However, if, after careful analysis, you decide on another type of rifle, then make sure to select one that seems to fit your needs. Not every purchaser of a semiautomatic, lever or pump rifle is making a mistake. For specific applications, the nonbolt rifles can prove quite adequate. For instance, if your shooting capability is such that you cannot do better than a 6-inch group at 200 yards regardless of the rifle used, then you would be a wise and sporting person if you refrained from ever shooting past 200 yards. For such shooting, almost any good rifle, regardless of action type, will prove adequate.

Variety   If, like many shooters, you find that your needs and requirements vary considerably, you may want more than one action type in your gun rack. The majority of all my rifles are bolt actions. But I do own one semiautomatic centerfire, several pump and semiautomatic 22s and several single-shot centerfire rifles.

Single-shots can often be tuned to shoot as accurately as most good bolt rifles. As a whole, however, when taken from the box, they appear to be somewhat less accurate, if only slightly so, than bolt-action rifles. Single-shots offer a unique challenge to the hunter, for there are no real disadvantages to using a single-shot unless you are a sloppy marksman. However, for dangerous game, a reliable bolt-action does offer a definite edge in personal security.

Popularity   Regardless of what type of rifle suits your style and needs best, do keep in mind that it pays to select those makes and models that are popular. Rifles in the gun shop always appear to suit the purpose, but in the field some become difficult to use or even balk at performing as expected.

Rifles seldom become popular if they are difficult to load or shoot or if they are prone to mechanical problems. Unless you are completely familiar with a less frequently encountered rifle, you may do best by confining your choice to those rifles that have proven extremely popular over a number of years.

In any event, consider the ease of loading and action operation with a gloved hand, the rifle's adaptability to your choice of scope or aperture sight and the ease of mounting sling swivels, if the rifle is not already so equipped.

Important Features   All else being equal, rifles with specific features are preferred to those without them. Easily and silently operated safeties; nonslip, unbreakable, hard rubber butt plates; recoil pads; factory-installed sling swivels or swivel bases—all are plus features. And if I have the choice between two models that are identical, I select the one with the best trigger pull rather than the one with the fanciest wood.

While the selection of a rifle might not need all the care of picking a spouse or home, it sure can come close to the care required in purchasing a new car. Think carefully about your specific needs in cartridges and accuracy. If in doubt, opt for a bit more cartridge and accuracy rather than for a bit less, because the selection made will have a very definite bearing on your capability as a marksman and hunter.

Weight and Length

The heaviest and longest rifles are best suited to target shooting. Among serious varmint shooters, rifles with heavy barrels are quite popular. These shooters don't walk much and frequently shoot from some sort of a rest. For such applications, the extra weight provided by a heavy barrel is an advantage in steadying the rifle or in offering a few tenths of an inch in increased accuracy.

For general hunting purposes, rifles with barrels of 22 to 24 inches and a maximum weight of 7½ to 8½ pounds will prove about right. In this weight include the scope mount and scope, sling and cartridges. Rifles that fit this category will be the easiest to shoot under a wide range of field conditions.

The Remington 700 Classic is, in my opinion, about the optimum in weight, length and balance. With this rifle or a similar one, the shooter will be able to do his best under the widest range of conditions without incurring the excess fatigue caused by carrying a rifle that is too heavy.

Nevertheless, there are hunting conditions best served by a short, lightweight, yet highly accurate rifle. When hunting steep, mountainous country, I have always found a light rifle a blessing. In the thin air of high altitudes, the shooter will do best if his burden of carrying a rifle is kept to a minimum. When you hunt in heavy timber or brush, it is often best to use a short rifle. If fast shots are the rule, a lightweight rifle will come to the shoulder quickest.

A short, light rifle is not always the best for long-range, offhand shooting. A heavier rifle simply will steady down a bit quicker. But for many hunting shots to about 200 yards, a short, light rifle can be best. When a secure shooting position can be assumed, a good light rifle can be amazingly devastating even at longer ranges.

The Winchester Model 70 Featherweight is a fine medium-weight rifle, suitable for a wide range of applications, though its 22-inch barrel is a bit long for use in "thick" country. For such applications, many shooters have found the Ruger 77 lightweight to be ideal. My favorite short, lightweight hunting rifle is the Remington Model Seven. Its 18½-inch barrel and its very short action result in an overall rifle length that is less than some popular lever-action carbines. Additionally, the diminutive Model Seven weighs less than many such carbines, yet this rifle is capable of a high level of accuracy. The bolt throw on this rifle is extremely short, which aids in making quick follow-up shots. Happily, the Model Seven's stock design closely duplicates that of its bigger brother, the 700 Classic. It is because of this excellent stock design that the Model Seven is easy to shoot accurately in the field.

Short, light rifles have a very definite hunting application. However, if I could own only one rifle for all of my hunting, I would select a moderate-length and -weight rifle such as the Remington 700 Classic. For a second hunting rifle

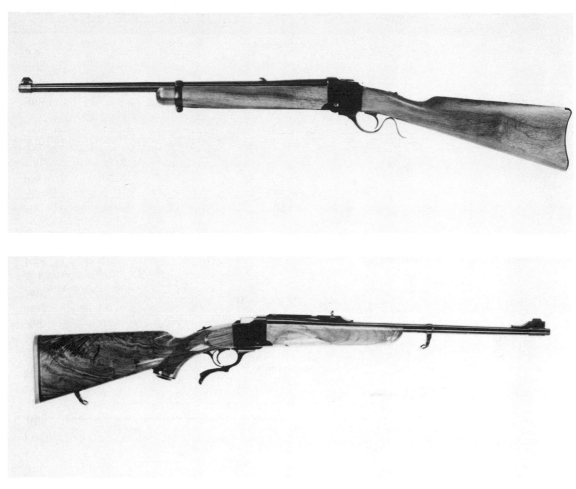

Single-shot centerfire rifles: Ruger No. 3 Carbine (above) and Ruger No. 1 Sporter.

I would always favor a short, light one, and the Remington Model Seven would be my choice.

Varmint hunters (as opposed to varmint shooters) will often find that a short, light rifle can add a great deal of pleasure to the days spent afield. I find that my Model Seven in 222 allows me to walk a great deal farther in search of woodchucks than I could manage comfortably with a heavier rifle. And its short length is darned handy when I'm crawling through cover to get within a reasonable range of my quarry. Coupled with a small 6-power Zeiss scope, this rifle is capable of taking varmints to 250 yards, yet has a minimum of bulk or weight to interfere with my often very long treks. But for those days when I want to sit

SOME SUGGESTIONS FOR SELECTING A RIMFIRE RIFLE

Requirement	Rifle Make & Model*	Caliber	Comments
Plinking	Remington Nylon 66 (S) Remington 572 (P) Remington 552 (S) Ruger 10-22 (S) Marlin 39 (L) Browning Autoloading (S)	22 L.R.	Use of long rifle ammo is suggested to protect chamber from erosion and to keep accuracy levels high.
Small game hunting, plinking, & varmint shooting	Remington 581 (B) H & R 865 (B)	22 L.R.	My Remington 581 rifle is surprisingly accurate.
Maximum accuracy requirements	Remington 541S (B) Anshutz 1422 (B) Ruger 77/22B Kimber 82 (B)	22 L.R.	My Remington 541S rifle is without doubt the most accurate rimfire rifle I have ever used. It is capable of ½″ 50-yard groups with most ammo.
Woodchucks & crows to 100 yds.	Kimber 82 (B) Mossberg 640K (B) Anshutz 1522(B)	22 Mag.	The Kimber is the most accurate of all the .22 Magnum rifles I have used.
Young shooters	Chipmunk Single Shot (B) Remington 581 Boys Rifle (B)	22 L.R.	Caution: The elevation screw on the rear sight of the Chipmunk is easily stripped.

NOTE: There are, of course, a great many other possible choices. The ones shown are suggestions based on the author's personal experience and preferences.

*S = semiauto
P = pump
L = lever
B = bolt

on a sunny hillside and take shots at anything up to 400 or more yards, I switch to a heavy, varmint-weight rifle with a high-powered scope.

Hunting is made up of many types of game, terrain and ranges. The selection of an appropriate rifle can add a lot of enjoyment to the hunt, allowing you to make the shots as they come. As stated, the one-rifle hunter is well advised to choose a medium-length, medium-weight rifle. A highly specialized hunter may be well off with a long, heavy gun or a short, light one, depending upon his purposes. When you have more than one rifle, it pays to have a standard weight, a lightweight and even a heavy one before you start to be concerned with rifles of widely varying calibers.

SOME SUGGESTIONS FOR SELECTING A CENTERFIRE RIFLE

Requirement	Rifle make & model	Caliber	Comments
Varmint hunting	Kimber 82 Classic	22 Hornet	Ideal cartridge for suburbia or hunting in proximity to homes.
Varmint hunting	Remington Model Seven	222 Rem.	Ideal rifle for extensive walking due to its light weight. Applications for all varmints to 250 yards.
Varmint shooting	Remington Model 700 Classic	22-250 Rem.	For all varmint shooting to about 350 yards.
Varmint shooting	Remington 700 Spl. Ruger 77 Varmint	243 Win. or 6mm Rem.	For the longest ranges.
Varmint hunting	Ruger 77 Ultra Light Remington Model Seven	243 Win. or 6mm Rem.	Good choice where a lot of walking is combined with long-range shooting.
Deer & antelope at long ranges	Remington 700ADL, 700 BDL, and 700 Classic Ruger 77 Winchester M-70 Featherweight	270 Win., 7mm-08 Rem. or 30-06	All will provide excellent accuracy.
Deer & black bear at short to medium ranges	Remington Model Seven Ruger 77 Ultra Light Ruger 77 International Remington Models Four & Six Winchester 70 Featherweight	7mm-08 Rem., 270 Win., 308 Win., or 30-06	All are comparatively light. The Model Seven Remington and the Ruger 77s will prove the handiest in heavy cover due to their short lengths.
Deer & black bear at short ranges only	Marlin 336 Winchester 94AE	30-30 Win., 307 Win., 356 Win.	Best suited for ranges of 150 yards or less.
Goat, sheep & caribou	Remington 700 Classic Ruger 77 Winchester 70 Featherweight	270 Win. 30-06	Ideal for any practical range with 130 gr. (270) and 150 gr. (30-06) bullets.
Elk & moose	Remington 700 Classic Ruger 77 Winchester 70 Featherweight	30-06, 300 H&H Mag., 300 Win. Mag.	Use of 180-grain bullets is suggested.
Grizzly bears & brown bears	Remington 700 Classic Ruger 77	300 H&H Mag., 300 Win. Mag., 338 Win. Mag., 375 H&H Mag.	The 300 H & H and 300 Win. magnum cartridges can be used for game as small as deer if the rifleman can handle the recoil.

NOTE: There are, of course, a great many other possible choices for rifles and cartridges. The ones shown are suggestions based on the author's personal experience and preferences. Not every model is available in all the listed calibers.

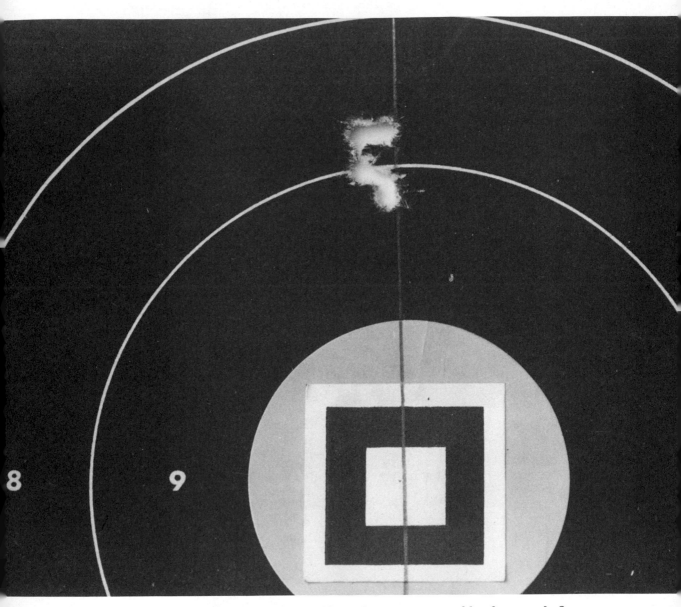

A properly tuned factory rifle and ammo are capable of extremely fine accuracy as evidenced by this less than ½ inch group fired with a Remington Model Seven and Remington Power Lokt ammo.

TUNING YOUR RIFLE FOR MAXIMUM ACCURACY

7

Within action style limits, most rifles are capable of acceptable accuracy. Only a few of those normally encountered are inherently inaccurate. However, rifles will seldom perform at the best possible level unless carefully tuned. Well-tuned rifles will shoot with a very high degree of accuracy and help make difficult shots relatively easy for the rifleman. A gun that consistently shoots small groups, that holds its point of impact under all conditions and that is easy to shoot will pay dividends in both the rifleman's confidence and his ability to make shots count.

Rifle accuracy requirements vary widely depending upon the terrain, the game hunted, and the ability of the individual rifleman. A whitetail-deer hunter in the heavy cover of a northeastern forest may find that a rifle capable of putting three shots into a 6-inch circle at 200 yards is all he requires. There would not be millions of lever-action 30-30 carbines being used if this level of accuracy were not suitable. However, a mule-deer hunter, in the sagebrush country of the West, requires a rifle capable of producing the same 6-inch group at 300 yards, and the serious antelope hunter may well demand similar groups at a full 400 yards. Varmint hunters frequently insist on a rifle capable of putting ten shots into 1 inch or less at 100 yards. Often the long ranges and small target area of their game make a rifle seem less than perfect if it's not capable of shooting groups of ¾ inch or less at 100 yards.

But even when 6-inch groups at 200 yards will get the job done, it makes sense to use a rifle that is capable of far more accuracy. A 6-inch group from the bench at the local range has a way of becoming a 12-inch group under field conditions. A rifle that is not properly tuned may shoot one, two or even three small groups and then a few very large groups. Obviously, consistency is important in a hunting rifle.

Because one needs to be able to count on every shot, not just a small random sampling of shots, serious shooters often use 10-shot groups to determine a rifle's real potential. But in practical terms for a hunting rifle, the average group size of five 5-shot groups will best reflect a rifle's potential performance.

Serious big-game hunters frequently use their rifles for off-season varminting. This enables them to keep in practice with the rifle they will use in the fall. Such off-season varminting places high demands of accuracy on a rifle. Only a rifle that has been carefully tuned will supply the required precision.

As important as accuracy is the rifle's ability to hold its point of impact. Small groups are nice, but if groups cannot be placed upon the point of aim, the rifle's worth is questionable. After carefully sighting in at the range, don't arrive at the moment of truth with the rifle delivering the bullet high, low, left or right of where it was shooting when it was sighted in.

Bedding When a rifle is bedded with some amount of upward pressure being applied by the fore-end against the barrel, any change in this pressure can cause the rifle to shoot to a different point of impact. And fore-end pressure will vary as the stock warps due to drying or moisture absorption as the seasons change. A stock soaked in a driving rain can absorb moisture very rapidly, and the point of impact can be altered notably during the hunt due to this absorption. It does not take much of a change in fore-end pressure to move the point of impact as much as 2 inches or more at 100 yards.

If a sling is used to help make difficult shots, you will be defeating your purpose if the rifle's barrel is bedded with any fore-end pressure. Proper use of a sling demands that considerable tension be put on it, and thus the fore-end will be pulled away from the barrel, altering the amount of pressure against it. The steadiness you gain by using the sling could be more than offset by the change in point of impact if the barrel is pressure-bedded.

Many shooters realize the potential problems caused by a pressure-point bedding system, but few take the steps necessary to relieve the problem. And while a majority of shooters can detect accuracy variations from group to group, they fail to take corrective action.

The most important step in improving accuracy and ensuring a consistent point of impact is a simple one: remove sufficient wood from the stock's barrel channel to ensure that the barrel does not touch the stock at any point. Enough wood needs to be removed to prevent the stock from coming into contact with the barrel at a later date as it warps with changes in its moisture content. Additionally, you will want to make certain that the use of your sling will not force the stock against the barrel.

Free-Floating Barrels Most rifles with barrels that are free of any wood contact shoot more accurately than those with barrels having one or more pressure points. I have noted only relatively few rifles that have shown no sign of improved accuracy when free-floated and have encountered none that performed less accurately after such free-floating. But even if a rifle gave superb accuracy without free-floating, it would still be subject to point-of-impact changes caused by stock moisture content or pressure changes resulting from the use of a sling. Free-floating will completely eliminate point-of-impact changes caused by changes in fore-end tension.

One might ask why the factories don't free-float barrels. The answer is that it would be very difficult, using machines, to remove sufficient wood to leave ample clearance while still not creating an unsightly gap. Also, some designers still believe that pressure bedding results in superior accuracy. But even if they were correct, the smallest groups in the world are of little value if the rifle's point of impact changes frequently.

A sheet of writing paper can be slipped between the stock and fore-end of a rifle that has been correctly bedded with a free-floating barrel.

The gap between a barrel and stock on a properly floated barrel is almost unnoticeable.

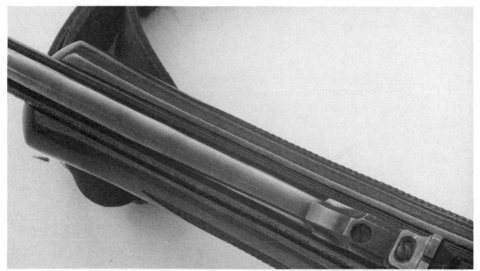

Most careful people can free-float rifle barrels by careful sanding of the stock's barrel channel with an 80-grit sandpaper. However, unless you are sure of your ability, I suggest that your first attempt to float a barrel be on a less-than-valuable rifle. It takes only a tad of misapplied enthusiasm to create an ugly gap between stock and barrel. If you have any doubts, find a good gunsmith or stockmaker to do the job.

A rifle owner who is interested in the beauty of his equipment may want no more than 0.007 inches of space between barrel and forearm. But with only minimum space, the stock could easily warp enough to bring the fore-end into contact with the barrel at some point in the future. A spacing of about 0.015 inches is more practical if you do not want to be bothered with the possibility of some future rebedding. Gaps of 0.020 inches or larger usually are unsightly and indicate less than ideal workmanship.

Any free-floated barrel should be checked from time to time by inserting a sheet of writing paper between fore-end and barrel. You should be able to move the paper up and down the barrel channel without any binding. Additional wood removal is called for if tight spots are noted.

Fitting Action to Stock   In addition to floating the barrel, there is another bit of fine tuning that can be accomplished while working on the stock. This involves the glass bedding of the recoil lug or the entire action. The fit of the action to the stock is critical to accuracy. If the action can move about during firing, accuracy will be less than optimum. The fit of the recoil lug is perhaps the most important area. Some factories, realizing this importance, are now glass-bedding the recoil lugs of their rifles. Examples of this are U.S. Repeating Arms' use of a bedding material for the recoil lug on the Winchester Model 70 and Kimber's glass bedding of the recoil lug on their Model 82 in 22 Hornet.

If you want to glass-bed only the recoil lug of a rifle, following the directions supplied with most glass-bedding kits will enable you to accomplish the task without undue problems. Again, however, I suggest that your first attempt be restricted to an inexpensive rifle. If you feel the entire action needs glass bedding because of poor factory fit, I strongly suggest that you allow a good stockmaker to do the job. Action fit to wood is critical not only with respect to accuracy but also in preventing it from splitting under recoil. Unless you have the necessary qualifications, it is wise to leave this part of rifle tuning to persons with plenty of experience.

You can, however, check to see if your action fits properly into the stock. Once the barrel has been completely floated, replace the barrel action into the stock and use only the front-action screw to lightly tighten the stock assembly to the rifle. Test for fore-and-aft or left-and-right shifting of the action in the stock by applying pressure to the barrel with your hand. Any movement or rocking means corrective measures are called for if you want the best in accuracy. Often, bedding only the recoil lug will correct any movement. But if there are doubts, the best procedure would be to have the entire action bedded in one of the various epoxy compounds.

A really good job of barrel floating and action bedding will provide substantial dividends in accuracy and uniform point of impact. In fact, uniformity can be made so consistent as to allow the removal and replacement of the stock without incurring a change in point of impact. Try that with a rifle that is fore-end pressure bedded, and your point of impact might shift as much as 6 inches at 100 yards.

Keep in mind that a mistake in using bedding compounds can result in the stock becoming hopelessly glued to the barreled action. If this happens, you will have to destroy the stock to separate it from the rifle. When you do your own bedding, carefully follow the directions supplied with the kit.

Proper Stock Fit   An important step in tuning your rifle is to ensure a good stock fit. If the stock is too long or too short, the gun will be difficult to shoot. Also, a stock that is too short will exaggerate recoil, so that shooting with any but the lightest cartridges will become painful. Almost surely a flinch will develop, and the ability to hit the target will disappear.

It is a simple matter to check to see if the length of pull from trigger to butt plate is correct for you. With the right arm bent at the elbow, hold the gun with the butt plate flat against the upper arm and the right side of the stock (for right-handed shooters) against the forearm. Place the trigger finger on the trigger.

Often a stock can be lengthened for correct fit by simply adding a slip-on recoil pad, such as this one made by Pachmayr.

You should find your arm and wrist nearly straight, with the trigger finger slightly bent. The pad of the trigger finger should be resting comfortably on the trigger. If you have to strain to reach the trigger, then the length of pull is too long. If you find you are bending your wrist and/or finger excessively, then the stock is too short.

Check the length of pull when wearing all hunting clothes. Checking the length of pull when wearing only a shirt will make a stock seem too short, when in fact, it may be just right for use with heavy clothing.

If you are going to use the same rifle for shooting in heavy winter clothing as well as summer dress, make the length of pull correct for the heavy clothing and learn to adjust when shooting in short sleeves. It is possible to adjust to a slightly short stock, but a long stock will slow down the mounting and sighting process considerably. Also, a slip-on recoil pad can be used when you're in shirtsleeves.

The proper fitting of a recoil pad or stock spacers, and the cutting shorter of a butt stock, are difficult tasks if fit and finish are to be the perfection most firearms owners demand. Such work is best left to a professional gunsmith.

Trigger Pull   After your stock has been properly bedded and fitted, you will have accomplished the most important steps in tuning. However, there are other points to be considered. The most important of these is the trigger pull. It is impossible to shoot your best if the trigger pull is excessively heavy or has take-up, creep or excessive backlash.

Trigger-pull adjustment is directly related to safety. An improperly adjusted trigger could cause your rifle to fire if it is bumped, dropped or otherwise subjected to rough handling. I have seen trigger-pull butchering that resulted in the rifle being fired whenever the safety was pushed to the off position. Because trigger and sear engagement is measured in thousandths of an inch and minute angles, no one should attempt to work on a trigger except a qualified gunsmith. Most shooters will do their best with a trigger pull between $2\frac{1}{2}$ to $3\frac{1}{3}$ pounds. When properly adjusted, a trigger should fire the rifle consistently at the same weight of pull, without perceptible movement.

Some triggers lend themselves to excellent adjustment. The triggers of most current centerfire bolt-actions can be easily adjusted for superb let-offs. But lever-action, semiautomatic and pump-gun triggers often cannot be adjusted satisfactorily. Also, a few less-than-well-designed bolt-action rifle triggers will defy tuning to an acceptable level.

Keep in mind that a crisp trigger pull is more important than a light one. A good trigger will let the sear go without perceptible movement, much like the breaking of a glass wand. Good triggers seldom have any notable amount of after-travel once the sear has been released.

Sights   The selection of a good scope and mount or suitable sights can be considered part of fine-tuning a rifle. Such selection is covered in detail elsewhere, but regardless of the type of sight chosen, it must be mounted to the rifle so as to be completely free of any possible movement. A less than snug screw can result in poor accuracy, as the sight or mount moves with the recoil of each shot. All mounting screws should be snugged up securely and checked from time to time.

Once you have tuned a rifle properly, it need not be done again. All that is required is that you slip a piece of paper between stock and barrel from time to time, to ensure that the barrel is indeed floating. Of course, all stock screws need to be kept tight. This should be checked each year prior to your annual sight-adjustment check.

An old gentleman of the shooting sports once said: "Only accurate rifles are interesting." I agree, and add that only well-tuned rifles will qualify.

Recoil pads, either of the slip-on type or permanently installed, can add a great deal of comfort when shooting your favorite rifle.

Not all recoil pads are gun-mounted. This shock absorber works very well when pinned to the clothing.

ACCESSORIES THAT MAKE RIFLE SHOOTING EASIER

8

Marksmen just don't happen. A high degree of proficiency with a rifle is often a direct result of good shooting habits and practice. Both form and repetition play vital roles in developing the skill of a marksman. But, as most serious shooters realize, there are a few accessories that can enhance the performance of most riflemen.

If one were to try and count the accessories offered to riflemen, the listing would be very long indeed. However, when one evaluates these accessories in light of their effectiveness in aiding the shooter to hit his target, the list is shortened considerably. Some shooting-improvement accessories are suitable only for target shooting, others only for limited hunting situations. Relatively few are suitable for almost all hunting applications.

Recoil Pads   One accessory that I firmly believe in is an honest recoil pad— not the hard rubber butt plate that some rifle manufacturers choose to call a recoil pad, but a rubber pad that actually is thick enough and soft enough to compress under the forces of recoil.

Few shooters realize how beneficial a recoil pad can be in preventing fatigue during practice sessions. This fatigue prevention will allow you to develop good shooting habits rather than poor ones. Additionally, by making shooting more comfortable, a recoil pad can actually result in your doing more shooting, and more shooting will mean greater proficiency. Any rifle that produces a recoil level equal to or greater than that of the 270 is best fitted with a recoil pad. Don't let any macho-type thinking get in the way of your using this accessory.

A recoil pad is especially beneficial and essential for young shooters, shooters of small stature, shooters who are overly affected by the fear of recoil, shooters who find recoil a painful experience and shooters who use rifles with the recoil of a 30-06 Springfield or greater. Also, hunters who are forced to take shots from awkward positions will find recoil pads beneficial.

To those who feel they are immune to the effects of recoil I would like to ask: "Is your car equipped with power steering, power brakes or an automatic transmission? How about air-conditioning?" These accessories make driving easier and more comfortable, thereby reduce driving fatigue and enable you to be a better driver and to drive well for longer periods of time. A good recoil pad, properly fitted, will do the same for your shooting. It will make your shooting more comfortable and thus reduce fatigue, thereby making you a better shot.

Those who shoot their rifles only occasionally have the most need of a recoil pad. Such shooters often unknowingly develop a slight flinch. These involuntary muscle jerks can raise havoc with your ability to hit a target.

I have often said that if I were a firearms manufacturer who wanted to develop a reputation for accurate rifles, the first step I would take is to install recoil pads on all rifles larger in caliber than a 257 Roberts.

If you have doubts as to what a recoil pad can do for your shooting, I suggest you purchase a good slip-on recoil pad and put it on your favorite rifle. These pads are inexpensive and will slip onto your rifle's stock quickly and easily. After a few shooting sessions, I would be quite surprised if you were not in the market for a permanent and thicker pad. Even the toughest shooters will be more comfortable with a good recoil pad. And more comfort means better accuracy for the majority of riflemen.

Slings The most difficult part of shooting any rifle is holding it motionless after the sights have been aligned on the target. Most shooters never achieve the ability to hold the rifle absolutely steady; instead, they settle for the minimum amount of barrel waving that they can make possible. Yet, there is an accessory that can greatly reduce muzzle wobble. Many hunters' rifles are equipped with this accessory, though they generally leave it unused when shooting. Frequently, this accessory, the sling, is used only when there is a need to have both hands free in order to drag a deer from the woods. Slings are a convenient way to free your hands from rifle carrying, as most shooters know. However, few shooters take advantage of the rifle-steadying capability of a properly used sling.

Difficult targets can suddenly become easier to hit if you use a sling properly. A hasty-sling position can be assumed without any delay during the mounting of the rifle to the shoulder. The military-sling position does take a few seconds to assume, but it can turn really difficult shots into not-too-hard-to-make shots.

Not every rifle is adaptable to the use of a shooting sling, but knowledge of sling types and how they are effectively utilized may well make the difference between a clean kill, a crippling shot or a miss on your next hunt.

Unfortunately, with some rifles, a sling is meant to be used only as a means of carrying the rifle, not as a shooting aid. Rifles that have the sling swivel anchored directly to the barrel are not suitable for use with a sling as a shooting aid. Proper shooting with a sling creates a lot of tension against the anchor points. If this tension is applied directly to the barrel, it will bend the barrel sufficiently to cause a considerable change in point of impact. If you doubt this, you need only carefully shoot a rifle equipped with a barrel-mounted swivel with and without use of the sling. As an example, the Ruger No. 1 single-shot features barrel-mounted swivels in certain variations and therefore should be equipped only with a simple carrying strap.

If you prefer a sling that has a wider section over the area where it contacts

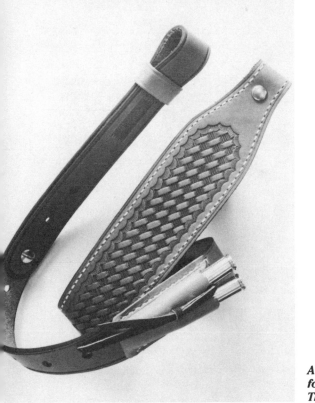

A good sling is essential for carrying the rifle comfortably and for holding it steady when shooting. The cobra style sling has a cartridge pouch.

your shoulder, a cobra-type sling can be used. Such a sling spreads the weight of the rifle over a greater area, thus preventing the sling from becoming uncomfortable. Cobra-style slings do add some bulk, which can prove a disadvantage if the sling is carried in the pocket while actually hunting.

Sling Positions   For any rifle where the forward sling swivel is not mounted to the barrel, a sling will always prove an asset in making shooting easier. The quickest sling position for hunting shots is often called the *hasty sling.* This position can be used with any style sling that has been adjusted to proper length.

To employ the hasty sling properly, carry the firearm muzzle down over your left shoulder, with the sights or scope at your back. (Left-handed shooters will carry the rifle over the right shoulder.) When a shot is to be made, insert the left hand between the sling and fore-end so that your hand enters the sling from the body side. As you grasp the fore-end, the sling should feel snug across the back of your hand. Swinging the rifle forward will allow the rear portion of the sling to drape over the upper arm. Then turn the rifle upright and bring it to the shooting shoulder. If the sling has been adjusted to the proper length for the clothes worn, it will form a snug anchor around the left upper arm and over the back of the left hand. The resulting tension will enable you to hold the rifle much steadier than could ever be accomplished without the aid of a sling. The secret of success is making sure the sling is tight across the upper arm and the

ASSUMING THE HASTY SLING POSITION, OFFHAND

1. Carry gun over left shoulder, muzzle down.

2. Place hand under sling and onto fore-end.

3. Swing gun across the body . . .

4. . . . and position buttplate firmly on shoulder.

back of the hand. Be sure the length of the sling is adjusted for the clothes being worn. Sleeve thickness of heavy hunting garments versus a light hunting shirt will require a notable change in overall sling length.

The hasty-sling position is very fast to use. When it is properly executed, the rifle can be brought to the shoulder as quickly as without a sling. However, despite its merits, the hasty sling cannot provide all of the rifle-steadying support of a properly executed military-sling position.

The military-sling position does take time to assume. But for prone, sitting, kneeling or offhand shooting it has no match. The increase in steadiness will enable you to hit targets that would normally be beyond your capability. However, the military-sling position cannot be accomplished with the popular carrying-type slings. A military-style sling such as the one offered by Uncle Mikes must be used.

To use this position, insert the left upper arm through the loop formed by the forward half of the military sling. Then pull down the keeper (a leather loop) against the upper arm, anchoring the sling in place. Put your hand on the fore-end by reaching from the left side of the sling and moving your hand over the sling. When the forearm is grasped, the sling will pass over the back of the left hand and around the inside of the wrist. The forward portion of the sling should be quite tight. If not, adjust the length of the forward loop until it is a tad difficult to get the hand into position. A military sling is most effective when as snug as possible. The rear loop of the military sling should be adjusted so that no tension is applied by it. Actually, the best rear-loop length adjustment is one that allows the use of a hasty-sling position when there is insufficient time to assume the military-sling position.

The use of a sling will not affect the point of impact on rifles with free-floated barrels. On rifles with barrels bedded with forearm pressure, you should check for point of impact variation at the range. Because the use of a sling as a shooting aid places a lot of pull on the fore-end, pressure from the fore-end will be reduced on nonfloating barrels, so that some change in point of impact is sure to occur. I favor a full floating barrel for all my hunting rifles for a number of reasons, the use of a sling being an important one.

Because the military-type sling can be used for both the hasty and military positions, it will prove the most practical. If your style of hunting or the terrain rules out the use of a military position, then a basic carry strap can be used effectively for the hasty-sling position.

Bipods and Unipods   Another accessory that can help make difficult shots easier is the modern adaptation of the crossed sticks used by buffalo hunters to steady their rifles. In modern format, these buffalo sticks take many forms, but they are basically divided into two categories: bipods and unipods.

Some bipods attach to the front sling swivel stud. Those with mounting methods that eliminate the sling are less than popular with me. Some shooting supports are not attached to the rifle in any way. They are simply carried hanging from the belt. When pressed into use, a spikelike leg is jammed into the ground. Obviously, such a rest, while effective, has limitations, not the least of which is the inability to be used on rocky terrain.

ASSUMING THE MILITARY SLING POSITION, SITTING

1. Slide keeper up to widen loop; slip arm through.

2. Pull loop tight.

3. Ready to shoot, with sling wrapped behind wrist.

A field rest is handy, especially for varmint shooting. This one is adjustable for a wide range of heights.

Shooting rests were at one time considered unsporting. However, more and more shooters have come to understand that it's not a bit unsporting to ensure a swift, clean kill, as opposed to a cripple that is lost to die a lingering death.

Shooting supports are highly practical for woodchuck and other varmint hunting. For most other types of hunting, however, they are often a burden to carry.

Set Triggers Another accessory that is beneficial, primarily to the varmint hunter, is the set trigger. Set triggers offer the advantage of a very light trigger pull—usually just a few ounces—when the trigger has been "set." Used without "setting," such triggers afford clean, crisp trigger pulls of normal weight. They are sold in two basic versions—a single-set style, in which the trigger is forced forward to engage the set feature, and a double-set trigger, which has two separate triggers—the rear trigger is pulled to set the front trigger to its lightweight let-off. Such triggers can improve accuracy on shots where the shooter can assume a very steady shooting position. From a less-than-solidly-supported position, this trigger should be used in its normal mode.

Summary: The Essentials It has been my experience that, among all the accessories for hunting rifles, those that actually help to make rifle shooting easier, and hence enable you to hit your target precisely, are limited to a soft recoil pad, a good leather sling, a shooting rest and a set trigger. I consider only the first two essential. For rifles smaller than .27 caliber, the recoil pad would be essential only if the shooter is particularly recoil shy, a not uncommon occurrence. A recoil pad will also help protect the rifle from damage by resisting the chipping, cracking or scratching that often occurs with plastic or metal butt plates. And if you are ever forced to stand the rifle in a corner, a rubber butt pad will help prevent the rifle from slipping and taking a finish-marring tumble to the floor.

The number of rifle accessories suitable for the target shooter is quite large compared to those that are practical for the hunter. Depending upon what type of shooting interests you, the list of options can be quite different. The small-bore position shooter will find such shooting aids as a well-padded shooting jacket, a sling keeper, a cuff and hook and a well-padded shooting glove essential to a high level of performance. The silhouette shooter, on the other hand, needs no accessories (nor are they generally even allowed) except a spotting scope or binocular for his spotter's use.

The main consideration is whether a specific accessory is practical in use and actually a positive aid in shooting. A serious benchrest shooter, for instance, will soon find that a fixed-position, sand-filled fore-end and butt stock rest is far less efficient than a well-made pedestal that is adjustable for height. The purchase of any accessory should be made only after the use of a similar item or, at the very least, recommendations by experienced and qualified shooters.

Externally mounted telescope apertures increase sharpness of the image when target shooting.

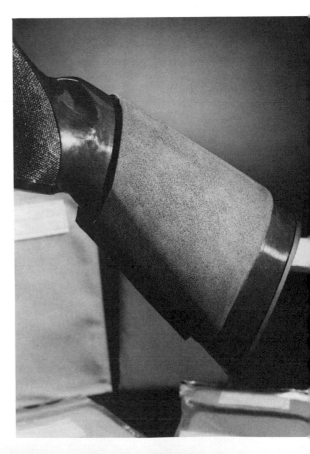

A cheek saver can reduce bruised faces on heavy recoiling rifles.

The following list may help you consider items that have proven beneficial to other shooters.

SOME USEFUL RIFLE ACCESSORIES FOR:

Benchrest shooting
1. Shooting pedestal, adjustable
2. Extra lightweight (pull) triggers
3. Fiberglass stock
4. Action sleeve
5. External telescope apertures (improve target sharpness)
6. Telescope sunshade

Small-bore target shooting
1. Padded rifleman's coat
2. Sling with hook and cuff
3. Fore-end stop
4. Padded shooting mitt
5. Spotting scope

Big-bore target shooting
1. Recoil pad
2. Spotting scope
3. Padded shooting jacket
4. Recoil shock eliminator (Action Products) in lieu of recoil pad
5. Cheek Saver pad (Action Products)

Hunting
1. Sling
2. Recoil pad (rifles over .26 caliber)
3. Shooting rest
4. Single- or double-set trigger

Gun Cases   Finally, one should keep in mind the value of a gun case. Often a shooter will spend $600 to $1,000 or more for a good hunting rifle with a scope, and then skimp on the price of a gun case.

A good case should afford sufficient protection during transportation of the rifle from home to the range or hunting territory. If you travel by car, a well-padded, soft leather case is ideal. It will take up no more room than absolutely necessary, yet protect the gun from all of the value-destroying hard knocks that can occur during an auto trip. The case will also protect your rifle from accidental abuse when it is not being used—if you remember to store your rifle in it.

For airline travel or travel in a bush plane, or even railway or bus transportation, nothing less than a good, hard, luggage-type case will suffice. Guns can be subjected to unbelievable abuse by baggage handlers, most of whom simply care nothing about your property. Even bush plane pilots, who should know better, will frequently pile a great deal of gear on top of a rifle case. Select a case no larger than needed to keep bulk at a minimum. If the case will be out of your sight, even for only a short while, sturdy locks are required. If the case will go directly from your car to a float place, then you can get along with a far less expensive case that does not incorporate locks. A good case for such purposes is the Gun Guard Special Edition case.

For use around or on the water, a waterproof case is a good investment. One in particular that appeals to me has an interior that is inflatable. The cushion of air not only protects a gun from knocks on rocks or in a canoe bottom, it also offers excellent protection from outboard motor vibrations. And if the case goes overboard, it will easily float an 8- or 9-pound rifle. This case, called the Solidaire, is made by Dart Manufacturing.

All good rifles and scopes deserve a hard luggage case for commercial travel. Additionally, a soft case should be available for auto and camp use. It makes little sense to abuse a rifle or let the effort of sighting in be destroyed for want of a good case. Buy the most rugged and well-padded cases you can possibly afford. Indirectly they will prove an accessory that indeed makes your shooting easier. Have you ever tried shooting with a broken stock or smashed scope?

Gun cases help to insure that your rifle will arrive at camp undamaged and sighted in. Waterproof and floatable Solidaire case by Dart (left) will prevent rifle loss on canoe trips. Hard aluminum case (center) will protect rifle on airlines. For auto travel, the all-leather, well-padded Weather Shield case (right) is ideal.

A good set of scope caps will protect lenses from damage both in transit and while hunting.

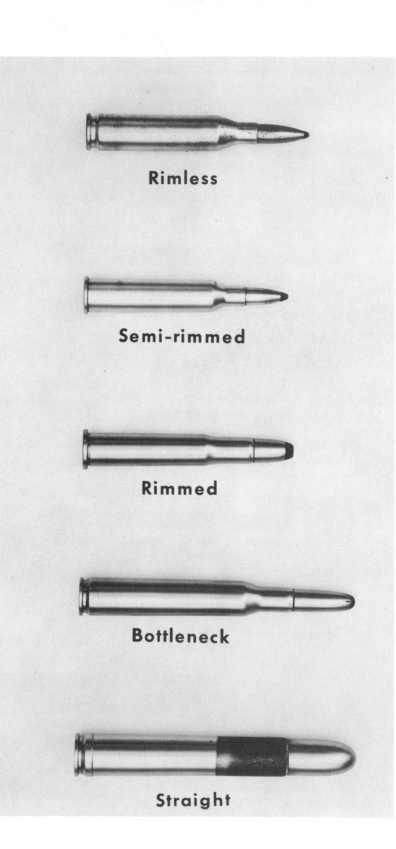

Rimless

Semi-rimmed

Rimmed

Bottleneck

Straight

Basic types of rifle cartridges.

BASIC BALLISTICS FOR THE RIFLEMAN

9

Cartridge ballistics vary widely, and the nomenclature applied to the various rounds cannot be interpreted as very meaningful. For instance, the word "magnum" is frequently abused, as can be noted by comparing one cartridge bearing the magnum name with another bearing the same name or, for that matter, with a standard, nonmagnum cartridge.

Magnums   If you review the following ballistics carefully, it should be obvious that all magnum cartridges do not produce magnum-type ballistics.

Caliber	Bullet wt. in grains	Muzzle vel. in ft/s	Muzzle energy in foot-pounds
264 Winchester Magnum	140	3030	2855
270 Winchester	130	3060	2700
280 Remington	150	2970	2935
375 H & H Magnum	270	2690	4335
44 Remington Magnum	240	1760	1650
444 Marlin	240	2350	2940

Obviously, the 264 Winchester Magnum's ballistics are ever so slightly superior to that of the 270 Winchester. But are they enough of a gain to rate the word "magnum"? If you compare the 264 Winchester Mag with the 280 Remington, you will find that the 264's bullet is lighter, going only 60 feet per second faster, and that its energy level is 80 foot-pounds less. Hardly magnum performance! But the 264 Winchester Magnum case has a magnum-style belt around its head and is called magnum whether or not the cartridge offers any real gain in ballistics over other similar, nonbelted cartridges.

But what about the listed 44 Magnum? It has no belt and is in fact a diminutive rimmed cartridge. And it uses the same 240-grain bullet as the 444 Marlin, at 590 feet per second *less* velocity and 1290 foot-pounds *less* energy. The 44 Magnum may be a "hot" round in a handgun, but when stacked up against rifle cartridges it is indeed puny in performance.

The listed 375 H & H Magnum's velocity is well below that of a great many cartridges. But when combined with its heavy bullet weight, it does produce magnum amounts of energy and recoil.

Obviously, a cartridge's name cannot be depended upon to be a true indication of its performance. Surely the muzzle velocity combined with bullet weight and the resultant muzzle energy are much better indicators of a cartridge's potential performance. But even here things can be deceiving. Look again at the foregoing ballistics. The 444 Marlin and the 270 Winchester ballistics, when compared, show the 444 Marlin with notably more muzzle energy than the 270 Winchester— some 240 foot-pounds more, to be exact. Hence, one might be inclined to accept the 444 Marlin as a more potent cartridge. The next chart compares the down-range performance of these two cartridges.

Cartridge	Bullet wt. in grains	Muzzle	At yards 100	200	300	400
			velocity in feet per second			
270 Winchester	130	3060	2775	2510	2260	2020
444 Marlin	240	2350	1815	1375	1085	940
			energy in foot-pounds			
270 Winchester	130	2700	2225	1820	1470	1180
444 Marlin	240	2940	1755	1010	630	470
			trajectory in inches			
270 Winchester	130		+2.0	+1.0	−4.9	−17.5
444 Marlin	240		+2.0	−2.9	−13.6	−31.3

The name of a cartridge doesn't always reveal its ballistics. Despite its nomenclature, the diminutive 44 Magnum (left) is considerably less potent than the larger 444 Marlin.

The 308 cartridge (left) is considerably more potent than the 45-70 (right) despite the latter's larger size.

After reviewing the full range of velocities, energies and trajectories from the muzzle to 400 yards, it is quite obvious that the 444 Marlin, for all its muzzle energy, is not anywhere near the equal of the 270 Winchester. The 444 Marlin has barely enough energy at 200 yards to be useful for deer, while the 270 has more than enough energy to get the job done at 400 yards (assuming you subscribe to the theory that it takes about 1000 foot-pounds of energy to kill a deer humanely).

Ballistics Comparisons   The shooter needs a source of ballistic comparison of all the various cartridges. And these comparisons need to be made at all the ranges at which the cartridge can be put to use. There is, therefore, a very definite need for ballistics tables. Without them, few shooters would ever be aware of the potential performance of one cartridge over another. We might be led to decide that a belted case means magnum performance or that large cases, such as the 45-70 Government, mean greater performance than smaller cases like the 308 Winchester. Ballistics tables quickly show that belted cases or cartridges called "magnum" are not necessarily indicators of performance. Nor does case size necessarily indicate performance levels.

The ballistics tables as presented in this chapter are therefore offered as an aid in allowing you to determine the relative performance of the various cartridges and bullet weights. The velocities and energies shown have all been rounded to the nearest 5 feet per second or 5 foot-pounds. However, do not assume that every shot fired will obtain the velocity or energy level listed. The ballistics tables merely represent a nominal or hoped-for average velocity and energy. The actual average of your velocity and energy could be somewhat higher or lower. But even more importantly, the shot-to-shot variation can be considerable. The very best ammunition will deliver relatively low shot-to-shot variations, while less desirable ammunition can produce surprising extremes.

To better acquaint you with exactly what can occur, let me give you the results obtained from the firing of two different lots of the same type ammo. Both used the same bullets and both were manufactured by the same producer. Dates of manufacture were different. Results are based on the firing of a 10-shot string with loads from each lot.

	Lot #1	Lot #2
Average velocity	2665 ft/s	2690 ft/s
Highest velocity	2704 ft/s	2718 ft/s
Lowest velocity	2626 ft/s	2656 ft/s
Extreme variation (1)	78 ft/s	62 ft/s
Standard deviation (2)	22 ft/s	21 ft/s

(1) Difference between highest velocity and lowest velocity.

(2) An analytical expression that indicates the relative uniformity of the ammunition. The lower the number, the more uniform the ammunition will be from shot to shot.

The two foregoing lots of ammunition were of average quality. Better ammunition is possible, and equally so, one can encounter far worse uniformity. When velocity variations are less than 50 feet per second, one can consider the ammunition to be of excellent uniformity. When variations of more than 100 feet per second are encountered in a 10-shot string, the ammunition may be performing at a substandard level. When handloading ammunition, I strive to maintain extreme variations well under 50 feet per second. But in that the standard deviation number is more indicative of long-run performance, I look for loads and procedures that will produce a maximum standard deviation of 25 feet per second. It is not uncommon to obtain standard deviations as small as 7, 8 or 9 feet per second when one assembles ammunition carefully with compatible components.

Uniform Performance   Obviously, ballistics tables will not tell you which cartridges perform the most uniformly. And if you do not own a chronograph, you have no way of measuring actual performance. But you can base your choice of cartridge somewhat on popularity. Cartridges that perform with consistent uniformity tend to gain the best reputations for accuracy and performance on game. Certain cartridges throughout the years persist in their popularity because of their ballistic merits. If you do not have sufficient exposure to enough shooting people to form a solid opinion as to which cartridges are most popular, you may want to consider my opinions, which are based on 37 years of hunting, industry and testing experience. The following calibers have proven to be ballistically uniform when combined with a good ammunition lot:

22 Hornet
222 Remington
223 Remington
22-250 Remington
243 Winchester
6mm Remington

250 Savage
257 Roberts
25-06 Remington

270 Winchester

7mm Mauser
7mm-08 Remington

280 Remington
7mm Remington Magnum

30-30 Winchester
300 Savage
308 Winchester
30-06 Springfield
300 H & H Magnum
300 Winchester Magnum

8mm Remington Magnum

338 Winchester Magnum

375 H & H Magnum

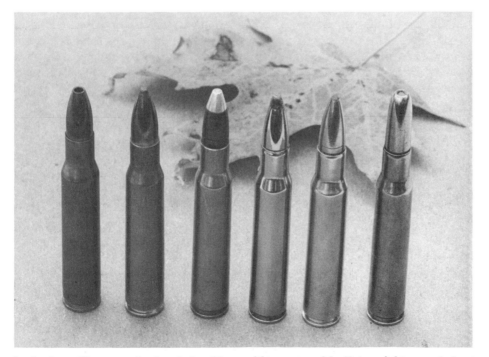

A single caliber can be loaded with a wide range of bullet weights, each best suited only to one specific application. The 30-06 Springfield cartridge is shown with a number of bullet weights (from left): 110 grain, varmints; 125 grain, varmints; 150 grain, light big game; 165 grain, light and medium big game; 180 grain, medium and heavy big game; 220 grain, very heavy big game.

But knowing the ballistics of each cartridge and which usually provide the most uniform results is still not enough. As an example, consider the following 30-06 Springfield ballistics:

Bullet wt in grains	Muzzle	Velocity in ft/s		
		100 yds.	200 yds.	300 yds.
125	3,140	2,780	2,445	2,140
150	2,910	2,615	2,340	2,085
180	2,700	2,470	2,250	2,040

Bullet wt in grains	Muzzle	Energy in foot-pounds		
		100 yds.	200 yds.	300 yds.
125	2,735	2,145	1,660	1,270
150	2,820	2,280	1,825	1,445
180	2,915	2,435	2,025	1,665

Different Ammunition for Different Game   Only one of the listed loads is suitable for heavier big game, one is ideal for deer and light game and one is meant for nothing bigger than varmints. Obviously, the ballistics tables, unto themselves, give no clue as to which bullet weights are suitable for what type of game. Bullets that are designed to expand rapidly on small woodchucks are useless for deer or larger game. The use of such bullets on deer-sized game would result in a hideous surface wound that would not be immediately fatal, allowing the animal to escape and die a lingering death. Additionally, a bullet designed to stop an 800-pound animal would shoot through a small 140-pound

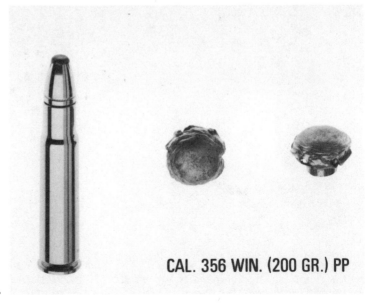

CAL. 356 WIN. (200 GR.) PP

An example of a well-expanded bullet.

deer without much expansion or transfer of energy. It is essential, therefore, to select the proper bullet weight and construction for your intended purpose.

In the 30-06 Springfield ballistic example, the 125-grain bullet is designed for varmints; the 150-grain bullet is ideal for light, thin-skinned game such as deer, antelope, goat and sheep; the 180-grain bullet is best chosen for game weighing 400 pounds or more.

Sometimes, as in this case, one can gain some insight into bullet use by the weight of the bullet. Light bullets are often for varmints, medium bullets for light big game and heavy bullets for heavy game. But frequently there are certain applications for which no bullet is suitable in a given caliber.

Those unfamiliar with bullet construction and the application of the various bullets may refer to the table on p. 121, which outlines basic recommended bullet usage. This table will make it possible for you to choose among the various bullets offered in a given caliber without danger of using a bullet for a nonsuitable application. The handloader will need to use discretion when selecting bullets, as this table applies only to factory-loaded ammunition.

Bullet Shapes   One other aspect of bullet selection is the actual nose shape of the bullet. Sometimes a given weight of bullet will be offered in a number of shapes and styles. For instance, the 30-06 Springfield is offered as a 180-grain bullet in a spitzer shape (very sharp point), a round nose (quite blunt) and quite a few configurations somewhere in between these two extremes. The best possible choice is evident from the following sample ballistics:

30-06 SPRINGFIELD BALLISTICS BASED ON BULLET SHAPE AS LOADED BY REMINGTON

Bullet wt in grs	Bullet style	Bullet shape	Velocity in ft/s (yds)				Energy in ft-lbs (yds)			
			Muzzle	100	200	300	Muzzle	100	200	300
180	Bronze Pt.	1	2700	2485	2280	2085	2915	2470	2075	1735
180	Pointed SP	2	2700	2470	2250	2040	2915	2435	2025	1665
180	Round nose	3	2700	2350	2025	1725	2915	2205	1635	1190

1 = very sharp nose   2 = sharp nose   3 = blunt nose

Note how rapidly the blunt, round-nose bullet loses its velocity and energy as the range increases. It makes far more sense to select the pointed bullets over the round nose, since game is seldom shot at the muzzle, the only place where bullet performance is similar. Then why are round-nose bullets available? In part, they owe their existence to a misconception that has persisted for many years, and in part, they are still made because bullet expansion was more reliable with the round-nose bullet designs of many, many years ago.

The misconception involved here stated that blunt-nose bullets, preferably of large diameter and low velocity, penetrated through brush, whereas spitzer bullets and those of smaller diameters or higher velocities would not penetrate brush as well. It has been proven many times that this has no basis in fact.

The late Lysle Kilbourn and I once conducted extensive brush-penetration tests. We used all types of bullet shapes, from spitzers to wadcutters, and all diameters, from .22 to .45 caliber. Bullet weights from 45 to 500 grains were tested at velocities from 1100 to 4000 feet per second. Our experiments proved, as have other similar tests, that no bullet performs better than another when penetrating through brush, regardless of its nose shape, speed or diameter. All bullets deflect with equal disregard to their shape, diameter or speed. And all bullets perform equally poorly when encountering brush obstacles on the way to the target.

Today's bullet manufacturers are able to design spitzer bullets that expand with reliability equal to any round-nose bullet. Thus, round-nose bullets continue to be available only because of customer demand based on an unfounded adage and the poor performance of spitzer designs made during the first half of the century.

As a knowledgeable rifleman, you will favor the bullets with sharper profile, thus ensuring the maximum in retained downrange velocity and energy. As

The round-nose bullet (left) may be equal to the spitzer at the muzzle, but as the range increases it becomes less potent than a sharper-pointed bullet of the same weight (the 180-grain 300 Savage is shown).

shown in the sample 30-06 ballistics, this can easily be as much as 360 feet per second and 545 foot-pounds of energy at 300 yards, even when bullets leave the muzzle with identical velocities and energies.

The ballistics tables included in this chapter are for most of the efficient bullet shapes generally available. For specific performance levels of different shapes, refer to the manufacturers' ballistics tables. Remember to consider the barrel length of the gun you will be using. All the manufacturers' ballistics are based on barrels of 24 inches, with the exception of the 30M1 Carbine, the 351 Winchester and the 44 Remington Magnum, which are based upon a 20-inch barrel length. Many sporting rifles have barrel lengths of 22 inches or less, in which case the actual ballistics obtained will be somewhat less than suggested by the tables. Some examples are shown in the table.

Caliber	Bullet wt in grs	Muzzle vel in ft/s	Muzzle energy in foot-pounds	Barrel length in inches
243 Winchester	80	3005	1600	18½
		3350	1995	24
243 Winchester	100	2690	1605	18½
		2960	1945	24
257 Roberts	100	2710	1630	22
		2900	1865	24
257 Roberts	117	2585	1735	22
		2650	1825	24
7mm-08 Rem.	140	2680	2235	18½
		2860	2540	24
307 Winchester	150	2680	2395	20
		2760	2540	24

The velocities from barrels shorter than the test 24-inch ones cannot always be predicted. However, you can make a close approximation of velocities for short barrels by using the following table:

Velocity range	Approx. change in velocity for each 1″ of barrel reduction from the nominal length
0 ft/s to 2000 ft/s	5 ft/s
2001 ft/s to 2500 ft/s	10 ft/s
2501 ft/s to 3000 ft/s	20 ft/s
3001 ft/s to 3500 ft/s	30 ft/s

Using the Tables   At best, this is an arbitrary approximation of the actual anticipated results. But the table will be sufficiently close in predicting actual results obtained with most commercially produced ammunition. Velocity variations will be encountered from lot to lot of ammunition or from one barrel to the next. Velocity variations of 100 feet per second, with identical ammunition, can occur between two barrels of the same make, model and length.

As you gain experience with the ballistics of the various cartridges and in the variations that can exist from the printed tables, you will become aware that the mere listing of an additional 50 to 150 feet per second velocity does not necessarily mean that a given cartridge will prove superior to another in the field. Take a look at the listed ballistics of the 243 Winchester and the 6mm Remington. On paper, one is a slightly superior cartridge, while in the field the two perform as ballistic twins.

For all practical purposes, you will need a listed velocity increase of at least 180 to 200 feet per second to notice any change in real performance in the field, all other things being equal. Or, on an energy level, an increase of 300 foot-pounds is required to make a notable difference in performance on big game.

So use the ballistics tables to make final evaluations of the various cartridge and bullet weights with respect to their potential field performance. For all practical purposes, when comparing cartridges, you can ignore velocity differences of less than 150 feet per second or energy differences of 200 foot-pounds. Comments to the contrary are pure hype rather than a realistic evaluation of field performance. Of course, any comparison must be based on an all-other-factors-being-equal condition. Remember that you must select the proper bullet for your intended purpose.

Despite their physical differences, some cartridges often perform identically in the field. The 243 Winchester and 6mm Remington are twins in actual field performance.

The shorter 7mm-08 Remington is ballistically superior to the longer 7mm Mauser.

Keep in mind also that all the velocity and energy in the world is useless unless you can deliver it accurately to the vital organs of the intended target. A 308 Winchester bullet fired from a highly accurate bolt-action rifle equipped with a good telescopic sight can prove far more effective than a 30-06 Springfield bullet fired from an inaccurate semiautomatic fitted only with iron sights, regardless of the ballistic superiority of the latter on paper. You and your rifle's capabilities as a combined team are of considerably more importance than a small gain in published ballistics.

Any rifleman who wants to investigate the worth of the ammunition he uses should consider the purchase of a good chronograph. Some, such as the Oehler Model 33, incorporate a program that allows for the computation of averages, extremes and standard deviations, which can be obtained at the push of a button.

WIND DRIFT TABLE

Caliber	Bullet wt. (grs.)	Muzzle velocity in ft/s	Drift in inches (approx.) for 10 mph wind (90°) at:		
			100 yds.	200 yds.	300 yds.
17 Remington	25	4040	1.4	6.3	15.7
22 Hornet	45	2690	2.9	13.5	34.9
222 Remington	50	3140	1.5	6.8	16.8
223 Remington	55	3240	1.3	5.7	14.0
222 Remington Magnum	55	3240	1.3	5.7	14.0
22-250 Remington	55	3680	1.0	4.3	10.2
243 Winchester	80	3350	1.0	4.3	10.4
243 Winchester	100	2960	0.9	3.6	8.4
6mm Remington	80	3470	1.0	4.1	9.9
6mm Remington	100	3100	0.8	3.3	7.8
250 Savage	87	3030	1.1	4.8	11.6
250 Savage	100	2820	1.3	5.6	13.5
257 Roberts	87	3170	1.1	4.5	10.8
257 Roberts	100	2900	1.2	5.3	12.9
257 Roberts	117	2650	1.5	6.5	15.8
25-06 Remington	87	3440	1.0	4.1	9.7
25-06 Remington	100	3230	0.9	3.9	9.3
25-06 Remington	120	2990	0.8	3.5	8.2
264 Winchester Magnum	100	3320	1.0	4.4	10.6
264 Winchester	140	3030	0.8	3.2	7.4
270 Winchester	100	3430	0.6	3.2	7.4
270 Winchester	130	3060	0.9	3.8	9.0
270 Winchester	150	2850	1.0	4.3	10.2
7mm Mauser	140	2660	1.1	4.8	11.5
7mm Mauser	175	2440	1.5	6.3	15.3
280 Remington	150	2970	0.7	3.1	7.3
7mm Remington Magnum	125	3310	0.9	3.8	9.0
7mm Remington Magnum	150	3110	0.8	3.4	8.1
7mm Remington Magnum	175	2860	0.7	3.1	7.2
30 Carbine	110	1990	3.4	15.0	35.5
30-30 Winchester	150	2390	2.0	8.5	20.9
30-30 Winchester	170	2200	1.9	8.0	19.4
300 Savage	150	2630	1.6	7.2	17.5
300 Savage	180	2350	1.7	7.5	18.2
308 Winchester	110	3180	1.5	6.7	16.6
308 Winchester	125	3050	1.1	4.7	11.2
308 Winchester	150	2820	1.0	4.4	10.4
308 Winchester	180	2620	0.9	3.9	9.2
308 Winchester	200	2450	1.2	4.9	11.5
30-06 Springfield	110	3330	1.4	6.2	15.2
30-06 Springfield	125	3140	1.1	4.5	10.8
30-06 Springfield	150	2910	0.8	3.5	8.4
30-06 Springfield	180	2700	0.7	2.8	6.6
30-06 Springfield	220	2410	1.1	4.5	10.6
300 H & H Magnum	150	3130	0.9	3.8	8.9
300 H & H Magnum	180	2880	0.8	3.4	8.0
300 H & H Magnum	220	2580	1.0	4.3	10.2
300 Winchester Magnum	150	3290	0.9	3.8	9.0
300 Winchester Magnum	180	2960	0.8	3.4	8.0
300 Winchester Magnum	220	2860	0.9	3.8	9.0

WIND DRIFT TABLE (*continued*)

Caliber	Bullet wt. (grs.)	Muzzle velocity in ft/s	Drift in inches (approx.) for 10 mph wind (90°) at:		
			100 yds.	200 yds.	300 yds.
32 Winchester Special	170	2250	1.9	8.4	20.3
338 Winchester Magnum	200	2960	1.0	4.2	9.9
35 Remington	200	2080	2.8	12.4	29.8
358 Winchester	200	2490	1.5	6.5	15.7
358 Winchester	250	2230	1.4	5.9	14.2
375 H & H Magnum	270	2690	1.1	4.5	10.7
375 H & H Magnum	300	2530	1.7	7.2	17.6
44 Remington Magnum	240	1760	4.0	17.2	38.6
444 Marlin	240	2350	3.1	14.1	35.3
45-70 Government	405	1330	2.8	10.8	23.2
458 Winchester Magnum	500	2040	1.5	6.3	15.0

CARTRIDGE AND BULLET WEIGHT APPLICATION TABLE

Caliber	Bullet wt. (grs.)	Applications
17 Remington	all	varmints
22 Hornet	all	varmints[1]
222 Remington	all	varmints
223 Remington	all	varmints
222 Remington Magnum	all	varmints
22-250 Remington	all	varmints
243 Winchester	80	varmints
243 Winchester	100	light big game
6mm Remington	80	varmints
6mm Remington	100	light big game
250 Savage	87	varmints
250 Savage	100	light big game[2]
257 Roberts	87	varmints
257 Roberts	100 & 117	light big game[2]
25-06 Remington	87 & 90	varmints
25-06 Remington	100 & 120	light big game
264 Winchester Magnum	100	varmints
264 Winchester Magnum	140	big game
270 Winchester	100	varmint
270 Winchester	130 & 150	big game
7mm Mauser	140 & 175[2]	big game
7mm-08 Remington	140	big game
280 Remington	150 & 165	big game
7mm Remington Magnum	125	varmints
7mm Remington Magnum	150	big game
7mm Remington Magnum	175	heavy game
30 Carbine	110	plinking & target
30-30 Winchester	150 & 170	light big game[2]
300 Savage	150 & 180	light big game[2]
307 Winchester	150 & 180	big game[2]
308 Winchester	110 & 125	varmint
308 Winchester	150	big game

CARTRIDGE AND BULLET WEIGHT APPLICATION TABLE
(continued)

Caliber	Bullet wt. (grs.)	Applications
308 Winchester	180 & 200	heavy big game
30-06 Springfield	55, 110 & 125	varmints
30-06 Springfield	150 & 165	big game
30-06 Springfield	180, 200 & 220	heavy big game
300 H & H Magnum	150	big game
300 H & H Magnum	180 & 220	heavy big game
300 Winchester Magnum	150	big game
300 Winchester Magnum	180 & 220	heavy big game
32 Winchester Special	150 & 170	light big game[2]
8mm Remington Magnum	185	heavy big game
8mm Remington Magnum	220	dangerous big game
338 Winchester Magnum	200	heavy big game
338 Winchester Magnum	225	dangerous big game
35 Remington	150 & 200	light big game[1]
356 Winchester	200 & 250	big game[2]
358 Winchester	200 & 250	big game
375 Winchester	200 & 250	light big game[2]
375 H & H Magnum	270 & 300	dangerous big game
44 Remington Magnum	240	light big game[3]
444 Marlin	240	light big game[2]
45-70 Government	300 & 405	light big game[1]
458 Winchester	500 & 510	dangerous big game

[1] For short ranges only (150 yards or less).
[2] For modest ranges only (200 yards or less).
[3] For extremely short ranges only (50 yards or less).

APPROXIMATE LEADS (in feet*) FOR GAME TRAVELING AT:
15 feet per second

Caliber & bullet wt.	100 yds.	200 yds.	300 yds.	400 yds.
30-30; 170 grs.	4¾	7¾	—	—
243; 100 grs.	1½	3¼	5¼	7½
270; 130 grs.	1½	3	4¾	7
30-06; 180 grs.	1¾	3¾	5¾	8
300 Win. Mag.; 180 grs.	1½	3½	5¼	7½

20 feet per second

Caliber & bullet wt.	100 yds.	200 yds.	300 yds.	400 yds.
30-30; 170 grs.	6½	10½	—	—
243; 100 grs.	2	4½	7	10
270; 130 grs.	2	4¼	6¾	9¼
30-06; 180 grs.	2¼	4¾	7½	10½
300 Win. Mag.; 180 grs.	2¼	4½	7¼	10

APPROXIMATE LEADS (in feet*) FOR GAME TRAVELING AT:
25 feet per second

Caliber & bullet wt.	100 yds.	200 yds.	300 yds.	400 yds.
30-30; 170 grs.	8	13	—	—
243; 100 grs.	2¾	5½	8¾	12¼
270; 130 grs.	2½	5¼	8¼	11¾
30-06; 180 grs.	3	6	9½	13¼
300 Win. Mag.; 180 grs.	2¾	5¾	9	12½

30 feet per second

Caliber & bullet wt.	100 yds.	200 yds.	300 yds.	400 yds.
30-30; 170 grs.	9½	15½	—	—
243; 100 grs.	3¼	6¾	10½	15
270; 130 grs.	3	6½	10	14
30-06; 180 grs.	3½	7¼	10½	16
300 Win. Mag.; 180 grs.	3¼	7¾	10¾	16

35 feet per second

Caliber & bullet wt.	100 yds.	200 yds.	300 yds.	400 yds.
30-30; 170 grs.	11¼	18¼	—	—
243; 100 grs.	3¾	7¾	12½	17½
270; 130 grs.	3½	7½	11½	16¼
30-06; 180 grs.	4	8½	13¼	18½
300 Win. Mag.; 180 grs.	3¾	8	12½	17½

NOTE: For different speeds, simply interpolate from the appropriate table. For example, for game traveling at 40 feet per second, double the 20-feet-per-second table leads. Or for game traveling at 50 feet per second, double the 25-feet-per-second table leads. For game at other speeds, combine two tables.

*to nearest ¼ foot

COMPARATIVE TRAJECTORIES

Caliber	Bullet Wt. (grs.)	Style	Muzzle vel. in ft/s	100 yds.	150 yds.	200 yds.	250 yds.	300 yds.	400 yds.
17 Remington	25	HP	4040	+2.0	+2.4	+1.7	−0.2	−3.7	−17.4
22 Hornet	45	SP	2690	+2.0	+0.6	−3.7	−14.0	−24.8	−73.2
222 Remington	50	SPS	3140	+2.0	+1.6	−0.4	−4.3	−10.6	−33.1
223 Remington	55	SPS	3240	+2.0	+1.5	+0.2	−3.5	−8.8	−27.1
222 Rem. Mag.	55	SPS	3240	+2.0	+1.5	+0.2	−3.5	−8.8	−27.1
22-250 Remington	55	SPS	3680	+2.0	+2.4	+1.3	−0.7	−4.3	−17.1
243 Winchester	80	SPS	3350	+2.0	+2.0	+0.9	−1.5	−5.4	−18.6
243 Winchester	100	SPS	2960	+2.0	+1.8	+0.2	−2.8	−7.5	−22.2
6mm Remington	80	SPS	3470	+2.0	+2.1	+1.1	−1.0	−4.5	−16.5
6mm Remington	100	SPS	3100	+2.0	+2.0	+0.6	−2.0	−6.1	−19.8
250 Savage	87	SPS	3030	+2.0	+1.7	⊕	−3.3	−8.4	−25.2
250 Savage	100	SP	2820	+2.0	+1.5	−0.6	−4.5	−10.4	−29.5
257 Roberts	87	SPS	3170	+2.0	+1.8	+0.4	−2.5	−6.9	−21.9
257 Roberts +P	100	SP	3000	+2.0	+1.7	−0.2	−2.2	−9.1	−26.8
257 Roberts +P	117	SP	2780	+2.0	+1.3	−1.2	−5.7	−22.6	−35.4
25-06 Remington	87	HP	3440	+2.0	+2.2	+1.1	−1.2	−5.1	−18.4
25-06 Remington	100	SPS	3230	+2.0	+2.0	+0.8	−1.7	−5.7	−18.9
25-06 Remington	120	SPS	2990	+2.0	+1.7	+0.2	−2.8	−7.4	−21.6
264 Win. Mag.	100	SPS	3320	+2.0	+2.0	+0.8	−1.7	−5.8	−19.4
264 Win. Mag.	140	SPS	3030	+2.0	+1.8	+0.4	−2.4	−6.6	−20.0
270 Winchester	100	SPS	3430	+2.0	+2.1	+1.0	−1.2	−4.9	−17.5
270 Winchester	130	SPS	3060	+2.0	+1.8	+0.4	−2.4	−6.8	−20.8
270 Winchester	150	SP	2850	+2.0	+2.0	−0.6	−4.5	−10.6	−30.4
7mm Mauser	140	SPS	2660	+2.0	+1.3	−1.0	−5.0	−11.1	−29.9
7mm Mauser	175	SP	2440	+2.0	+0.7	−2.7	−8.8	−17.6	−46.1
7mm-08 Remington	140	SPS	2860	+2.0	+1.6	−0.2	−3.4	−8.4	−23.9
280 Remington	150	SPS	2970	+2.0	+1.7	+0.2	−2.9	−7.5	−22.4
7mm Rem. Mag.	125	SPS	3310	+2.0	+2.1	+1.0	−2.1	−4.9	−17.0
7mm Rem. Mag.	150	SPS	3110	+2.0	+1.9	+0.6	−2.1	−6.1	−19.3
7mm Rem. Mag.	175	SPS	2860	+2.0	+1.7	⊕	−3.2	−7.9	−22.7
30 Carbine	110	SP	1990	+2.0	−1.5	−9.5	−23.3	−43.9	−100.8
30-30 Winchester	55	Accel.	3440	+2.0	+1.8	⊕	−3.8	−10.2	−35.0
30-30 Winchester	150	SP	2390	+2.0	+0.3	−4.2	−12.0	−24.0	−64.5
30-30 Winchester	170	SP	2200	+2.0	⊕	−4.8	−13.0	−25.1	−63.6
300 Savage	150	SP	2630	+2.0	+1.0	−2.0	−7.5	−15.1	−43.5
307 Winchester	150	SPF	2760	+2.0	+1.2	−1.6	−6.7	−14.7	−42.7
307 Winchester	180	SPF	2510	+2.0	+0.7	+1.0	−8.4	−17.1	−45.1
308 Winchester	110	SPS	3180	+2.0	+1.8	⊕	−3.5	−9.3	−29.5
308 Winchester	125	SPS	3050	+2.0	+1.7	⊕	−3.2	−8.2	−24.6

Cartridge	Wt.	Type	Velocity						
308 Winchester	150	SPS	2820	+1.0	+1.5	-0.6	-4.3	-10.0	-28.1
308 Winchester	180	SPS	2620	+2.0	+1.2	-1.2	-5.5	-11.7	-31.3
308 Winchester	200	SP	2450	+2.0	+0.9	-1.9	-7.5	-15.4	-39.7
30-06 Springfield	55	Accel.	4080	+2.0	+2.4	+1.9	+0.5	-2.1	-11.7
30-06 Springfield	110	SPS	3330	+2.0	+1.9	+0.4	-2.7	-7.7	-25.6
30-06 Springfield	125	SPS	3140	+2.0	+1.8	+0.4	-2.5	-7.1	-22.2
30-06 Springfield	150	SPS	2910	+2.0	+1.7	-0.2	-3.5	-8.8	-25.4
30-06 Springfield	165	SPS	2800	+2.0	+1.5	-0.6	-4.3	-9.9	-27.5
30-06 Springfield	180	SPS	2700	+2.0	+1.4	-0.8	-4.7	-10.5	-28.6
30-06 Springfield	220	SP	2410	+2.0	+0.7	-2.7	-8.7	-17.5	-45.4
300 H & H Magnum	150	SP	3130	+2.0	+1.9	+0.6	-2.1	-6.3	-20.0
300 H & H Magnum	180	SPS	2880	+2.0	+1.6	-0.2	-3.5	-8.3	-23.7
300 H & H Magnum	220	SP	2580	+2.0	+1.2	-1.4	-5.9	-12.6	-33.5
300 Win. Mag.	150	SPS	3290	+2.0	+2.0	+0.9	-1.5	-5.3	-17.8
300 Win. Mag.	180	SPS	2960	+2.0	+1.7	+0.2	-2.7	-7.6	-20.5
300 Win. Mag.	220	SP	2860	+2.0	+1.3	-1.0	-5.0	-11.0	-29.5
32 Win. Spl.	170	SP	2250	+2.0	+0.1	-4.5	-12.5	-24.3	-62.8
8mm Rem. Mag.	185	SPS	3080	+2.0	+1.9	+0.4	-2.5	-7.0	-21.7
8mm Rem. Mag.	220	SPS	2830	+2.0	+1.5	-0.4	-3.9	-9.1	-25.5
338 Win. Mag.	200	SP	2960	+2.0	+1.7	⊕	-3.2	-8.2	-24.3
338 Win. Mag.	225	SP	2780	+2.0	+1.1	-1.4	-5.3	-11.1	-27.8
35 Remington	200	SP	2080	+2.0	-0.7	-7.3	-18.3	-35.1	-89.7
356 Winchester	200	SPF	2460	+2.0	+0.6	-3.0	-9.4	-18.9	-49.6
356 Winchester	250	SPF	2160	+2.0	⊕	-4.7	-12.4	-23.7	-58.4
358 Winchester	200	SP	2490	+2.0	+0.7	-2.6	-8.5	-17.1	-47.2
358 Winchester	250	SP	2230	+2.0	+0.3	-3.9	-10.9	-21.6	-52.7
375 Winchester	200	SPF	2200	+2.0	-1.0	-8.1	-19.4	-35.9	-85.8
375 H & H Mag.	270	SP	2690	+2.0	+1.4	-1.0	-5.1	-11.5	-31.4
375 H & H Mag.	300	FMC	2530	+2.0	+0.7	-2.6	-8.6	-17.6	-47.1
44 Rem. Mag.	240	HP	1760	+2.0	-2.9	-13.6	-31.3	-57.1	-137.5
444 Marlin	240	SP	2350	+2.0	-0.1	-5.4	-15.7	-31.8	-87.4
45-70 Govt.	300	HP	1880	+2.0	-1.6	-8.8	-20.4	-38.3	-87.5
45-70 Govt.	405	SP	1330	+2.0	-5.7	-20.6	-43.2	-74.4	-164.4
458 Win. Mag.	500	SP	2040	+2.0	-0.3	-5.6	-14.1	-26.4	-64.0
458 Win. Mag.	510	FMC	2040	+2.0	-0.6	-6.4	-15.9	-29.7	-73.1

ABBREVIATIONS:

Rem. = Remington

Win. = Winchester

Mag. = Magnum

+P = plus pressure – loaded to higher pressure and velocity than older types of ammo.

H & H = Holland and Holland

Spl. = Special

Govt. = Government

HP = hollow point

SP = soft point

SPS = soft point spitzer

Accel. = Accelerator, a 22 caliber bullet encased in a 30 caliber plastic sabot.

SPF = soft point flat nose

FMC = full metal case

⊕ = bullet strikes point of aim

AVERAGE VELOCITIES AND ENERGIES FROM A 24" BARREL

Caliber	Bullet Wt. (in grs.)	Style	Velocity in feet per second at yards: Muzzle	100	200	300	400	Energy in foot-pounds at yards: Muzzle	100	200	300	400
17 Remington	25	HP	4040	3285	2645	2085	1605	900	600	390	240	145
22 Hornet	45	SP	2690	2040	1500	1130	950	725	415	225	125	90
222 Remington	50	SPS	3140	2600	2125	1700	1350	1095	750	500	320	200
223 Remington	55	SPS	3240	2745	2305	1905	1555	1280	920	650	445	295
222 Rem. Mag.	55	SPS	3240	2750	2305	1905	1555	1280	920	650	445	295
22-250 Remington	55	SPS	3680	3135	2655	2220	1830	1655	1200	860	605	410
243 Winchester	80	SPS	3350	2955	2595	2260	1950	1995	1550	1195	905	675
243 Winchester	100	SPS	2960	2695	2450	2215	1995	1945	1615	1330	1090	880
6mm Remington	80	SPS	3470	3065	2695	2350	2035	2140	1665	1290	980	735
6mm Remington	100	SPS	3100	2830	2575	2330	2105	2135	1775	1470	1205	985
250 Savage	87	SPS	3030	2675	2340	2035	1755	1775	1380	1060	800	595
250 Savage	100	SP	2820	2465	2140	1840	1570	1765	1350	1015	750	545
257 Roberts	87	SPS	3170	2800	2460	2145	1855	1940	1515	1170	890	665
257 Roberts +P	100	SP	3000	2635	2295	1980	1695	2000	1540	1170	870	640
257 Roberts +P	117	SP	2780	2410	2070	1760	1490	2010	1510	1115	805	575
25-06 Remington	87	HP	3440	2995	2590	2220	1885	2285	1735	1295	955	685
25-06 Remington	100	SPS	3230	2895	2580	2285	2015	2315	1860	1480	1160	900
25-06 Remington	120	SPS	2990	2730	2485	2250	2030	2380	1985	1645	1350	1100
264 Win. Mag.	100	SPS	3320	2925	2565	2230	1925	2445	1900	1460	1105	820
264 Win. Mag.	140	SPS	3030	2780	2550	2325	2115	2855	2405	2020	1680	1390
270 Winchester	100	SPS	3430	3020	2650	2305	1990	2610	2025	1555	1180	875
270 Winchester	130	SPS	3060	2775	2510	2260	2020	2700	2225	1820	1470	1180
270 Winchester	150	SP	2850	2505	2185	1885	1620	2705	2085	1585	1185	870
7mm Mauser	140	SPS	2660	2435	2220	2020	1650	2200	1845	1535	1265	1035
7mm Mauser	175	SP	2440	2135	1855	1605	1380	2315	1775	1340	1000	740
7mm-08 Remington	140	SPS	2860	2625	2400	2190	1990	2540	2140	1795	1490	1230
280 Remington	150	SPS	2970	2700	2445	2205	1975	2935	2425	1990	1615	1300
7mm Rem. Mag.	125	SPS	3310	2975	2665	2375	2105	3040	2460	1970	1565	1230
7mm Rem. Mag.	150	SPS	3110	2830	2570	2370	2085	3220	2665	2195	1790	1450
7mm Rem. Mag.	175	SPS	2860	2645	2440	2245	2055	3180	2720	2315	1955	1645
30 Carbine	110	SP	1990	1565	1235	1035	925	965	600	375	260	210
30-30 Winchester	55	Accel.	3400	2695	2085	1570	1185	1410	885	520	300	170
30-30 Winchester	150	SP	2390	1975	1605	1305	1095	1900	1295	860	565	400
30-30 Winchester	170	SP	2200	1895	1620	1380	1190	1825	1355	990	720	535
300 Savage	150	SP	2630	2245	1895	1585	1325	2305	1680	1200	835	585
300 Savage	180	SP	2350	2025	1730	1465	1250	2205	1640	1195	860	625
307 Winchester	150	SPF	2760	2320	1925	1575	1290	2540	1795	1235	825	555
307 Winchester	180	SPF	2510	2180	1875	1600	1360	2520	1900	1405	1020	740
308 Winchester	110	SPS	3180	2665	2205	1795	1445	2470	1735	1190	785	510

Cartridge	Bullet Wt. (grs.)	Type										
308 Winchester	125	SPS	1185	1560	2020	2580	1535	1790	2065	2370	2695	3050
308 Winchester	150	SPS	1050	1345	1705	2135	2650	1775	2010	2265	2535	2820
308 Winchester	180	SPS	1270	1555	1895	2290	2745	1780	1975	2180	2395	2620
308 Winchester	200	SP	1095	1385	1740	2165	2665	1570	1765	1980	2210	2450
30-06 Springfield	55	Accel.	530	765	1075	1485	2035	2085	2500	2965	3485	4080
30-06 Springfield	110	SPS	575	880	1320	1915	2710	1530	1900	2325	2800	3330
30-06 Springfield	125	SPS	955	1270	1660	2145	2735	1855	2140	2445	2780	3140
30-06 Springfield	150	SPS	1130	1445	1825	2280	2820	1845	2085	2340	2615	2910
30-06 Springfield	165	SPS	1220	1535	1910	2350	2870	1825	2045	2285	2535	2800
30-06 Springfield	180	SPS	1360	1665	2025	2435	2915	1845	2040	2250	2470	2700
30-06 Springfield	220	SP	990	1300	1710	2215	2835	1420	1630	1870	2130	2410
300 H & H Magnum	150	SP	1345	1705	2140	2650	3260	2010	2265	2535	2820	3130
300 H & H Magnum	180	SPS	1585	1925	2325	2785	3315	1990	2195	2410	2640	2880
300 H & H Magnum	220	SP	1415	1765	2185	2675	3250	1700	1900	2115	2340	2580
300 Win. Mag.	150	SPS	1425	1825	2315	2900	3605	2070	2340	2635	2950	3290
300 Win. Mag.	180	SPS	1860	2195	2580	3010	3500	2155	2345	2540	2745	2960
300 Win. Mag.	220	SP	1625	1995	2425	2925	3510	1825	2020	2230	2450	2860
32 Win. Spl.	170	SP	520	710	1000	1395	1910	1175	1370	1625	1920	2250
8mm Rem. Mag.	185	SPS	1525	1965	2495	3130	3895	1925	2185	2465	2760	3080
8mm Rem. Mag.	220	SPS	1785	2200	2690	3255	3910	1915	2125	2345	2580	2830
338 Win. Mag.	200	SP	1540	1975	2505	3135	3890	1860	2110	2375	2660	2960
338 Win. Mag.	225	SP	2005	2385	2815	3305	3860	2005	2185	2375	2570	2780
35 Remington	200	SP	445	575	840	1280	1920	1000	1140	1375	1700	2080
356 Winchester	200	SPF	730	1020	1435	1985	2690	1285	1515	1795	2115	2460
356 Winchester	250	SPF	935	1210	1570	2030	2590	1300	1475	1680	1910	2160
358 Winchester	200	SP	845	1150	1565	2095	2755	1380	1610	1875	2170	2490
358 Winchester	250	SP	1050	1345	1725	2195	2760	1375	1555	1760	1990	2230
375 Winchester	200	SPF	525	715	1035	1505	2150	1090	1270	1525	1840	2200
375 H & H Magnum	270	SP	1745	2230	2810	3510	4335	1705	1930	2165	2420	2690
375 H & H Magnum	300	FMC	1140	1600	2260	3140	4265	1305	1550	1845	2170	2530
44 Remington Mag.	240	HP	410	500	660	1015	1650	880	970	1115	1380	1760
444 Marlin	240	SP	470	630	1010	1755	2940	940	1085	1375	1815	2350
45-70 Govt.	300	HP	810	1015	1355	1815	2355	1105	1235	1425	1650	1880
45-70 Govt.	405	SP	760	860	1000	1225	1590	920	975	1055	1170	1330
458 Win. Mag.	500	SP	1840	2310	2925	3690	4620	1235	1440	1625	1825	2040
458 Win. Mag.	510	FMC	1515	1970	2640	3545	4710	1155	1320	1525	1770	2040

ABBREVIATIONS:

Rem. = Remington
Win. = Winchester
Mag. = Magnum
+P = plus pressure – loaded to higher pressure and
velocity than older types of ammo.
H & H = Holland & Holland
Spl. = Special
Govt. = Government

HP = hollow point
SP = soft point
SPS = soft point spitzer
Accel. = Accelerator, a 22 caliber bullet encased in a 30
caliber plastic sabot.
SPF = soft point flat nosed
FMC = full metal case

SHOOTING THE SHOTGUN

PART II

SELECTING A SHOTGUN 10

Choosing a shotgun is a very personal decision. A shotgun must fit you, it must balance well for you and it must shoulder, point and swing quickly for you. The obvious important consideration is *you*.

When you choose a shotgun, it makes little difference what some authority might prefer. You must select a gun that fits you comfortably. Most shooters can find a number of guns that have the proper length of pull and drop at comb and heel and correct balance. Therefore, understanding the advantages of various shotgun features may be of help in making your selection.

Weight and Length You should first consider the weight and length of a shotgun, especially if you hunt in heavy cover. A New England woodcock and partridge hunter would quickly become discouraged with a long-barreled and heavier-than-necessary shotgun. For brush country, short and light are always best. However, a pass-shooting waterfowler, who walks little and who shoots heavy loads, may find a long-barreled, heavy shotgun ideal. Such a gun will help him point as sharply as possible, and once he gets it swinging, it will keep on moving with a minimum of effort. In addition, extra gun weight will help tame recoil. On the other hand, for shooting over decoys, a light, short shotgun may be just right for the fast shooting involved.

Gauge Shotguns with an overall length of 41 to 43 inches are about ideal for almost any upland application. Each inch past 43 proves more of a handicap than an asset for such shooting. An overall length up to 48 or 49 inches is satisfactory for waterfowl shooting. More length gains you nothing, except perhaps the accidental banging of the gun into parts of the blind or boat.

Shotguns weighing between 6¼ and 7½ pounds seem to be satisfactory for most shooters. If you walk extremely long distances during a hunt, the lighter weights will prove to be advantageous. Also, if your shooting demands rapid gun mounting, the light shotguns will shoulder just a bit more quickly than heavier models, especially when you are somewhat fatigued. However, the heavier shotguns will cut down on perceived recoil, thus may be desirable if you shoot a steady diet of magnum loads. On pass shooting, the heavier guns, once started, continue on long swings with somewhat less shooter effort. Thus, for pass shooting, a 7¼- or 7½-pound gun may prove to be an advantage. Eight-pound shotguns are a burden for almost any application, and guns under 6 pounds are hard to control while swinging, since they tend to float about.

To make a sensible selection, it is also necessary to decide upon the gauge gun you require. For most shooters, the 410 and 28 gauge can be eliminated, as these are highly specialized shotguns best suited to smaller game birds at relatively short distances. The 16 gauge, while efficient for many tasks, has become almost obsolete in this country, with but a few guns being manufactured in this bore size. The 10 gauge are also very specialized shotguns, because of their heavy weight, very heavy loads and the high cost of ammo. It takes a highly skilled shotgunner to gain any advantage from this monster gun. The 10 gauge is best restricted to extremely long-range waterfowl shooting and perhaps turkey hunting.

This narrows most shooters' choice to the 12 or 20 gauge. At one time, if you wanted a lightweight, well-balanced shotgun, it usually meant a 20 gauge. If you wanted a shotgun to do almost everything a shotgun could, then a 12 gauge was mandated. However, today's gunner has a broader choice. It is now possible to select a 12-gauge gun that is short, light and well balanced. The Remington 1100 "Special Field" shotgun is a good example. And 20-gauge shotguns with 3-inch chambers, though less than ideal, can be used for waterfowling or even turkey hunting in a pinch.

Chapter 16 covers the basics of shotshell ballistics. After reading it, the shooter should have a good idea as to what size shot and charge weight are required for his heaviest hunting needs. Equipped with this knowledge, the choice between a 12- or 20-gauge gun should be easy. However, if you are a one-shotgun hunter, I recommend without reservation that you select a 12-gauge gun—unless you know that your hunting will always be restricted to light upland game. If deer, turkey, waterfowl or pheasant are on your list of intended applications, then a 12 gauge will prove best.

In the tradition of fine English doubles, the Winchester 23 Lightweight is a fine choice in a side-by-side shotgun for all-around use.

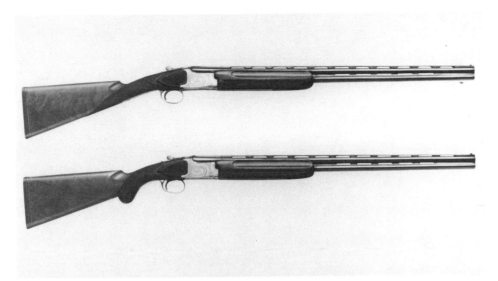

Over-and-under shotguns, such as these Winchester Model 101's, are extremely popular with U.S. sportsmen.

The short-barrelled (21-inch) Remington 1100 Field Special is highly favored by the author for field shooting.

Perhaps the most popular shotgun in the world, the Remington 1100 is also available in a left-handed version as shown.

The most popular pump shotgun ever built, the Remington 870 is available in all gauges from 12 to 410.

Inexpensive single shots are popular with budget-conscious shooters as well as beginners. This is the Stevens Model 94.

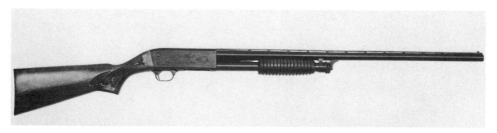

The Ithaca Model 37 is an old-timer light enough to satisfy any shooter.

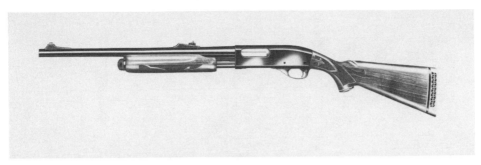

A fine deer gun for lefties and slugs is the Remington 870 Brushmaster (available in right-handed models also).

Naturally, the recoil-sensitive shooter might justifiably want to select a 20-gauge gun. However, if he then uses 1⅛-ounce baby magnum loads, he will be enduring more recoil than he would get with light 1-ounce or light 1⅛-ounce 12-gauge loads. By selecting the proper loads, you can have less of a recoil burden with a 12 gauge than with a 20 gauge. The recoil-sensitive shooter is ahead of the game with a 20 gauge usually only if he restricts himself to ⅞-ounce loads.

For the upland hunter interested only in woodcock and partridge and who must negotiate almost impossible thicket tangles in search of his quarry, the shortest and lightest possible shotgun makes sense. The natural choice for such a hunter is a 20 gauge.

Choke   After you decide upon the gauge, the selection of the appropriate choke or chokes is essential. Basically, choke need is dictated by the ranges at which you will be taking game. Choke is the constriction of the shotgun's bore at the muzzle. It works much like the nozzle on a garden hose. When the garden hose is opened to its largest diameter, the water sprays forth in a large-diameter circle but goes only a short distance. When the nozzle is adjusted to its tightest constriction, the water is sprayed in a very narrow circle and travels the maximum distance.

So it is with chokes. A wide diameter at the muzzle allows the shot to disperse in a wide pattern, making it easier to score hits at short ranges. However, as the range increases, the pellets continue to spread and the distance between pellets becomes greater and greater. At some point, the pellets are spread so far apart that it becomes impossible to hit the target with the multiple pellets necessary to bring it to bag.

A tight choke holds the pellets close together for as long as possible, making the pattern at short ranges very narrow and dense. But scoring hits at short ranges is extremely difficult, and any game so taken will receive a great many more hits than necessary. A partridge shot at 15 yards with a full choke may simply be blown to a ball of feathers, leaving the hunter with no edible meat. Yet, at ranges past 35 yards, the full-choke patterns are opened up enough to provide just the right density of pellets to ensure game-taking capabilities without excessive destruction of meat. But even with the tightest choke, pellets

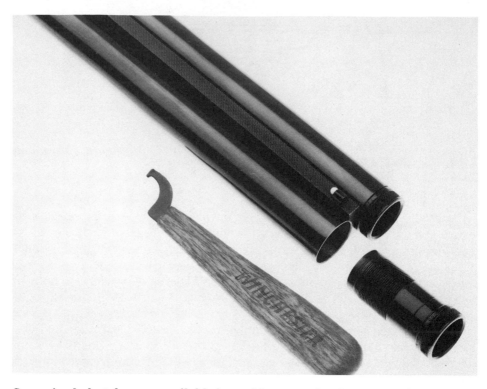

Screw-in choke tubes are available in a wide range of makes and models and add a great deal of versatility to any shotgun.

eventually become so spread apart as to make shooting at a given range completely impractical.

Chokes are normally encountered in a wide range of constrictions. The common choke designations are, from the most open to the tightest:

> cylinder (no constriction)
> skeet (often the same as improved cylinder)
> improved cylinder
> modified
> improved modified (sometimes called improved trap)
> full
> extra full

The ideal range applications of these chokes, assuming that game, shot size and shot charge weight have all been matched correctly, are appropriately as follows:

Range	Suggested choke
15–25 yards	cylinder
20–30 yards	improved cylinder (skeet)
25–35 yards	modified
30–40 yards	improved modified
35–45 yards	full choke
40–50 yards	extra full

Shooting at ranges under 15 yards will often result in too many pellets in the game regardless of what choke is used. However, at such short ranges, excessive hits can be reduced by switching to a very light charge. Also, by using magnum shot charges, maximum ranges shown can be extended by approximately 10 yards. For instance, a 12-gauge full-choke gun with a 1¼-ounce charge of No. 4s normally would prove satisfactory for waterfowl at ranges from 35 to 45 yards. However, by switching to a magnum load of 1½ ounces of No. 4s, the maximum practical range becomes about 55 yards.

All too frequently, shotgunners tend to overestimate the capability of shotshells when combined with various chokes. The preceding table suggests ranges at which you will encounter no difficulties with either mutilated game or crippled game if you select the appropriate-size shot and charge weight. Expert shooters may be able to stretch the suggested maximum ranges by perhaps 5 yards. But if you need to shoot at any longer range, you should switch to a magnum shot charge weight and/or a tighter choke.

The shotgun purchaser will find that not every choke designation is available in every model shotgun. Field guns are normally offered only in improved cylinder, modified and full choke. Cylinder chokes are found usually only with police riot guns or barrels specifically bored for shooting shotgun slugs. Skeet chokes are offered only on skeet guns, while improved modified chokes usually can be found only in conjunction with trap guns. Extra-full chokes are not normally available except on guns that have removable choke inserts, and then only in 12 gauge.

Guns that have screw-in tubes to allow the shotgunner his option of choke are extremely practical. Such tubes allow the shotgun to be matched to specific needs without the costly expense of owning extra barrels.

Barrel Length
Having decided upon gauge and choke, you might then want to consider the length of barrel you need. Traditionally, the choice of choke settled the question of barrel length. The manufacturers generally offered the improved cylinder only in 26-inch length, the modified choke only in a 28-inch barrel and the full choke in a 28- or 30-inch barrel. However, in repeating shotguns, even barrels of 26-inch length often prove excessively long for hunting in heavy cover. Since the early 1980s, shotgun manufacturers have begun to respond to the shooter demands for shorter barrels. Ithaca, for instance, offers its pump Model 37 English UltraLite in 20 gauge with a 25-inch barrel in improved cylinder, modified or full chokes. And Remington offers its Model 1100 "Special

Field" semiautomatic with a 21-inch barrel in any of the same three chokes. The 1100 "Special Field" is available in both 12 and 20 gauge with this short barrel length.

Experience has shown that a 20–23-inch barrel seems about right on a repeating shotgun. If I were making the decision, all repeaters would be available with a 21-inch barrel as the standard length regardless of choke. Optional would be 26-inch modified and full-choke barrels for waterfowlers who find a longer barrel a bit easier to point precisely for shooting at extreme range.

Short barrels do, of course, reduce the muzzle velocity of a given load. However, this reduction seldom exceeds 15 feet per second per inch of barrel. In practice, a 21-inch shotgun barrel usually produces only about 75 feet per second less velocity than a 28-inch barrel. At 40 yards, the difference in remaining velocity between the two barrel lengths is only about 20 feet per second, depending upon the pellet size used. A velocity difference of 20 feet per second goes unnoticed by both game and shooter.

Short barrels offer advantages in gun handling, in gun weight and in negotiating tight cover. The disadvantage of velocity loss can be considered insignificant. Thus, only the serious long-range waterfowl hunter may require a slightly longer barrel to help his pointing be as sharp as possible, and here a 26-inch barrel will prove sufficiently long. The user of a short-barreled gun is less likely to jam the muzzle into the snow or mud and thus set the scene for a burst barrel at the next shot.

Not every manufacturer offers shotguns with realistic barrel lengths. You may be forced to accept a 26- or 28-inch barrel, depending upon the specific shotgun you choose. But more is not always better.

Barrel lengths on double-barreled shotguns, be they side-by-side or over-and-under, are usually 26 or 28 inches. Because such guns lack the receiver and the resulting extra length of a repeater, 26-inch barrels will prove a good choice. And the 25- or 25½-inch barrels sometimes offered are about ideal for providing short overall length combined with good balance and pointability. I find 28-inch barrels a bit longer than needed on a double, except perhaps for waterfowl hunting.

Actions   Which shotgun type is best suited to you—pump, semiauto or double? Pumps frequently appeal to the budget-minded shooter. They also appeal to those who prefer a repeating shotgun but who do not like to strip-clean guns frequently. Semiautomatics offer less apparent recoil than fixed-breech shotguns, and thus they appeal to a lot of shooters. Hunters who routinely use the heaviest loads find the recoil-reducing effect of semiautomatics, especially the gas-operated models, a desirable asset. But semiautos do demand frequent strip-cleaning if they are to function reliably.

Infrequent shooters may find semiautos to be actually more reliable than pumps. Shooters who use their shotguns only occasionally may not fully pump their guns, thereby incurring a feeding jam or an empty chamber. If you fit into the occasional-usage group, a semiauto may well be a wise choice.

Because of their cost, double guns are less frequently encountered today than they once were. Nevertheless, such shotguns offer a grace and positiveness of functioning that is unsurpassed in any other style shotgun. But unless you can afford to spend at least $700 for a new shotgun, a repeater will prove the better buy. Cheap doubles seldom prove satisfactory because all sorts of mechanical problems occur after only limited use. On the other hand, a good double gun will last longer than most shooters and their children.

Sights and Stocks Shotgun sights are frequently misunderstood. When a new shotgunner first inspects his gun, the single front bead often leaves him with the impression that it must be difficult to aim a shotgun. On the other hand, knowing that many shooters do well with such guns may make the shooter decide that shotguns throw such large patterns that it must be difficult to miss the mark.

Experience quickly shows that shotguns are not difficult to point but that hits do require a fair level of proficiency—even experts miss some targets. When using a shotgun, the shooter should realize that the front bead is only one-half of the sighting system. The rear sight is actually the shooter's eye. In order for this sight system to work, the shooter must mount the gun in such a way as to position his eye in exactly the same location shot after shot. If his eye is higher or lower than, or to the left or right of, the normal position, his pattern will be centered higher or lower, left or right of the normal point of impact.

Because the position of the eye is critical to a centered point of impact, it is vital that a shotgun stock fit the shooter correctly. If the stock is a poor fit, the shooter will be unable to mount the gun quickly and have it cheeked in the proper position to ensure correct positioning of his eye. The shotgun's buttstock serves as the base for the rear sight (your eye) and is thus an important part of the shotgun's sighting system.

Stock length, or, more correctly stated, the trigger pull length, which is the distance from the face of the trigger to the center of the back edge of the butt plate, should be of a dimension that allows the shooter to position his head comfortably. This length will always correspond to one that allows the pad of the first joint of the trigger finger to rest comfortably centered on the trigger when the shotgun is held against the upper arm. There is some tolerance to this dimension, and serious shooters often can get along well with a stock that is ¼ to ⅜ inch longer or shorter than ideal. My experience has been that it is best to opt for a slightly longer stock rather than one that is too short. However, if a stock is on the long side to begin with, it may prove to be far too long late in the season, when a heavy coat is worn.

More important for proper sighting than the exact length of the stock is the amount of drop it has. The drop in a stock is the distance below the center of the bore line to the top of the stock. This measurement is usually taken at the comb and heel of the stock. Too much drop on a stock will prevent the shooter from seeing the front bead correctly positioned on the top center of the receiver when the shotgun is properly mounted. With too little drop, too much of the barrel will show above the receiver. A gun with too much drop will force the shooter to raise his head away from firm contact with the stock. In that he then has no positive stop to bring his head into position, the amount he raises his head will vary slightly from shot to shot. Therefore, his performance with such

To measure trigger pull, hold shotgun with buttplate against upper arm. Pad of trigger finger should rest comfortably on trigger. This stock is too long.

The shooter's eye is the rear sight of a shotgun and therefore must be positioned exactly for each shot.

a poor fitting stock will vary because he sees a different sight picture with each shot.

It is easier to use a stock that has too little drop than one with too much drop. With a stock that has insufficient drop, the shooter at least can bring his head into the same firm contact with the stock each time. He then needs only to learn how much he should hold below the target for the proper sight picture to score consistent hits. As most trap shooters know, a comb with extra height is ideal when shooting rising birds, since you can hold on the bottom edge of the target and score a hit. With a stock of lower height, you may need to pass your barrel above the bird (thus blocking it momentarily from view) in order to score a hit. This is a less-than-ideal sight picture.

It is for this reason that I favor stocks with rather high and straight combs, similar to trap stocks, for all of my shotgun shooting. On crossing birds, I simply swing 6 to 12 inches below my target; on rising birds, I can hold on the bottom edge of the bird. The only shots that need special care are those when a bird is descending, in which case I need to hold quite a deal lower than if I used a shotgun with the "normal" comb height.

I prefer the sight picture offered with high combs to swinging the muzzle through the center of crossing birds or to having to shoot above rising birds. With a high comb stock, the sight picture will show about 3 inches of muzzle protruding above the receiver, with the front sight bead sitting squarely in the middle of the receiver, although somewhat above it. You also may find high stocks a positive step in increasing your effectiveness in pointing your shotgun.

Some shotguns, most often target or high-grade varieties, are fitted with a smaller second bead about one-third or one-half of the way down the rib of the gun. This second bead can be highly functional in ensuring that you have positioned your head and eye correctly on the stock. The proper sight picture when a shotgun is equipped with two beads is to have the beads form a figure eight. The smaller rear bead should be placed so that it blocks out the bottom half of the front bead, with the remainder of the front bead sitting on the top of the rear bead, thereby forming a figure eight. When properly positioned, the rear bead will ensure positive left and right alignment of your eye as well as provide a visual check on the height of your eye above the comb.

Shotgun beads, while effective with shot loads for small game and birds, are not the thing to use when hunting big game with slugs. The front bead alone or even in conjunction with a middle bead cannot afford the positive aiming required to place your slug in the vital area of your quarry.

For slug shooting, the front bead should be combined with an open rear sight or an aperture-type sight. The shortcomings of the open sight and the virtues of the aperture sight have been covered fully in Chapter 1 of this book. It is often less than practical to attempt to mount a peep or open sight on a shotgun. Often it makes sense to purchase an extra barrel that is especially bored and choked for accurate slug shooting. Such barrels are fitted at the factory with a rifle-type ramp front sight and an adjustable, open rear sight.

The open rear sight used on slug barrels is far less of a handicap on a shotgun than it is on a rifle. This is because accuracy limitations restrict the use of a slug gun usually to somewhere between 75 and 100 yards. It is a rare lot of slugs

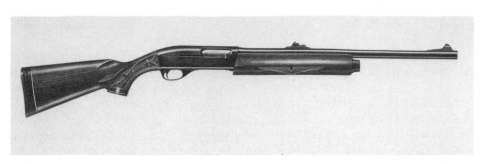

Shotguns intended for use with slugs on big game are available with factory-fitted rifle-style sights such as those shown on this Remington 1100.

A peep sight can make any shotgun an effective big-game weapon.

and slug gun that will hold the required 6-inch group past the 100 yard mark.

Nonetheless, many slug shooters do mount telescopes on their shotguns. For one thing, a scope helps the hunter to locate antlers when he hunts during buck-only seasons. And in heavy cover, a scope can oftentimes help him pick a hole in the brush to prevent slug deflection from interfering limbs. Most important, the scope-equipped slug gun will enable the hunter to place his shot with far more certainty than he could ever accomplish with iron sights.

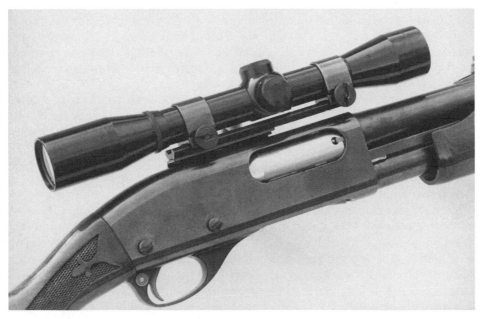

This Weaver mount is especially designed for a quick two minute installation on any Remington 870 or 1100.

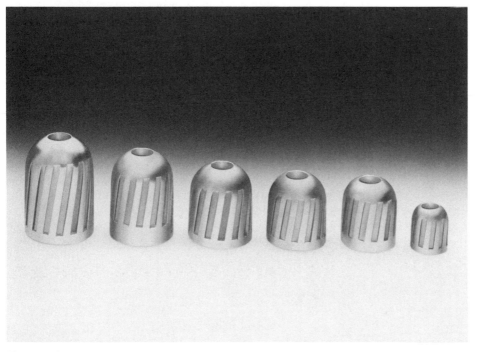

Federal Super Slugs are available in six hollow-point rifled slug loads from 10 gauge, 3½-inch Magnum to .410.

Because of the limitation on range forced by slug accuracy, there is little point in equipping any slug gun with a scope of more than 4 power—2½ or 3 power will work equally well. In brush and heavy cover, the 2½- or 3-power scope could well prove to be advantageous, since its wider field of view can make for slightly faster shooting when ranges are short.

I have frequently used a Leupold 1½–5-power variable scope on my slug guns. I find the extra-large field of view afforded by this scope when it is set on 1½ power to be a real asset for the extra-short ranges I often encounter when hunting in my home state of Connecticut.

My less-than-perfect eyesight appreciates the ability to turn the scope up to 5 power when looking for antlers, and at this setting I can pick a hole in the brush that would go unnoticed at 2½ or 3 power.

Owners of Remington Model 1100 or 870 shotguns have a very easy task when mounting a scope if they use the Weaver mount system especially made for their shotguns. To install this mount, one needs only to remove the two pins that hold in the trigger group and slip into place two replacement screws, which securely attach the scope base side plate. The top-mount base comes factory-assembled to this side plate, and it takes only about two minutes to install the mount. Of course, each time the mount is removed and installed, the gun should be carefully sighted in. Owners of other shotguns may find that a gunsmith's services are needed to install a scope and mount. Some shotgunners object to having holes drilled into their bird guns. For such hunters, a replacement slug barrel usually affords the best solution for sights when hunting with slugs.

Those who do not use a slug barrel should keep in mind that the best slug accuracy will usually occur with cylinder, skeet or improved-cylinder chokes, while the worst accuracy most often occurs with full-choke barrels. Slugs, of course, can be used safely with any choke.

If you elect to have a peep sight installed on your shotgun, Williams offers a fine one with a large aperture especially designed for the poor light conditions and short ranges often associated with slug hunting. But when mounting a peep, be certain to select a shotgun with a barrel that does not have a middle sight, which would interfere with the use of your chosen sight.

When sighting in a slug gun, adjust your sight so that you are hitting 3 inches high at 50 yards. This will put you dead on at 100 yards or perhaps 1 inch low, depending upon the exact velocity you obtain with your shotgun's barrel length. This applies regardless of the gauge of your shotgun. Your slug will then be about 2 inches high at 25 and 75 yards. Such sighting in will allow you to ignore the trajectory of your slug when hunting at all practical ranges.

SKEET: BEST WAY TO LEARN SHOTGUNNING

11

One of the best places to learn how to shoot a shotgun is on the skeet field. A fast-moving game, skeet offers a variety of angles on both incoming and outgoing birds. Also, it is a game that is easily mastered with limited practice, so that all shotgunners can participate.

The skeet shooter has a definite advantage when upland-game season rolls around, especially if he hunts with the same gun he has been using for skeet. His skeet shooting will have his reflexes well tuned for shots in the field.

Guns for Skeet

If you already have a field shotgun, you can use it for skeet shooting regardless of its gauge or choke. However, because of the short range at which skeet is shot, a tightly choked shotgun will prove a handicap. Cylinder (skeet I) and improved cylinder (skeet II or skeet) are the most appropriate chokes.

Skeet shooting will quickly prove that you can hit targets easier with a 12-gauge gun than with any smaller gauge. And you will find the 20-gauge gun quite easy to score with compared to the diminutive 28 gauge or the extremely difficult-to-master 410 bore. Because of this, many beginning skeet shooters start with the 12 gauge and move to the smaller gauges only after they have mastered it.

Some shooters, however, would do well to start with a gun that produces only a modest level of recoil. The 12 gauge can be abusive to a shooter who is a novice or is of small stature. The gun's recoil can actually prevent these shooters from developing any level of proficiency. The result is often a discouraged shooter who quickly loses interest in what amounts to no more than a painful experience. A novice who first masters the essentials using a 20 gauge can later graduate to the heavier recoiling 12 gauge or the harder-to-hit-with 28 gauge or 410 bore.

In competition, skeet shooters are segregated by ability and by gauge of the gun used. This helps keep competitors on an equal footing. There is, however, no classification for the dying 16 gauge. In fact, a great many skeet ranges do not inventory 16-gauge shells. If you elect to shoot skeet with a 16-gauge gun, be sure to bring along your own ammunition. Users of the 16 gauge will be grouped with 12-gauge shooters in formal competition.

Skeet guns can be of any action type you prefer. Semiautomatics are most

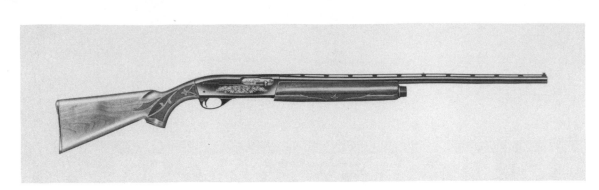

The most popular skeet gun ever manufactured, the Remington 1100 swings smoothly, recoils lightly and breaks lots of targets. Shown is a 20-gauge lightweight.

Over-and-unders, such as this Remington 3200, are popular with skeet shooters.

MODEL 23 WINCHESTER WITH WINCHOKES

This side-by-side Winchester 23 with skeet tubes makes a fine skeet gun; with a change of choke tubes it becomes a fine field gun.

commonly used because they reduce perceived recoil level and leave the shooter free from any gun manipulation between shots when shooting doubles. Gas-operated semiautomatics are more popular than recoil-operated guns because they tend to create a lighter perceived recoil. Also, many shooters find the shuffle of the barrel moving back and forth on recoil-operated shotguns quite annoying and even distracting.

Large numbers of pump guns and over-and-under doubles are used by skeet shooters, who prefer their slightly more reliable functioning as compared to semiautomatics. Side-by-side doubles are sometimes used. If you shoot skeet often, you will eventually see almost every type of shotgun in use on the field.

The purchaser of a shotgun to be used specifically for skeet should consider one of the various skeet models offered by most major firearms manufacturers. Skeet models always feature a ventilated rib barrel. The vent rib helps dissipate heat waves coming off the barrel, to a large extent preventing mirage distortion along the sighting plane. All skeet models are equipped with a second bead sight, placed about halfway down the barrel. This second bead aligns itself behind the front bead of a properly shouldered (mounted) gun, allowing the shooter to verify that he has indeed brought the gun to his shoulder correctly and that his head is in the correct position on the stock.

Being considerably smaller in diameter than the first bead, the second bead forms a sight picture with the first that looks like a figure eight. However, keep in mind that shotgun beads should never be used as true sights. They are there only to assist in assuring that you have the gun properly shouldered and cheeked.

Skeet-model guns, in addition to having ventilated ribs and middle beads, often incorporate slight modifications of field stock dimensions. Their beavertail forearms are sometimes larger in order to keep fingers away from hot barrels and to afford more positive control of the gun. The comb of the buttstock often has somewhat less drop than a field stock, and the butt plate often will be a good recoil pad. The straight comb will help you break more targets, while the recoil pad will reduce fatigue and prevent the butt from slipping on your shoulder.

Trap Stocks   Tall or long-necked shooters will do best with a trap stock installed on their skeet (and field) shotguns. Or they can simply replace the barrel of a trap gun with one intended for skeet. Standing almost 6 foot 3, I have found that it pays big dividends to equip all of my shotguns with trap-dimension stocks. I suggest that any shooter 6 feet or taller will break more targets and take more game when using a trap stock.

Many shooters find a trap stock advantageous regardless of their height. The straight comb of the trap stock helps reduce perceived recoil because it does not pound into the cheek. Also, the high comb lets you swing just below birds rather than through them, thus enabling you to retain a more open sight picture.

The extra length of a trap stock will prove uncomfortable for shooters 5'6" or less or for the shooter 5'7" or less wearing bulky clothing.

Summary   The final selection of a shotgun for skeet should incorporate a well-fitting gun that you can operate and swing easily. It should be choked very open, either cylinder or skeet or perhaps improved cylinder. And you should select either a 12- or a 20-gauge gun, depending upon your tolerance for recoil.

Keep in mind that skeet is frequently shot in shirtsleeves and that 25 shots are fired in about 25 minutes. A 12-gauge gun that proves comfortable with a heavy coat and for a few shots at game may prove to have too much recoil for the beginning skeet shooter.

A specialized skeet gun is of course the best choice, but, as stated, any field gun can be used. It is better to start becoming a good shot by shooting skeet now, rather than waiting until you have the ideal gun.

Finally, a deer-slug barrel with its short length and open choke makes a fine skeet barrel. Use its sights to confirm proper gun mounting, then ignore them while you swing and shoot.

Shot

Skeet shooting is traditionally done with No. 9 shot—indeed, some skeet ranges restrict shooting to this shot size. However, for informal shooting with a 12 or 16 gauge, No. 8 or even No. 7½ shot will serve equally well. In the smaller gauges, No. 9 shot is essential for the high pellet count required to maintain adequate pattern density.

Relatively light shot-charge weights are used in skeet shooting in order to keep recoil levels low. Standard charges are 1⅛ ounces for 12 gauge, 1 ounce for 16 gauge, ⅞ ounce for 20 gauge, ¾ ounce for 28 gauge and ½ ounce for 410 bore. A number of 12-gauge shooters are wisely switching to the lighter recoiling, yet almost equally effective 1-ounce target load for 12 gauge.

Relatively low-velocity shells, 1,145 ft/s or 1,200 ft/s, are used for skeet loads. Both velocity levels are available in 12 gauge as 2¾ drams equivalent or 3 drams equivalent shells. The slower 2¾ drams equivalent (1,145 ft/s) shell is all that will ever be required. This load has the advantage of producing less recoil than the 1,200 ft/s (3-dram) load. All the smaller gauges are loaded to a 1,200 ft/s velocity level. If you reload your own shells, you will find that a velocity of 1,140 to 1,150 ft/s is perfect for all skeet shooting.

Factory-loaded skeet rounds are usually put together as target-grade ammunition. But standard-velocity field ammunition that meets the shot-charge requirements with suitable-size shot can be successfully employed for informal shooting.

Fundamentals of Shotgunning

The fundamentals of shotgunning—foot position and stance; gun mounting; body swing; leading; trigger control; and follow-through—can all be learned on the skeet field. In fact, they are more easily learned at skeet because the shooter is motivated by the game itself.

The rules of skeet are simple. The shooter fires 25 shots from eight prescribed stations at targets traveling a constant course. In the beginning, novices can expect to break anywhere from three to seventeen birds.

Foot Positions   When firing a shotgun, the position of the feet is all-important. Stand with your feet comfortably spaced, your forward foot (left foot for right-handed shooters) pointing at the place where you expect your shot to intercept the target. Your rear foot should be a half-step behind the front one, at approximately a 45-degree angle to it. This proper placement of the feet is vital to your success. You must do it consistently and exactly. Correct foot placement is equally important in all skeet, trap or field shooting.

Mounting the Gun   When the feet are properly placed, bring the shotgun to your shoulder as follows: The fore-end hand grip should be at a comfortable angle, with the elbow of the fore-end hand at about a 45-degree angle to the horizon. The pistol grip or wrist of the stock should be gripped firmly but not tightly, as the gun is swung up to bring the butt to a point some 2 inches away from your shoulder, with the muzzle about 30 degrees above the horizon. Then pull the butt back against your shoulder while bringing the muzzle down to a target-level position, placing your cheek firmly in contact with the stock. Do not stretch or bend your neck other than perhaps to tilt your head down just a bit. The sight picture you see when the gun is properly mounted is the front bead fully centered on the top of the barrel or rib. The rear bead must be directly behind the front bead, with the top half of the front bead showing clearly above it. This position requires that you be looking over the top rear edge of the receiver. If your shotgun is not equipped with a middle bead, simply picture an imaginary bead, half the diameter of your front bead, sitting on the middle of your barrel or rib. This imaginary bead should cover the bottom half of the front bead when the gun is properly mounted.

Do not cant—that is, tip—the gun to the left or right. The gun should be level when it is properly mounted.

Gun mounting must become habit, so that you consistently mount the gun the same way every time. If you do not, the sight picture and your sights (your shooting eye and the muzzle) will not align in the same relationship for each shot. Under such conditions, one shot may go high, low, left or right as compared with another. You cannot consistently break birds unless each shot is fired with exactly the same sight picture.

Stance   When mounting the gun, lean slightly into the shot. You can accomplish this by shifting your body weight forward onto the front foot as you break the forward knee slightly. The rear leg should remain straight, bent only at the ankle.

The elbow of the trigger arm should be at about a 90-degree angle to the body when you assume a shooting stance. The exact position of either elbow or the distance between your feet can be varied slightly for comfort. But once you decide what position is most comfortable, you must be able to assume the same position for every shot. Do not alter the suggested elbow or foot-placement angles by more than 15 degrees, or you will interfere with the smooth swing required for hitting birds consistently. Beginners should use the suggested stance exactly, until they reach at least a medium level of proficiency. Earlier changes could lead to poor shooting habits. Experienced shooters can decide how much

These photos show skeet champion Phil Murray demonstrating proper shotgun form. (*Photos by Bryan Hendershot*)

1. *At ready position for high house bird, Murray stands with his feet approximately a shoulder length apart, the forward foot pointing at place he expects shot to intercept target. For low-house bird, his right foot would drop back about 6 inches.*

2. *Mounting his gun, Murray points muzzle a short distance from house in readiness for release of bird.*

3. *As Murray's eyes pick up the bird, he swivels his torso, and swings his gun. He does not lift his cheek from the stock until the target breaks.*

THE SWING SEQUENCE SEEN FROM A DIFFERENT ANGLE.

1. Ready position.

2. Pointing position.

3. Swinging and shooting.

SWING SEQUENCE SEEN FROM BE-
HIND, HIGH HOUSE IN BACK-
GROUND.

1. Ready position.

2. Pointing position.

3. Swinging and shooting.

improvement their shooting requires and how close to the described stance they can come with comfort.

The shooting stance is vital to success. It must be repeated exactly for each shot, just as the gun must be mounted in exactly the same way each time. Variations will result in a missed (lost) bird. The only variation that should be used is for station-8 shots, where the bird passes almost directly overhead. (This variation will be discussed later.)

After mounting and stance are mastered, you must remember that the forward foot should always be pointing at the location where you expect to break the target (kill the bird). The ideal place to accomplish this is in the center of the field. This point is marked by a stake. Therefore, at any shooting position from station 1 to station 7, the forward foot should always be pointing at this stake.

Body Swing Now that you can mount your shotgun properly, using the correct stance and with your lead foot pointing at the center stake, you must learn how to swing. All left and right movement should be accomplished only in one manner. Think of your body as a tank. From the waist down, you are the tank proper; from the waist up, you are the tank's turret. All left and right movement should take place at the waist—none below, none above. In practice, some very slight body movement may occur above and below the waist, but it should be kept to an absolute minimum.

Up-and-down movement is also accomplished at the waist, with back, head and gun staying in a constant position. When this type of movement is mastered, you will be well on the way to success.

The Skeet Game Skeet is shot on a field that is roughly laid out as a half-circle. The target-release houses sit on each end of the field at the junction of the chord and the circumference. Stations 1 through 7 begin at the first target-release house (the high house) and proceed at intervals, along the circumference, to the second target-release house (the low house). The eighth station is halfway between high house and low house, along the chord. (See the accompanying diagram.)

At stations 1 and 2, the shooter first fires on a high-house bird (a clay target), then on a low-house bird (singles). He then fires at two birds (doubles) released simultaneously, one from each house. From stations 3, 4 and 5, the shooter fires both at high- and low-house singles. At stations 6 and 7, there are both singles and doubles. Only singles are fired upon from station 8.

When shooting doubles from stations 1 and 2, the shooter fires first at the high-house target, then at the low-house "bird." From stations 6 and 7, the order of firing at doubles is reversed, with the shooter firing at the low-house bird first. The sequence is easy to remember if you always shoot your first doubles shot at the bird released from the house nearest to you. In singles, however, the first shot is always at the high-house bird, the second at that from the low house.

The flight of the clay target released from either the high or low house is toward the outer edge of station 8. A stake is usually placed in the ground directly beyond this station, below the path of the bird. One simply proceeds

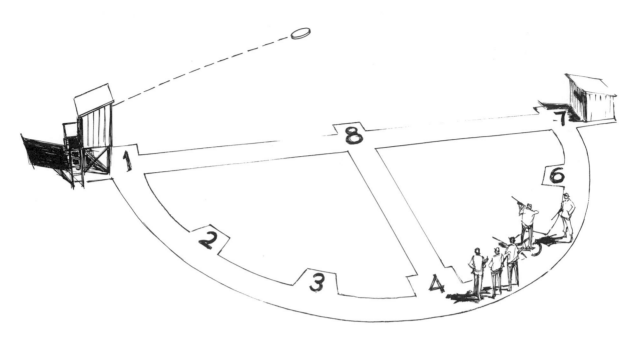

Layout of a skeet field.

from station 1 through station 8, firing four shots from stations 1, 2, 6 and 7 (two each at singles and two at doubles) and two shots each from stations 3, 4, 5 and 8.

The first shot missed is repeated. If you break 24 straight birds, your 25th shot is then taken from station 8 at a low-house bird. Variations on the 25th (optional) shot are sometimes allowed or required, depending on the club at which you are shooting.

Lead and Follow-Through Now you must learn where to start the gun, when to begin the swing, how much to lead the bird and when to press the trigger. All four of these points must come together properly or the bird will break only by chance. In addition, you must know how to follow through.

Committing gun-start position and leads to memory will help immensely. The spot at which the gun is pointed (gun-start position) while calling for a bird is constant regardless of the station from which you are shooting. This spot is an imaginary point some 10 feet from the release house along the path of the bird. Point the lead foot at the center stake, mount the gun and assume the shooting stance, pointing the gun where the bird will pass over the stake. Then wind up your body by swinging from the waist only, and bring your muzzle to a point about 3 inches below the imaginary spot described. This means your shotgun will be pointed some 10 feet from the release house, 3 inches below the path of the released bird. The only exceptions to this position are at station 1, high-house bird, station 7, low-house bird, and station 8, both birds. At both station

1 high-house and station 7 low-house birds, the gun should be pointed approximately halfway between the station and the center stake, directly along the bird's flight line.

If it is hard to imagine the 10-feet-from-the-house gun position, it is a point on the bird's flight path, directly in front of station 2 for high-house birds and station 6 for low-house birds. Remember to keep the gun about 3 inches below the bird's path. If a trap stock is used, hold about 6 inches below the bird's path.

The Eight Stations You should now be ready to call for a bird ... Pull! When the bird passes the stationary muzzle (which is pointed at the gun-start position), begin your swing. But be certain the bird has passed the muzzle *before* beginning any gun movement. If the swing is started early (jumping the bird), you will not shoot well. One of the secrets to success is to let the bird pass the muzzle, *then* to pass the bird with the muzzle, obtain the correct lead and shoot.

How much lead? That's simple. Commit the following to memory:

Station	High-House Lead	Low-House Lead
1	6 inches under	1 foot
2	pass & shoot	2 feet
3	3 feet	3 feet
4	4 feet	4 feet
5 (same as 3)	3 feet	3 feet
6 (same as 2)	2 feet	pass & shoot
7	1 foot	shoot right at bird
8	pass & shoot	pass & shoot

Little discussion is required regarding these leads. Every expert shooter asked will have some variation, but by using those shown, the novice shooter can learn to break a perfect score. So remember: Station 2, low—2 feet. Station 3, high and low—3 feet. Station 4, high and low—4 feet. Station 5, high and low—back to 3 feet. Station 6, high—back to 2 feet. One can learn quickly to associate the station number with a specific lead.

The pass and shoot stations may require some clarification. This simply means that after the bird passes the gun-start position, the shooter quickly swings the gun past the bird. The instant he is conscious of having passed the bird, he presses the trigger. For most shooters, this means pulling the trigger when the bird cannot actually be seen. The bird is there in view, but your eyes will not register it. The muzzle will be about 6–12 inches in front of the bird when the gun goes off.

It is most important that the gun be moved smoothly and quickly. If the shooter swings too slowly, he will require greater leads, if he swings too fast, less lead will be needed. Just swing naturally. Your pace will slowly but surely come to the right speed level.

A most important point to remember is to press the trigger instantly, without hesitation, when the lead is right. Attempting to hold a constant lead in order to make sure the lead is correct will result in a great many missed birds, and you will require longer leads. Never, never stop the gun swing when firing. In

Shooter displaying good form at station 1.

fact, exaggerate the follow-through by swinging well past the point of firing. It is all too easy to stop the swing. I prevent this by swinging my gun all the way to the opposite house, be the shot a hit or miss. It is a good habit that can totally eliminate lost birds due to stopping the gun.

Station 8 is unique. It is perhaps the hardest shot (along with 2 high and 6 low) for novice shooters. However, once learned, it becomes one of the easier shots. In the beginning, it seems as though there is not enough time to make the shot, but after just a limited amount of shooting practice, the bird can be broken without any effort. The proper gun-start position for station 8 is 6 inches below the opening of the house, at the outside edge of the *window.*

The proper stance for this station is the same as described earlier, except there is no stake at which to point the lead foot. Ideally, the bird will be broken when it has traversed two-thirds of the distance from the house to the shooter. Feet and gun should be pointed accordingly, and the body should wind up so that the gun then points at the position just below and on line with the outside edge of the house window. Then combine this with a major stance change. Break both knees considerably, so as to assume almost a crouching position. Then, when the bird is released, straighten the knees while swinging. This will accomplish a great deal of the rapid elevation gain needed to catch up with and pass the bird.

Because of the angle at which the shooter swings on a station-8 bird, he will be unable to see the bird once the muzzle has passed it. Just as soon as the bird is blotted from view, pull the trigger—but keep the gun moving.

Practice and Play   Skeet shooting demands that the shooter practice good gun mounting, stance, proper gun start, swing and follow-through. Yet, it is easy to learn and a sport that can be enjoyed from childhood through the senior citizen years. In addition, good skeet shots have a notable advantage in the

This shooter at station 2 has his cheek firmly pressed against the stock of his shotgun as he swings and fires at the fast-moving bird.

hunting field. Every shotgun owner should give skeet a try. Novice shooters should stick with it until they can consistently break 18 to 20 birds each round. If you choose not to shoot skeet regularly, then at least shoot three or four times prior to hunting season to sharpen your reflexes.

There are no shortcuts to becoming a good skeet shooter. Practice the fundamentals discussed often enough, and suddenly everything will fall into place. One word of caution: Skeet shooters are a helpful bunch and are quick to point out shooting errors, if asked. But if you want instruction, select a competent person and stick with that instructor. More than one instructor tends only to confuse the matter and often will hinder your progress. Everyone shoots a little differently—to hear most shooters tell it, you would think they were shooting different games.

The techniques described in this section have been used to teach a very large number of new and not-so-new shooters to become excellent skeet shots. If you follow these instructions carefully, you also can become a good or better skeet shot.

SHOOTING THE SHOTGUN IN THE FIELD

12

Hunting with a shotgun is an enjoyable sport only if you have attained some degree of proficiency. You cannot simply pick up a shotgun and walk through the fields and woods, expecting to bag game when it flushes.

Fundamentals of Shooting Game

In order to score hits with a shotgun, you must understand and practice the fundamentals: stance, gun mounting, pointing, swinging and the all-important follow-through. As I've suggested, perhaps the best way to learn these fundamentals is to shoot skeet. Skeet is easy to learn, and because each shot is at a bird from a known release point, traveling a known path, you can put all of your concentration on the positioning of your feet, mounting the gun properly, pointing the gun at the right starting place, swinging, firing and following through. The basics required to accomplish these tasks have been covered extensively in the previous chapter.

I cannot overstress the importance of learning all the fundamentals. Actually, a shooter who learns to do well at skeet will do reasonably well in the field. I know a number of shooters who, with each field shot, try to equate the quarry's flight path to a specific skeet shot, then proceed to lead and shoot as though the target were a clay bird. It works often enough to allow these shooters to bag a respectable percentage of the game at which they fire.

Field shooting can be as easy as skeet or a great deal more difficult than crazy quail shooting (see Chapter 14). The field shooter does not always have the advantage of a level shooting station, and as often as not his feet are pointing in the wrong direction when his quarry is flushed. He may be fatigued, out of breath, hung up in the brush or bent over in an awkward position as he steps below some overhanging limb, while his foot is slipping on a muddy place—or some combination of all of these.

Leads on Moving Game   Wing shooting is part mathematics. You must understand that you simply cannot shoot directly at a moving target. If you do, by the time your shot pattern arrives where it has been aimed, the target will have moved some distance beyond the place in space being occupied by your shot. Shot has a very definite velocity. It does not arrive at the target at the same exact microsecond the gun discharges. Leaving the muzzle at a velocity somewhere between 1,100 and 1,350 feet per second, shot quickly begins to lose its velocity. It may take a shot charge as much as two-tenths to three-tenths of a second to reach some distant target. Now, that's not much time, but it is sufficient time for a flying bird to move 10 to 30 feet. With an effective pattern diameter of, say, some 3 feet, and assuming you centered the bird well, the extreme edge of your effective pattern would be some 8 to 28 feet behind your target.

Once you begin to realize that you must lead moving game, then you have a number of options. You could, of course, simply pick out a point in front of your quarry and shoot at that imaginary mark. And on occasion you would bring a bird to bag. But not very often, because birds fly at varying speeds, and the distance covered by the bird varies with that speed. The shooter, however, would be unable to determine flying speeds and leads required in the limited time available to take the shot.

Some shooters score a fair number of hits by using what is called a sustained lead. They start the gun on the target, swing ahead of the target and then maintain a specific distance of lead, pulling the trigger sometime during the period of sustained lead. This kind of shooting requires substantially shorter leads than simply pointing at a spot in front of the target, since the gun is also moving at the same speed as the target. While a good number of targets can be hit with a sustained lead, there are drawbacks to such a method. For one, it takes a comparatively long time to establish and maintain a sustained lead. During this time, a target could conceivably fly out of sight or out of range. Sustained lead shooting is fine if the shooting conditions are not difficult. But if a bird changes directions slightly when a shooter is using a sustained lead, the change will often go unnoticed, and the result is an inevitable miss.

There is a better way to hit game, and that is the swing-through method described in the previous chapter. But field conditions demand more than just the right kind of swing. For instance, where is the gun started for a field shot? How does one compensate for uneven terrain and awkward positions?

Stance   The first step in hitting any target is always to assume a proper stance. A right-handed shooter who finds his right foot forward when a bird flushes or a rabbit darts forward should always—I mean always—take a half-step forward to position the left foot correctly under the left arm. And placing the left foot out in front is not in itself enough. As the left foot comes forward, it must be positioned so that a straight line drawn across the front edge of the right foot will fall directly across the front edge of the left foot. When extended, this line will be pointing at the place you expect to hit the bird or other target. More often than not, this means that the position of the right foot also must be changed. Movement of the right foot is most often best executed by pivoting on it without actually ever completely lifting it from the ground.

Proper foot placement needs to be thought about and deliberately executed until it becomes an automatic reflex. For those who do not get sufficient shooting opportunities, positioning of the feet may involve a conscious effort right up to the day we fire the last shot.

I have found that one of the best ways to ensure proper foot position is to make no attempt to mount the shotgun until after the proper position is assumed. This awareness in keeping the gun down somehow helps me take the half-step and to pivot on my right foot as required. For most shotgunners, bringing up the gun after the proper foot position has been assumed is the first step in learning the *art* of shooting, but a lot of field practice is required in order to accomplish this.

Should your left foot be forward when a target explodes from cover and heads for a distant place, you still must align that imaginary line across the toes of both feet so that it is pointing to the spot where you expect to hit your target. To accomplish this, you may have to move the left foot a number of inches forward or backward and perhaps change its position to the right or left. Pivoting on the right foot should be accomplished simultaneously. Only when the feet are positioned correctly should the gun be moved to the shoulder.

Mounting the Gun   As the gun is mounted, you must execute the shouldering precisely the same each and every time. As discussed earlier, your eye is the rear sight, and thus it must be positioned in the exact same spot with relationship to its height above the stock's comb and its left and right adjustment over an imaginary line drawn through the center of your bore and receiver. In the case of a side-by-side shotgun, the centerline of the rib between the barrels is the reference point over which the eye must be positioned. If you place your eye too high above the comb, your shot will go high. If you get too close to the comb, your shot will be low. An eye positioned to the right or left of proper alignment will cause the shot to go off in that direction. Therefore, the mounting of the shotgun should be deliberate and precise.

Gun Fit   Because field shooting places a great demand upon speed, one should use a shotgun with stock dimensions that require no deliberate head or neck movements to assume a consistent head position on the stock. Ideally, as the gun is shouldered, the head will be in the correct position on the stock. In practice, to compensate for the differences in neck lengths and face proportions, some small amount of neck bending or head positioning may be required. However, if you must enter into any notable movement to see just a little barrel with the bead centered clearly in the middle of both barrel and receiver, then you should consider having your stock altered to suit your build.

Frequently, stock fit can be adjusted merely by learning to position the butt higher on the shoulder. A great many shooters find that this style of butt positioning helps their scores considerably. The reason for this is that when the gun is positioned high on the shoulder, it is difficult to lift the head off the stock, thus preventing the shooter from getting his eye out of its vertical alignment. To prove this point, try shouldering your shotgun so that half the butt plate protrudes above your shoulder. You will note that the comb is being pushed up hard against your cheek, preventing you from lowering your head and eye position in relationship to the gun. Also, because your head is fully erect, you cannot lift it from the comb any farther, and thus your eye cannot be raised from its position relative to the comb. When shooting, what you are trying to

Positioning the butt of the shotgun high on the shoulder will eliminate the tendency to lift your head from the stock before shooting.

effect is a positive and consistent eye position in relationship to the bore of your shotgun. It is the uniform position of your eye that enables you to "aim" the shotgun uniformly. Without such uniform positioning, your shots will be directed to different places. Your eye is the rear sight. If you move the rear sight on a rifle, the point of impact changes. If you move your eye when shooting a shotgun, so also will the point of impact change.

The most consistent game shot always positions his shotgun on his shoulder so as to assure positive wood-to-cheek contact without any notable bending of the head. Perhaps the best way to accomplish this is to mount the gun as high on the shoulder as possible. Trap-style stocks help accomplish the same end, since their higher combs contact the face sooner. Thus, when a trap stock is positioned identically on the shoulder as a fieldstock, the comb will be higher and the head will be held more upright, ensuring a more positive alignment of the eye. For this reason, I always try to buy trap-grade guns and then fit them with barrels of the appropriate chokes. Of course, this is not always possible, and one can learn to shoot a standard comb stock very, very effectively. I just find things a tad easier with a stock that has a higher-than-normal comb.

Swing and Follow-through After the feet have been properly positioned and the shotgun properly mounted, you must start your shotgun at some point of reference and then swing through your target, obtain the correct lead, fire and follow through with your swing. Where you start your shotgun will have a decided effect on whether your shot will hit the intended target or simply become another miss.

It would be almost impossible to start your gun, as in skeet or trap, by aligning it on some imaginary point in relationship to the target's release point. After all, the target is already on the move, and its starting point is now of little consequence. Wherever you start your gun, it must be somewhere behind your target if the swing-through and lead are to be properly executed. Perhaps one of the best systems ever devised for accomplishing a uniform gun-starting position is the "apparent vertical clock" method. I first saw this method discussed in a handbook published by the Committee on Promotional Activities of the Sporting Arms & Ammunition Manufacturers Institute. If memory serves me, the book was dated late 1930s, and therefore you are not apt to have one on hand for reference. Let me explain the method as I have used it for more than 37 years.

Aim Imagine, if you will, that you have sighted your quarry, which is rising and going away from you while moving to your right. You quickly assume the correct foot position and then begin to mount your gun. The problem now is where to have that gun pointing once it is correctly mounted. If that imaginary point is always the same, matters become somewhat simpler. So when pointing your gun, always start at the center of an imaginary vertical clock directly in front of you (see diagram). This clock's vertical position can be such that its center may vary somewhat, depending upon the elevation of the target with respect to the height of your shoulder. If the game is well above you, move the center of the clock to an imaginary position well above your head. The important point is that the center of the clock be behind the position of the game at the moment the gun is mounted and that it be along a line drawn from the clock's outer edge through the target's current path. The accompanying illustrations will serve to clarify this point.

The black dot at the center of the clock is where you point your gun in order to begin a proper swing-through on your target. Your swing will be in a straight line, assuming the gun was started correctly and that the target is moving in a straight line. This style of shooting keeps shotgunning to the minimum basic essentials.

Remember: Position your feet, mount the gun while simultaneously pointing at the center of the imaginary clock, begin swinging on the line corresponding to the target's direction, pass the target and pull the trigger when the lead looks right. But never forget to keep swinging even after the shot. Such follow-through will prevent you from stopping the gun at the moment you pull the trigger.

Passing through the target from the rear and then moving out ahead of it assures that your gun is moving faster than the target. By making the gun move more quickly than the target, you reduce the amount of required lead to an absolute minimum.

These drawings depict imaginary field situations in which you would have to lead a moving target. When the target appears, imagine a clock with a black dot in the center. You would point your gun at the dot, begin your swing toward an imaginary numeral, swing through the target and fire when your lead looks right. Field shots can often be visually associated with skeet (or trap) shots.

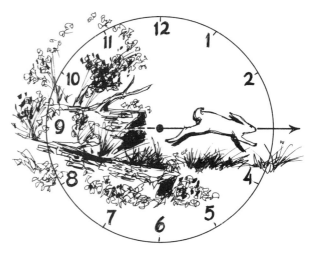

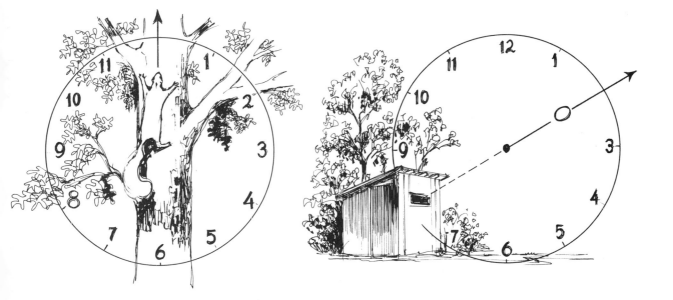

Getting It All Together   While target speed, angle and distance are essential parts of mathematically calculating the required lead, the art of successful shotgunning is to reduce the mathematics to an instinct that tells you when the lead is right. For targets up to 25 yards away, using skeet leads on birds and game traveling at the same approximate angle as a specific skeet shot will work well enough to get you started on connecting with your target. Thus, on birds going straight away, you would hold just below by perhaps 6 inches. For targets traveling at a modest angle, you would lead perhaps by 1½ or 2 feet. At greater angles, you can increase the lead to 2 or 3 feet. On crossing shots, a lead of 4 feet would be a good beginning.

As the range increases, so will the necessary lead. On distant crossing ducks, I have often led as much as 12 feet in order to score a hit. Gaining the ability to determine the necessary lead for field shooting is not difficult. You simply need to practice often enough to develop the required skill. Unlike some art forms, successful shotgunning can be learned by almost anyone who practices the basic essentials: proper stance (foot placement), gun mounting, pointing, swing, lead and follow-through. After that, it is only a matter of sufficient application in order to gain the necessary skills.

Finally, it is important to realize that you can shoot no better than you can see. Therefore, it makes sense to keep both eyes open when shooting. This is not possible for every shooter. Some, regardless of how hard they try, find that shooting with both eyes open results in them not looking down the barrel as they should. Such shooters will do best to forget the both-eyes-open advice.

Keep in mind that, in field shooting, game can frequently change directions even while you are swinging. You must keep alert to such changes and correct your swing accordingly. Do not forget to consider that your body above the waist should be moved like a gun turret. Once your feet have been properly placed, all swing, be it vertical or horizontal, should take place at the waist. If you attempt to obtain the correct swing by moving only arms and shotgun, you will more often than not forget to keep your head positioned exactly on the stock. Swinging from the waist will allow you to keep your head tight against the stock, so that your eyes will not move in relationship to the bore line of your shotgun.

Practice   Few of us possess a natural shooting ability that seems not to be affected by a lack of practice. Therefore, it is important to do at least some shooting with your field gun prior to hunting season. A few rounds of skeet and trap or some hand-trap-thrown clay targets can give you the opportunity to brush up on the basics. Serious shooters will find themselves shooting clay targets frequently, all year long. And why not? Properly approached, a shotgun shooting game can be as much fun as a day afield. I enjoy my practice sessions doubly, as they give me pause to reflect on the coming days afield. And if, during the course of the season, I miss a few easy shots, I will interrupt my hunting and head for the skeet or trap range to sharpen up a bit.

If you miss a shot, try to recall the position of the barrel and target in relationship to one another. If you cannot, perhaps there was none, and your shot was made by rote rather than by actually swinging through the target and obtaining a positive lead.

Be certain you are looking down the barrel of a properly mounted gun. This should be done as you point the shotgun at the imaginary clock center. Then be sure you see the muzzle clearly as it passes through your target. If you are not seeing the muzzle end of your shotgun over the receiver and the target, in relationship to the muzzle, you can bet you're not putting everything together and hence will miss more often than not. When the misses occur too frequently, it's time to review your shooting from the basics.

If you seldom miss, you need only to practice frequently to maintain a high degree of field shooting skill. Field shooting is difficult only if the shooter refuses to put the basics to work on each shot. If you try to hurry a shot, you are sure to forget something. Take your time to do it all. One well-taken shot will produce better results than two or three hasty, half-executed shots.

13 TRAP SHOOTING

Trap shooting is more difficult to learn than skeet shooting. In skeet, you have targets traveling at known angles, but in trap, the angle of the target can vary considerably. Because the birds are released some 16 yards away from the shooter, and because they travel in a direction that takes them still farther away, trap shooters usually break their targets at considerable distances. Those who shoot very quickly may sometimes find a modified choke sufficient. Other quick shooters may select an improved modified choke, sometimes called modified trap choke. But the greatest majority of experienced trap shooters favor a full choke.

Trap is a very old shooting game that is shot year-round. A trap field consists of an arc of five stations spaced 3 yards apart. The release point for the bird is some 16 yards directly in front of station 3. Legal birds released from the trap house are thrown straight away from the shooter or at any angle up to 22 degrees to the left or right of a straightaway target from station 3.

Trap Guns   Because the bird is a rising target, trap stocks have higher and straighter combs and somewhat longer lengths of pull. Without the higher comb stock, one would have to point above the rising bird in order to score a hit. With a trap-dimension stock, it is possible to hold for the bottom edge of the rising bird and score a hit *if* the gun is moving with the target. Field-dimension stocks require that the gun be pointing above an obscured target in order to hit it.

Because of the long ranges at which trap birds are broken, a long barrel will help facilitate the exactness of pointing required for good scores. Barrel lengths of 28 to 32 inches are frequently used, with a 30-inch barrel being the most popular. And because trap is a fast-paced game, a ventilated-rib barrel is almost a must. Heat rising from a hot barrel often causes mirage conditions that can optically distort the apparent position of the target. Even when such position distortion does not occur, the shimmering heat waves themselves can cause the shooter to break his concentration on the target and, hence, to miss birds. The ventilated rib will lessen this problem greatly.

Of course, trap can be shot informally with almost any shotgun, using at least 1 ounce of No. 8 or No. 7½ size shot and with a barrel choked modified or

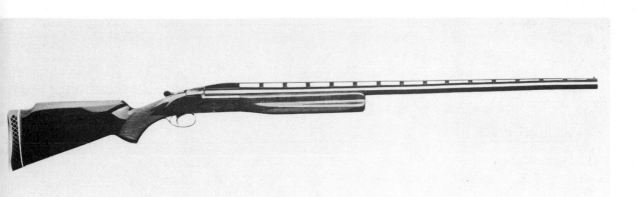

The Browning single shot BT99 is popular with many trap shooters.

Extremely popular, the Remington 870 TA trap gun is available with a standard trap stock (shown) as well as Monte Carlo style.

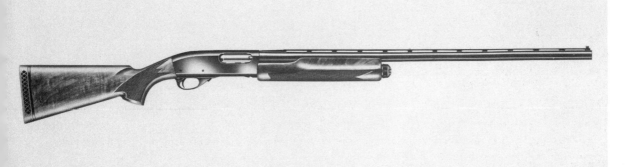

Unique among trap guns, the Remington 870 Competition trap gun is a pump single shot that incorporates a unique gas-actuated recoil reducing system in what otherwise would be the magazine.

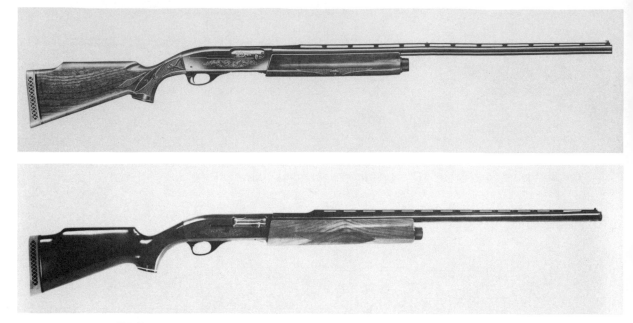

While perhaps the least popular action style, semiautos do have a following with trap shooters who like recoil to keep at a minimum. Shown are the Remington TA with Monte Carlo stock (125a) and the S & W Model 1000 also with Monte Carlo stock (123b).

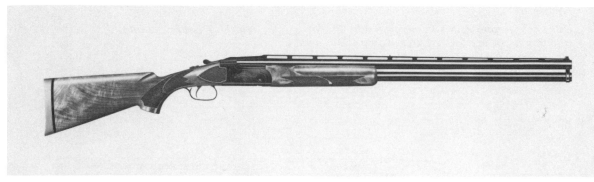

Over-and-under shotguns have a strong following among trap shooters.

tighter. But for consistently high scores, a 12-gauge gun using 1⅛ ounces of shot and having a tightly choked ventilated-rib barrel, along with a trap stock, is essential.

Gauging the Angles   Because trap is a game where the target is released at an unknown angle, one cannot be taught where the bird will appear. By the time the bird clears the trap house and the shooter's eyes register its departure, it may be traveling at an angle 22 degrees left of a line drawn from station 3 to the center of the trap house. Or it may be traveling at an equal angle to the right of the same line, or anywhere between these two points.

To increase the degree of difficulty, the angle at which a given bird is traveling, in relationship to the shooter, varies depending upon the station at which the shooter is positioned. A bird that is a straightaway target for a shooter on station 3 becomes a slight left-angle target for a shooter on station 2 and a slight right-angle target for the station-4 shooter. The same birds seen from stations 1 and 5 would be a harder angle. By the same token, a bird that would be a right-angle shot from station 3, could be a straightaway from station 1.

Because of the unknown angles at which the bird can be released, the successful trap shooter must learn to start his shotgun from a position that will allow him to see each bird quickly as it is released. At the same time, he must be able to determine exactly at what angle it is traveling in relation to his shooting

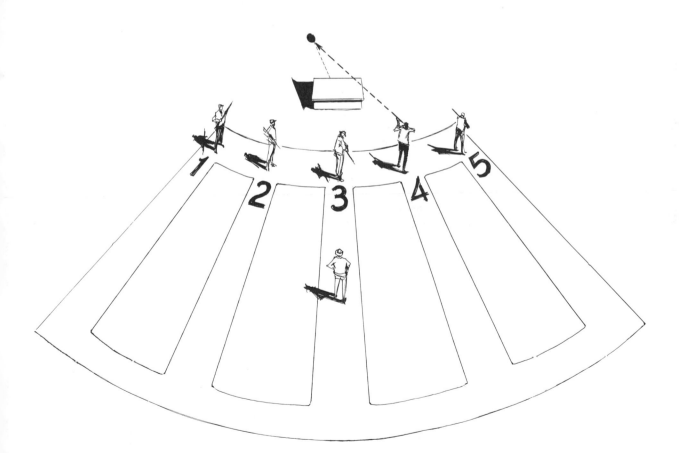

Layout of a trap field.

station. To do this consistently, the shooter must start the gun low enough so that he can see the bird as soon as it clears the trap house, and he must start it in a position that will allow him a positive visual reference (compared to the position of the barrel) to establish the exact angle of flight. There is a very exacting way to accomplish this from each of the five stations.

Aim and Leads From station 1, after shouldering the shotgun, point it about 1 foot below the top left edge of the trap house. Hold this position when calling for a bird. When the bird appears, if it rises straight over the barrel, it will be going straightaway and require no left or right lead. Birds going to the left or right of the barrel should be gauged as to the extent of the angle of departure. In the beginning, it helps many shooters to break the birds' flight into basic categories: straightaway, slight left angle, moderate left angle, hard left angle, and slight, moderate and hard right angles.

As one becomes proficient at handicap trap, he "earns" yardage and is slowly moved back from the 16-yard station in 1-yard increments until he reaches a maximum distance of 27 yards. The amount of horizontal lead required will naturally increase as one moves farther back along the handicap distances. For our discussion here, we will consider the leads required only from the first position of 16 yards. When a shooter becomes proficient enough to earn a handicap yard or more, the ability to determine the necessary increase in lead will come quite naturally.

In the beginning, it would be well to use a 1-foot lead on slight-angle birds, a 2-foot lead on moderate angles and a full 3-foot lead on the hard-angle birds. From station 1, the extreme left-angle bird will require perhaps a 4-foot lead— ditto for the extreme right-angle bird from station 5. The exact amount of lead will, of course, vary with the speed of your swing.

From station 2, the gun should be pointed at an imaginary spot 1 foot from the top edge of the trap house and one-third of the way into the house from the left edge. At station 3, the gun should be started at a point 1 foot below the edge of the house along a line drawn vertically through its center. From station 4, start the gun at a point 1 foot below the top edge of the house and one-third of the way in from the right side. From station 5, again use the same elevation, but start the gun at the right edge of the house.

When starting the gun 1 foot below the top edge of the house, do not use the closest edge of the roof line, but rather the farthest edge of the roof.

Five shots are fired from each of the five stations when shooting trap "singles." When calling for a bird, be sure not to move the gun from its starting position when seeing the bird in flight—wait until you are certain of its angle of travel. Decide whether the bird is traveling straight away or at a slight, moderate or hard angle. On stations 1 and 5, also decide if the bird is traveling at the extreme possible angle. When deciding upon the angle at which the bird is traveling, mentally relate that to a required vertical lead of 0, 1, 2 or 3 feet, and on stations 1 and 5 perhaps a 4-foot lead, for the extreme left- or right- angle birds respectively. Only after seeing the bird, deciding upon its course and selecting a required lead should the shooter begin moving his gun.

Obviously, there is not a great deal of time in which to make all of these

Trap shooter calling for a target from station three with the gun properly held on the center of the trap house.

observations and a decision. After a few seconds the bird will begin to fall, indicating that its distance from the shooter has become relatively great. Once the bird begins its fall, he will have to shoot below it in order to hit it. At such ranges, patterns have opened up sufficiently to make hitting the small target rather difficult. To score well in trap, the bird must be shot while it is still rising. The faster the shot, the smaller the specific lead required. Also, when increasing the distance between shooter and target, as when using handicap yardage, the shooter who has learned to shoot quickly will have the advantage in firing at a bird that is much closer than it would be if he were slow in accomplishing his task.

Speed and Swing   Speed, of course, is vital when you first decide upon shooting doubles (two birds released simultaneously). For such shooting, the traps are secured into position so that the birds will travel at a known angle.

When beginning the swing on the bird, it is best, in my opinion, to swing through the arc created by the bird's flight, passing just underneath the bird and firing when the lead is correct for the angle. Pass no more than 6 inches below the bird, and remember to keep swinging even after the trigger is pulled. Unless the shooter follows through in this manner, he will miss the target. It is almost impossible to hit a bird with a motionless gun. The lead and swing will always include an upward movement to compensate for the rising bird. If the bird begins to fall before the shot gets to it, quicker shooting is required.

The beginner should strive for no more speed in shooting than is required to get shot to the target before it begins to fall. A certain amount of deliberate concentration, the swing and the lead are more important than breaking the bird as soon as it clears the house. With practice, a pace best suited to the individual's style of shooting can be developed. If shots can be made quickly, an improved modified choke or perhaps even a modified choke may be tried. But stay with the full choke at least until 85 percent or more of the targets are consistently broken. By then, you will know what choke is best for your style of shooting without actually using each of the various chokes. If you will not be participating in highly competitive matches, then there is little reason to investigate chokes other than full. A full choke is almost mandatory for the second shot on doubles or for shooting single birds when a handicap is the 22-yard mark or greater.

Practice   Perhaps the best way to learn to shoot trap is first to learn skeet. Once the swing, lead and follow-through required for skeet are mastered, trap targets will not seem quite as difficult. These essentials are, of course, a vital part of any kind of shotgun shooting.

It takes a lot more practice to become proficient at trap than it does for skeet shooting, at least for most shooters. This practice is required because of the unknown angles. Unlike skeet, where someone can tell you exactly where the next bird will come from and how much it will need to be led, each shot in trap demands that the shooter determine the direction of the target and the amount of lead required to hit it.

None of this is to say that trap is unduly difficult. It simply requires that most of us practice a bit more than we might do for skeet if we wish to be reasonably skilled. Perfect scores are not nearly as common when shooting trap as they are when shooting skeet. Yet, there are far more registered trap shooters than there are skeet shooters. At least for me, the satisfaction of a perfect 25 is most rewarding when accomplished in trap shooting. I enjoy skeet shooting, but trap is indeed the greater challenge.

The shotgunner who wants to be proficient in the field should shoot both skeet and trap at least a half-dozen times a year. An upland hunter who uses a wide, open-bored shotgun at short ranges would be served well with just skeet practice, while a shooter who hunts wild, flushing birds in open country, could get along fine with only trap practice. But the shooter who wants to be able to hit birds in the field under widely varying conditions will be served best if he divides his target shooting equally between trap and skeet.

Loads   For most trap shooting at single targets from 16 yards, a 1⅛-ounce, 2¾-dram load of either No. 8 or No. 7½ shot will do perfectly. For shooting from extended handicap ranges, you may find No. 7½ shot preferable. Many shooters prefer 3-dram loads, but the reduction in lead provided by the extra 50 feet per

Action at a trap-shooting tournament. These shooters are shooting in the 16-yard event. When competing in the handicap event, they would shoot from different yard markers depending on their ability.

second muzzle velocity of these loads is rather small. The 2¾-dram loads have less recoil and therefore will not fatigue the shooter as much. I suggest use of the lighter 2¾ drams equivalent loads in the beginning. Later, as skill is developed, the decision to use a faster load can be made.

For shooters of light stature or for those who are particularly recoil shy, the newer 1-ounce target loads may prove highly desirable. Regardless of what load you shoot, the actual ammunition performance will not vary greatly at the normal target breaking distances.

Keep in mind that all of the points covered for gun handling, mounting and swinging in the chapter dealing with skeet are equally applicable to trap shooting. They have not been repeated in order to prevent redundancy. But, if you skipped the skeet chapter because your interest was only in trap, it will be necessary to go back and read the skeet chapter in order to get a full discussion of all the fine points of proper gun mounting, swinging, lead and follow-through.

14 CRAZY QUAIL AND OTHER SHOTGUN GAMES

Crazy Quail

Crazy quail is perhaps the hardest shotgun game ever devised, yet it is the most fun. There is only one shooting station in crazy quail, and a full round consists of only ten shots. Sound easy? If you think so, consider the following:

The clay target (bird) is released from a pit 16 yards away. The angle of the bird can be anywhere in a 360-degree circle. To further compound the difficulty, there is usually a hedge or fence erected around the release pit preventing the shooter from seeing the bird until it clears the obstruction. The hedge may be some 3 to 5 yards from the pit.

Targets and Technique   Thus, the shooter may receive a target that is thrown directly at him, directly away from him, at a 90-degree angle or anywhere else in a 360-degree circle. Incoming birds clearing the hedge may be no more than 11 yards away when first seen. By the time the shooter's mind sets everything in motion, the bird will be even closer. After he mounts the shotgun and swings, the chances are that the bird may be no more than 4 or 5 yards away. This kind of shooting is best served with a cylinder or skeet choke.

The next target called for could well be a straightaway bird, which may be a full 22 yards away before seen. Reaction time plus mounting and firing will have the tiny target at least 30 to 35 yards away when you try to break it—or perhaps considerably farther if you are a somewhat slow and deliberate shooter. It is necessary to fire at the bottom edge of a going-away bird or as much as a foot over it, depending upon the stock dimensions of the shotgun. On the other hand, if your reflex time is slow and the bird has begun to fall, it may be necessary to shoot a foot under it. Outgoing birds are trap-type shots, best accomplished with a full choke.

Incoming birds will need to be blocked out like station-8 skeet birds. There will also be shots requiring leads varying from 6 inches to as much as 4 feet. Shooters who fire quickly will need to be concerned with rising birds only and need not worry about leading falling birds. Some shots will be best taken with cylinder or skeet chokes, others are best suited to a modified choke and still other shots are served properly only with a full choke. Thus, for all practical

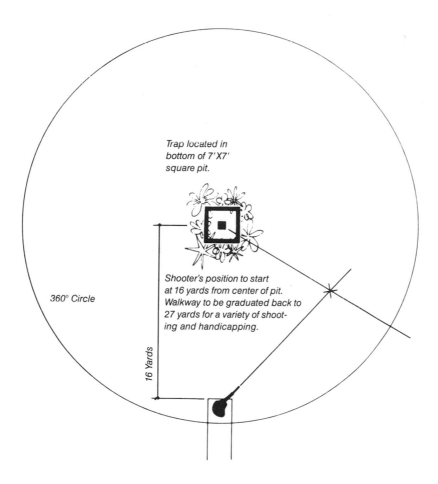

Trap located in bottom of 7'X7' square pit.

Shooter's position to start at 16 yards from center of pit. Walkway to be graduated back to 27 yards for a variety of shooting and handicapping.

360° Circle

16 Yards

purposes, crazy quail shots will simulate a good variety of field situations. I strongly favor a modified choke, and I try to shoot quickly to prevent the bird from getting too far away or too close, in order to have an optimum pattern at the range I break the birds. I can also attest to the fact that a full choke works well for shooters who can point very sharply on all of the incoming birds. For shots at close ranges, the pattern diameter will be measured in inches, so if even a small error is made, the bird will escape unharmed. A skeet choke may make the incoming birds easier to hit, but those going straight away, or nearly so, will be out of practical range by the time you get on them.

It helps to start the gun straight away and pointed perhaps 1 foot below the edge of the hedge or fence. This will allow you to see the bird as quickly as possible and also help you determine if the bird is actually going straight away or at a slight angle.

I shot crazy quail on one range for over eight years. During that time only two dozen perfect tens were shot by anyone. I have often broken as many as nine birds, but I'm beginning to believe that ten, for me, is an impossible accomplishment.

Variations on the Game   A variation on crazy quail that speeds up the game is miss-and-out. Each shooter fires until he either misses or breaks ten straight. At the first miss, the shooter leaves the box in favor of the next shooter. It is amazing how often shooters must leave the shooting box after firing only one shot.

Any incoming bird must be fired upon before it passes the shooter. No shots should be taken, for obvious safety reasons, at any bird that passes the shooting station. Birds not fired upon, because the shooter failed to see them, are scored as misses. Such birds are not as infrequent as one might think. Just the moment your eyes are scanning the right side of the field, is frequently when a hard-left-angle bird will be released. By keeping the gun below the hedge and watching the entire circumference of the hedge, such lost birds can be kept at an absolute minimum.

Some crazy quail ranges are set up to add a handicap to the shooter, as though it's really needed! In handicapped crazy quail, the shooting station starts at 16 yards from the release point and progresses back to 30 yards. Shooting from a distance of 22 yards or more makes a full-choke gun a must.

Just when a shooter feels that he has gotten the edge, don't be surprised to find the trap operator down in the pit trying to throw targets at angles at which he has the greatest difficulty in scoring hits.

Hunters' Clays

Another shotgun shooting game that has seen a fair amount of exposure is hunters' clays. In this game, the shooter stands in a wire cage, and the birds are released from a trap located at ground level to his left and from an elevated platform to his right. The birds can be released at varying angles and at varying trajectories. When a bird is called, it is up to the pullers to decide whether the bird will be released from the ground-level trap, the tower-height trap or both. Throw in unknown angles, and hunters' clays can be a very exasperating experience. However frustrating, practice at hunters' clays will make a shooter a better field shot; if he becomes serious about it, his field shooting will improve notably.

By the time the shooter sees the bird or birds, they will have traveled a fair distance, so using a modified choke seems about right. A full choke can also perform well, especially on the second bird when doubles are thrown. I prefer to use a trap gun with an improved modified choke or a double gun with modified and full-choke barrels. On doubles, the best scores are shot by those who can quickly decide which bird is closest, break it and then concentrate on breaking the second bird before it travels out of range. Despite the difficult nature of hunters' clays, most shotgun hunters find the game very enjoyable. Hunters' clays lends itself to a wide range of variations that can be employed to satisfy the shooters involved. A round can consist of 10, 15, 25 or any other number of shots, at the option of the shooters. Those who have shot a great deal of skeet and/or trap will usually prefer a 25-shot round. However, if you prefer your frustration in easy doses, as few as ten birds may prove a satisfactory round.

Because the shooter never knows when two birds will be released simultaneously, two shells are always loaded into the gun. Often only one shot is taken; therefore, proper gun handling becomes a serious part of the game. The shooters' station is usually fully enclosed on three sides and the top with cyclone-type fencing, to prevent the shooter from swinging his gun in any direction except out in front. This helps to ensure the safety of spectators and scoring and trap personnel.

Riverside Skeet

Another shotgun game, Riverside skeet, has seen limited popularity. This game was developed in 1948 by shooters at the Riverside Yacht Club in Riverside, Connecticut. In this game, five stations are arranged as in trap. However, the targets are released from two traps—one at the left, the other at the right, of the firing line.

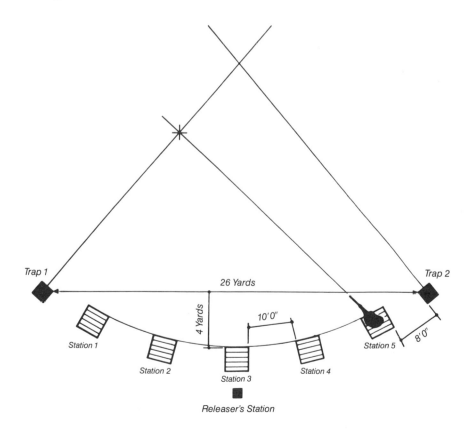

The shooter on station 1 first fires at a left-trap bird and then at a right-trap bird. The third shot is a bird released from either trap, at the option of the releaser. After completion of three shots at station 1, shooting then rotates to the shooters on stations 2 through 5. When all shooters have fired three shots, the shooter on station 1 fires on a pair of birds released simultaneously. Shooting then rotates to the other shooters in turn. When all have fired a total of five shots, the shooters each move to the next station, with the shooter on station 5 moving to station 1, as in trap. A round consists of 25 shots, five from each station. From 1948 to approximately 1969, only twelve perfect scores were shot at the Riverside Yacht Club. Riverside skeet is not an easy game.

The traps are arranged so that when birds are released in pairs, they will cross about 25 yards in front of station 3. Thus, a skeet or improved cylinder choke will be about right.

Other Games

Other shotgun shooting games do exist on local levels throughout the country. But if there is no nearby shotgun shooting range, you can still enjoy shooting clay targets in any open field where it is safe to shoot. All you need is an inexpensive hand trap and a case of clay targets. A shooter and thrower can invent their own games and sharpen up their skills for hunting season. Owning a shotgun can be a lot of fun. You simply need to get out and use it on clay targets in order to enjoy the pleasures of shotgunning. Birds thrown with a hand trap are the very best targets for the beginner or for polishing rusty skills. The basics can be taught quickly with a few boxes of shells and a case of clay targets.

SHOTGUN ACCESSORIES THAT MAKE SENSE

15

A shotgun requires very little in the way of accessories to enhance its performance. The most common and useful accessory for a repeating shotgun is the extra barrel. An extra barrel or two or even three can allow you to participate in a very wide range of shooting activities with exactly the right choke or sights.

Barrels   A slug barrel equipped with rifle-type sights will afford the maximum possible accuracy when shooting slugs for big game. Ideally such barrels are essentially cylinder bores, having one continuous diameter from breech to muzzle. While the diameter of a slug barrel may not exactly match that of a true cylinder barrel, the patterns thrown by it when shooting shot will effectively duplicate those of a cylinder bore shotgun. Thus slug barrels can do double duty, serving both your slug needs and shot needs to ranges of 25 yards or so. A slug barrel, especially a short 20- or 22-inch one, will prove ideal for close-in bird hunting in heavy cover. It will also work very well on the skeet range. I have broken many a perfect skeet score with a 12-gauge Remington 870 equipped with a slug barrel. Some slug barrels are improved cylinder choke.

An improved cylinder barrel will prove satisfactory for most bird shooting and can serve admirably on the skeet field. And if you use a scope for slug shooting, the improved cylinder barrel will prove almost as accurate as a cylinder bore or slug barrel.

Modified barrels should be selected whenever the ranges will run predominately between 25 and 35 yards. A modified choke is as tight a choke as should be used by a less than very good shot.

When used by experienced shooters, full-choke barrels can prove ideal for long-range waterfowl shooting and crow shooting. Full-choke guns can be used for all turkey hunting, as most shots are at a stationary target. Turkeys are hard to kill, and a tight pattern is needed to get the job done.

Screw-in Chokes   If you have a barrel that accepts screw-in chokes, such as the Winchester Winchoke, then a full selection of all tubes available makes good sense. Tubes for 12-gauge guns are usually available in skeet, improved cylinder, modified, improved modified, full and extra full. For 20-gauge shotguns, one can usually purchase skeet, improved cylinder, modified and full-choke

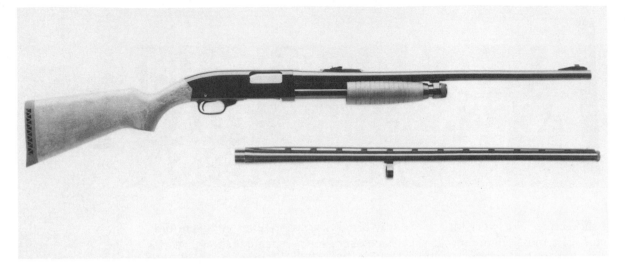

Extra slug barrels are useful for turning the shotgun into a big-game "rifle" and can double nicely as a short range (up to 30 yards) upland game barrel.

Screw-in chokes can be added to many guns or the shooter can start with a gun so equipped. Such chokes are the handiest of all shotgun accessories.

tubes. Interchangeable choke tubes are far more handy than extra barrels. They can be carried in the pocket, allowing you to switch chokes on a moment's notice, whereas extra barrels are usually left at home or are locked in the car trunk.

I have used interchangeable choke tubes extensively in several shotguns and find that the skeet and improved cylinder tubes in my Winchester Model 23 double gun are the ideal selection for most upland shooting. They have proved to be far more practical than the normally encountered fixed-choke combination of improved cylinder and modified. For waterfowl shooting over decoys with the same gun, I switch loads and install a modified and improved modified tube. When the ranges will be long, I use the improved modified and extra-full choke. For turkey, I prefer the full and extra-full tubes. Regardless of how the hunting conditions may vary, a pocket containing two or more extra choke tubes can keep your shotgun perfectly matched to the shooting.

Adjustable Chokes   Adjustable chokes are also available. However, such choking devices have fallen from popularity with the advent of screw-in choke tubes. These tubes match the barrel contour and are either almost or completely hidden within the barrel itself, whereas adjustable chokes add bulk to the end of the barrel. Shooters often find that the size and weight of an adjustable choke not only detract from their gun's appearance, but also alter the point of impact noticeably, because of the change in sight picture caused by the raising of the front sight in relationship to the bore line. This, for many shooters, results in a low point of impact. Of course, some gunsmiths do "straighten" barrels equipped with adjustable chokes to correct the problem. But many shooters object to the idea of bending a barrel to correct such difficulties.

I agree that adjustable chokes are ugly and detract from a gun's pointing and handling. I far prefer interchangeable choke tubes or extra barrels. Of course, interchangeable choke tubes are not necessary for every hunter. If your shotgunning is basically of one type at a relatively constant range, you may find that one choke is all you need. Or if you change from close-in woodcock to ducks, you may prefer an extra barrel in order to obtain a longer sighting plane. The ability to change chokes is put to best advantage by shooters who use their guns for widely varying conditions. I have one double gun, a 12 gauge, with interchangeable choke tubes, but all of my other doubles have fixed chokes. Because each of my repeating shotguns is used for a specific purpose, I prefer interchangeable barrels for the few occasions when I want to use a specific shotgun for slug shooting or what-have-you.

Slings

For a long time, Europeans have been using one accessory that Americans avoid on shotguns—a sling. Slings on shotguns are unattractive to most American hunters. But there are times when a sling can prove advantageous to

A sling on a shotgun, while alien to most U.S. sportsmen, can prove very handy at times.

a shotgun hunter. A waterfowl hunter carrying shells, lunch, coffee thermos and decoys might find that a shotgun equipped with a sling can be slipped over the shoulder and forgotten, leaving hands free to lug all the other gear. A deer hunter will find a sling useful when dragging a buck out of the woods. Having both hands free is often a blessing in a number of other routine hunting situations, such as erecting a blind on a muddy flat, negotiating some difficult terrain or simply on the long walk back after a full limit. If a sling-mounted shotgun offends you, then avoid its usage. But do consider the benefits before deciding to allow aesthetics to become the only reason for a judgment.

I don't use slings on my bird guns but have frequently used them on waterfowl shotguns. I insist upon a sling on any shotgun that is used exclusively for deer.

Vent Ribs   Perhaps not a true accessory, but rather an option at the time of purchase, is the ventilated rib barrel. Vent ribs, as mentioned in the skeet and trap chapters, are almost a must for serious clay target shooters. They are, however, of limited value for the hunter, and vent ribs do add a bit of weight to a barrel. However, for a shooter who tends to be a bit sloppy when mounting his shotgun, the vent rib can serve as a means of helping direct the eye down along the centerline of the bore. Also, during warm weather and fast shooting, such as might occur during a good dove hunt, a vent rib can help eliminate the problem of heat waves coming off the barrel.

And, of course, there are many hunters who just plain like the appearance of a vent rib. As shotguns have become lighter, the installation of vent ribs on them

A ventilated rib adds beauty and practicality to some shotguns.

has become more common. You will simply have to decide whether a vent rib has any practical value or aesthetic appeal for you. I find such a rib most helpful with respect to hunting on the shorter barrels, which I so prefer to use. On repeating shotguns with barrels of 21 inches or on double guns with barrels of 26 to 25 inches, a rib does help to sharpen up my pointing. However, on long-barreled waterfowl guns, I find the vent rib to be of no practical value. Indeed, for saltwater hunting locations, a vent rib seems simply to be a place under which rust can form, because of the difficulty in effectively cleaning beneath the rib.

Cleaning Materials Of course, the most common shotgun accessory is a cleaning kit. While modern shells with plastic sleeves around the shot seldom cause leading in the bore, a good bronze brush should still be part of your cleaning equipment. Such a brush is necessary to remove plastic residue from the bore and to keep chambers clean, especially in semiautomatics. A cleaning rod, patches, solvent and non-gumming oil will complete your cleaning needs. Select the best rod you can find, avoiding any with hollow plastic handles, which surely will break before much usage.

Recoil Pad One item that most shotgunners will enjoy and derive benefit from is the recoil pad. This accessory is often installed when a stock is shortened or lengthened or when the pitch of a gun is to be changed. However, because the recoil pad reduces shooting fatigue, it is a practical accessory for many shooters. For recoil-shy shooters, the improvement in shooting when using a recoil pad can be quite noticeable. Even a slip-on pad can be a giant step for such shooters.

Gun Cases Last but not least, a well-padded luggage-style case is a necessity for any shotgun that will be subjected to the rigors of public transportation. I can tell you from experience that airline personnel who handle luggage with respect of any kind are indeed very, very rare. I have seen much better treatment by the personnel who work for out-of-the-way train lines. But such train travel often includes a great number of bumps and bangs. A soft, well-padded case is handy for car transportation and camp use. If you're a waterfowl hunter, a waterproof case will greatly extend the useful life of your shotgun.

Summary There are other shotgun accessories ranging from inserts that will allow you to shoot .410 shells in your 12-gauge all the way to compasses that screw into the buttstock. However, most of these fall into the gimmick category. I consider extra barrels, choke tubes, adjustable chokes, slings, vent ribs, cleaning kits, and recoil pads the only shotgun accessories that make sense—not counting, of course, the huge amount of special clothing I have for various types of shotgun hunting. And surely you don't want to count the thousands of dollars I have invested in boat, motor, related equipment, boat trailer and several hundred duck and goose decoys as being money I have spent on accessories. Those items are essentials!

If you can think of other items essential to your shotgun shooting equipment, by all means invest in them. I firmly believe in anything that will help someone enjoy his days afield.

BASIC BALLISTICS FOR THE SHOTGUNNER

16

It has been my experience that of all groups of shooters, shotgunners know the least about the ballistics of the ammunition they choose to use. This is un-doubtedly as much the fault of the ammunition manufacturers as anyone else. The velocity of shotshells is virtually an unknown factor to most shotgunners.

Dram Equivalent One of the underlying reasons for this lack of knowledge is that ammunition manufacturers do not often publish data on shotshell bal-listics. But perhaps the main reason is because the ammunition industry con-tinues to perpetuate the archaic system of referencing the relative velocity of shotshells to the ridiculous dram-equivalent system. Dram equivalent is perhaps the least understood ballistic terminology ever used, yet it appears on almost every box of shotshells produced in this country. So, just what is a "dram equivalent"?

The industry definition of a dram equivalent is "The accepted method of correlating relative velocities of shotshells loaded with smokeless propellant to shotshells loaded with black powder." The black-powder load chosen as the main point of reference is the three-dram charge with 1⅛ ounces of shot in a 12-gauge case with an *assumed* velocity of 1,200 feet per second.

If you can see some mighty big holes in this definition, I'm not surprised. First, who really cares about black-powder loads? The comparison may have been valid during the transition from black powder to smokeless powders, but that transition occurred many generations ago. Second, a three-dram charge of *one* specific brand of black powder would have produced a velocity level notably different from a similar charge of black powder of *another* make. Must we assume that the vague reference refers to DuPont FFg, which, by the way, has not been manufactured for a good number of years? Third, the use of different kinds of wadding produces varying velocity levels. So much for the granite solidity of the industry standard definition for velocity ratings!

You may be extremely disappointed to know that the dram-equivalent system based on the assumed 1,200 feet per second was decided upon long after the discontinuance of black powder usage. However, in that the industry persists in marking shotshell boxes by dram equivalent, you should be aware of what velocity levels these dram equivalents represent. On shotshell boxes marked

All three shells contain 1¼ ounces of 7½ shot yet each will perform at a different level of ballistics. Understanding the dram equivalent system will allow you to determine the ballistic level of each shotshell.

Dram Equivalent - Max or Maximum Dram Equivalent, the shooter will have to be doubly alert. This is vagueness at its height because the ammo companies frequently load ammunition heavier than these so-called maximum equivalent loadings. For instance, some high-velocity 12-gauge 1¼-ounce loads frequently bear a max-equivalent rating. Yet you can purchase 1½-ounce loads in the same gauge. Consider also that the 12-gauge 1¼-ounce load in its high-velocity form has a rating of 3¾ drams equivalent and that the factories have in the past produced four-dram equivalent loads in 12 gauge. So what does the "maximum" rating mean? The dram-equivalent system must be analyzed with respect to each of the components in the listing—that is, gauge, shot weight and dram equivalent—if any real sense is to be made of the system.

The accompanying dram-equivalent charts will give you an exact average expected velocity level of all shotshell loads except those marked *Maximum* or *Magnum.* In the case of such a listing on your box of shells, you will need to know specifically to what the manufacturer is referring. In most cases, such markings will be found on so-called high-velocity loads or magnum loads and refer to an average velocity as follows:

All four shells are magnum yet their shot charges vary from 1¹/₈ ounces to 1¹/₄ ounces and finally 1⁷/₈ ounces. Proof indeed that the term magnum can be very misleading.

Shot charge weight differences are grapically depicted in this photo. From left to right are charge weights of: ⁷/₈ ounce, 1 ounce, 1¹/₈ ounces, 1¹/₄ ounces, 1³/₈ ounces, 1¹/₂ ounces, 1⁵/₈ ounces and 1⁷/₈ ounces.

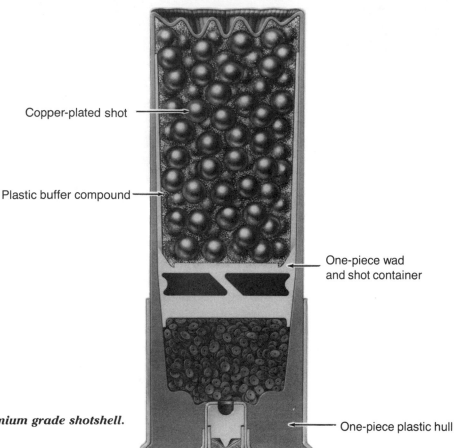

Copper-plated shot

Plastic buffer compound

One-piece wad
and shot container

A cutaway of a premium grade shotshell.

One-piece plastic hull

Gauge	Shot weight and type		Velocity	Dram equiv.
12 ga.	1½-ounce magnum	=	1,260 ft/s	"MAG"
12 ga.	1¼-ounce high vel.	=	1,330 ft/s	"MAX"
16 ga.	1¼-ounce magnum	=	1,260 ft/s	"MAG"
16 ga.	1⅛-ounce high vel.	=	1,295 ft/s	"MAX"
20 ga.	1⅛-ounce magnum	=	1,175 ft/s	"MAG"
20 ga.	1 ounce high vel.	=	1,220 ft/s	"MAX"
410 bore		=	1,135 ft/s	"MAX"

Comparisons of Velocity   It becomes easier to compare shotshells as one begins to comprehend the various levels of velocity. The included table lists all the loads available at this writing from the three major ammunition manufacturers. Shown are the listed dram equivalents and the actual nominal velocity to which the shells are loaded. Those loads indicated as MAX are those that normally carry a *Max Dram* equivalent rating on the shell box. Not every manufacturer loads each load listed, nor does every manufacturer always load all the shot sizes shown.

For each specific load shown, a number of variations are often possible. For example, the 12-gauge 1½-ounce 3¾-dram load (frequently referred to as a Max Load) can be purchased as:

A standard high-velocity loading
A load using extra-hard shot
A load using extra-hard shot and a granulated polyethylene filler
A load using copper-plated, extra-hard shot and a granulated polyethylene
filler

10-GAUGE DRAM-EQUIVALENT CHART
(velocity in feet per second)

Shot Wt. (ounces)	3¾	4	4¼	4½	4¾
1¼	1270	1315	1360	1405	1450
1⅜	1245	1290	1335	1380	1425
1½	1220	1265	1310	1355	1400
1⅝	1195	1240	1285	1330	1375
1¾	1170	1215	1260	1305	1350
1⅞	1145	1190	1235	1280	1325
2	1120	1165	1210	1255	1300
2⅛		1140	1185	1230	1275
2¼		1115	1160	1205	1250

12-GAUGE DRAM-EQUIVALENT CHART
(velocity in feet per second)

Shot Wt. (ounces)	2½	2¾	3	3¼	3½	3¾	4
⅞	1160	1215	1270	1325	1380	1435	1490
1	1125	1180	1235	1290	1345	1400	1455
1⅛		1145	1200	1255	1310	1365	1420
1¼		1110	1165	1220	1275	1330	1385
1⅜			1130	1185	1240	1295	1350
1½				1150	1205	1260	1315
1⅝				1115	1170	1225	1280
1¾					1135	1190	1245
1⅞					1100	1155	1210
2						1120	1175

16-GAUGE DRAM-EQUIVALENT CHART
(velocity in feet per second)

Shot Wt. (ounces)	2¼	2½	2¾	3	3¼	3½	3¾
⅞	1145	1200	1255	1310	1365	1420	1475
1	1110	1165	1220	1275	1330	1385	1440
1⅛		1130	1185	1240	1295	1350	1405
1¼			1150	1205	1260	1315	1370
1⅜			1115	1170	1225	1280	1335

20-GAUGE DRAM-EQUIVALENT CHART
(velocity in feet per second)

Shot Wt. (ounces)	2	2¼	2½	2¾	3	3¼	3½
¾	1145	1200	1255	1310	1365	1420	1475
⅞	1100	1155	1210	1265	1320	1375	1430
1		1110	1165	1220	1275	1330	1385
1⅛			1120	1175	1230	1285	1340
1¼				1130	1185	1240	1295
1⅜					1140	1195	1250

28-GAUGE DRAM-EQUIVALENT CHART
(velocity in feet per seond)

Shot Wt. (ounces)	1¾	2	2¼	2½	2¾
¾	1115	1205	1295	1385	1475
⅞		1160	1250	1340	1430
1		1115	1205	1295	1385

FACTORY LOAD SPECIFICATIONS

Gauge	Slug or shot wt. (ounces)	Advertised dram equivalent	Avg. velocity ft/s ± 35 ft/s	Shot sizes and types	Shell type and length (inches)
10	2¼	4½	1205	BB,2,4	Magnum, 3½
10	2	4¼	1210	BB,2,4,5,6	Magnum, 3½
10	1¾	max.	1280	Slug	Magnum, 3½
10	18 pellets	max.		00 Buck	Magnum, 3½
10	54 pellets	max.	1100	4 Buck	Magnum, 3½
10	1¾	max.	1280	BB, 2 (steel)	Steel, 3½
10	1⅝	4¼	1285	BB, 2 (steel)	Steel, 3½
10	1⅝	4¾	1330	4	H.V., 2⅞
12	1⅞	4	1210	BB,2,4,6	Magnum, 3
12	1⅝	4	1280	2,4,6	Magnum, 3
12	10 pellets	max.	1225	000 Buck	Magnum, 3
12	15 pellets	max.	1250	00 Buck	Magnum, 3
12	24 pellets	max.	1040	1 Buck	Magnum, 3
12	41 pellets	max.	1220	4 Buck	Magnum, 3
12	1½	4	1315	BB,1,2,4 (steel)	Steel, 3
12	1⅜	3½	1245	BB,1,2,4 (steel)	Steel, 3
12	1¼	3½	1275	1,2,4 (steel)	Steel, 3
12	1½	3¾	1260	BB,2,4,5,6	Magnum, 2¾
12	1¼	3¾	1330	BB,2,4,5,6,7½,8,9	H.V., 2¾
12	1¼	3¼	1220	6,7½,8,9	S.V., 2¾
12	1⅛	3¼	1255	4,5,6,7½,8,9	S.V., 2¾
12	1	3¼	1290	6,7½,8	S.V., 2¾
12	1¼	max.	1490	Slug	H.V., 2¾
12	1	max.	1600	Slug	H.V., 2¾
12	12 pellets	max.	1325	00 Buck	H.V., 2¾
12	20 pellets	max.	1075	1 Buck	H.V. 2¾
12	34 pellets	max.	1250	4 Buck	H.V., 2¾
12	8 pellets	max.	1325	000 Buck	H.V., 2¾
12	9 pellets	max.	1325	00 Buck	H.V., 2¾
12	12 pellets	max.	1300	0 Buck	H.V., 2¾
12	16 pellets	max.	1250	1 Buck	H.V., 2¾
12	27 pellets	max.	1325	4 Buck	H.V., 2¾
12	1⅛	3½	1310	9 (target load)	Spl.Target,2¾
12	1⅛	3¼	1255	7½,8 (target loads)	Spl.Target,2¾
12	1⅛	3	1200	7½,8,9(target loads)	Hvy.Target,2¾
12	1⅛	2¾	1145	7½,8,8½,9(target loads)	Lt.Target,2¾
12	1	2¾	1180	8,9 (target loads)	Spl.Target,2¾
12	1¼	3¾	1330	BB,1,2,4 (steel)	Steel, 2¾
12	1⅛	3¾	1365	1,2,4 (steel)	Steel, 2¾
16	1¼	3¼	1260	2,4,6	Magnum, 2¾
16	1⅛	3¼	1295	4,5,6,7½,9	H.V., 2¾
16	1⅛	2¾	1185	4,5,6,7½,8,9	S.V., 2¾
16	1	2½	1165	4,6,7½	S.V., 2¾
16	⅘	max.	1600	Slug	H.V., 2¾
16	12 pellets	max.	1225	1 Buck	H.V., 2¾
16	1	3¼	1330	4 (steel)	Steel, 2¾
20	1¼	3	1185	2,4,6,7½	Magnum, 3
20	18 pellets	max.		2 Buck	Magnum, 3
20	1⅛	2¾	1175	4,6,7½	Magnum, 2¾
20	1	2¾	1220	4,5,6,7½,8,9	H.V., 2¾
20	1	2½	1165	4,5,6,7½,8,9	S.V., 2¾
20	⅞	2¼	1155	6,7½,8,9	S.V., 2¾

FACTORY LOAD SPECIFICATIONS *(continued)*

Gauge	Slug or shot wt. (ounces)	Advertised dram equivalent	Avg. velocity ft/s ± 35 ft/s	Shot sizes and types	Shell type and length (inches)
20	¾	max.	1600	Slug	H.V., 2¾
20	20 pellets	max.	1200	3 Buck	H.V., 2¾
20	⅞	2¼	1200	8,9 (target loads)	Target, 2¾
28	¾	2¼	1295	6,7½,8	H.V. 2¾
28	¾	2	1200	9 (target load)	Target, 2¾
410	11/16	max.	1135	4,5,6,7½,8,9	H.V., 3
410	½	max.	1135	4,5,6,7½,9	H.V., 2½
410	½	max.	1200	9 (target load)	Target, 2½
410	⅕	max.	1830	Slug	H.V., 2½

H.V. = high velocity   Hvy.Target = heavy target
S.V. = standard velocity   Lt. Target = light target
Spl.Target = special target

From the included table, one can quickly see that a 20-gauge, 3-inch magnum load pushing 1¼ ounces of shot is not equivalent to a 12-gauge high-velocity load using 1¼ ounces of shot or, for that matter, to a 12-gauge standard velocity load with the same shot weight. The difference is velocity. The 20-gauge, 3-inch, 1¼-ounce magnum load leaves the muzzle at 1,185 feet per second, whereas the 12-gauge, high-velocity, 1¼-ounce load leaves the muzzle at 1,330 feet per second and the 12-gauge standard-velocity load is traveling at 1,220 feet per second when it leaves the muzzle. The point is, don't be misled by identical shot charges or names like *magnum, high-velocity* or *standard-velocity* until you know just what they mean in relationship to the specific load. The following table shows clearly how such information can be misleading:

VELOCITY COMPARISONS

Name type used	Gauge and load specs	Actual velocity (ft/s)
Magnum	10-ga. 3½", 2¼ oz.–4½ drams	1205
Magnum	12-ga. 3", 1⅞ oz.–4 drams	1210
Magnum	12-ga. 2¾", 1½ oz.–3¾ drams	1260
Magnum	20-ga. 3", 1¼ oz.–3 drams	1185
Magnum	20-ga. 2¾", 1⅛ oz.–2¾ drams	1175
High-velocity	12-ga. 2¾", 1¼ oz.–3¾ drams	1330
High-velocity	20-ga. 2¾", 1 oz.–2¾ drams	1220
High-velocity	410-bore, 3", 1 1/16 oz.–Max.	1135
Standard-velocity	12-ga. 2¾", 1¼ oz.–3¼ drams	1220
Standard-velocity	12-ga. 2¾", 1 oz.–3¼ drams	1290
Standard-velocity	16-ga. 2¾", 1 oz.–2½ drams	1165

It is obvious that when one high-velocity load has a velocity of only 1,135 feet per second (410 bore), and when one standard-velocity load has a velocity of 1,290 feet per second (12 gauge) and when a magnum load has a velocity of 1,175 feet per second (20 gauge), that names are somewhat meaningless unless you know exactly what velocity is being implied.

You might ask, "Does the ammunition I buy actually duplicate the velocities shown in the tables?" Yes and no. The manufacturer strives to obtain an average as close to the nominal listed velocity as possible. And normally, the actual average velocity obtained will be within 25 feet per second of the listed nominal velocity. But the velocity of each individual shot will vary above and below the average velocity level. Ballistically, it is impossible to load ammunition that will produce a uniform given velocity shot after shot. A good lot of shotshell ammunition will include shells that vary by as much as perhaps plus or minus 35 feet per second from the average velocity. And a less than ideal lot of ammunition may show deviations of 50, 60 or more feet per second from the average velocity level. In a ten-shot string, it is unlikely to find any two shells that produce an identical velocity except in instances of extremely uniform ammunition or sheer chance.

So what velocity levels do you require for specific shotgun applications? The accompanying shot applications table lists the minimum average velocity that has proven effective under a wide range of circumstances. Included in this table are recommendations for the all-important shot size and the minimum shot charge weight. These factors are far more important than the velocity of the load.

SHOT APPLICATIONS

Shot size	Minimum shot charge wt. (ounces)	Minimum suggested velocity (ft/s)	Suggested applications
BB	1½	1210	Geese, turkey, fox, similar-size game
2	1⅜	1210	Geese at shorter ranges, turkey, fox and large ducks such as mallards, blacks and white-wing scoter
4	1¼	1260	All ducks, small geese, pheasants, turkey, squirrel and rabbit[1]
5	1¼	1185	Duck shooting at 30 yards or less, pheasants, large grouse and rabbit[1]
6	1⅛	1165	Pheasant at 30 yards or less, grouse, doves, pigeons, partridge, squirrel, crows, and rabbit[1]
7½	1	1165	Crows, woodcock, snipe, large rails (clapper), doves, pigeons, grouse, quail, partridge and rabbit[1]
8	⅞	1135	Quail, small grouse, partridge, woodcock, snipe and large rails (clapper)
9	¾	1135	Quail, woodcock, snipe and all rails
11	¾	1135	Small rails (sora)

1 = For rabbit a minimum average velocity of 1,135 ft/s is adequate

For skeet shooting, No. 9 shot in charge weights from ½ ounce to 1⅛ ounces at velocities from 1,145 to 1,200 feet per second are usually used. For trap shooting, No. 8 and No. 7½ shot in a charge weight of 1 or 1⅛ ounces at velocities of 1,145 to 1,200 feet per second are normally used.

The importance of shot size is best demonstrated by the rapid loss of velocity and energy of the smaller sizes of shot. No. 6 shot and all smaller sizes quickly lose their velocity and energy and therefore have shorter practical maximum hunting ranges than the larger sizes. The table shows the maximum effective range of each pellet size, assuming it meets the minimum average muzzle-velocity requirement.

MAXIMUM PRACTICAL HUNTING RANGES FOR THE VARIOUS SHOT SIZES

Shot size	Minimum charge wt. (in ounces)	Minimum muzzle velocity (in ft/s)	Maximum range (in yards)
BB	1½	1210	60
2	1⅜	1210	55
4	1¼	1260	50
5	1¼	1185	47
6	1⅛	1165	45
7½	1	1165	40
8	⅞	1135	37
9	¾	1135	35
11	¾	1135	25

Note: Naturally, if this table is to have any real value, you must properly apply the correct size shot to the correct game.

Pattern density is dependent upon the size shot and the total weight of the shot charge. There are far fewer No. 4 pellets in a 1-ounce charge (137 pellets) than there are No. 7½ pellets in a 1-ounce charge (352 pellets). This is a result of the difference in pellet diameter between the two sizes. The following table shows pellet diameters and weights of individual pellets. The table is based on shot having an antimony content of 0.5 percent.

Shot size	Diameter (in inches)	Weight (in grains)	Approx. number of pellets per ounce
BB	0.180	8.75	50
2	0.150	5.03	87
4	0.130	3.37	130
5	0.120	2.57	170
6	0.110	1.99	220
7½	0.095	1.28	341
8	0.090	1.09	401
8½	0.085	0.92	475
9	0.080	0.77	568
11	0.060	0.32	1367

Exterior Ballistics   How shot loses its velocity and hence its energy is shown in the tables. It will be quite apparent when reviewing these tables that only the larger pellets retain sufficient energy at longer ranges to supply adequate penetration of game to ensure swift, clean kills. Large birds and quadrupeds require high levels of pellet energy if wings or bones are to be broken. The paradox here is that the larger pellet sizes result in fewer pellets per load. Thus, at long ranges, low pellet count can result in a pattern density too sparse to ensure bagging your target. It is thus obvious that a shotgun's maximum range depends upon pattern density (size and total weight of pellets), game size and, to a lesser extent, the muzzle velocity of the load. Therefore, good sportsmanship requires that you follow the suggestions in the charts and refrain from shooting at game beyond the capabilities of your equipment.

EXTERIOR BALLISTICS TABLE
For Shot Size #4 (.13″ diameter @ 3.37 grains)

Range	Vel.	Energy	Vel.	Energy	Vel.	Energy	Vel.	Energy	Vel.	Energy	Vel.	Energy
3 feet	1330	13.2	1315	12.9	1295	12.6	1240	11.5	1220	11.1	1200	10.8
20 yards	1015	7.7	1010	7.6	995	7.4	965	7.0	950	6.8	940	6.6
40 yards	820	5.0	815	5.0	805	4.9	790	4.7	780	4.6	770	4.4
60 yards	690	3.6	685	3.5	680	35.	670	3.4	660	3.3	655	3.2

EXTERIOR BALLISTICS TABLE
For Shot Size #5 (.12″ diameter @ 2.57 grains)

Range	Vel.	Energy	Vel.	Energy	Vel.	Energy	Vel.	Energy	Vel.	Energy	Vel.	Energy
3 feet	1330	10.1	1315	9.9	1295	9.6	1240	8.8	1220	8.5	1200	8.2
20 yards	995	5.7	990	5.6	975	5.4	945	5.1	935	5.0	920	4.8
40 yards	795	3.6	790	3.6	785	3.5	765	3.3	755	3.3	745	3.2
60 yards	665	2.5	660	2.5	655	2.4	645	2.4	635	2.3	630	2.3

EXTERIOR BALLISTICS TABLE
For Shot Size #6 (.11″ diameter @ 1.99 grains)

Range	Vel.	Energy	Vel.	Energy	Vel.	Energy	Vel.	Energy	Vel.	Energy	Vel.	Energy
3 feet	1330	7.8	1315	7.6	1295	7.4	1240	6.8	1220	6.6	1200	6.4
20 yards	975	4.2	965	4.1	955	4.0	925	3.8	915	3.7	905	3.6
40 yards	770	2.6	760	2.6	755	2.5	735	2.4	730	2.4	725	2.3
60 yards	635	1.8	630	1.8	625	1.7	620	1.7	615	1.7	605	1.6

EXTERIOR BALLISTICS TABLE
For Shot Size #7½ (.095″ diameter @ 1.28 grains)

Range	Vel.	Energy	Vel.	Energy	Vel.	Energy	Vel.	Energy	Vel.	Energy	Vel.	Energy
3 feet	1330	5.0	1295	4.8	1240	4.4	1220	4.2	1200	4.1	1145	3.7
20 yards	935	2.5	915	2.4	890	2.3	880	2.2	870	2.2	840	2.0
40 yards	720	1.5	710	1.4	695	1.4	685	1.3	680	1.3	660	1.2
60 yards	585	1.0	580	1.0	570	0.9	565	0.9	560	0.9	550	0.9

The ballistics tables clearly indicate that varying velocities within the nominal range of speeds change downrange energies only slightly. The size and weight of the shot are far more important than muzzle velocity in supplying sufficient downrange energies. As can be seen from the charts, a No. 4 pellet at 60 yards has roughly 40 percent more energy than a No. 5 pellet at the identical range, when both leave the muzzle at the same velocity. One can quickly understand why No. 4 shot performs so much better than No. 5 shot on waterfowl. While there are more No. 5 pellets in a given charge weight compared to No. 4s, there are not enough to make up for the difference of 40 percent more pellet energy with the larger size shot. The increased energy of the bigger pellets enables them to break big wing bones or penetrate deeply at ranges where No. 5 pellets just won't get the job done. The lesson to be learned is always to use as large a pellet size as is consistent with adequate pattern density for the game you wish to bring to bag.

Lead Content   Perhaps the aspect of ammunition performance most often discussed by shotgunners is the amount of lead required with different loads and for different game. The lead required for a specific shot is based on two specific variables, the time of flight for the shot to reach the target and the speed of the target. Time-of-flight charts are included in this chapter, as well as a waterfowl-speed chart. To determine specific leads one need only be able to calculate the distance to the target, the time of flight for the shot to reach the target and how far the target will move during the time it takes the shot to reach it. The distance the target moves during the time of flight for the shot is the amount of lead required. Of course, such calculations are impractical if not impossible to make in the field.

SHOT TIME OF FLIGHT #2 SHOT (IN SECONDS)
Muzzle velocity (ft/s)

Range (yds.)	1,330	1,315	1,295	1,240	1,220	1,200
20	.051	.052	.053	.054	.055	.056
40	.115	.116	.117	.121	.123	.125
60	.191	.193	.194	.201	.203	.205

SHOT TIME OF FLIGHT #4 SHOT (IN SECONDS)
Muzzle velocity (ft/s)

Range (yds.)	1,330	1,315	1,295	1,240	1,220	1,200
20	.052	.053	.053	.056	.056	.057
40	.119	.120	.121	.125	.127	.128
60	.199	.201	.203	.209	.212	.214

SHOT TIME OF FLIGHT #5 SHOT (IN SECONDS)
Muzzle velocity (ft/s)

Range (yds.)	1,330	1,315	1,295	1,240	1,220	1,200
20	.053	.053	.054	.056	.057	.058
40	.121	.122	.124	.128	.129	.131
60	.205	.206	.208	.215	.217	.219

SHOT TIME OF FLIGHT #6 SHOT (IN SECONDS)
Muzzle velocity (ft/s)

Range (yds.)	1,330	1,315	1,295	1,240	1,220	1,200
20	.054	.054	.055	.057	.058	.058
40	.124	.125	.126	.130	.132	.134
60	.211	.212	.215	.221	.223	.226

SHOT TIME OF FLIGHT #7½ SHOT (IN SECONDS)
Muzzle velocity (ft/s)

Range (yds.)	1,330	1,295	1,240	1,220	1,200	1,145
20	.055	.056	.058	.059	.060	.062
40	.129	.132	.136	.137	.139	.142
60	.223	.227	.233	.235	.238	.245

WATERFOWL SPEED OF FLIGHT (IN FT. PER SEC.)

Species	Speed Range
Canvasback	90–100
Green-wing teal	80–90
Blue-wing teal	80–90
Redhead	75–95
Brant	70–90
Canada goose	70–90
Gadwall	70–80
Widgeon	70–80
Pintail	60–80
Spoonbill	50–90
Black duck	50–90
Mallard	50–90

So what does the shooter do to learn how to lead and by how much? Skeet and trap shooting are the best ways I know for the shooter to learn the fundamentals. After one becomes proficient at these games, leading becomes easier. The use of a swing-through type lead will also make things go smoother. This method is discussed in Chapter 12, Shooting the Shotgun in the Field. But to give you an idea of how little leads change with the loads of varying speeds, the following are examples of leads required for a duck crossing at a right angle at 20, 40 and 60 yards using shells loaded with No. 4 shot at 1,330 feet per second and at 1,240 feet per second.

LEAD REQUIREMENTS
(IN FEET)
(Based on an assumed bird speed of 70 feet per second.)

Range	Muzzle velocity (ft/s)		Difference
	1,330	1,240	
20 yds.	3′8″	3′11″	3″
40 yds.	8′4″	8′9″	5″
60 yds.	13′11″	14′8″	9″

Anyone who believes he can see, hold and maintain a lead difference of 3 inches at 20 yards or 5 inches at 40 yards or even 9 inches at 60 yards is at best an extreme optimist. If you can see, hold and maintain a lead within plus or minus 2 feet at 60 yards, you are a rare and expert shotgunner.

The shotgunner can, for the most part, ignore trajectory. The amount shot drops in travel over its useful range is relatively little compared to the effective pattern diameter. At 60 yards, the effective pattern, even with a full choke, is more than 48 inches high, while shot drop varies from 7 to 12 inches, depending upon the muzzle velocity and size of the shot used. It would be extremely difficult to compensate for this small amount of drop at these extreme ranges. The shooter would be better served in trying to center the game in his pattern. At 40 yards, a more practical range for most shotgunners, pellet drop ranges between 3 and 4 inches for almost any load. This is a relatively minute amount in a pattern that is effective for a diameter of 30 inches or more.

The next three tables graphically list pellet trajectories for velocities from 1,330 feet per second to 1,145 feet per second and for pellet sizes 2, 4, 5, 6 and 7½.

TRAJECTORY # 2 and # 4 SHOT
(DROP TO NEAREST INCH)
Muzzle velocity (ft/s)

Range (yds.)	1330	1315	1295	1240	1220	1200
20	1	1	1	1	1	1
40	3	3	3	3	3	3
60	7*-8°	7*-8°	7*-8°	8	8*-9°	8*-9°

* = #2 shot   ° = #4 shot

TRAJECTORY #5 and #6 SHOT
(DROP TO NEAREST INCH)
Muzzle velocity (ft/s)

Range (yds.)	1330	1315	1295	1240	1220	1200
20	1	1	1	1	1	1
40	3	3	3	3	3	3
60	8	8	8	9	9*-10°	9*-10°

* = #5 shot   ° = #6 shot

TRAJECTORY #7½, #8 & #9 SHOT
(DROP TO NEAREST INCH)
Muzzle velocity (ft/s)

Range (yds.)	1330	1295	1240	1220	1200	1145
20	1	1	1	1	1	1
40	3	3	4	4	4	4
60	10	10	10	11	11	12

The adage "let the buyer beware" is very appropriate when purchasing shotshell ammunition. Therefore, it makes good sense to determine beforehand exactly what size shot and velocity level you need for your purpose. Match these requirements to the listing of factory-loaded ammunition, noting the dram-equivalent rating and shot weight for the load. Then you will be able to sensibly purchase a load that will get the job done without paying for more shell than you need. It is, of course, better to err on the side of too heavy a load rather than too light a load.

SHOOTING THE HANDGUN

PART III

SELECTING A HANDGUN 17

Handguns are selected for a number of purposes including various kinds of target shooting, hunting and personal defense. The intended application will dictate the configuration of the handgun chosen as well as the appropriate caliber. However, before discussing what features are required or desirable for specific applications, let's first try to put some meaning into the long-debated merits of the revolver versus the semiautomatic.

Comparing Revolvers and Semiautomatics

In the U.S., the revolver reigned as the unchallenged preferred handgun for a great many years. But over the past decade, a large number of shooters have been turning to the semiautomatic pistol as their preferred choice. Indeed, great improvements in the reliability of semiautomatics have occurred. Perfect or near-perfect semiauto designs have been combined with near-perfect manufacturing. Revolvers reached a similar development some time ago. From this one might assume that the two types are equal in anticipated performance levels. Nothing could be further from the truth.

Accuracy　The first item considered when reviewing the merits of the semi-automatic-versus-revolver argument is often accuracy. This is so simply because accuracy is easily determined by a skilled shooter. It has been proven many times that poorly designed automatics provide poor accuracy and that well-designed but poorly built automatics provide only fair accuracy. However, a well-designed and well-built automatic has a potential for accuracy actually greater than does a revolver of like quality.

The semiautomatic's barrel and chamber, being one single unit, contribute greatly toward accuracy. On the other hand, the revolver's barrel is separated from its six individual chambers by an air gap. This arrangement causes problems, since each chamber will not align in exactly the same position in even the most carefully built revolver. Nor will the chambers be equal to one another with respect to dimensions. Of course, stiff, heavy barrel on a revolver can go a long way toward providing accuracy. But the lighter barrels used on most semiautos have, as with rifles, been refined to a high level of capability. On the

SOME SUGGESTIONS FOR SELECTING A HANDGUN

Requirement	Handgun make & model	Caliber	Comments
General fun shooting, camp gun, plinking	S & W Kit gun Model 34 S & W Combat Masterpiece Model 18 (revolvers)	22 L.R.	4-inch barrel suggested; kit gun offers very compact size, but the larger K frame will prove easier to shoot well.
Target shooting, including rimfire silhouettes & small game	Ruger Mark II (semiauto)	22 L.R.	5½-inch bull barrel is very accurate and steady to hold; very modest retail price makes this a real bargain.
Target shooting, including rimfire silhouettes & small game	S & W K-22 Masterpiece Model 17 Colt Diamondback (revolvers)	22 L.R.	6- or 8⅜-inch barrels available; suggest red-ramp front and white-outline rear sights as well as target trigger, target hammer and target stocks.
Competitive target shooting	S & W Model 41 (semiauto)	22 L.R.	5½-inch bull barrel provides best accuracy.
Target shooting, small game, plinking	S & W Combat Magnum Model 19 and Model 586, Colt Python (revolvers)	357 Mag.& 38 Spl.	6-inch barrel, red-ramp & white-outline rear sights, target trigger and hammer are all suggested.
Competitive target shooting	S & W 38 Master Model 52 Colt Gold Cup (semiautos)	38 Spl. (mid-range)	These highly accurate target-grade autos function only with flush-seated wadcutter ammo.
Hunting big game	S & W Model 29 & 57 (revolvers)	44 Mag. 41 Mag.	8⅜-inch barrel is suggested.
Silhouette shooting	S & W Model 29 Silhouette	44 Mag.	10⅝-inch barrel plus four-position front sight for silhouette targets.
Home protection	S & W Model 19 & Model 36 Chiefs Special (3" bbl), Colt Detective (3" bbl), Ruger Service Six (2¾" bbl) (revolvers)	357 Mag. 38 Spl.	2½-inch barrel length with red-ramp front and white-outline rear sight suggest for S & W 19 (this has round butt and smooth combat trigger as standard items).
Personal protection (carry)	S & W Lightweight Bodyguard Model 38	38 Spl.	Extremely compact, alloy-frame revolver that can be carried easily.

NOTE: Naturally, there is a large number of other selections possible. Those shown reflect the author's personal tastes and preferences.

whole, the accuracy potential of quality automatics has proven to be better than that of similar revolvers, so that the semiautos have become the preferred choice of extremely serious target shooters.

A semiautomatic is also easier to shoot if the grip angle and size are correct. This is because there is no need to move the gripping hand to cock the hammer. A handgun, be it a semiauto or revolver, responds to even small changes in the grip of the shooter.

Shooters often complain that handguns do not seem to have consistent points of impact from one group to another. More enlightened shooters may realize that the problem does not lie with the handgun but rather with themselves. Some of these shooters mistakenly decide that the problem must be the way they see the sights from group to group, when in reality the problem is that they are not gripping the gun identically for each group. Change the grip, and the point of impact will surely move. Obviously, when you shoot heavy recoiling cartridges in a semiauto, the grip changes during recoil and, hence, the auto can then offer no specific advantage. But with light or moderate loads, the relatively mild recoil will not interfere with a consistent grip. Thus, with all but the heaviest loads, the auto offers an additional advantage.

Recoil   Another point in favor of the automatic is an apparent reduction in recoil. A given load fired in a semiauto will create less apparent recoil than if it were fired from a revolver of identical weight. This is because the semiauto spreads out the recoil over a greater period of time, turning sharp, quick jabs into prolonged pushes.

Firepower   Still another plus for the semiauto is the potential for a rather large magazine capacity. Most autos hold at least seven rounds of ammunition. Magazine capacities of nine, ten, twelve or even fifteen rounds are not uncommon. Police officers must sometimes engage in firefights with criminals. When the opponent has a fifteen- or sixteen-shot 9mm auto, the police officer often feels outgunned with his six-round revolver. Under such circumstances it would be hard to convince the officer that his accuracy capability is far more important than firepower. Indeed, the officer could easily snap back with: "My opponent can simply keep pulling the trigger. With fifteen shots he's bound to get lucky and hit me with one of them." Maybe so. But not if the officer makes his first shots count.

The semiauto will often give the peace officer who is poorly trained in marksmanship a false sense of security based on the amount of firepower he carries. Fifteen rounds in the handgun and two extra clips on his belt put forty-five shots at the policeman's disposal rather than the usual six in a revolver and perhaps twelve rounds carried in his belt loops (which must be inserted one at a time). Even if the officer is equipped with a speed loader, the actual insertion of six rounds simultaneously can still take notably longer than the insertion of a fully charged clip containing perhaps more than twice as many rounds. Speed of loading is certainly an advantage of the autoloader. With a semiauto the police officer can quickly bring his gun up to full capacity at any point simply by

REVOLVERS

Fixed-sight small-frame revolvers, such as this S & W Model 650 chambered for the 22 rimfire magnum, are ideally suited for heavy duty.

Target style, fully adjustable sights plus a target hammer, target trigger and target stocks, are standard equipment on the Colt Python 357 Magnum revolver.

Short-barrelled, fixed-sight revolvers in 38 Special caliber are ideal for personal defense by occasional shooters as they are easily mastered without excessive practice.

The versatility of this frontier-style single-action revolver is greatly enhanced by its adjustable rear sight.

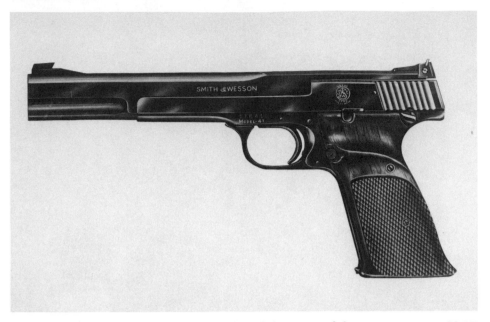

This S & W Model 41 is, in the author's opinion, one of the most accurate 22 LR pistols available.

The S & W Model 52 is the ultimate target pistol in 38 Special.

The 9mm S & W Model 46 is the ideal choice for those who want a semiautomatic for personal protection.

The S & W Model 639 is a fine 9mm auto in a full-size pistol and incorporates a fully adjustable and well-shrouded rear sight.

The S & W Model 459, because of its fixed sights, is well suited for heavy duty and is chambered for the potent 8mm Luger cartridge.

The ever popular Colt 1911 semiautomatic in 45 ACP is shown in a superb target version—the Colt Gold.

dropping the partially used magazine and replacing it with a fully charged one.

Certainly a good semiauto offers some very positive advantages. Intelligent people have put forward convincing arguments about why semiautos are preferred—convincing enough that quite a few local, county and even state police forces have switched to semiautomatics of some kind. The Smith & Wesson 9mm double-action autos have been quite popular with many police departments. And indeed, the S & W is perhaps the best semiautomatic selection possible for a wide number of reasons. More recently, at least one state police department has adapted a foreign-built semiauto 9mm.

Reliability   But despite the semiauto's virtues, it does have several serious drawbacks. The first of these is that, by design, parts in a semiauto are more subject to failure. And a broken part often means that the weapon is put out of service. Picture, if you will, a firefight in which one of the semiauto combatants has an extractor break or an ejector fail. The round fired prior to the breakage would perhaps be the last round the combatant would ever fire again.

If one doubts the higher frequency of broken parts in semiautos, he need only talk to a busy gunsmith or ask someone who has industry knowledge. In fact, significantly fewer revolver parts are replaced compared to semiauto parts. Combine this finding with the obvious fact that there are a great many more revolvers in use than semiauto handguns, and a point in favor of revolvers becomes quite evident.

The pistol folks will argue that even though semiautos do break down more frequently, the rate of incidence is so low as to be inconsequential. Again, that may be so. I even heard one fellow argue that if one peace officer's life were lost every ten years because of a broken-down auto, it would be a small price to pay for all the auto's features that could save other officers' lives. I wonder if his argument would hold water if that one police officer who dies was a member of his family.

Training and Experience   The auto pistol's second disadvantage is that it takes far more training to produce a fast and accurate shooter than it does with a revolver. First, the semiauto user must be taught how to disassemble and reassemble the auto to keep it clean enough to guarantee that it will function when required. The amount of skill needed far exceeds that which is required of a revolver owner. Second, the auto pistol user needs to learn and to commit to memory the removing of the gun's safety when putting it into action. Revolver users need not be concerned with this since there are usually no manual safeties employed on their handguns.

Regardless of the skill of the shooter, it will always take a split second longer to unholster a semiauto pistol and fire the first shot as compared to a revolver, simply because the safety must be removed. Yes, it can be pushed off as the gun is being brought into position for the shot. But the mental and physical action required will result in some delay. Regardless of how small that delay may be, it could mean the difference between life and death.

Ponder whether or not the semiauto user who, when placed under the great stress of having to defend his life or the life of another, grabs his handgun and tries to start shooting. Will he always remember to remove the safety?

Removing the Safety
I have talked to far too many shooters who forgot to remove their safeties prior to taking a hunting shot, a target shot or even a shot at a tin can. Certainly, no undue stress was present and no fear was involved as they tried and failed to get off a shot. I have literally shot many thousands of game birds and invariably, about once a year, I still mount, swing and pull my trigger only to find a bird escape my skill simply because I forgot the safety. Revolver shooters never forget safeties! And therein lies the first major advantage of the revolver.

Magazines
Revolver shooters never lose their magazines. Many semiauto pistol users have found that a pistol can be separated from its magazine unknowingly. The same button that allows the shooter to release the magazine can be inadvertently pushed. The owner may lean or bump into something that will cause the magazine to release, or perhaps it may be released in a scuffle. To make matters worse, many auto pistols incorporate a magazine safety. When the magazine is out of the gun, the pistol will not fire the round in the chamber. Thus a fifteen-shot capacity handgun can be reduced to a single shot that cannot be fired.

Consider a firefight. The first magazine having been emptied is dropped to the floor and a fresh one is being inserted. In the excitement it is dropped. What then? Additionally, a magazine, if not fully inserted, will cause the same problems as a missing magazine, or it may fall to the ground with the first shot.

Revolver users never contend with lost magazines or partially inserted ones. Again, another real advantage of the revolver is its lack of the semiauto's disadvantages. The revolver cannot be put out of action through a loss of its ability to hold cartridges.

Variations in Ammunition
Another advantage of the revolver is associated with the ammunition used. There is no such thing as perfect ammo. Having spent a great number of years in the firearms and ammunition industry, I suspect I have seen everything possible that can go wrong with ammo. Even if the shooter of a semiauto carefully inspects each round as it is loaded into a magazine, he has no way of knowing if it will perform as intended. A ruptured or split case could occur upon firing. This may well cause the auto pistol to jam. Or the cartridge could be without a powder charge or have been loaded with only a partial powder charge. Again, a jammed or out-of-action auto! Or perhaps the primer is missing the anvil or priming pellet. Such a condition means the auto won't fire and that the faulty cartridge must be cleared by working the slide and feeding a new round into the chamber. And what would the assailant be doing while time was being taken to clear a jam or eject a faulty cartridge? Modern automatic pistol cartridges are very well made. Indeed, they represent a level of reliability far greater than the ammo of years ago. But cartridges cannot be mass-produced or even handloaded that can be guaranteed to work every

time. A certain percentage, small though it may be, will fail. Additionally, a cartridge may be rendered inoperative simply because it has been contaminated by oil applied by a well-meaning but overzealous firearm owner.

All of these ammunition problems are little consequence to the revolver shooter. When a cartridge case splits, or even if it fails to fire, the revolver owner simply needs to pull the trigger again. This will rotate a new chamber into place with a fresh cartridge being acted upon by the firing pin. The only ammunition malfunctions that can stop the revolver are a blown gun or a bullet lodged between the barrel and cylinder, preventing the cylinder's rotation. But the occurrence that caused such a problem would equally stop a semiauto pistol.

A bullet that stops partway down the barrel of an automatic means that insufficient power was developed to fire the auto. If a fresh round is fed into the chamber and fired, almost invariably the light barrel of an auto will rupture, rendering the gun useless.

However, as many revolver owners have found, bullets that are stuck in the barrel have often been driven from the barrel by the next shot. Heavy revolver barrels, while dangerously bulged from such an occurrence, often have been inadvertently fired extensively after such a happening.

Summary   In conclusion, revolvers are quicker to press into service, are less prone to mechanical problems and are impervious to most stoppages caused by faulty ammunition. Thus, for *defensive* purposes, be it personal or the defense of another, the revolver is and will remain the best possible choice in a sidearm. For military *offensive* purposes, where firepower remains supreme, the semiauto pistol is the most logical selection.

But, among nonmilitary shooters, few if any applications of handguns are related to military offensive type usage. Defensive application, however, is often the legitimate intended purpose of a civilian handgun.

For a handgun to be used solely for target shooting, either type will serve the purpose efficiently. And if the handgun is to be used for hunting, again, either can be selected wtihout hesitation. But if there is even a remote chance that the handgun may someday be used for self-defense, a good revolver is without question the logical choice.

Caliber

The selection of caliber is very broad for handguns. There are sufficient cartridges to fit any real or imagined application. The target shooter, interested in paper targets only, could well decide that a 22 rimfire handgun is his best choice. Ammunition is inexpensive, and the 22 produces little noise and almost no recoil. All this adds up to a cartridge that makes plenty of practice feasible.

For a gun to be used for target shooting, plinking and perhaps self-defense in the home, a 38 Special might be ideal. With light, mid-range wadcutter loads, the 38 Special makes an excellent and accurate target gun. With high-speed hollow points, it will do an admirable job if needed for personal protection. And there is a wide selection of in-between loads that allow the 38 to be used for a great many purposes.

Anyone interested in the 38 Special cartridge would do well to purchase a 357 Magnum, as any revolver chambered for the 357 Magnum may be used with all 38 Special loads. Thus, one has the option of light 38 target loads, heavy 357 Magnum loads for defense or short-range deer hunting and plenty of in-between loads.

For serious big-game hunters who use handguns, the 44 Magnum is the most powerful selection that can be made. This cartridge is also a perennial favorite among silhouette shooters. However, the 44 Magnum is more than can be mastered by a good number of shooters. Its noise and recoil are nothing short of horrendous, compared with almost all other handgun cartridges.

Obviously, with cartridge selections running from the diminutive 22 to the giant 44 Magnum, care must be taken when analyzing the requirements for a handgun. The profusion of cartridges does complicate selection. But the process can be made easier by elimination of the many handgun rounds that have little practical value.

Between 22 and 38

The 22 rimfire cartridge is, of course, a great selection for targets, plinking and even short-range small-game hunting. However, between the 22 and the various 38 calibers is a host of 25, 30 and 32 caliber cartridges that have no legitimate application. They are all inadequate for either target shooting (poor accuracy), self-protection (too little power) or hunting (inaccurate and too little power). The sole exception is the 32 S & W long cartridge. Recent interest by international target shooters has shown that this cartridge is quite accurate and ideal for paper target shooting, especially when minimum recoil is important.

The next caliber of practical consideration is the 9mm Luger, which is a fine cartridge having excellent power and accuracy. It is ideally suitable for personal defense and does very well for target shooting and hunting.

The diminutive 380 auto cartridge has perhaps some usefulness for those who insist on a small pocket-size automatic for personal defense. It is, however, borderline in both power and accuracy.

The 38 Special

A cartridge that has proven its worth for target and small-game hunting is the 38 Special. And the newer hollow points and higher-velocity ammo make it a very respectable cartridge for personal defense. Many shooters find that the 38 Special combines a tolerable level of recoil and noise with adequate power for most applications. The new, higher-velocity Plus-P 38 Special ammunition has added a good deal of performance to this old cartridge.

Heavier Rounds

After the 38 Special cartridge come a number of calibers that have considerably more recoil and noise accompanying their increase in power. For some shooters, these cartridges will prove impossible to master with respect to shooting skills. But with sufficient practice, the 357 Magnum, 44 Special, 45 auto and 45 Colt cartridges can prove to be very wise choices for those who take handgun hunting seriously. Of course, each of these cartridges makes a fine personal-defense round.

Still heavier rounds, such as the 357 Maximum or the 41 and 44 Remington Magnums, are available. These rounds are ideally suited to the sport of handgun silhouettes and to short-range big-game hunting. However, few shooters can master these noisy and heavy-recoiling cartridges.

A Dozen Potentials   By eliminating all other handgun rounds and making your selection from among the 22 long rifle, 32 S & W Long, 380 Auto, 38 Special, 9mm Luger, 357 Magnum, 357 Maximum, 41 Remington Magnum, 44 Special, 44 Remington Magnum, 45 Colt and 45 Auto, you can reduce the confusion to a dozen potentials. And if you are not interested in centerfire handgun silhouette

The selection of the proper handgun can lead to a great deal of shooting enjoyment.
Here the author and his family are divided in their choice of semiauto or revolver.

shooting or big-game hunting, the 357 Maximum, 41 Remington Magnum and 44 Remington Magnum can be eliminated, thus leaving but nine cartridges from which to choose. The marginal 380 Auto is best forgotten, and the 44 Special and 45 Colt cartridges are somewhat obsolete. Despite their merits, few guns are chambered for these rounds. Also, few good guns are found for the 32 S & W Long, except for some very high-priced international-match-grade guns. This brings the average handgunner to a choice between a 22 long, 9mm Luger, 38 Special, 357 Magnum or a 45 Auto. Those who prefer a semiauto may wisely choose the 22 and the 9mm Luger. The 9mm, with today's rapidly expanding bullets, has justifiably replaced the older and heavier-recoiling 45 Auto cartridge.

When approached from the hard light of logic, handgun cartridge selection becomes a relatively simple matter. It can boil down, as shown, to the selection of 22 rimfire and either a 357 Magnum or 9mm Luger, depending upon your personal preferences. There's not much magic or romance in such a simple selection. But few will regret such a choice, and most will enjoy a great many years of a wide variety of shooting with such selections. The silhouette shooter or big-game hunter will, of course, need to add a 44 Magnum to his selections.

Brand Names

When you have made your decision on whether you want a revolver or automatic and which cartridge or cartridges you desire, then comes the selection of the specific gun or guns. I may be somewhat old-fashioned, but I still like my handguns to say S & W, Ruger or Colt. All of the handguns made by these manufacturers are normally quite well made. I have particular fondness for 22s in the following configurations: S & W Model 41 (semiauto), S & W K-frame revolvers with 6- and 8⅜-inch barrels and the Ruger Mark I and Mark II semiautomatics. In the 357 Magnum, I prefer the S & W Models 19 and 27 with barrel lengths from 2½ to 8⅜ inches. For a pocket gun, the S & W lightweight Bodyguard in 38 Special is my favorite. The S & W 9mm autos and the Colt autos in the same caliber are highly proven designs. Also for target shooting, the S & W and Colt match-grade semiautomatics in 38 Special are hard to beat for accuracy and reliability.

Whatever model you choose, do purchase the best quality you can possibly afford. A good handgun can be a lifetime investment. A poor one will soon prove ineffective for anything more than tin-can shooting.

HANDGUN SIGHTS | 18

Handgun sights are critical to the shooter's performance. Some handguns come equipped only with fixed sights. These sights cannot be adjusted to compensate for differences in the shooter's eyesight, in his manner of gripping or in the ammunition used. Yet such sights can and do serve a positive need.

Fixed Sights

For personal-defense situations, a handgun is seldom pressed into service at ranges longer than the distance across a large room. About 7 yards would cover more than 90 percent of all self-defense encounters with the actual range often being considerably less. For such application, fixed sights will prove more than adequate for effective placement of shots to be accomplished. Fixed sights offer the advantage of noticeably reducing the cost of a revolver. Thus, for home protection or short-range personal defense in the street, a fixed-sight revolver will get the job done while being somewhat less costly than a similar revolver with an adjustable sight. Trappers who use a 22 will also find that fixed sights are all they need for their short-range purposes.

Fixed sights are also ideal for applications where the handgun will see a good deal of hard use or perhaps even abuse. A dropped handgun can often result in adjustable sights being damaged beyond use, while a fixed-sight gun subjected to the same treatment may sustain no more damage than the finish being marred.

When fixed sights are selected for heavy-duty use or abuse, it is extremely important that the shooter take the time to find a load that, combined with his eyesight and grip, will strike within 2 inches of his aiming point at 25 yards. This degree of accuracy cannot always be obtained without returning the fixed-sight handgun to the manufacturer. I have shot a few such handguns that, regardless of ammunition used, would not hit closer than 6 inches to my point of aim at 25 yards. Yet, I own a Smith & Wesson 38 Bodyguard lightweight that will print certain 125-grain hollow points, 148-grain wadcutters and most 158-grain lead bullets all within 1 inch of my point of aim at this range. Such handgun capabilities are not common because of the variations in shooters' eyes, gripping methods and ammo. But accurate handguns can be found if the shooter is willing to try three, four or maybe more guns until he finds one that is right for him.

219

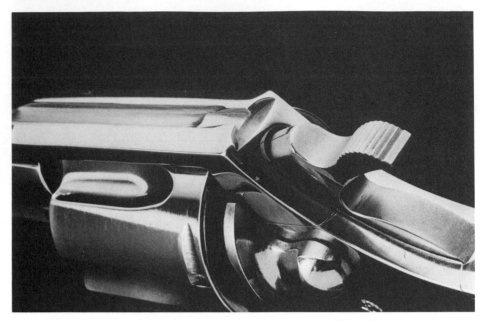

On weapons to be used for self-protection at close range, fixed sights are adequate. This is the Colt Detective Special.

Two white dots on this rear sight help the shooter's eye to align the front sight (which also contains a white dot) between the blades.

Left or right point-of-impact variations can sometimes be corrected by a gunsmith or the factory by turning the barrel on its threads a slight amount. A gun that shoots low can also be corrected by reducing the height of the front sight. For the most part, however, fixed sights are intended only for very short-range use in which the ultimate in precision is not required. For ranges up to 7 or 8 yards, a fixed-sight gun will often prove entirely adequate.

Adjustable Sights

For target shooting of any type or for hunting, adjustable sights are not only desirable but usually essential. If you plan to use a variety of different loads—say, 110-grain bullets for varmint, 125-grain bullets for personal protection and perhaps 158-grain bullets for deer hunting (actual weight would vary with caliber)—then adjustable sights are mandatory. For any application where precise bullet placement is important, you must have a handgun equipped with sights that are adjustable for both windage and elevation.

The use of "Kentucky windage," wherein the shooter simply holds left, right, high or low to compensate for the bullet's point of impact, will result in, at best, ho-hum accuracy. It is simply impossible consistently to hold a specific number of inches to one side or the other when there is no specific aiming point for reference.

Adjustable sights come in a wide range of types and styles. Most frequently, both elevation and windage adjustments are accomplished in the rear sight. Some handguns separate these adjustments. The 22 rimfire H & R 999 revolver, for example, has the windage adjustment located in the rear sight and the elevation adjustment in the front sight.

Some so-called adjustable sights are rather crude. Windage may be adjusted, for instance, by driving the rear sight to one side or the other in a dovetail slot using a hammer and punch, or by loosening a screw on one side and then tightening one on the other side. Crude adjustments, while better than none, are useful primarily to the handgunner who uses only one specific load. Frequent adjusting of such sights could be a costly proposition in ammunition used if one often varied the load used. Adjusting crude sights often becomes a matter of trial and error, and errors frequently dominate the sighting-in session.

The best adjustable sights have click-type adjustments, which allow an exact amount of movement of the point of impact for each click. Regrettably, even on some of the finest guns, the hoped-for clicks are not present because of poor workmanship. However, even when the normally audible click is not present, these sights usually offer a precise visual reference. The careful shooter, who keeps record of such things, can often go from a zero setting for one weight and speed of bullet to another zero setting for different ammo, then back to the original zero, simply by counting clicks of elevation and, if required, windage. However, even the best record keeper should verify such adjustments with an actual firing test.

The adjustable rear sights on this Llama big-bore pistol are rounded off. This is an asset when drawing the gun from a holster.

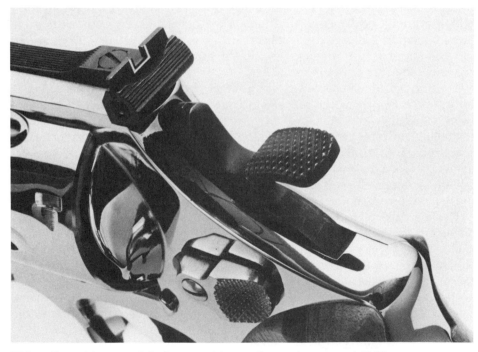

This adjustable rear sight has a white outline to improve visibility.

Rear Sights   Large, flat-faced rear-sight blades, such as are used on the 5½-inch heavy barrel Smith & Wesson Model 41, are to be preferred over small-faced rear sights, such as are used on Smith & Wesson revolvers. The large, flat-faced rear sight prevents distraction and annoying glare from marring a multilevel sight picture. One needs to use such a sight for only a short time to appreciate its virtues. Unfortunately, the shooter seldom has a choice in rear-sight styles, since usually only one style is available on a given model with a specific barrel length.

Black sights have always been favored by target shooters, and when the light conditions are right, such sights do give a clear, sharp silhouette. But when the light conditions vary greatly, such as when hunting or even silhouette shooting, a flat, black sight may well be a poor choice. Sights that incorporate colors to make them more visible under varying conditions can then become the ideal selection.

Front Sights   Ramp front sights with rectangular red inserts are available on a number of revolvers. Some manufacturers also offer gold bead sights of varying styles. Replacement front blades of yellow, orange, red, green or blue are available for specific revolvers from such firms as Magnum Sales Limited. All these allow for easy pick-up of the front sight against a wide range of varying

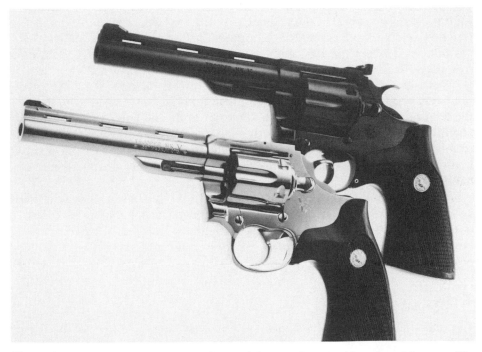

These Colt Mark V revolvers have front sights equipped with colored inserts. The inserts enable the shooter's eye to pick up the front sight in poor light.

backgrounds and light conditions. The best color is, of course, determined by the shooter's ability to see color and the type of background and light conditions that will be encountered when shooting. Red or yellow are perhaps the best selections for most shooter's eyes. Colors don't always appear the same from shooter to shooter, so there is a need actually to look at the various sights under differing light conditions.

When a colored front sight is enhanced by a white line around the rear-sight notch, the shooter then has a set of sights that will provide the highest possible visibility for a very wide range of conditions. Smith & Wesson, for one, offers such sights (red ramp/white outline rear) on many models. I prefer this type of sight over all others for hunting and silhouette target shooting. But for indoor use or shooting paper bull's-eyes, I still do best with a plain square post and rear sight. The differences are small, however, and if I were to select sights for a handgun to be used for varying purposes, a red-ramp or gold-bead front sight combined with a white-outline rear sight would be chosen without hesitation. Such sights are well suited to shooting in poor light and in personal-defense situations because they are quickly seen and offer very rapid alignment.

Some handguns offer only windage adjustments. To my way of thinking, this is somewhat akin to offering half a crutch to a man with a broken leg.

Telescopic Sights

Telescopic sights are becoming more and more commonplace on handguns. Hunters learn quickly that the alignment of iron sights at any but the shortest range is seldom very exact. The scope offers the handgun shooter all of the advantages it offers the rifle shooter, except one. The optical sight can offer magnification, a clear, sharp picture of both sight and target and very precise adjustments for centering the sights on the target. However, because of the relatively great distance at which a handgun telescope is located from the eye, the field of view is rather small. A by-product of this situation is a slowness in aligning the sight and target until the shooter has had sufficient practice to enable him to get the task done as quickly as possible. Because the serious hunter is often very deliberate, this bit of slowdown does not present a real handicap.

For target shooting, the use of an optical sight is a big plus, and a great many serious shooters today use some sort of handgun scope. For most types of hunting or target shooting, the scope is a definite advantage. For moving targets, however, the pistol scope is a poor choice because of its very restricted field of view.

Alignment

The alignment of nonoptical sights is a relatively simple matter for those with 20/20 or better vision. But for others with less perfect vision, pistol sights can be a nightmare, appearing as hard-to-see, indistinct blurs. Yet, even when sights are difficult or nearly impossible to see, a shooter can do amazingly well if he understands what is required.

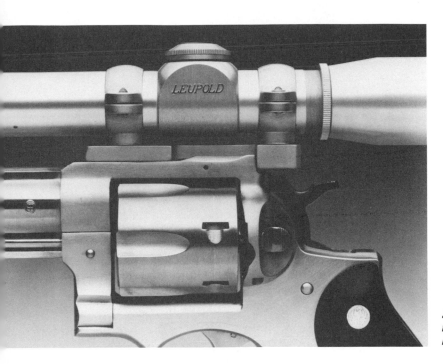

Sturdy mounts are essential for mounting a scope on a centerfire handgun.

This scope-equipped Stalker is an ideal hunting handgun.

Problems   Even with the best eyesight, when one attempts to look at three widely separated objects (rear sight, front sight and target), one or more will be blurred, while only one of them can be sharp and distinct. Knowing this, some shooters, mostly those with better eyesight, will attempt to achieve a compromise that allows them to see the front sight clearly located in a slightly fuzzy rear sight, both sights aligned on a slightly fuzzy target. Others opt for a fuzzier target and sharper sights. This latter method works well for target shooting.

Solutions   Some (like me) are unable to see the sights in any but an extremely blurred picture when they can see the target. Yet, they are able to shoot quite well. Regardless of your own level of visual acuity, if you use the sights properly, good accuracy is possible at ranges up to 35 yards or more. The secret to success is to align the front sight as precisely as possible in the rear sight notch without visual reference or concentration on the target. Get the front sight spaced properly in the rear notch, with an equal amount of light on both sides. Get the top edge of the front sight exactly level with the top edge of the rear sight. Even if you have poor eyesight, you can accomplish this if your eyes are focused on the sights alone and you forget the target. When the sights have been brought into proper alignment, they should be kept so aligned as the gun, hand, wrist and forearm, as a unit, are brought to bear on the target.

While the handgun is thus being brought into alignment with the target, shift your eye focus to the target. The sights will then blur. Depending upon your visual acuity, the amount of blur may range from slight to great, but your eye will retain a memory of the correct sight alignment even in the most blurred sight picture.

This method works and works well. I can assure you that it is impossible for me to see more than a badly blurred outline of a rear sight and an almost equally fuzzy front sight when I can see my target. But by first focusing on the sights as best I can, I can bring them into alignment. Then, moving gun, hand, wrist and forearm as a unit, I bring the sights into alignment on the target while shifting my eye focus to the target. I have no undue difficulty in hitting 2-inch bull's-eyes at 50 yards. In fact, putting aside false modesty, I do quite well at rimfire silhouette-target shooting, a most difficult test of marksmanship. Poor eyesight does not have to mean poor marksmanship with a handgun.

Practice   Of course, this method of shooting, like any other, requires a fair amount of practice to master. But for any shooter who wishes to gain a high level of proficiency, it is one of the easiest methods to learn. Once you have selected a good set of sights, it makes little sense not to learn how best to use them.

Keep in mind that colored front sights with white-outline rear notches tend to be more visible in a blurred sight picture. The less able you are to see the rear and front sights, the greater the advantage to having red and white handgun sights.

Using Scopes   Of course, scopes eliminate all visual problems, since both reticule and target are placed on the same sight plane. The magnification of a scope, however, exaggerates the normal amount of wobble and tremble present. Thus, scopes are best suited to use from very steady positions or by skilled handgunners who have trained enough to be able to hold a handgun at arm's length without a great deal of movement. Pistol scopes are best selected in low powers, from 1½ to a maximum of 4. More magnification would create too much enhancement of the ever-present wobble and would, therefore, usually be self-defeating.

No attempt should be made to use a scope until all the fundamentals of pistol shooting have been mastered. The shooter using a scope must be careful not to begin yanking the trigger when target and reticule are in alignment. This is a tendency common to shooters who have not committed grip, breathing and trigger squeeze to rote.

Keep in mind that any easily adjusted handgun sight is a lot more prone to damage than a fixed sight. It is necessary to prevent accidental knocks from damaging or misaligning such sights. A good holster that offers positive protection of the sights affords the best insurance that your handgun sights will be pointing where you want when you next use them.

Selection   There are a great many adjustable sights sold separately for installation on fixed-sight guns. Such sights require varying degrees of gunsmithing to install. A few are rather simple to put into place, while some require a great deal of skill. Such sight conversions can turn a favored handgun into an accurate revolver or automatic. However, not infrequently, the cost of such sights exceeds the cost involved in trading in the old fixed-sight handgun for a newer one with adjustable sights.

As with all sighting systems, there is little point in having more than you need. For a home-defense handgun, fixed sights are all that is required for what will probably be a point-and-shoot application. In this case, adjustable sights add nothing but cost to the firearm. Nor does it make sense to install a scope on a handgun that will be used for informal target shooting, plinking or short-range small-game shooting. Under such conditions, most shooters will find that the extra weight of the scope and mount, along with its slowness in alignment, actually detracts from the enjoyment of shooting. For most serious target shooters and dedicated big-game-with-a-handgun shooters, a scope sight will often add a great deal of pleasure and accuracy. However, a handgun equipped with a scope does become bulky and generally unsuitable to any application other than targets, big-game and varmint hunting.

In summary, the selection of handgun sights must be closely related to the intended application of the handgun. For all-around use, nothing will beat adjustable open sights, especially if they incorporate a colored front post or blade with a white-outline rear notch. For defense or any short-range (maximum 8 yards) purpose, fixed sights will do just fine. The scope is best suited to paper targets and long-range hunting.

19 TUNING THE HANDGUN FOR ACCURACY

Handguns, by their nature, do not allow for a great many improvements to be made using the equipment in the average home workshop. However, by keeping after the essentials, the shooter can maintain his handgun in the best possible condition to allow for maximum accuracy.

Fit of the Grips   Perhaps the most important and probably the most often overlooked aspect of keeping a handgun in tune is the fit of the grips. As mentioned in Chapter 18, any change in a shooter's grip on the handgun can create a change in the point of impact, even if such a change goes unnoticed. (If the shots are dispersed randomly over a 12-inch bull's-eye, it's hard to determine the center of any single such group, let alone establish a point-of-impact change.) Equally, the point of impact can shift from group to group or even from shot to shot if the handgun grips move about on the frame. Obviously, then, one should keep all grip screws securely tightened.

But tight is not always enough. Some grip screws, especially those on many revolvers, tighten one grip panel against the other. Often the grip screw can be snug, yet the grips will not bear securely against the frame. To test for such a condition, hold the grips in one hand and grasp the barrel with the other. Then, by twisting the barrel in various directions, see if you can feel any motion of the handgun within the grips. Such a problem will prevail only on grips that totally encompass the grip frames, such as large, target-style grips. To correct this problem you may have to shim the grips or use a longer locating pin.

Short or undersized locating pins can cause problems in almost any handgun with almost any style of grip. Locating pins should snugly fit into the corresponding hole on the inside surface of the grip. If there is excess play, it often can be cured by filling in the holes with a suitable material. In extreme cases, either the grips and/or the locating pin may need to be replaced.

Tightness of Screws   On handguns with adjustable sights, frequent use may cause retaining screws to back out. Heavy recoiling cartridges may cause screws to work loose in as few as fifty shots, while light-caliber guns are often fired thousands of times before a screw will begin to loosen. If a sight-retaining screw loosens up a bit, the shooter may well find it impossible to hit the same

Check for grip looseness by twisting the gun while holding the grips tightly.

A loose grip often can be corrected by the use of carefully placed shims.

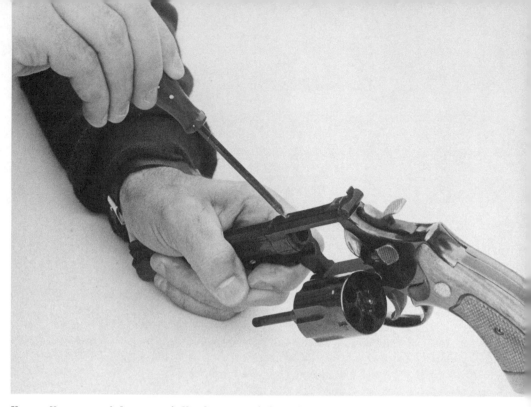

Keep all screws tight, especially those retaining sights.

spot twice in a row. The cure is obvious. However, prevention works better, and it pays to check all handgun screws for tightness after each shooting session.

Proper-fitting screwdrivers are necessary to avoid damaging the often delicate heads of handgun screws. Too, one must learn that it's not necessary to twist off the screwhead in order to ensure that it is properly tightened. On handgun screws, finger-tight is usually sufficient.

Cylinder Alignment

Revolver cylinders should lock up tight with little movement. And positive alignment is required for peak accuracy. While there is little the average owner can do to correct a loose cylinder or misalignment, he can check to see that everything is functioning as intended, seeking the aid of a gunsmith when changes are necessary.

It makes little sense to check a cylinder for tight locking when the gun is at a "rest" position. Nor should you check for tightness with the hammer at full cock. Check for cylinder play only when the trigger has been pulled and is held in its rearmost position. The hammer should be down in the fired position with the cylinder hand-tight against the back of the cylinder. Pulling the trigger in the double-action mode (empty cylinder, of course) will bring all the parts into the proper positioning—if you make certain that the trigger is held in the rear-most position. Then, with your free hand, attempt to move the cylinder by trying to rotate it and also trying to move it left and right. Any excessive play should be removed by a gunsmith.

Cylinder misalignment will make itself known if lead bullets are used frequently. Excessive lead buildup on the inside surface of the frame is a sure indicator of misalignment. However, the key word is *excessive*. All revolvers will have a small amount of lead buildup on inside surfaces of the frame and front end of the cylinder. This is a result of the inevitable vaporization of small amounts of lead from the bullet base, caused by the heat and pressure of the burning powder. If this lead buildup is not cleaned away after each use, eventually it might appear excessive. If you clean your revolver after each use and are able to remove the leading with modest application of a bronze brush, then the chances are that the leading is not excessive. On the other hand, if the firing of fifty rounds of lead-bullet ammo leaves you with a deposit that must be removed with a sharp instrument, chances are the buildup is excessive.

If you use only jacketed bullets, there will be no lead buildup. Users of jacketed bullets who suspect misalignment should engage the services of a very competent gunsmith who has all the necessary gauges. Some shooters make their own alignment gauge. All you need is a highly polished steel rod that just fits into the barrel of your revolver. The rod is pushed gently down the barrel and into the cylinder. If the rod's sharp shoulder contacts the cylinder face before

Check for excess cylinder play by attempting to rotate the cylinder and to move it left and right. The trigger should be at its rearward-most position, the hammer fully forward.

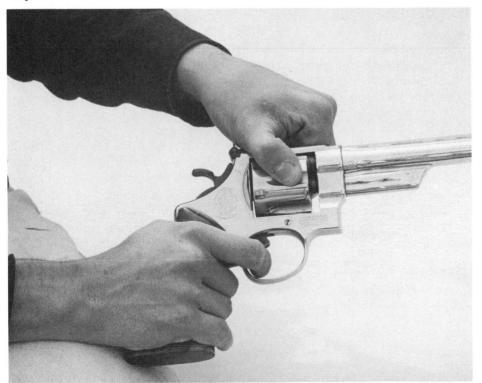

entering the cylinder, your gun is suffering from serious misalignment.

Because of the funnel-like throat at the breech of the barrel, minor misalignment will cause no serious problem. However, when accuracy is less than desired and no other cause can be found, sometimes the removing of any misalignment will effect a noticeable improvement.

Semiautomatic pistols of a type similar to the Colt 1911 model can have accuracy notably increased with the relatively simple installation of a new "accuracy" barrel bushing. These bushings help eliminate any space between barrel and bushing, thus more positively aligning the barrel within the bushing from shot to shot. A longer link installed on the barrel will also help improve accuracy by forcing the barrel to rise to its uppermost position as the gun goes into battery.

Trigger Pulls   Handgun trigger pulls that are crisp, clean and reasonably light (about 3–3½ pounds) can help your shooting. However, handgun trigger pulls should not be altered by just anyone—only qualified gunsmiths should do the job. The lightening of mainsprings or trigger-return springs is not an acceptable approach to obtaining a lighter trigger pull. When mainsprings are altered, the inevitable result will be at least an occasional misfire caused by too light a hammer fall. Anyone who suggests that mainspring tension should be reduced either by alteration or the backing off of a strain screw is not well qualified as a gunsmith.

Customizing   Of course, extensive work on the accuracy of handguns is possible for specialized gunsmiths. However, such customizing, while appropriate for highly skilled shooters who use their handguns only for target shooting, is often less than practical for the casual shooter, informal or infrequent shooting participant or hunter.

One bit of factory customizing that can pay big dividends is the installation of the special sights often offered by the factories. These sights were discussed in the previous chapter. Of course, the best time to get such sights is when the handgun is purchased. It's cheaper to do it this way, since you are not paying for two sets of sights and an extra installation charge.

Cleaning and Tuning   Commonplace as it may seem, one step that all handgunners can take to increase accuracy is to keep their pistol or revolver clean. Fouled or leaded barrels adversely affect handgun accuracy. A good bore cleaner is a necessity, especially when jacketed bullets are used.

No firearm is forever. Parts do wear, and worn parts result in a decrease in handgun accuracy. A revolver that has been fired 10,000 times or more may well need a new cylinder bolt or locking rod to restore its original accuracy. Likewise, a semiautomatic that has fired a similar number of rounds may require a new barrel, barrel bushing and barrel link (if so equipped). If your favorite handgun's accuracy begins to fall off, and if a thorough cleaning doesn't restore it, it's probably time for a first-class tune-up by the factory or a top-quality gunsmith.

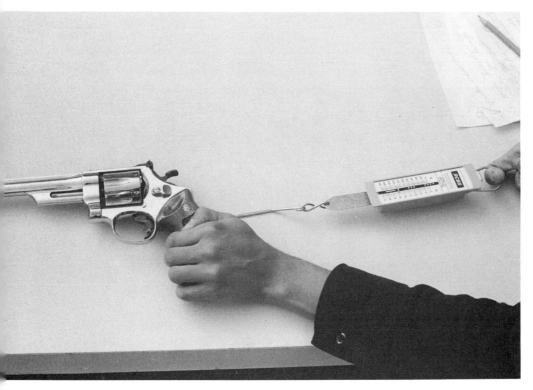

A crisp action trigger pull of 3 to 3¹/₂ pounds will help accuracy.

20 BASIC BALLISTICS FOR HANDGUNNERS

Handgun cartridges are used for many purposes, and each one requires a different level of ballistics. For target shooting, little value is placed on energy levels. Rather, the shooter is justifiably concerned with light recoil and moderate noise levels combined with a high degree of accuracy. The shooter interested in personal defense of home, property and loved ones, on the other hand, is concerned with a good level of energy combined with a properly expanding bullet to transmit energy effectively. And a hunter requires not only sufficient energy to reduce his quarry to possession, but also a sufficiently flat trajectory to enable him to score hits at all practical ranges. Obviously, the hunter, like the target shooter, has a keen interest in accuracy.

Achieving Accuracy

Accuracy is not something one can look up in a ballistics table. Assuming the shooter has the necessary skill, handgun accuracy is a function of the firearm chosen and the cartridge for which it is chambered. The use of a quality handgun being assumed, accuracy potential varies according to the worth of the cartridge and ammunition used.

Performance Standards   The ammunition industry has long applied a certain level of performance to handgun cartridge accuracy. This is the minimum level at which ammunition is expected to perform. More accuracy is nice but frequently impractical, especially in the light of production costs. Less accuracy is not acceptable but, alas, does on occasion occur for whatever reason. The following table outlines the expected accuracy level of various handgun cartridges. This table can be an aid in selecting a cartridge or load, or it may be used to determine if your gun and ammunition are performing at least at a minimum level of accuracy.

Variations in Guns   Keep in mind that when lead bullets are being used, the condition of the bore plays a large part in accuracy. Some ammunition leaves large deposits of lead in the bore. Such "leading" can quickly build up and destroy any hope for accuracy. A 25-yard group from a clean gun with such ammo may show five or six shots in a 2-inch circle. Twenty-five rounds later, bullets may be actually hitting the target sideways, if at all, owing to accumulated lead deposits. While such conditions are to be avoided, only experience will enable you to know which brands and loads will produce excessive leading in your gun. Once heavily leaded, a gun will require a fair amount of scrubbing with solvent and a bronze brush before the barrel can be restored to its original condition and accuracy.

Cartridge	Bullet wt. and style	Range (in yards)	Expected accuracy (in inches)
22 Short	29 grs.-lead	25	3
22 Long	29 grs.-lead	25	3
22 Long Rifle	40 grs.-lead	50	2
22 Remington Jet	40 grs.-jacketed	50	3
221 Remington Fireball	50 grs.-jacketed	50	2
256 Winchester	60 grs.-jacketed	50	3
30 Luger	93 grs.-FMC	25	3½
32 ACP	all	25	3
9mm Luger	all	25	3
380 Auto	all	25	4½
38 ACP	all	25	3
38 Super Auto	all	25	3
38 Special	all service loads	50	4½
38 Special	148 and 158 grs.-target loads	50	2½
357 Magnum	all	50	4
41 Remington Mag.	all	50	6
44 Remington Mag.	all	50	6
45 ACP	all	50	3

Variations in Ammunition Ammunition that exceeds the listed performance level is frequently encountered. Ammunition that does not come to the listed levels of performance can be considered among the worst products of the ammo-making industry. A careful handloader can usually improve on the listed handgun cartridge performance by some amount, but increases in accuracy will not be as notable as with rifle ammunition.

Handgun loads, like rifle ammunition, do not provide identical velocities and energies from shot to shot. Very good ammunition may show as little extreme variation as 25 feet per second in a ten-shot string. More likely would be an extreme variation on the order of 50–100 feet per second in a ten-shot string, while poor-performing ammo might have a variation of 150–175 feet per second within a ten-shot string. Thus, velocity and energy figures used to depict expected performance levels are listed as averages. The next table shows average figures for expected velocities and energies from a test barrel of a specific length. Actual values obtained from a specific firearm or ammunition lot can vary from the values indicated by the table.

The interior dimensions of all firearms vary slightly because of manufacturing tolerances. These variations can be such that a revolver with an 8⅜-inch barrel might give no more velocity than a revolver of the same make and model with a 6-inch barrel. Or the longer barrel could well produce notably more velocity, depending upon such factors as actual bore diameter, land diameter, cylinder-to-barrel gap and actual chamber dimensions, to mention just some of the variables.

To illustrate this point I offer the evidence of having measured a great number of 380 automatic barrels for a particular bit of research I once conducted. I measured groove diameters as large as .362 inches on some guns and as small as .358 inches on others. Combine this with a nominal bullet diameter measurement of .355 inches, and it is obvious that some barrels will develop different levels of ballistics because of a better gas seal and the technicalities of bullet fit to barrel.

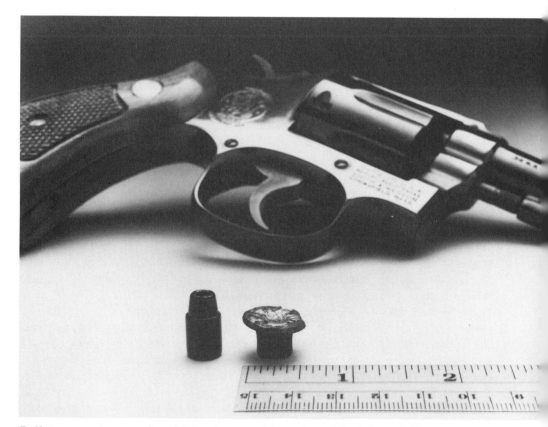

Bullet expansion can be obtained even with a short 2-inch barrel if the proper loads are used. The Federal 125-grain Nyclad 38 Special is an example of an efficient cartridge with an expanding bullet.

Winchester Silvertip hollow-point bullets offer reliable expansion from cartridges which traditionally have been considered nonexpanders, as evidenced by this photo of 32 Auto and 380 Auto bullet performance.

Cartridge Selection   The novice picking a cartridge might do well to consider certain minimum levels of performance if the ammunition is intended to be used for personal defense. An energy level of 200 foot-pounds at the range at which you would use your handgun is a number often used as a minimum requirement. More energy is of course always better to the extent that the shooter can control additional recoil and noise. However, energy levels in excess of 400 foot-pounds would, for the most part, prove to be overgunning for the task.

Hunters need all the energy they can handle if large game is to be hunted. For such applications, 500 foot-pounds of energy is needed for the maximum range at which you will shoot game. This means the 357 Magnum with the right loads may prove satisfactory to perhaps 25 yards, the 41 Magnum to 100 yards and the 44 Magnum to possibly 125 or 130 yards.

Handgun bullets that will reliably expand are becoming more commonplace. Such bullets are vital for hunting or self-defense purposes. However, the mere presence of a hollow cavity in the bullet nose does not guarantee expansion. Much depends upon the velocity obtained from the barrel being used. In general, lead hollow-point bullets offer the best expansion potential. Specific bullet types, such as the Winchester Silvertip, also offer reliable expansion. Jacketed hollow points will offer expansion when fired from 4-inch (or longer) barrels if the lighter bullet weights are selected. The heaviest jacketed hollow points or soft points expand most reliably when fired from 6-inch or longer barrels. For 2–2½-inch barrels, only the lead hollow-point and the very lightest jacketed hollow-point bullets will provide expansion.

Target shooters cannot gain much insight from ballistics tables. The most accurate cartridges, however, include the 22 Long Rifle, 32 S & W (with wadcutter bullets), 38 Special and the 45 ACP.

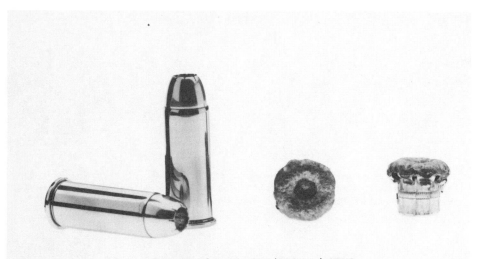

CAL. 44 S&W SPECIAL (200 GR.) STHP

The Winchester Silvertip hollow point is also a good bullet in heavy calibers. Shown are two expanded 44 Special bullets.

Not all hollow- or soft-point bullets will actually expand, as shown by these fired bullets. Be sure to test your ammunition in your gun to assure that you are getting the results you expect.

These CCI 38/357 shot loads have limited applications, but are quite effective on small pests to about 30 feet.

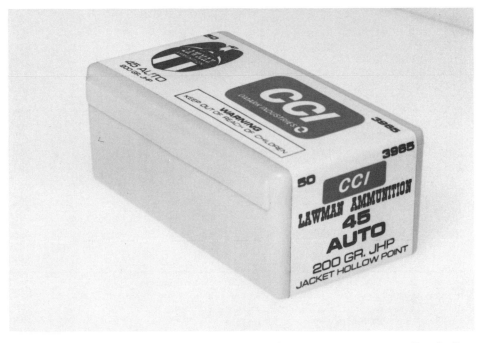

When selecting ammunition for self-defense, always choose an expanding bullet.

EXTERIOR BALLISTICS TABLE FOR HANDGUN CARTRIDGES[1]

Caliber	Bullet Weight in grs.	Type	Velocity in ft/s at: 0 yds.	50 yds.	100 yds.	Energy in ft-lbs at: 0 yds.	50 yds.	100 yds.	Max.(2) Range in yds.	PIR(3) at 0 yds.
22 L.R.	40	lead	1060	—	—	100	—	—	—	22
22 Rem. "Jet"	40	JSP	2100	1790	1510	390	285	200	2334	117
221 Rem. Fire Ball	50	JSP	2650	2380	2130	780	630	505	2667	232
25 Auto	50	FMC	760	705	660	65	55	50	1400	17
32 S & W	88	lead	680	645	610	90	80	75	1334	23
32 S & W Long	98	lead	705	670	635	115	100	90	1434	27
32 Colt Short	80	lead	745	665	590	100	80	60	1400	25
32 Colt Long	82	lead	755	715	675	100	95	85	1400	25
32 Auto	71	FMC	905	855	810	130	115	95	1467	32
32 Auto	60	HP	970	895	835	125	105	95	—	42
380 Auto	88	JHP	990	920	870	190	165	145	—	53
380 Auto	95	FMC	955	865	785	190	160	130	1467	54
9mm Luger	95	JSP	1355	1140	1010	385	275	215	—	144
9mm Luger	115	JHP	1155	1045	970	340	280	240	1867	129
9mm Luger	124	FMC	1110	1030	970	340	290	260	1900	95
38 Super Auto	115	JHP	1300	1145	1040	430	335	275	—	160
38 Super Auto	130	FMC	1215	1100	1015	425	350	300	2034	125
38 Colt Short	125	lead	730	685	645	150	130	115	—	42
38 S & W	146	lead	685	650	620	150	135	125	1467	42
38 Special	95	JHP	1175	1045	960	290	230	195	—	108
38 Special	110	JHP	995	925	870	240	210	185	1800	86
38 Special	125	JHP	945	900	860	250	225	205	—	92
38 Special	148	LWC	710	635	565	165	130	105	1634	52
38 Special	158	lead	755	725	690	200	185	170	1834	56
38 Special	158	LSWC	755	725	690	200	185	170	1834	63
38 Special	158	LHP	890	855	825	280	255	240	—	107
38 Special	200	lead	635	615	595	180	170	155	1934	49
357 Magnum	110	JHP	1295	1095	975	410	290	230	—	152
357 Magnum	125	JHP	1450	1240	1090	585	425	330	—	217
357 Magnum	158	JHP	1235	1105	1015	535	430	360	—	199
357 Magnum	158	JHP	1825	1590	1380	1170	885	670	—	435
41 Rem. Mag.	210	lead	965	900	840	435	375	330	2234	151
41 Rem. Mag.	210	JHP	1300	1160	1060	790	630	525	2367	322
44 Special	200	HP	900	860	820	360	330	300	—	147
44 Special	246	lead	755	725	695	310	285	265	1734	96
44 Rem. Mag.	180	JHP	1610	1365	1175	1035	745	550	—	424
44 Rem. Mag.	240	lead	1000	945	900	535	475	435	—	218
44 Rem. Mag.	240	JHP	1180	1080	1010	740	625	545	—	304
44 Rem. Mag.	240	LSWC	1350	1185	1070	970	750	610	2500	397
45 Colt	225	HP	920	875	840	425	385	350	—	175
45 Colt	250	lead	860	820	780	410	375	340	1800	132
45 Auto	185	MCWC	770	705	650	245	205	175	1467	89
45 Auto	185	JHP	940	890	845	365	325	295	—	155
45 Auto	230	FMC	810	775	745	335	310	285	1700	107
45 Auto	230	lead	810	770	730	335	305	270	1634	107

(1) All velocities rounded to nearest 5 ft/s, and all energies rounded to nearest 5 foot-pounds
(2) Maximum range based on an assumed muzzle angle of 35 degrees and calculated for bullets with a tangent ogive nose of 0.8 caliber radius, cylindrical bearing and a flat base at the nominal listed velocity.
(3) PIR is Power Index Rating; for full explanation, see accompanying text.
  JSP = jacketed soft point; FMC = full metal case; HP = hollow point; JHP = jacketed hollow point;
  LWC = lead wadcutter; LSWC = lead semiwadcutter; MCWC = metal case wadcutter.

Mid-range traj. from bore line (in inches)		Barrel length used to establish ballistics	Mid-range traj. from bore line (in inches)		Barrel length used to establish ballistics
50 yds.	100 yds.	(in inches)	50 yds.	100 yds.	(in inches)
—	—	6	2.0	8.3	4
0.3	1.4	8⅜	2.0	8.3	4
0.2	0.8	10½	1.4	6.0	4
2.0	8.7	2	2.8	11.5	4
2.5	10.5	3	0.8	3.5	4
2.3	10.5	4	0.6	2.8	4
2.2	9.9	4	0.8	3.5	4
2.0	8.7	4	0.4	1.7	10½
1.4	5.8	4	1.3	5.4	4
1.3	5.4	4	0.7	5.4	4
1.2	5.1	4	1.4	5.9	6½
1.4	5.9	4	2.0	8.3	6½
0.7	3.3	4	0.5	2.3	4
0.9	3.9	4	1.1	4.8	6½
1.0	4.1	4	0.9	3.7	4
0.7	3.3	5	0.7	3.1	4
0.8	3.6	5	1.4	5.6	5½
2.2	9.4	6	1.6	6.6	5½
2.4	10.0	4	2.0	8.7	5
0.9	3.9	4	1.3	5.5	5
1.2	5.1	4	1.7	7.2	5
1.3	5.4	4	1.8	7.4	5½
2.4	10.8	4			

Power Index Rating (PIR)   Perhaps the hardest task in the appraisal of ammunition performance is to rate the potential of the various handgun loads for personal defense. Two loads may prove to have identical energy, yet in use, one will far outperform the other. The difference can be caused by one load having a full-metal-case bullet that fails to expand and the other having a bullet that expands violently, thereby transferring all of its energy to the target. Also, the actual diameter of the bullet has an effect, although a minor one, on what kind of wound channel is created, and bullet profile also plays a part in effectiveness.

The PIR (Power Index Rating) values in the handgun chart signify the relative effectiveness of handgun cartridges for self-defense. This rating system uses the bullet's kinetic energy plus the bullet's diameter and its ability to expand as a means of forecasting a load's effectiveness. Those interested in the full details of this system are referred to the feature article in the *1984 Gun Digest,* "Rating Handgun Power." In brief, this system expands on simple kinetic energy figures by allowing for the varying ability of a bullet to transfer its energy to the target. Obviously, a full-metal-case bullet that passes through its target and expends most of its energy on the landscape is not being efficient at its intended purpose. But a rapidly expanding bullet that creates a large wound channel and stops within the target is indeed most efficient at accomplishing its goal.

To calculate the PIR value of any handgun load, one needs to know the following: bullet velocity in feet per second; bullet weight in grains; bullet diameter in thousandths of an inch; bullet profile; and whether or not the bullet will expand when fired from the specific barrel length being used. The formula used to calculate the PIR value is:

$$\text{PIR} = \frac{V^2 ETv\, Bg}{12111} \times Dv$$

In this formula, V is velocity in feet per second; ETv is the energy transfer value (from the ETv table); Bg is the bullet weight in grains; and Dv is the diameter value of the bullet (from the Dv table).

ETv TABLE

For all bullets that actually expand[1]	= 0.0100
For nonexpanding bullets with a flat nose equal to 60% of bullet diameter	= 0.0085
For all other nonexpanding bullets	= 0.0075

[1]Determined by actual test at range and velocity for which Power Index Rating is desired.

Dv TABLE

Actual bullet diameter (in inches)	Value
.200 to .249	0.80
.250 to .299	0.85
.300 to .349	0.90
.350 to .399	1.00
.400 to .449	1.10
.450 to .499	1.15

PIR values have been calculated for all the loads shown on the ballistics table based on actual test of the bullet's ability to expand in test media at point-blank range. To calculate the PIR value of any other load, simply use the formula and tables presented.

In the PIR system, a value of 24 or less indicates a load that is suitable only for target shooting or plinking and that should never be used for personal protection.

PIR values between 25 and 50 require very exact bullet placement if used for personal defense. If a perfect shot is not accomplished, the only result might be to heighten the rage of the antagonist. Loads in this group could prove satisfactory for small game but must be considered less than satisfactory for personal defense.

Loads having a PIR value of 55 to 94 are quite popular as defense loads. However, experience has shown that they are marginal even when good hits are made. Many police departments are armed with loads from this group. However, more than one peace officer has lost his life when an assailant failed to be stopped by a load from this group. Loads in this category are marginal at best.

A rating of 95 to 150 will meet the requirement of almost all military applications. It will also prove adequate for police departments that wish to use a load that will, in all likelihood, prove adequate and effective under almost any circumstance. Of course, all loads within this category will prove ideal for personal defense as well as for hunting small game and varmints.

A 151 to 200 rating in the PIR system will take the fight out of any opponent, often with only fairly placed hits. Loads in this power range do, however, produce heavy recoil and a great deal of noise. As a result, only a few shooters can use these loads because of the amount of skill required to master such ammunition.

A load with a PIR value of 201 or more can only be described as overkill with respect to personal defense. Such loads are best suited to hunting or defense against bears gone crazy. Very few shooters can develop the necessary skills to handle the huge amounts of recoil and noise produced by ammunition from this grouping. However, these loads are indeed ideal for centerfire handgun silhouette shooting.

It is, of course, impossible to place a specific value on a load for any specific application, unless all the criteria are known beforehand and are fully evaluated. However, the PIR value system will afford the shooter general guidelines to handgun load performance that far exceed the previous simple listing of kinetic energy.

Energy in foot-pounds at:					Mid-range trajectory at 200 yds.	Barrel length
0 yds.	25 yds.	50 yds.	100 yds.	200 yds.		
340	305	280	240	190	18.0″	4″
295	280	270	250	215	24.5″	4″
450	400	365	310	245	15.5″	5″
535	475	430	360	280	16.0″	4″
790	700	630	525	410	15.0″	4″
970	860	765	630	480	14.0″	4″
420	400	380	345	285	28.5″	5½″
335	320	310	285	240	31.0″	5″

LONG-RANGE BALLISTICS FOR SELECTED HANDGUN CARTRIDGES

Caliber	Bullet Weight (in grains)	Type	Velocity in feet per second at: 0 yds.	25 yds.	50 yds.	100 yds.	200 yds.
9 mm Luger	115	FMC	1155	1095	1045	970	865
38 Special	158	SWC	915	895	880	845	785
38 Super Auto	130	FMC	1245	1180	1120	1035	920
357 Magnum	158	JSP	1235	1165	1105	1015	900
41 Remington Mag.	210	JSP	1300	1225	1160	1060	935
44 Remington Mag.	240	JHP	1350	1270	1200	1085	950
45 Colt	255	lead	860	840	820	780	710
45 Auto	230	FMC	810	795	775	745	690

Velocity and energy rounded to nearest 5 ft/s or nearest 5 foot-pounds.
FMC = full metal case; SWC = semiwadcutter; JSP = jacketed soft point; JHP = jacketed hollow point.

USEFUL HANDGUN ACCESSORIES

21

Handguns need only a few accessories to improve their performance. Only those accessories that offer positive assistance in accuracy improvement will be discussed. Those that do not allow for improvement in your ability to hit what you aim at seldom prove to be more than gimmicks.

For revolvers, the three "Ts" are the most essential accessories. A target trigger, target hammer and a set of target stocks are offered on a great many revolvers as original-equipment options. Some better-grade revolvers have these three Ts as part of their standard equipment.

Target Triggers   A target trigger is notably wider than average and is usually checkered or serrated. This simple accessory allows the shooter to more accurately center the first pad of his trigger finger on the trigger, thus allowing better trigger control. However, wide serrated target triggers are best used only for single-action shooting. The double-action shooter will find a smooth-faced trigger, one about midway in width between a standard trigger and the target variety, to be best suited to his needs. In double-action shooting, the finger must slide slightly on the face of the trigger as it is pulled from its farthest forward position to its extreme rearward position. A smooth trigger surface allows the finger to slide naturally without hesitation. During extensive double-action shooting, a grooved trigger may actually irritate the shooter's finger until it becomes quite tender. Special "combat"-style triggers have the medium width and smooth surface ideal for double-action shooting.

Before selecting a trigger type, decide upon the style of shooting that will be your primary method. For single-action shooting, the extra-wide target trigger with its serrations will be best. For double-action shooting, or for a mixture of double- and single-action shooting, the smooth, mid-width, combat-type trigger will be the best selection. The standard trigger will, of course, work for either purpose, but it will be more difficult to control in single-action shooting because of its very narrow width. Also, the grooves on most standard triggers are less than well suited to extensive double-action shooting.

A word of caution: Some shooters install relatively inexpensive trigger shoes over standard triggers to come up with a target-style trigger without using the services of a gunsmith. Accidents have happened in the use of guns equipped

A wide, serrated target trigger can add a lot of comfort to single-action shooting.

A smooth combat trigger is ideal for double-action shooting.

with such trigger shoes. The extra width of these shoes often protrudes well beyond the edge of the trigger guard. There have been many cases where a handgun was accidentally discharged as it was holstered because the shoe snagged on the holster. Additionally, I am aware of a number of instances where trigger shoes have worked themselves partially loose and then wedged against the trigger guard, preventing further use of the handgun until the offending trigger shoe was repositioned or removed. Avoid problems and danger by using only triggers designed by the manufacturer for the specific handgun being used.

Target Hammers   A target hammer offers a lower and much broader spur than a conventional hammer. The position and width of a target hammer spur greatly facilitates the ease and speed of cocking the gun for single-action firing. Such hammers offer no disadvantages and are well worth the price on any gun that will be used, even only occasionally, for single-action shooting. Of course, a target hammer would add nothing but cost to a handgun used exclusively for double-action shooting.

Target triggers, combat triggers and target hammers are usually offered only in conjunction with revolvers. Semiautos, for the most part, come equipped with only one type of trigger or hammer, with no accessory replacements being available.

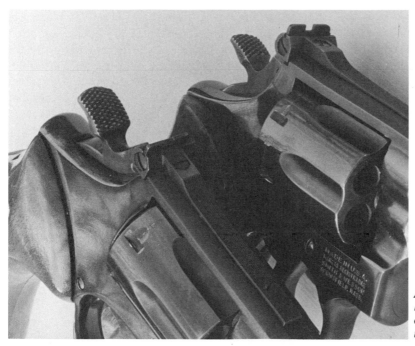

A target hammer has a wide and low spur that facilitates easy, one-handed cocking compared to a standard hammer.

Target Stocks   Target stocks for revolvers and semiautomatics are offered in almost as many configurations as there are handguns. Large, oversized, checkered wood grips are the most common and will suit the needs of most hunters and target shooters. Smooth wooden grips of similar size and shape are also available. These are frequently favored by shooters using handguns with very heavy recoil, such as the 44 Magnum. With very heavy loads, recoil can force the coarse checkering of target stocks painfully against the hand. Smooth grips do away with this discomfort.

Some target grips incorporate finger grooves, which can be an aid in positioning the gun for each shot. But unless they fit the individual shooter's hand, they could easily be more of a hindrance than a help.

Combat Grips   Combat-style grips are offered by many manufacturers. These grips are usually midway in size between standard stocks and target stocks. Most often, such stocks incorporate finger grooves or at least a pinkie groove. Combat-style stocks are designed for double-action shooting, whereas target stocks are meant for single-action shooting. Combat stock configuration varies widely, and such stocks are often offered in wood or rubberlike material. Some of the rubber combat grips are surprisingly comfortable and particularly well suited to the intended purpose. The most important aspects to look for in combat grips are recoil control and a size conducive to smooth, double-action shooting. Fit is important. Smaller hands will require a notably smaller combat grip to accomplish the task.

There are no shortcuts to determining the correct size combat grip. The grip must be installed on the handgun and used for a period of time to determine its effectiveness. However, if a wooden grip is chosen and it proves too large, often it can be rasped and sanded down to give a perfect fit. Shooters most often err by selecting too large a grip. If the hand cannot comfortably wrap around a grip rather completely, the chances are that the grip will be too large for double-action shooting.

Several cautions on combat grips: If a revolver is to be effective in combat situations, you must be able to empty the fired cases and reload without wasted time or motion. Some combat- (and target-) style grips are so bulky that they prevent the extracted case next to the frame from falling clear of the revolver unless the cylinder is rotated. These same grips often interfere with the use of speed loaders. Any combat grip should allow ample clearance for ejection of empty cases and the rapid reloading of fresh cartridges. Finally, avoid any combat grip that would easily be damaged should the gun be dropped.

Safeties   Left-handed pistol shooters will, for the most part, require the installation of left-handed safeties on their chosen semiautomatics. Of course, an ambidextrous safety will work nicely for any shooter, regardless of which hand he uses to hold a handgun.

Tangs   Some semiautomatics tend to pinch the skin between the tang and the hammer as the slide pushes the hammer to its lowest and rearmost position.

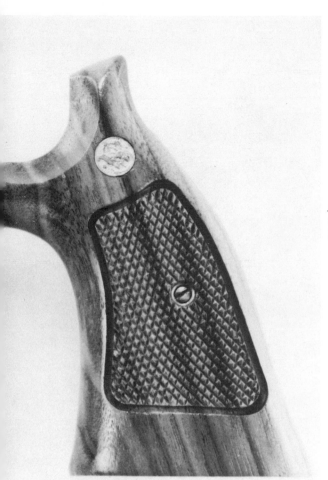

An oversized grip, such as this S & W checkered stock, is a useful addition to any gun that will be used for single-action shooting.

A smooth grip is a good choice for a heavy, recoiling handgun. This type of grip doesn't have the "bite" of checkered grips during recoil.

Two excellent combat grips, Pachmayr's Gripper and Compac with pinky groove. These grips are designed for double-action shooting.

There are longer or extension-type tangs available for some pistols, but not all. Shooters with large hands are likely candidates for tang/hammer pinch; they would be wise to select a semiauto for which longer accessory tangs are available, or one that has a sufficiently long tang as original equipment.

Magazines   Of course, spare magazines are essential to the pistol shooter. No magazine will last forever, sooner or later its ears, which hold the cartridges in place and guide them to the feed ramp, will become damaged. At that point, jams may begin to occur, signaling that time has come to replace the magazine. Also, in that rapid reloading is one of the advantages of a semiauto, it makes good sense to have at least one spare magazine.

If a semiauto is to be used for combat police shooting, on the range or street, padded magazine extensions are good investments. These pads can help ensure that the magazine is driven fully into the pistol when loading; they will also protect the magazine from most of the damage that can occur when magazines are released and allowed to fall to the ground.

Extra Barrels   Another accessory that will appeal to owners of certain semiautomatic pistols is extra barrels. For example, the S & W Model 41 is available in a heavy (bull) barrel configuration with a 5½-inch length. It also comes with a 7⅜-inch barrel with a lighter profile and a different-style rear sight blade. Some shooters find that for specific applications the ability to change barrel lengths will add to their enjoyment and marksmanship. Some semiautomatics can be changed from one caliber to another by replacing the barrel and several other parts.

Speed Loaders   Revolver owners may wish to consider the usefulness of the various kinds of speed loaders. Some allow the shooter to load six rounds simultaneously into the cylinder. However, these units are bulky and therefore not easily carried on the person. A very simple, inexpensive and effective alternative is the Bianchi Speed Strip loader. This flexible nylon unit is nothing more than an adaptation of a rifle stripper clip. It holds six cartridges in a single row without any notable bulk. The cartridges can then be moved from the pocket to the back of the cylinder en masse for rapid loading. The shooter can quickly load the rounds, either singly or in pairs, without fumbling or dropping rounds. This unit is darned handy for carrying extra cartridges, even if you're not interested in the advantage of rapid reloading.

Gun Cases and Holsters   Padded gun cases or shooting boxes that securely hold the handgun in position can protect sights from being damaged or inadvertently moved. Therefore, at the least, each handgun should have a well-fitting and well-padded case for storage and transportation.

Good holsters are, of course, an important part of the handgunner's equipment. Because of their importance, they will be dealt with in depth in Chapter 26.

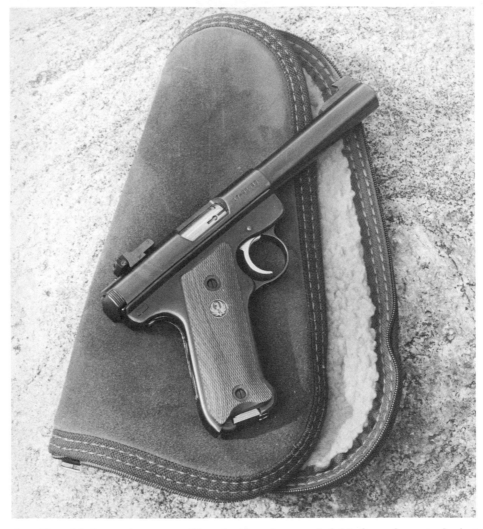

A well-padded carrying case will protect handgun and sights from damage during storage or transportation.

Gun Locks Perhaps the most important accessory for the handgun is one that will prevent its becoming the plaything of innocent persons or being turned into an instrument of assault against its owner. Regardless of where I have secured my handguns in my home, I was always concerned with them being found by a burglar. Should I ever walk in on a burglar, would he have found my guns and ammo? And would he use them against me? Also, what about the children of guests who might inadvertently find my handguns during their play?

The perfect answer to these problems is the Gunsafe made by Lasco, Inc. This little steel chest allows you to lock up a handgun in a well-padded box. Any unauthorized person finding the box can only carry it away with him, hoping to break into it at a later date to discover its contents. Yet, the design of the box will allow anyone who knows its combination to open it instantly, even in the dark.

The box has five raised push buttons. One or all in any sequence can be used to open the box. The exact number of buttons and the proper sequence required to open the box are determined by the owner. Also, the box's design will quickly allow the owner to determine if it has been tampered with.

The enterprising owner of a Gunsafe can add to its potential security by bolting it to a closet or any other site selected. Every owner of a handgun is morally bound to try and prevent its theft and misuse. The Gunsafe is the ideal solution to what otherwise may be a very difficult-to-solve problem.

Every owner should keep all handguns secure. The Gunsafe shown here keeps unauthorized persons from gaining quick access yet allows the owner to retrieve his gun quickly even in the dark.

22 SINGLE-ACTION SHOOTING

Single-action shooting, in which the hammer of the handgun is cocked prior to squeezing the trigger, allows for the maximum in accuracy potential. Because very little trigger and finger movement is required to discharge the handgun, the shooter will find it easy to realize full accuracy capabilities.

Some revolvers cannot be fired in any manner other than single-action. Ruger's Single Six and Blackhawk revolver models are examples of single-action-only revolvers. Semiautomatic pistols are single-action guns once the hammer has been cocked. A few semiauto pistols are also capable of double-action shooting, wherein a single pull of the trigger will cock and release the hammer.

Single-action shooting is the method most often used by hunters and by target shooters, whether they are punching holes in paper or attempting to hit a distant steel silhouette. Therefore, the fundamentals of single-action shooting should be mastered by all who use a handgun.

Proper Grip   As with any style of handgun shooting, the shooter must first learn the basics of properly gripping a handgun. One cannot simply pick up a handgun and begin shooting with any kind of accuracy. The handgun responds to the way it is held. If you grip it differently each time, it will strike a different point with each change in your grip.

The variation in point of impact can be as much as 2 inches at 25 yards. The reason for the change in point of impact is recoil. Because of the relatively low velocity of handgun cartridges, bullets travel through the barrel rather slowly, ballistically speaking. Thus, a handgun actually begins its recoil while the bullet is still moving through the bore. This is easily demonstrated by standing a revolver upside down, on a flat table, resting on its sights. Careful inspection will show that the sight line (the level table surface) and the bore line never intersect. The barrel of a handgun that has been sighted in will always be pointing away from the line of sight. When the revolver is resting on its sights on the flat table, the bore line will always be angled upward toward the ceiling. When the gun is held right side up and the sights aligned on a target, the bore line will be angled away from the sights and pointing downward toward the ground. Obviously, the bullet could never hit the target unless the bore-line angle changed.

254

The S & W, with its target trigger, target hammer and target stocks, is ideally suited to single-action shooting.

This is accomplished when the gun begins to recoil and the barrel is tilted upward.

Point of impact can be varied to the left or right, too, if the wrist and forearm are not positioned directly in line with the bore. With the wrist and forearm positioned to one side of the bore line, the handgun will tend to twist away from the wrist during recoil, causing the shot to go wide of its mark.

As you might expect, if recoil is increased, the effect of grip variations will be more notable. The exception is when increased recoil is also accompanied by increased velocity. The quicker the bullet exits the barrel, the less effect a varying grip will have. This is because the bullet is in the barrel for a shorter period of time, so that most of the recoil movement takes place after the bullet has left the barrel.

Obviously, then, it is important to grasp a handgun exactly the same each time it is picked up. And the grip must be maintained exactly for each shot. Since heavy recoil will tend to cause the handgun to move within your grip, properly fitting grips are important to control gun movement during recoil. Additionally, if you keep your elbow slightly bent, some of the recoil energy will be used raising your forearm. If the shooter locks his wrist and elbow in a straight and rigid position, the gun, wanting to move under recoil, will tend to twist downward in his grip rather than rise with the forearm as a unit.

To grasp a handgun identically each time, it is best to pick up the gun with

Positive grip control begins by placing the handgun into the shooting hand with deliberate pressure and exact positioning.

In assuming the proper grip, you should make sure that only the pad of the first finger joint rests on the trigger, after the gun has been cocked.

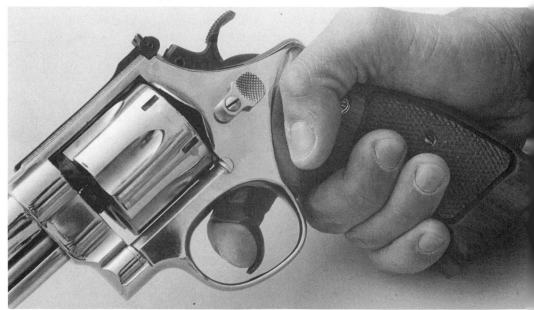

the nonshooting hand and firmly and exactly push it into the shooting hand. Ideally, this is accomplished by grasping the barrel with the left hand (for right-handed shooters). For short-barreled or semiauto guns, the left hand can, of course, grasp portions of both barrel and receiver. Never allow the left hand or any portion of the body to be placed in front of the muzzle. Then press the gun into the web, between thumb and trigger finger of the shooting hand, positioning your hand so as to obtain a comfortable trigger finger position. If the gun is grasped too high, the trigger finger will be cramped; if the position is too low, the finger will be forced to stretch in order to reach the trigger.

By deliberately grasping the revolver with extremely low and high grips, you will be able best to appreciate what is meant by the words "cramped" and "stretched." Find the position that's most comfortable for you, with the first pad of the trigger finger resting centrally on the trigger *after* the gun has been cocked. Assume this grip exactly each time. Of course, the handgun will not be cocked as you grasp it. But when it is cocked, the trigger finger will come to rest comfortably on the trigger.

A proper grip requires that the individual shooter sit down with each of his handguns and, by trial and error, find the most comfortable grip and commit that to memory. Then, each time the gun is placed by the nonshooting hand into the shooting hand's grip, it should be pressed into position firmly and exactly.

Regripping If the load being used causes a recoil that moves the gun in the shooting hand, the original grip should be restored before the next shot is taken. Some shooters can accomplish this easily by walking the gripping hand down the grips. Others will find that they do best by repositioning the gun with the nonshooting hand. Regardless of the method chosen, it is imperative, for safety's sake, that the revolver not be cocked again until after it has been re-gripped. With semiautomatics, the gun will be cocked automatically after each shot, so caution must be used when adjusting your hold.

Cartridges for the 22 rimfire to the 38 Special mid-range wadcutter loads can usually be controlled sufficiently during recoil to negate any need for regripping. However, even light-recoiling cartridges can cause the handgun to move within the shooter's grasp if the stocks do not fit well. For single-action shooting, large grips are usually the best, since they spread recoil over a larger area of the hand and thus reduce the handgun's tendency to pivot.

Cocking the Hammer On revolvers, where the hammer must be cocked between each shot, the importance of a target-style hammer is obvious. Few shooters can cock a standard hammer without a goodly amount of movement in the shooting hand. Thus, changing from a shooting grasp to a cocking grasp and back to a shooting grasp is required. Such excess movement is bound to cause variations in the grip, and along with these will come inaccuracy caused by point-of-impact changes.

On the other hand, most shooters can reach the lower and wider spur of a target hammer without altering their grip on the revolver. Shooters who cannot

The one-hand grip has been traditional for shooting single-action revolvers, but greater accuracy can be achieved with the two-hand hold.

In an alternate form of the two-hand hold, favored by many shooters, the left index finger is wrapped around the trigger guard, pulling the gun firmly into the right hand.

An important feature of the two-hand hold is the position of the left arm. As shown, the elbow should be bent slightly and positioned almost below the right elbow.

accomplish the cocking motion without repositioning the gripping hand sometimes can correct the problem with a different style of stock. If hand proportions are such that a new stock does not help, often using a gun with a smaller or larger frame gun will correct the problem. When all else fails, a semiautomatic will do away with the problem entirely.

When it's practical, one can also cock the hammer with the nonshooting hand. I do all of my long-range accuracy testing of revolvers using this method. It works well and is also a practical method of cocking the hammer of an auto pistol for the first shot.

For single-action shooting, the handgun traditionally has been gripped with one hand. In the past, some competition was done one-handed, and at some matches this method still prevails. Too, when shooting a handgun in self-defense, only one hand may be available for the task. Thus, it is important to be able to shoot with one hand. However, greater accuracy can be obtained using a two-handed hold and therefore such a grip is preferred whenever possible. For either one- or two-handed gripping, the method of holding the revolver or automatic is always the same for the first hand. As noted earlier, this is a matter of trial and error in locating the best position for your hand with a specific gun and set of grips.

The proper two-handed single-action hold begins with securely grasping the handgun's butt with the shooting hand in a comfortable position. The pinky of the shooting hand will usually fall close to the bottom edge of the grip. The thumb often is most comfortable and effective in controlling the handgun, if it can be pressed down against the upper portions of the grip, or thumb rest. The two-handed hold will be completed by resting the shooting hand in the palm and then wrapping the fingers of the second hand around the knuckles of the gun-holding hand. In that single-action stocks are often quite large, the grip used cannot exactly duplicate the double-action, two-handed hold which will be discussed later. Seek a supportive position for the second hand that will help steady the handgun. Keeping the second elbow somewhat lower than the first will help accomplish this objective. The accompanying illustrations will help elucidate the idea of a comfortable and steady two-handed hold usable from a prone, sitting or standing position. The first illustration shows a good one-handed hold and the second, the better hold afforded by using both hands.

Placing the Trigger Finger   Having learned to grasp the handgun correctly for each shot, the shooter then must concentrate on positioning the trigger

A target-style hammer with its low, wide spur is a great advantage on a single-action revolver, enabling the shooter to cock the weapon without severely altering his grip.

finger's first pad centrally on the trigger. If too little or too much finger is stuck into the trigger guard, little stresses will be created that will result in shots going wide of the aiming point. By placing only the pad of the first joint on the trigger, you will be able to supply the necessary pressure rearward in a straight line.

Aligning the Sights   With the handgun properly grasped, the hammer cocked and the trigger finger in place, the shooter then needs to align the sights, first with one another and then with the target. This, of course, is a critical point, and it must be properly executed. In that proper sight alignment has been covered extensively in Chapter 18, it will not be repeated here. Suffice to say that sight alignment is not what a great many shooters think. The *sights* are first brought into alignment with one another and then the gun, hand, wrist and forearm as a unit are brought into alignment with the target so as to present the proper sight picture.

Trigger Squeeze   With the sights showing the correct sight picture, the single-action shooter can then begin to apply pressure to the trigger. If or when the sight picture deteriorates and the sights start to move high or low, left or right, trigger pressure should cease to be increased, but all the pressure previously applied should be maintained. As the sights again show the correct sight picture, begin to apply additional trigger pressure.

Regardless of how often the sight picture deteriorates or improves before you get the shot off, proper trigger pressure will result in the gun going off only while it is in perfect alignment with the target. Good trigger control doesn't just happen; it takes a great deal of practice. Squeeze only when the sight picture is right, and hold when it's not. Apply more pressure only when the sights are again right, and so on. The results will be gratifying.

A small amount of follow-through is required. While the hammer is falling, during ignition and bullet travel through the bore, the revolver must be maintained in alignment. Granted it all happens quickly, but unless the shooter consciously follows through, accuracy will suffer.

Handgun shooting with a good degree of proficiency does require a reasonable amount of physical ability. The gun must be held as motionless as possible. The less movement that occurs, the easier it will be to have the trigger release the hammer when everything is properly aligned. Thus, the shooter needs to be concerned with his ability to hold the handgun at arm's length, to control his breathing and to assume a comfortable position that will afford the maximum stability.

Proper Stance   The proper stance for single-action shooting will vary slightly with each shooter. But the basics are the same. The feet should be spread comfortably apart, perhaps 18 inches, with the body weight supported equally by both. The feet should be pointing approximately 90 degrees away from the target. To find the best position for yourself, start as outlined and bring your revolver into alignment with the target by holding it at arms' length. Then begin to shift the feet in small increments (10 or 15 degrees) toward the target while maintaining the handgun's alignment with the target. Take particular notice of the amount of stress felt in the muscles that run over the shoulder and into the uppermost portion of your arm. As you shift your feet, the tension will either increase or decrease. The foot position that results in the least amount of tension in the shoulder is the best for you.

Foot position usually will need to be varied as the shooter gains skill and stamina with practice. Do take the time occasionally to check for a change in proper foot position if you shoot frequently. Once your muscles are well tuned to the task, your foot position will remain constant. The infrequent shooter (once a month or less) will do best to maintain the feet in the same position as first decided upon.

Control of Breathing   Breathing should be controlled. For best results, begin by inhaling before you align the sights. Exhale partially just prior to alignment, and then hold your breath as you bring the gun to bear on the target. Your breath should be held until the gun discharges.

If you do everything as described, the shot will be a good one. However, if you jerk or yank at the trigger or apply pressure when the sight picture is less than perfect, the shot will go elsewhere than the intended point of impact. Actually, the discharge of the gun should come unexpectedly. If you try to anticipate the release of the hammer, invariably you will be guilty of a flinch, allowing the sights to drift from alignment, relaxing too soon or making one of the hundred or so other mistakes that are possible.

By practicing the described basics to the exclusion of any improper action, you will become a more than satisfactory shot. Practicing until you attain the fullest muscle tone and mental coordination will result in your becoming an accomplished handgunner. And once you develop a satisfactory level of skill, you will need to practice frequently to maintain it.

Practice   By practicing the described basics to the exclusion of any improper action, you will become a more than satisfactory shot. Practicing until you attain the fullest muscle tone and mental coordination will result in your becoming an accomplished handgunner. And once you develop a satisfactory level of skill, you will need to practice frequently to maintain it. If you shoot infrequently, you will need to apply an extraordinary amount of concentration with respect to the basics. If you shoot frequently, much of the basics will become rote. However, even then, you will need to concentrate sufficiently to be certain that your rote actions are indeed executed with exactness.

Handgunning is not difficult. Yet, by the same token, good shots do not occur without the expenditure of a certain amount of effort and the necessary practice. As in all athletic endeavors, those who put in the most effort tend to reap the rewards of higher levels of performance.

Finally, it pays to do a substantial amount of dry firing at home. Go through the entire drill with an empty gun, and concentrate on where the sights are when you hear the hammer fall. This procedure will help you improve on your stance, trigger control and follow-through. Only your grip techniques will be left out of this form of "shooting" practice.

If a shooter is serious about becoming a good all-around handgun shot, I feel it best that double-action revolver shooting be mastered prior to undertaking any extensive single-action shooting. However, the basics of single-action shooting need to be understood before one can become an accomplished double-action shooter.

Whatever form of target shooting you engage in, the basic principles of single-action shooting remain the same. Adhere to them and practice sufficiently, and you will attain a noteworthy proficiency.

DOUBLE-ACTION SHOOTING 23

Advantages

Double-action shooting, wherein the hammer is cocked and released by a single pull of the trigger, has several very positive advantages over single-action shooting. The most important of these advantages are faster speed in firing the first shot and, with revolvers, faster speed for each successive shot and safety in stress situations.

Easy Movement   The method by which the handgun is fired in the double-action mode eliminates any unnecessary hand movements during shooting, since trigger-finger pressure is all that is required to cock and fire the gun. As the trigger is pulled, the hammer is forced back and then released. Because the tension of the mainspring must be overcome, the weight of the trigger pull will increase notably. It's not uncommon for a trigger pull of 3 pounds in the single-action mode to jump to 9 pounds or more in the double-action mode. This increase in weight of the trigger pull makes it beneficial to use a two-handed hold. The combination of not having to move the hand to cock the gun and the extra support of the two-handed hold are two very positive steps in maintaining a consistent and uniform grip on the handgun and thereby obtaining a high degree of accuracy.

Obviously, if the act of cocking the hammer is eliminated, the revolver or semiauto can be fired far faster for the first shot. Of course, after the first shot, a semiauto would automatically go into a single-action mode, as the hammer is spontaneously cocked during the gun's functioning. However, those semi-automatics that offer a double-action mode for the first shot have a distinct advantage over single-action-only semiautos. Should a cartridge fail to fire because of a hard or insensitive primer, often the offending cartridge will fire with a second blow of the firing pin. To accomplish this second shot, a single-action semiauto must be manually cocked, whereas the user of a double-action semi-auto need only pull the trigger again.

Of course, double-action shooting is the method to use for fast, successive shots from a revolver. For this reason, double-action shooting is preferable for personal defense, police work or combat-style shooting whenever a revolver is used.

Safety   In any stress situation, a double-action pull is a great safety factor in preventing unintentional firing of the handgun. Picture an armed victim being accosted by a thug, or perhaps a police officer entering a highly volatile situation. A handgun, be it a revolver or a semiauto pistol, that has been cocked into single-action firing mode requires only a slight pressure of 2 to 4 pounds to be fired. Being excited, nervous and even frightened has caused more than one individual to discharge a handgun unintentionally in a stress situation, simply because it was already cocked. However, firing a gun in the double-action mode requires a very deliberate and relatively long trigger pull. The trigger must be pulled back perhaps one-half to three-quarters of an inch, and as much as 8 to 12 pounds of pressure must be applied. Compare this with the $\frac{1}{32}$ of an inch and 2- to 4-pound trigger-pull requirements of most handguns when they are cocked and ready to be fired via a single-action trigger pull.

A sudden movement or extra surge of adrenaline caused by fright or alarm could easily bring about the discharge of a handgun ready for single-action firing. On the other hand, a shooter has to really want to fire a double-action setup, and a sudden surge of adrenaline is highly unlikely to bring about an unintentional firing.

Therefore, any shooter who may use a handgun for self-protection or the protection of others should learn double-action shooting. Its speed and safety are extremely desirable in any stress situation.

Disadvantages

What drawbacks exist with double-action shooting? Only one—a decrease in shooter precision. I deliberately did not say a decrease in accuracy. Despite what many less-than-fully-trained shooters believe, double-action shooting can be accomplished with sufficient accuracy to keep all shots within a 6-inch bull's-eye to 25 yards. Even shooters who practice only occasionally can accomplish this level of accuracy.

I have trained a great many new shooters to be proficient in the usage of a handgun in as few as three hours and with as little as 100 rounds of ammo when using the double-action method. I have also watched some of these shooters on the range at a later date. With practice sessions of fifty to 100 rounds once every three months, their proficiency level was maintained. Any shooter who can keep all of his rapid-fire double-action shots in a 6-inch circle at 25 yards is more than qualified for any nonsport use of a handgun or, for that matter, to participate in the various types of combat pistol shooting competition.

Selecting a Gun   Double-action shooting, of course, begins with the selection of a handgun. Good double-action shooting cannot be managed by most shooters with cartridges that produce excessive recoil. For this reason, the 44 Magnum and 41 Magnum cartridges are not ideal selections. In that someday the use of double-action shooting potentially may be against an armed antagonist, one should select a cartridge suitable to the purpose. The 38 Special cartridge is the minimum that should be considered. A 38 Special revolver capable of handling the new Plus P type of ammo is perhaps the ideal. A Plus P 38 Special cartridge, using a lead hollow-point bullet of 125 to 158 grains, can be formidable. The 357 Magnum with lead hollow points usually produces about the upper reaches of recoil for most double-action shooters.

It makes little sense to select a more potent cartridge, for it will be difficult for the shooter to control it in double-action shooting. Making poor hits or tearing holes in the landscape with a superpowerhouse round is not nearly as effective as making good hits with a cartridge of modest power.

The 357 revolver is perhaps the best double-action revolver for 95 percent of all shooters. With a revolver chambered for 357 Magnum, the shooter can start his training with mild 38 Special wadcutters and quickly master all the necessary skills. He then can graduate to full-service loads, becoming accustomed to the increase in noise and recoil. When the shooter can control the standard 38 Special loads to his satisfaction, he can begin using 38 Special Plus P loads. As shown in our ballistics tables, the 38 Special Plus P 158-grain lead hollow point is a load that will get the job done under most circumstances, having a PIR value of 107. (As explained on page 243, a value of 95 is darned effective for defense purposes.) Then, if the shooter becomes proficient enough to master full-power 357 Magnum loads, he can make this final upgrade in his ammunition selection. With PIR values ranging from approximately 150 to over 200, the 357 is up to any and all defensive applications, yet recoil and noise are still moderate enough to be mastered by a good shooter.

While it has been the vogue to downplay the effectiveness of the 38 Special standard loads, there is no reason to badmouth the Plus P 38 Special or 357 Magnum cartridges. I sometimes feel that the condemnation of these two cartridges comes mostly from people who have never carried a gun for a living or from superqualified experts who have lost sight of the average citizen's capabilities and opportunities to practice. Not everyone can shoot several times a week, and frequent practice is the only way heavy recoil and muzzle blast can be mastered and that mastery maintained.

Perhaps the best revolver to use to learn proficient double-action shooting is one of the K-frame S & W models chambered for the 357 Magnum cartridge. It is true that with a steady diet of 357 loads the relatively light K-frame revolvers will eventually shoot loose. But most practice can be done with light wadcutter loads. One needs to shoot only enough magnum loads to adjust the sights and to become accustomed to the noise and recoil. But more often than not, most shooters will stay with Plus P loads because the magnum loads will prove to have too much noise and recoil for their taste. With Plus P loads, the K-frame revolvers will withstand many thousands of rounds of usage. I have literally shot that many rounds through my two S & W Model 19 2½-inch-barrel revolvers, and no notable change in their tightness has yet occurred.

If a revolver is to be carried concealed on a daily basis, the Model 19 will prove too large and heavy for most individuals. For these shooters, an S & W Bodyguard or similar J-frame revolver will be a good choice. The J-frames are chambered for the 38 Special and not recommended for use with Plus P cartridges. Perhaps the best load for these revolvers is the Federal 125-grain Nyclad

The S & W Model 19 round-butt revolver, chambered for the 357 Magnum, is the ideal handgun for double-action shooting.

The S & W Model 547 round-butt revolver is a fine double-action gun and is chambered for the potent 9mm Luger round. Because of its fixed sights, it is ideally suited for rugged duty.

The S & W 49 (or its lightweight version Model 38) is a fine pocket gun, well-suited to double-action shooting.

Chief's Special load. Even from a 2-inch barrel, the load will offer positive expansion at all practical ranges and thus be as effective as possible for the standard 38 Special cartridge.

Grips   Having selected a suitable revolver, you will need to consider the grips. In a gun that is to be carried concealed, often the best grips are those that come as standard equipment. Their small size helps keep the revolver concealable. Oversize combat-style grips can, however, make double-action shooting a bit easier if the grips fit the hand well. The best double-action grip is one that fills your hand, yet still allows you to encompass the grip completely with palm and fingers.

The proper grip for double-action shooting is to grasp the butt securely with your shooting hand. Ideally, the bottom edge of the pinkie is positioned flush with the bottom edge of the butt. This pinkie position is, of course, dependent on grip and butt size. A Smith & Wesson K-frame, round-butt revolver such as the Model 19 is ideally suited to the average hand. With the shooting hand properly positioned, rest the gun in the palm of your other hand. Wrap the index finger of the nonshooting hand just in front of the knuckles of your shooting hand. The remaining three fingers on the nonshooting hand should wrap around the back of your shooting hand just behind the knuckles.

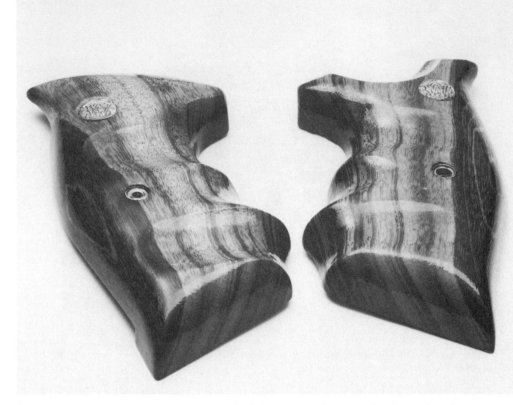

Finger grooved grips help a great deal in controlling recoil when shooting a double-action revolver.

It is important that the thumb of the shooting hand be laid over the middle finger of the same hand. The tip of the nonshooting hand thumb should be placed onto the thumbnail of the shooting hand, with pressure being applied simultaneously downward and rearward. The off arm should be positioned with the elbow down. The shooting hand should grip the gun quite tightly, and the supporting hand should be just short of snug. When properly gripped, the revolver will remain nearly motionless as the trigger is being pulled. I cannot overstress the importance of proper grip, without which accurate double-action shooting is extremely difficult. Study the accompanying photo to see what the proper grip looks like.

Trigger Squeeze   The actual pulling of the trigger must be one smooth, continuous pull. Do not try to interrupt the pull just prior to the hammer falling. This is a bad habit that could cost your life in a combat situation, because anticipating hammer fall, stopping to align sights and then finishing the trigger pull cost a great deal in time. Once you've started the trigger pull, complete it in one smooth, continuous movement. In the beginning, strive to maintain as good a sight picture as possible. The gun will move about somewhat, until you have practiced enough to anchor it rock-steady. During the trigger pull, the trigger finger will actually slide ever so slightly across the trigger. While this movement is minute, it nonetheless must occur, or else you will be forced to cramp your trigger finger excessively and thus cause some gun movement.

Make no effort to time your trigger pull to the best possible sight picture. Just start the pull and complete it without hesitation. Smoothness and the maintenance of a good sight picture can be learned very quickly, usually during the very first few hours of practice.

Once you begin to fire, continue until the revolver is emptied, mentally counting your shots so that you do not fire the gun on an empty chamber. This is

The proper double action, two-handed grip. Note the thumb of the left hand pulling the right thumb downward and rearward.

A pair of Mustang grips can add a great deal of recoil control for shooters with medium to large hands.

essential. If you are ever involved in a firefight, the time wasted pulling the trigger, when a fired case is being positioned below the hammer, could well be the most precious moments in your life. Also, firing a full cylinder is the only way to learn to control the progressive effects of recoil. Just align sights, hold the sight picture as best you can while pulling the trigger, then recover from recoil, align sights and so on.

With a good grip and 38 Special wadcutter ammo, you will have no difficulty in controlling recoil. As your ability increases, be sure to work up to the heavier loads. Extensive double-action practice need not be conducted with full-power loads. You should, however, finish each practice session with two cylinders of the loads you intend to use for serious business. This will keep you proficient and experienced with the additional noise and recoil.

Most shooters would be well advised not to purchase any special combat-style grips for double-action shooting until they have attained a fair degree of proficiency with the original equipment grips. By so doing, the shooter will be in the best position to know what he requires in a grip. In the gun shop, all grips feel great: on the range, very few seem to be just right.

Practice   Double-action shooting is not difficult. With just a few hours of practice, proficiency will begin to take on real meaning. Start your first shooting at a very short range, no more than 7 yards. When all shots are staying well inside of a 6-inch bull's-eye, move back another 5 yards or so. Keep reviewing in your mind the basics: supported hand grip, sight alignment, trigger pull.

The proper stance can help things come together more quickly. I suggest you face the target squarely, your feet well apart and your knees bent ever so slightly. The gun should be at shoulder height. With about two to three hours of practice, doing everything right to the exclusion of any bad form, you should be able to keep your shots in a 6-inch bull's-eye at 25 yards. However, do not attempt to cram the entire two or three hours of shooting into a single session. Fatigue will lead to a host of bad habits, not the least of which is flinching. Also, tired arms cannot hold the gun as motionless as required.

After each cylinder of cartridges is fired, empty the fired cases, reload and then holster the gun. Take at least a few minutes' rest before shooting again. This will prevent fatigue from occurring too quickly. Stop shooting just as soon as your arms feel tired. Doing so will keep you from learning bad habits. Continue your practice at another time—another day is best. If you want to get in as much shooting as possible in one day, sit down and relax for at least forty-five minutes before continuing. Pushing too hard *always* leads to bad shooting habits.

If practice is approached with the right outlook and stopped before fatigue (physical and mental) sets in, the maximum benefit will be gained. Following the outlined procedure should result in an acceptable level of proficiency prior to completing a full three hours of shooting. If it does not, something is being done incorrectly. A full review of the undertaking is then in order, since any additional shooting time may well result in the learning of some bad form. Habits learned are difficult to unlearn. Therefore, it is important to do everything right from the very beginning.

It helps a great deal if the sights are aligned on a specific dime-size spot on the target rather than attempting to aim at a whole bull's-eye or silhouette. If the target has no distinguishing feature to aim at, mentally project one. Aiming at the smallest possible spot will increase accuracy in any type of shooting, since you must concentrate and work harder to hit the small target.

It has been my experience that new shooters learn double-action shooting very quickly—especially those who have no preconceived notions on how to shoot. Experienced shooters often refuse to accept the simplicity of double-action shooting while forcing into their attempts some previously learned shooting style. It sometimes takes a great many sessions of instruction simply to get these shooters to execute the correct style. Once they stop trying to employ their older habits and accept what must be done, proficiency comes surprisingly quick.

A good double-action shooter will seldom find any need for cocking his handgun into the single-action mode. Only when ranges exceed 25 yards will there be such a need. However, the shooter who practices extensive double-action shooting often will be fully capable of 50-yard shots when urgency demands a no-wasted-time shot.

Accuracy capability with double-action shooting is such that unless I can assume a rest position against or over some heavy, immobile object, I will not consider a single-action shot. I simply can hit anything double-action that I can hit with a single-action shot if the range is 35 yards or less. This degree of proficiency is easily acquired and maintained. Just forget any impression you may have of double-action shooting being difficult. It is not. Almost anyone can learn fast and accurate double-action shooting in a very short time.

SILHOUETTE SHOOTING WITH A HANDGUN

24

Silhouette shooting can be a great deal of fun. It is even more enjoyable if the learning process can be shortened and geared to prevent frustration. The purchase of expensive equipment (that is soon discovered to be less than ideal) can be very discouraging. And therein lies part of the purpose of this chapter: to help you select the handguns and other equipment that have proven most suitable to the sport. The remainder of my purpose is to pass along a few tips that will help you understand some of the requirements for becoming a successful handgun silhouette shooter. This information should prove of value to you whether you chose to participate strictly on an informal basis or to become a serious competitive shooter.

Using 22 Rimfires

A great deal has been written about silhouette shooting with respect to centerfire rifles and centerfire handguns. However, very little has appeared in print about the shooting of iron targets with 22 rimfire handguns. This has been an injustice. Not everyone can participate in centerfire silhouette shooting. A great many potential participants in this sport find the recoil of the required cartridges much more than they can tolerate, let along enjoy. Still another large group has found that the cost of ammunition required, even if they reload, is prohibitive. In 22 rimfire handgun silhouette shooting, there is literally no recoil involved, and the cost of ammunition is minuscule in comparison to the cost of centerfire ammunition. The shooting of silhouettes with a 22 handgun is a sport in which every shooter, young, old, weak or strong, can participate. Therefore, rimfire handgun silhouette shooting will be covered in detail.

Range and Targets Twenty-two caliber silhouette shooting can be enjoyed anywhere that you can find 100 meters of shooting space with an adequate backstop. You can use almost any rimfire equipment. But if you want to enjoy real satisfaction from the sport, you will need a durable set of targets, a quality handgun, good ammunition and a few accessories. Let's start with the required targets.

A typical rimfire silhouette range, with steel targets resembling chickens, pigs, turkeys, and rams. It is important to shoot a handgun/cartridge powerful enough to topple the targets.

A full set of silhouette targets consists of 10 each of the following animals: chickens, pigs, turkeys and rams. The size of the targets and their weights should conform to the standards set by the International Handgun Metallic Silhouette Association (IHMSA) or by the NRA. One can start with fewer targets, but I have found that a full set cuts down on the time spent walking back and forth to set up targets and allows one to practice in a fashion that will duplicate actual competition conditions. Regrettably, silhouette targets are not available in every gunshop. Those shooters unable to find their needs locally can write to Metallic Silhouette Company, 2222 Peavy Circle, Dallas, Texas 75228. This company's targets have proven extremely satisfactory; I expect mine will last at least several lifetimes. Another source is Titan Metallic Silhouettes, 5740 Tichy Blvd., Commerce City, CO 80022.

Toppling Targets   To enjoy silhouette shooting, you should be able, after an initial learning period, to knock over between sixteen and twenty-one of the steel targets (in a forty-shot string) from the standing position. Less than this will leave you feeling that something is drastically wrong. To be able to accomplish this level of marksmanship, you need a very accurate handgun that is comfortable to hold and easy to shoot. You will also need terminal ballistics that deliver enough energy to topple the targets. Nothing is more frustrating than to hear the metallic clink of a bullet striking the target and watching it spin or wobble but not fall over. Such a hit is scored a MISS, because in silhouette shooting you haven't "killed" the target unless it falls over and plays dead.

I recall an early match in which my son, Eric, and I tied for first place. He still talks about the pig he hit on the nose that simply spun around 180 degrees but did not fall over. He felt that having hit one target more than his father entitled him to win. We both quickly found out that the judges (using IHMSA rules) break such ties by determining who knocked over the greatest number of the most distant targets (rams at 100 yards). Our tied score (18 each) was broken into a win for dad and a second place for his son. The lesson is that the targets not only have to be hit but also knocked over.

In that the rams are the hardest to topple, I began intensive testing to determine the minimum energy required to knock over these targets. Since energy is a direct result of velocity, I concluded that a 4-inch revolver simply wasn't enough gun to ensure that the hits made would result in a large percentage of the rams falling over. To reduce a lot of shooting into a few words, I soon discovered that a 6-inch barrel was necessary on a revolver, a 5-inch barrel on a semiautomatic. The need for a slightly longer revolver barrel is based on the fact that a revolver is somewhat less efficient than a semiautomatic (or single-shot) in producing velocity, because of its cylinder/barrel gap. Any length barrel from 4 inches on up would suffice for shooting the chickens at 25 meters and the pigs at 50 meters. The turkeys at 75 meters are the most difficut to hit, and a longer sighting radius than supplied with a 4-inch barrel is a very definite asset. The 100-meter rams demand a sufficient amount of energy, and only barrels of the minimum lengths I have specified will prove satisfactory.

Note: Ranges sometimes are reduced from meters to yards to accommodate existing facilities, which are often set up for targets at 25, 50, 75 and 100 yards.

What about longer barrels? I have used S & W revolvers with 8⅜-inch barrels and have found them quite suitable. Some shooters, however, find the longer barrels difficult to hold steady and prefer to stay with a 6-inch barrel on revolvers or the usual 5½-inch barrel on semiautomatics. With semiautos, I have found that 5½-inch bull-barrel pistols usually provide better accuracy than longer and thinner barrels.

Selecting a Gun   There are, in my opinion, only a very limited number of 22 handguns that provide the necessary accuracy combined with the feel and balance so necessary to enable you to shoot well. My rather extensive silhouette shooting has left me with the following list as being representative of those guns that I feel are best suited to the sport of 22 handgun silhouette shooting:

SEMIAUTOMATICS

Brand	Model	Barrel length (in inches)
Ruger	Mark I Target	5½ bull or 6⅞
Ruger	Mark II Target	5½ bull or 6⅞
Smith & Wesson	Model 41	5½ bull or 7
High Standard	Victor	5½ bull
High Standard	Trophy/Citation	5½ bull or 7¼
High Standard	Sharpshooter	5½ bull

REVOLVERS

Brand	Model	Barrel length (in inches)
Smith & Wesson	Model 17	6 or 8⅜
Colt	Diamondback	6
Colt	Trooper Mk III	6 or 8

SINGLE SHOT

Brand	Model	Barrel length (in inches)
Thompson Center	Contender	10 bull

While many shooters choose other makes and models, I have found the handguns listed to be the ones best able to deliver the accuracy and shootability needed to ensure success. And they all will stand up very well to the thousands upon thousands of rounds that an addicted silhouette shooter will undoubtedly fire through them.

The Ruger Mark I has been discontinued by the manufacturer. My own Mark I has proven to be a very satisfactory handgun for silhouette shooting. I did, however, install a set of Ruger checkered walnut thumbrest grips. These grips not only are an asset to my capability of scoring hits, they also "dress up" the pistol very nicely. The Mark I is extremely reliable and very, very accurate. I do have a very definite preference for the 5½-inch bull barrel in this pistol. I have found this heavy barrel to be slightly more accurate than longer but thinner barrels. It also balances better for most shooters. However, shooters with eyes that are more advanced in age may prefer the longer sighting radius of the 6⅞-inch barrel. The clip for this Ruger is somewhat difficult to load if you are inexperienced or have fingers that are weak or adorned with long nails. This handgun is easy to maintain and requires only an occasional cleaning to keep it going. If you already own a Ruger Mark I target grade, you have all the pistol you will need to be successful at silhouette shooting. Do try a pair of thumbrest grips. They helped my shooting noticeably.

All good choices for rimfire handgun silhouette shooting are (top to bottom): High Standard Sharpshooter, S & W Model 17 with 8⅜-inch barrel, High Standard Victor, and the Ruger Mark 1.

The Ruger Mark II target pistol is definitely an improvement over the Mark I. This new semiautomatic has an automatic slide stop (missing on the Mark I) and an improved trigger. The former is a great convenience, and the latter enhances the shootability of this handgun. The pistol is also somewhat easier to cock because of the shape of the new receiver. The Mark II also uses a new style of magazine that is quite a bit easier to load than the earlier model, because of the change in the type of magazine spring used. This Ruger is the lowest priced handgun suitable for silhouette shooting. However, don't let its low price fool you. It is as competitive as guns costing hundreds of dollars more.

One of the most accurate—and surely the easiest to shoot—22 handguns I have ever fired is the Smith & Wesson Model 41. I have used the 5½-inch bull barrel and a 7-inch barrel on this gun. The bull barrel is somewhat more accurate than the longer length, and, as is true for the Ruger, the shorter barrel offers a better balance. The grips that come with the Model 41 are of a modified thumbrest type suitable for either right- or left-handed shooting. These grips are excellent and will prove ideal for the two-handed hold usually employed in the standing silhouette-shooting position. The S & W Model 41 is an extremely accurate 22 handgun, in part because of its match-grade chamber dimensions. However, it is these same tight chambers that make both of my barrels quite finicky about ammunition. I encountered one lot of ammunition that simply would not function at all in this pistol. Almost every shot resulted in a jammed gun with an empty case firmly stuck in the chamber. At the other extreme, another lot of the same make ammo functioned flawlessly in the pistol and provided the best accuracy of any ammunition I ever used in it. If you select the Model 41 S & W, you will have an extremely accurate handgun with a superb trigger pull, excellent balance and a great sight picture. Sooner or later, however, you will run into ammunition that will not function well in the pistol. If you don't mind checking ammunition lots, then the S & W is a very wise choice.

At one point, I failed to make an initial purchase of a few boxes of ammunition from a specific lot in order to test my 41. The result was that I owned two cases (10,000 rounds) of an ammunition of the lot mentioned earlier, which simply would not function in my handgun. I found that the hardest part of this dilemma was trying to explain to my wife why I needed to purchase more 22 ammunition when I had nearly two full cases on hand. She simply could not understand the refusal of a suspicious dealer to take back what I described as defective ammunition. After all, it worked fine in his test revolver, and he felt that the problem must have been my S & W Model 41 barrels.

The S & W 41 is a very easy gun to cock, and the clips load easily. This will delight a number of shooters who have difficulty in handling these aspects on other semiautomatics.

The most popular centerfire handgun and silhouette cartridge is the Smith & Wesson Model 41. This special version incorporates a heavy $10^{5/8}$-inch bull barrel and a four-position front sight (one for each range).

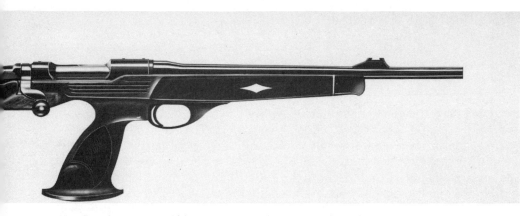

The Remington XP-100 bolt-action silhouette pistol is used by a number of centerfire silhouette shooters. Reloading is a must for its non-standard cartridge.

The High Standard automatics, as shown in our list, were all very difficult to cock when their hammers were in the fired position. The Sharpshooter was the easiest to cock, but even this model would not be suitable for most female and young shooters. Only those with strong hands will be satisfied with these handguns. All of the tested High Standard pistols shoot very well and have a nice balance, especially when equipped with the 5½-inch heavy barrels. The sight picture on these pistols is every bit the equal of the S & W Model 41, and the trigger pulls are excellent. The Victor includes a trigger that is adjustable for both weight of pull and overall travel. Its walnut thumbrest grips are quite comfortable, and the large grip makes a two-hand hold quite easy except for those with small hands. The Trophy model does not have the ventilated rib of the Victor. The Citation is simply a slightly lower priced (less frills) Trophy. The Sharpshooter is the only semiautomatic I suggest for silhouette shooting on which the rear sight moves back and forth with the slide. The lack of a fixed, nonmovable sight base does detract slightly from the accuracy level of the pistol, but despite this handicap, the handgun shoots very well. The Sharpshooter that I tested came in what High Standard calls a survival pack. This means that the pistol has an electroless nickel plating, a spare clip and a padded carrying case. With its wide-open breech, the Sharpshooter is the easiest of the tested semi-automatics from which to clear a jam.

I have found that one of the real advantages to the semiautomatic silhouette handgun is the ease of reloading during a match. You can have a sufficient number of clips on hand to allow you to shoot the entire course of fire without having to stop and load a clip. Having eight clips (five shots in each) on hand and ready to go prevents distractions. Nor will any cartridges be dropped to the ground. When using semiautomatic handguns during a match, I use the loading pauses to relax and to think about shooting my best. Some shooters, however, seem to get along nicely with only one magazine.

Revolvers   The number of suitable revolver choices is, in my opinion, somewhat more limited than the selection of semiautos. The Smith & Wesson K-frame Model 17 is a superb revolver that will serve perfectly for silhouette shooting with either the 6-inch or the 8⅜-inch barrel lengths. For best results, this revolver should be equipped with the optional target hammer, target trigger and target stocks (the 3 Ts). I prefer the checkered target stocks, but I admit to having made a subjective decision in this matter. Some shooters indicate that the S & W smooth combat stocks, with their finger grooves, provide a definite advantage for silhouette shooting. Smith & Wesson also offers a number of variations in front and rear sights. For most shooting, the standard adjustable rear sight and a plain patridge blade front sight will offer the best sight picture. I favor these sights under many conditions. On dark cloudy days, however, a red-ramp front and a white-outline rear sight can be a definite plus. I solved this selection problem by having one of my S & W revolvers equipped with the patridge front sight and my other S & W revolver fitted with a red-ramp front and white-outline rear sight. If you decide upon only one S & W revolver, then the red-ramp and white-outline rear may be best if you shoot under varying light conditions.

When choosing a Smith & Wesson revolver, be concerned primarily with the cylinder lockup and tightness and the action smoothness rather than with whether the gun has a 6-inch or an 8⅜-inch barrel. Picking the tightest gun you can find with a smooth action is far more important than deciding on barrel length. A Smith & Wesson Model 17 equipped with the 3Ts will prove a good investment.

The Colt Diamondback revolver is available only with a 6-inch barrel. This handgun is an excellent revolver, but the trigger pulls are usually too heavy on Colt guns to suit my personal taste. A factory trigger-pull job started at $60 the last time I checked. I believe this custom work is essential to make Colt revolvers suitable for 22 caliber silhouette shooting, with but few exceptions. The Colt Trooper Mk III is somewhat lower priced than the Diamondback. Both Colt models include target-style hammers, triggers and grips.

Usually, the best choice for young or inexperienced shooters is the revolver, in that it is easy to load and cock and there is never a problem with clearing a jam. Even the most experienced shooter may favor a revolver if he is the type who dislikes the occasional ammunition problem that will jam even the finest 22 semiautomatic pistol.

The Thompson Center Single Shot is in a category by itself. While this pistol, when chambered for centerfire cartridges, is quite popular for the big-bore silhouette events, few 22 shooters seem to employ it in silhouette shooting. Nonetheless, this pistol is very suitable for the purpose.

For my own use, I have settled on a Ruger semiautomatic with a 5½-inch bull barrel, a Smith & Wesson Model 17 with an 8⅜-inch barrel and a Smith & Wesson Model 17 with a 6-inch barrel. Obviously, I am not one to let decisions get the best of me!

The author's most used rimfire silhouette handguns include a 5½-inch-barrelled Ruger Mark I and a S & W Model 17 with 8⅜-inch barrel and the 3Ts.

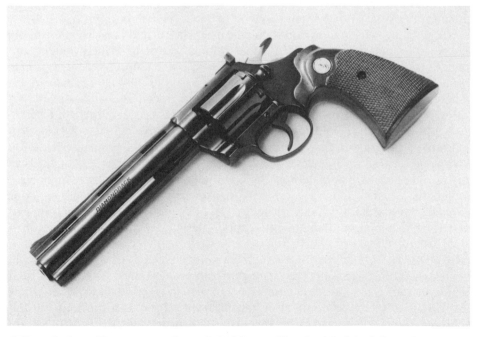

A fine rimfire silhouette revolver: Colt Diamondback with 6-inch barrel.

Ammunition   Rimfire ammunition quality can vary greatly from lot to lot. The lot number for any given batch of ammunition is usually stamped prominently on the inside flap of the cardboard box or somewhere on the label when the ammunition is packaged in plastic containers. The lot number is also usually prominently indicated on the outside of the 5,000-round case. A lot number indicates a homogeneous quantity of ammunition usually equal to one day's production.

Lot numbers are meaningful to rimfire shooters, especially 22 handgun silhouette shooters. I have found that ammunition of the same make and type can vary as much as 2 inches in its point of impact at 50 meters from lot to lot. And accuracy can range from superb in one lot to awful in another lot of the same kind of ammunition. Therefore, the serious shooter will first purchase only a box or two of any new ammunition lot and carefully test it in his gun or guns. When an acceptable lot is found, he will often purchase 5,000 or 10,000 rounds in order to avoid frequent sighting-in sessions and testing of new lots. A sample of an ammunition lot should provide you with at least 1¼-inch average group sizes at 25 meters. Small samples of ammunition that do not group into this average will not prove up to the chore of staying inside the 4.7-inch-diameter imaginary bull's-eye of the 100-meter ram target. Test firing of ammunition lots can be done also at 50 meters, where a maximum 2½-inch average group size should be your criterion. At long ranges, there is too much human error involved in aligning the sights of a handgun to give a clear evaluation of a given lot of ammunition's potential accuracy.

All testing should, of course, be done from a suitable benchrest. A sandbag support should be used for the wrist and forearm only. If you are to obtain a valid, practical evaluation, the gun must be gripped in the same two-handed manner that you will use when shooting offhand.

Only 22 long-rifle ammunition should be used. Shorts and longs will not supply the accuracy and energy required. Either standard-velocity or high-velocity ammunition may be used. I try to use high-velocity ammunition whenever I can, so as to obtain the extra energy to help knock over the 100-meter rams. But the difference in energy is very small, and if I find a more accurate batch of standard-velocity ammunition, I will use it in preference to a less accurate lot of high-speed ammunition. I would advise against any of the *extra*-high-velocity or *extra*-long-rifle-style rounds that are now being marketed by various ammunition companies. These rounds have never provided me with the accuracy levels of the normal long-rifle ammunition. Also, at the 100-meter range, the lightweight bullets have lost so much velocity that their energy level is no longer superior to even the standard-velocity 22 long rifle. With no gain in energy and less accuracy, this type of ammunition is a poor choice.

Sighting in   After you have selected a suitable lot of ammunition, you will need to sight in your handgun. The sighting-in process must be repeated each time you start a new lot of ammunition. Occasionally, you will find that a new lot will shoot to the same point of impact at all ranges as a previous lot. But such occasions will be somewhat rare. You must also check the new lot's point of impact at 50, 75 and 100 meters. Velocity differences from lot to lot are sometimes subtle enough that no changes in trajectory may be apparent at 50 meters, but at 75 and 100 meters a difference of several inches might be noted in the trajectory curve, in addition to any basic change in point of impact.

Sighting in should be done on paper targets that duplicate the exact silhouette of your metallic targets. These paper targets are also excellent for practice sessions, to cvaluate where your groups are centering and where the misses are going. You can then correct your hold to get the group centered so as to take advantage of the normal dispersion of your shots. Such targets are offered by Outers (Omark Industries) and are quite inexpensive.

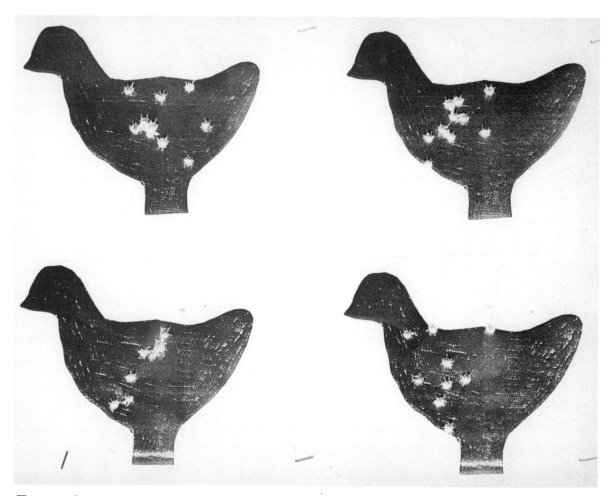

The use of paper targets is essential in sighting in your handgun and insuring that the centers of impact of are well within the bull's-eye area. These paper targets are evidence that the shooter is ready to move on to steel.

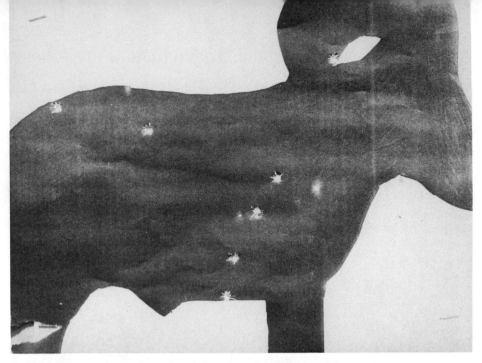

Seven hits out of ten shots is mighty fine shooting on the ram target.

The preferred method for sighting in will allow you the advantage of a good sight picture while preventing excessive holdover at the longer ranges. Because it is not often practical to attempt to readjust your sights for each range, this method will give you the best possible advantage for the four different ranges at which you will be shooting. When sighting in at the 25-meter range, you preferably should hold at the exact bottom edge of the chicken's leg. If, like mine, your aging eyes will not allow you to see clearly the small bottom edge of the chicken's leg, then you can use the bottom edge of the chicken's body to square off the top of your sights. Adjust your sights so that your group is centered on the 2.3-inch-diameter imaginary bull's-eye on the chicken. Attempting to shoot at the whole animal rather than the imaginary bull's-eye will result in substantially lower scores. (Please note that all references to targets and imaginary bull's-eye sizes are based upon regulation IHMSA targets.)

If you use the bottom of the chicken's leg as an aiming point, your shots should be grouping about 2 inches high. If you use the edge of the chicken's body as an aiming point, as I do, then your shots should be grouping 1.15 inches high in order to be properly centered on the chicken's imaginary bull's-eye. The advantage to using the bottom of the chicken's leg will become more obvious as the ranges increase with each target type.

Having properly sighted in at 25 meters, you should next determine where to hold at 50 meters in order to group your shots in the center of the pig's imaginary bull's-eye, which is 3.9 inches in diameter. The center of the bull's-eye is just forward of the rear edge of the pig's front leg. You should hold for a point halfway between the top of the pig's nose and the tip of its tail with respect to your left and right orientation. How high you have to hold will vary with the lot of ammunition used. With most lots of high-speed ammunition you will be able to hold on the center of the imaginary bull's-eye if your sighting-in point was at the base of the chicken's foot. If you used the edge of the chicken's body for an aiming point, then you will need to hold at a point approximately 1 inch above the center of the imaginary bull's-eye. For practical purposes, this means that you will be holding either roughly on the center of the pig's body (up and down) or roughly one-third of the way down into the pig's body, from the top of its back. The center hold will be more easily maintained.

The imaginary bull's-eye on the turkey at 75 meters is only one-tenth of an inch larger than the 50-meter imaginary bull's-eye being exactly 4.0 inches in diameter. The vertical center of this bull's-eye is just inside the front edge of the turkey's leg. The horizontal center is just about in the middle of the turkey's body. The aiming point for a gun sighted in at the bottom for the chicken's leg is approximately 1 inch over the turkey's back (or about halfway up the neck). For a gun sighted in using the edge of the chicken's body, the aiming point is slightly more than 2 inches over the turkey's back (or almost equal to the turkey's eye level). The proper sight picture is to see the appropriate amount of turkey neck (or head) extending from the top right or left corner of your front sight. Obviously, it will be far easier to hold with half of the turkey's neck protruding above the corner of your sight, rather than just the tip of its head. It is at this range that the real advantage of the lower 25-meter zeroing hold becomes obvious.

Shooting Technique Keep in mind that actual trajectory varies slightly with barrel length, individual ammunition lot and even to some extent the individual gun. It is imperative that you determine the correct hold for your gun with each lot of ammunition. This is best done on paper targets, which will allow you to see all of your shots as a group. Only in this way can you determine the best hold for placing the maximum number of shots on the target's imaginary bull's-eyes as frequently as possible.

At the 100-meter range, your hold will be either approximately 2½ to 3 inches over the ram's back (almost a line drawn through the upper portion of the ram's horns) or approximately 4 inches over his back (a point some ¾ of an inch higher than the tip of the ram's horns), depending upon your original sighting-in point at 25 meters. If you used a low zeroing hold at 25 meters, you should be just able to see the very edge of the ram's horns at the top right or left edge of your front sight. If you used the higher 25-meter sight hold, you will be squaring off your sights completely over the ram—in fact, you will have no reference point on which to hold. My own shooting is proof that this feat can be accomplished. However, it is far better to hold so that you can see some portion of the ram. Of course, some shooters attempt to adjust their sights for each range, but my experience has shown this to be a greater challenge than learning how to hold on the various targets with a single sight setting.

The imaginary bull's-eye on the ram is 4.7 inches in diameter. The vertical center of this bull's-eye lies approximately 1¼ inches off the center of the distance from the animal's nose to tail, favoring the animal's stern end. The horizontal center is exactly midway between the top of its back and bottom of its body.

When checking the center of your groups on paper animal targets, it pays to have some precut bull's-eyes of 2.3-, 3.9-, 4.0- and 4.7-inch diameters to place over the targets. By doing so, you will quickly be able to determine just how many of your shots are good hits or simply lucky hits. Of course, the misses will also be obvious. The heavy use of paper targets at the beginning of each new lot of ammunition is essential to determine just where you must hold in order to hit the 50-, 75-, and 100-meter animals after you have properly sighted in on the 25-meter chicken. There is no substitute for such target sessions. Once you know where to hold at each range for a specific lot of ammunition, you can then switch to offhand shooting at the steel targets.

The only valid advice I can give for this portion of your shooting is to shoot as often as possible and as much as possible. I usually shoot from 300 to 800 rounds per session. The amount of shooting must, of course, be geared to your personal desires, goals and physical stamina. The satisfaction of toppling a target will prove sufficient reward for all of your efforts. When you are knocking down an average of seven chickens, four pigs, two turkeys and three rams per session, you will be well on your way to becoming proficient in offhand 22 caliber handgun silhouette shooting.

Accessories   As with all sports, certain accessories are required to ensure total satisfaction from your efforts. Thankfully, not many are needed for silhouette shooting. Basically, you will need a good holster and/or handgun case to protect your pistol or revolver. Seven extra clips (a total of eight) are a nice plus if you use a semiautomatic for your shooting. A set of sandbags (to be placed on a suitable benchrest) is essential for sighting in and checking trajectory for each new lot of ammunition. Of course, shooting glasses and ear-protection devices are required, as in every shooting sport. A small screwdriver to adjust sights, a cleaning kit and targets, both paper and steel, are also essential. You will also need a spray can of flat black paint for touching up targets when they become silver colored from all of your hits.

Twenty-two handgun silhouette shooting is an affordable sport that can be enjoyed by almost everyone who has an interest in shooting. You should be aware that matches are conducted in standing position and in freestyle, where almost any position is legitimate.

Using Centerfire Guns

Centerfire metallic silhouette shooting can be a great deal of fun, too. However, because of the large mass of the silhouettes used and the distances at which this sport is shot, only heavy-caliber handguns will suffice.

The 44 Magnum has reigned the undisputed favored revolver cartridge. A wide

The silhouette shooter should aim at the center of an imaginary bull's-eye, as depicted by the white cardboard overlays on these silhouette targets.

Centerfire silhouettes are clearly larger than rimfire silhouettes (IHMSA or NRA size), but are shot at longer ranges.

range of heavy cartridges, including several wildcat cartridges, can also be used in the Thompson Center Single Shot pistol. Unfortunately, the popular 357 Magnum cartridge has proven less than adequate for turkey and ram targets, because it lacks sufficient energy to ensure a high percentage of knockdowns when the target is hit. The 357 Maximum cartridge is a recent attempt to provide the silhouette shooter with a cartridge of adequate power yet enable the shooter to use standard 38 Special or 357 Magnum ammo in his revolver for other types of shooting.

Regardless of the cartridge you select for other purposes, a centerfire handgun silhouette cartridge will need to be among the more potent ones if your hits are to knock over targets. The 41 Remington Magnum is as light a standard revolver cartridge as can prove consistently effective, and the 44 Magnum should be favored. At this writing, the 357 Maximum has yet to prove itself, however, based on my limited experience with it, I believe it does have promising potential.

Centerfire silhouette targets for handgun shooting are considerably larger and heavier than those used for rimfire shooting. In fact, they are the same size as the targets used for centerfire rifle silhouette shooting. They are, of course, set up at shorter ranges for the big-bore pistols: 50 meters for the chickens, 100 meters for the pigs, 150 meters for the turkeys and 200 meters for the rams. The same source listed for rimfire targets, Metallic Silhouette Company and Titan Metallic Silhouettes can provide the full-size big-bore targets.

Special factory ammo, often using full metal-cased bullets, is available for handgun metallic silhouette shooting. However, because of the need for extreme accuracy, most shooters prefer to load their own ammo, carefully tuning their loads for the best possible performance in their handgun.

Techniques   All the basics discussed for rimfire silhouette handgun shooting apply to the centerfire sport. For instance, you must learn to shoot at an imaginary bull's-eye on each animal. On centerfire pistol targets, the imaginary bull's-eyes are 6 inches for the chicken, 9¼ inches for the pig, 10½ inches for the turkey and 12 inches for the ram.

The trajectory of each load will, of course, vary considerably, depending upon the cartridge used, the bullet weight employed and the exact muzzle velocity for the load used in the specific handgun. The shape of the bullet finally settled upon will also affect trajectory. However, the principle of using a low aiming point on the chicken still applies. It will be necessary to learn where to hold on the longer-range targets by experimentation with your favorite load and handgun. But do remember to sight in using a hold at the bottom of the chicken's leg and to adjust your sights so that you are hitting the center of its 6-inch imaginary bull's-eye.

Of course, because of the huge helpings of recoil involved with suitable loads, the centerfire handgun silhouette shooter will need to practice frequently in order to master the chosen gun.

Centerfire handgun silhouette shooting, because of the requirement for heavy loads, is not for every shooter. It is, however, a sport that can provide the shooter with a great deal of enjoyment when the heavy recoil and muzzle blast are mastered. Hitting and knocking over a ram at 200 meters can be very satisfying indeed.

Smith & Wesson has a handgun specifically geared to the needs of the handgun silhouette shooter. This handgun, as could be expected, is a long-barreled, 10⅜-inch 44 Magnum. Its most appealing feature is a four-position front sight. Assuming you sight in on chickens using a dead-on hold, you need simply snap the front sight into the appropriate position for pigs, turkeys and rams. This enables using a dead-on hold for each animal and eliminates the need to be concerned with holdover and trajectory. To be 100-percent effective, the sight must of course have benefit of a load that very closely duplicates the trajectory of factory 240-grain ammunition.

If you wish to become highly proficient at centerfire metallic silhouette shooting, you would be wise to begin with rimfire silhouettes. After you have mastered these targets, try the centerfire game. Beginning in this manner will enable you to learn the proper techniques. Centerfire loads, with all their noise and recoil, often hide poor shooting habits. But trigger jerks, flinches, failure to follow through and a host of other faults are easily noted when shooting the 22 rimfire.

25 SHOOTING THE HUNTING HANDGUN

Shooting a hunting handgun is, in some ways, quite different from any other handgun shooting. In that the maximum in precision is essential, the hunting handgun is almost always used in the single-action mode. Of course, all the essentials of grip, sight alignment, trigger squeeze and follow-through remain constant. However, the hunting handgunner should always take advantage of any possible means to steady his gun. Shots taken from prone and sitting positions should be the norm. When game is the target, there is little excuse for attempting any shot unless the range and shooter's ability add up to 100-percent certainty of putting the shot exactly where intended.

Long barrels and heavy-frame revolvers seem to work out best for most hunting situations. A heavy gun will steady down more quickly when being shot from a position of solid support, while the longer barrels will result in higher velocity and, of course, increased energy levels. Barrel lengths of 7½ to 10½ inches are about right for most hunting.

The serious handgun hunter would be well advised to consider the use of a long eye-relief scope. Scopes and mounts developed for use with handguns can add measurably to the shooter's ability to take both small and big game at ranges up to 100 yards. Suitable cartridges must be used, and, of course, extremely rugged mounts are required for use on heavy recoiling revolvers.

Only a relatively few handguns are ideally suited to hunting for big game. The Smith & Wesson N-frame revolvers with 8⅜-inch barrels, chambered for the 44 Magnum or 41 Magnum cartridges, are excellent choices. Also, the Ruger Super Blackhawk in 44 Magnum makes a fine selection.

A firm called Mag-Num Sales offers a specially converted 44 Magnum Super Blackhawk, which they call the Stalker, that is ideal for the handgun hunter. Chambered for the hard-hitting and kicking 44 Magnum, the customized single-action Stalker revolver has a Mag-Na-Port barrel. Small gas-escape ports milled into the top front end of the barrel allow for the upward venting of a small percentage of gas. The net effect is that muzzle jump is notably reduced, and therefore perceived recoil is lessened. This makes the 44 Magnum round a bit easier to master. The Stalker is equipped with a very sturdy scope mount, among other custom features. Three scope rings rather than the usual two ensure that the scope will not slip in the rings during recoil. A Leupold M8 2-power extended

The S & W Model 29 (44 Magnum) is perhaps the most popular hunting handgun with big-game hunters.

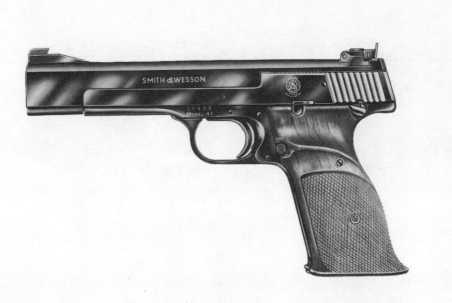

The S & W 5½-inch heavy-barreled Model 41 is a superbly accurate 22 semiautomatic well-suited for small-game hunting.

REMINGTON MODEL XP-100
Bolt action, single shot, center fire pistol
Caliber: 221 Remington Fireball

Remington's XP-100 chambered for the 221 Remington Fireball is perhaps the very best varmint hunting handgun.

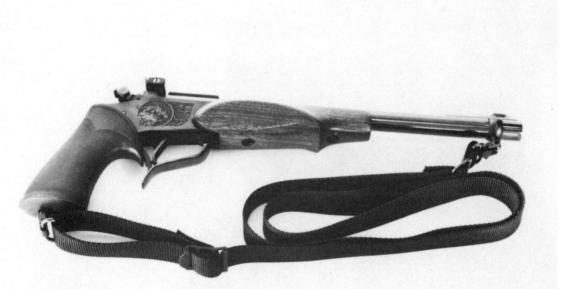

The Thompson Center pistol, shown here with a Williams Peep sight and an Uncle Mike's sling, is available in a wide range of hunting calibers from the 22 Long Rifle to the 30-30 and 35 Remington.

eye-relief scope is included with this pistol as standard equipment. Carefully executed trigger-pull work and the Mag-Num installed swivels and sling give the hunter the final touches in a handgun designed specifically for hunting.

A serious big-game hunter can purchase any suitable handgun. But the chances are that sooner or later he will have his gun equipped with a good scope and mount, sling and swivels, as well as having the action carefully tuned for the best possible trigger pull. Starting with a handgun like the Mag-Num Sales Stalker will eliminate the need for later customizing.

For small game or varmints, most shooters will do best with a cartridge that produces only a modest level of recoil. In today's market, one of the best handguns for varminting is without a doubt the bolt-action Remington Model XP-100. Chambered for the 221 Remington Fireball cartridge, this handgun offers ballistics approaching the 222 Remington caliber. Owners of the now-discontinued Ruger Hawkeye single-shot pistol will find its 256 Winchester cartridge ideally suited to small game and varminting. Of course, any revolver chambered for the 357 Magnum cartridge can be used very effectively for varmints and small game with the lighter-weight bullets of 110 to 125 grains.

For small game, anything from the 22 rimfire to the 357 Magnum can be used if the handgun chosen is sufficiently accurate. Of course, the very modest ballistics of the 22 rimfire cartridge require that its use be restricted to comparatively short ranges—25 yards seems about it for sporting shots. In 357 Magnum revolvers, 38 Special mid-range wadcutter loads are perfect for all small game to about 50 yards. These flat-nosed bullets do a very effective job of transmitting shock to the quarry. They are also extremely accurate, as many serious target shooters know. But for larger game such as woodchuck or fox, the wadcutter provides insufficient energy. For these applications, the use of high-speed Plus P 38 Special loads is a minimum—357 Magnum loads are preferable.

Shooting at game requires rock-steady sight alignment. To ensure this, one should make every attempt to get into the steadiest possible shooting position. No attempt to support the handgun directly should be made. If the barrel or any other part of the gun is rested directly against a supporting object, almost assuredly the point of impact will be moved. The gun must always be supported only by the shooting hands. To obtain the required rock-solid steadiness, only the forearms or wrists should be placed against any available support.

The shooting position most often employed when hunting with a handgun is the sitting posture. When taking a "sitting" shot, the forearms (not elbows) should be braced across the top of the knees. A major improvement on this position is to have the back braced solidly against some form of support, perhaps a tree or boulder. With forearms resting across the knees and the back well supported, I can shoot pretty near as well as from a bench with my forearm braced on a sandbag. In my opinion, this braced-back sitting position is the best possible for a shot at any type of game, be it woodchuck or deer.

Some shooters find that a prone position works well. The problem here is that hunting terrain seldom allows prone shooting. Brush, rocks and long grass will often obscure game when a prone position is assumed. Sometimes, a semiprone

Magnum Sales Stalker 44 Magnum handgun is a customized Ruger that features a Mag-Na-Port barrel (to reduce recoil), a rugged scope and mount, sling swivels and sling (not shown) as well as a specially tuned action.

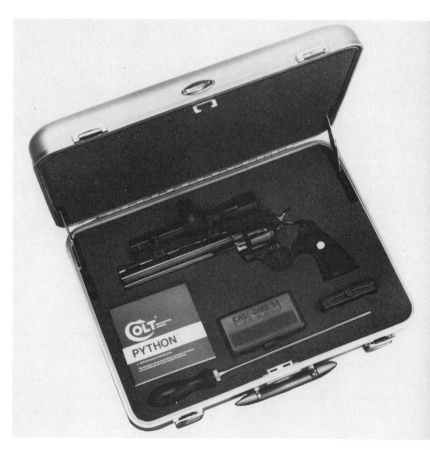

Colt has offered the shooter a completed hunting handgun set which includes a carrying case, a Colt 357 Magnum Python revolver, a scope and mount, and other accessories.

position can be taken by draping oneself over a rock or downed tree trunk. The added height thus gained will often clearly expose the quarry.

Offhand shooting is the least desirable position. Few shooters ever attain sufficient proficiency to allow for positive shot placement past 50 yards when shooting offhand.

A two-handed hold (as used for double-action shooting) is recommended for any hunting shot, regardless of the position assumed. If open sights are used, a two-handed sitting position will enable most shooters to be very precise in shot placement to about 50 yards. A 2-power scope will allow shots to about 100 yards to be taken with confidence. However, the trajectory and terminal energy of any handgun cartridge is such that no sportsman should attempt shots much past 100 yards. Sure, steel silhouette targets can be hit at 200 yards, but in hunting, a shot on nonvital areas is worse than not hitting at all. Crippled game is not acceptable to any hunter worthy of the name.

Finally, never attempt to use a handgun carrying sling as a shooting aid. Any pressure applied by the sling to the handgun will usually cause a drastic change in point of impact. Slings are handy for carrying hunting handguns, but they will prove detrimental to accuracy if they are misused as shooting aids.

The shooter who selects the 44 Magnum for his hunting handgun should keep in mind the wide variety of loads offered for this cartridge. For instance, Remington offers five different loads, each intended for a specific application. The 240-grain "medium loading" is intended for light applications where the shooter wishes to keep recoil at a minimum. This lead bullet load develops 535 foot-pounds of energy and has PIR value of 218. The 180-grain jacketed hollow-point load with a muzzle velocity of 1,610 feet per second and a muzzle energy of 1,035 foot-pounds (PIR 424) is designed for rapid expansion and proves ideal on varmints. The 240-grain jacketed hollow point with a muzzle velocity of 1,180 feet per second and an energy level of 740 foot-pounds (PIR 304) is the best heavy bullet load (using a jacketed construction) for handgun hunting. Its bullet offers a fine combination of penetration and expansion in handgun-length barrels. This load is a good choice for deer hunting. The 240-grain lead bullet with gas check produces velocity of 1,350 feet per second with 970 foot-pounds of energy and a PIR value of 397. At 100 yards, this load has more energy than any other commercial handgun load. The lead bullet will, of course, expand well. The 240-grain jacketed soft-point will produce velocities and energies equal to the 240-grain jacketed hollow point, but it will provide less expansion with deeper penetration. This load is best suited for use in rifle-length barrels.

In my test with the Stalker 44 Magnum, I obtained superb accuracy with all five Remington loads. All grouped at 4¾ inches or less at 100 yards. The 180-grain JHP load produced an average group size of only 3⅛ inches (based on five five-shot groups). The 240-grain lead bullet "medium loading" did shoot to a somewhat different point of impact than did the other three 240-grain bullets. By selecting the appropriate load, the 44 Magnum user can gain the maximum potential from his handgun.

When hunting always assume the best possible position to support the handgun. The author (298) here looks uncomfortable but his gun is rock steady. Hunter at uses a tree and his left hand to form a solid rest.

HOLSTERS | 26

Holsters are almost as old as handguns. The concept of being able to carry a gun on one's person without it becoming a burden is a good part of the reason handguns exist, and obviously a holster allows this concept to be practical.

Holsters are available in a very wide range of styles, and one suitable for a particular purpose is seldom worth much for another purpose. If you desire a holster to be used solely as a means of carrying a handgun and if supplying the maximum possible protection for gun and sights, a well-designed flap holster is the best possible choice. But a flap holster is bulky and therefore cannot be carried in a concealed position. And by nature, drawing a gun from a flap holster is a slow process, thus eliminating this style from any application where the handgun must be put into service quickly. Nonetheless, a soft-lined, leather flap holster, such as the Bianchi #16L, is still the best means of affording protection to any handgun.

Hunting Holsters   A flap holster is a good choice for big-game hunting. The gun generally is carried for a long time before actuallly being needed in the hunt, and most often the hunter has plenty of time to draw his handgun before taking a shot. The flap holster will help ensure that handgun and sights are in the expected condition when finally pressed into service.

For small-game hunting, a somewhat quicker-to-use holster is appropriate, as the gun may be drawn from the holster and reholstered frequently during the course of a hunt. A basic safety-strap holster will prove best for this type of usage. Ideally, the holster should be lined with a soft leather or leather suede to protect the finish of the gun. It also should have some form of guard to protect the sight from being damaged or moved inadvertently during the rough going that is often part of small-game hunting with a handgun. An ideal choice of a holster for this application is the Smith & Wesson Model 22. Regardless of the exact holster chosen, do select one that covers as much of the handgun as possible. When hunting, the gun will take a lot of abuse if it is not adequately protected.

Two other holster styles work out well for hunting, the S & W Model 27 and the Uncle Mike's Sidekick holsters. The Model 27 offers good protection and incorporates a thumb-release safety strap. The advantage of this holster over

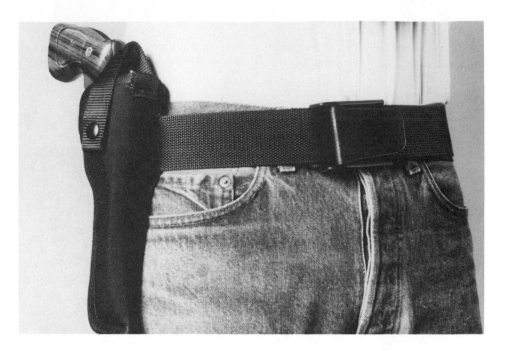

The Uncle Mike's Sidekick holster is an inexpensive yet effective holster that keeps bulk to a minimum (300). It is available for a wide range of revolvers and semi-automatics (300).

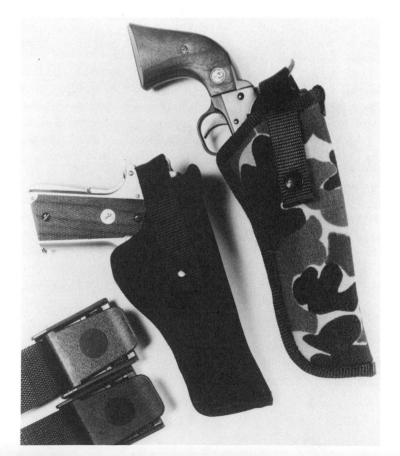

Cross-draw holsters can keep the gun on your off-side and help prevent undue damage.

the similar S & W Model 22 is that the hammer of the gun is completely covered by the leather of the thumb-release safety strap. However, I find the standard safety strap of the Model 22 far more convenient for field use.

The Uncle Mike's Sidekick holster is unique in that it is made of an extremely durable nylon-type material. This holster is well padded and offers all the protection of a leather holster. Its standard-style safety strap is adjustable for length. Thus, as is not the case with leather holsters, when the safety strap stretches, it can be easily adjusted to the correct length. Uncle Mike's Sidekick holster covers a great deal of the handgun and the rear sight, making it highly practical for field use. Perhaps its best feature is the relatively low cost—less than one-quarter of the price of a good-quality, leather-lined holster.

Holsters that do not protect the rear sight should not be selected for any but the lightest duty. The Smith & Wesson Model 21 holster offers a great deal of protection for the handgun but leaves the rear sight completely exposed. Thus, despite its other merits, this is a holster only for easy use when there is no danger of damaging the sight. One feature of this style holster that I dislike is its snap-off belt loop. A snap on the outside of the holster allows it to be put on and off a fastened belt. This can be convenient, but the drawbacks can be a lost gun and holster.

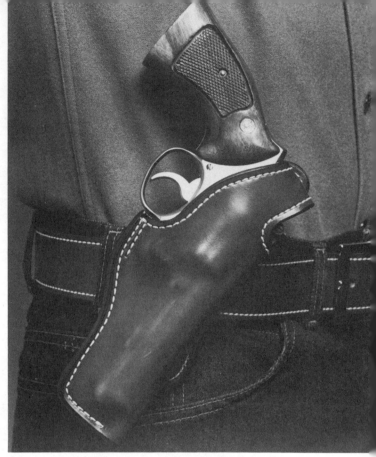

A good holster keeps the handgun butt tight against the body to prevent it from hanging up in brush or being damaged by bumping into obstacles.

A flap holster like this Bianchi will give any handgun maximum protection.

The Bianchi Lightning is the best holster for short barrelled revolvers, offering good concealment and plenty of protection.

Years, many years ago, I carried a Smith & Wesson 4-inch kit gun on my belt in such a holster. Along the way, I sat to take a shot with my 222 varmint rifle at a distant woodchuck. Unknown to me, the end of the holster was wedged against the ground as I sat, opening the snap and pushing the holster above my belt. I never heard the gun and holster fall to the soft ground as I stood. Hours later, I discovered the loss and spent a long time looking for the gun. Fortunately, no one else had happened along on the site where the handgun lay, and I found it. If you choose this style of holster, check the snap frequently. In my opinion, any holster that uses snaps of any kind to hold the belt loop can represent the potential of a lost handgun.

On the topic of potential problems with holsters, another point comes clearly to mind. I carried an S & W Model 41 automatic in one holster for quite some time. When I first lost a clip, I suspected that I had not pushed it fully into place. When I lost the second clip, I could not believe my carelessness. Then, one day, as I was bending over, I heard the soft click of the magazine-release button. A little investigation quickly revealed that this button could be actuated by the holster. When the outside of the holster was pressed against something, it forced the gun inward until the magazine release was pressed tightly against the inside of the holster, releasing the magazine. I complained to the manufacturer, but my efforts fell upon deaf ears. So, when selecting a holster for any semiauto with a push-button magazine release, be sure that there is absolutely no way for the release to be actuated while the gun is in the holster.

When a handgun is to be carried for the protection of the wearer or others, even more thought must go into holster selection. For uniformed police officers, the most important consideration is security. It is imperative that the handgun not be subject to being torn from the patrolman's holster in a scuffle or by someone who is simply bent on grabbing a handgun. There are a great many styles offered to accomplish the required security. Those with mechanical releases are the poorest choices, since the parts of such devices can be jammed by foreign matter and prevent the withdrawal of the handgun when it is urgently needed. The best of the security holsters require that the wearer's thumb be forced between holster and revolver in order to free the cylinder of a leather retaining lip.

Concealed Holsters

For off-duty police, plainclothes police and the citizen who carries a gun daily, holster choice can be made from a great many suitable types. The Uncle Mike's nylon Sidekick holster represents the least expensive, yet highly practical design. For a short, 2-inch barreled revolver this holster offers a minimum amount of bulk and ample gun protection, while holding the gun tightly to the body for maximum concealment.

For large-framed handguns, holsters like the Smith & Wesson Model 29L will keep the gun snug against the body and riding quite high. Both of these features are desirable when the wearer wishes to keep the handgun concealed beneath a short jacket. The famous "FBI tilt" is incorporated on many holsters of this type, and thumb-break safety straps are also usually standard. These two features mean that a rapid, no-fumble draw of the gun can be accomplished easily.

For small-frame revolvers, the most effective holster I have ever used is the Bianchi #55L Lightning. This holster offers an unusually high degree of handgun protection not often found in small holsters. Also, the safety strap goes over the back of the trigger guard rather than over the hammer. It is released by pressure with the middle finger. This feature is unusual enough to confuse many of those who might want to attempt to snatch a gun from a holster, yet the user will incur no delay in drawing the gun. The handgun rides high and very tight to the body in this holster, making it an ideal selection for concealment. The Bianchi Lightning is also available for larger-frame revolvers and works well for them. This holster is my unquestionable favored choice for a belt holster that is to be worn on a daily basis. Its only disadvantage is that the safety strap is a bit awkward to engage when returning the gun to the holster. This is of minor consequence since a gun that is carried daily is seldom pressed into service. When needed, the concern is for a fast draw rather than a quick application of the safety strap after returning the gun to the holster.

Another style of holster that is popular for carrying a concealed handgun is the so-called waistband holster. This is a simple sheath worn inside the pants.

The Rogers Double Agent shoulder holster is light, comfortable and conceals easily.

These holsters do indeed conceal the handgun as much as possible while still allowing for a fairly rapid draw. In years gone by, such holsters were most often equipped with a leather loop that held them in place when the pants' belt was placed through it. And such an arrangement worked fine. Today, however, this style of holster is most often equipped with a metal spring latch that simply snaps over the belt. On two different occasions when bending over, I have had such holsters ride up over my belt and free of my waistband. Both times, gun and holster fell to the ground. After the second mishap, I removed the offending clip and now use the holster as a pocket holster. When the gun is placed in my side pants pocket, the holster protects it from the ravages of sweat and keeps the gun from tilting into awkward positions that would prevent rapid draw. It also prevents telltale bulges by providing a smooth, undistinguishable bump in my pocket.

A holster style that can be superbly effective for concealment is the shoulder holster. A well-designed shoulder holster will allow a small-frame revolver or semiautomatic to be effectively concealed beneath as little as a summer-weight sport shirt. Medium-frame revolvers or large-frame semiautos can be concealed beneath a light jacket if the shoulder holster is properly designed.

A poorly designed shoulder holster can be a nightmare of discomfort to the wearer. And a few specimens require the wearer to be a contortionist to free the gun from the holster. One of the best-designed shoulder holsters I have ever used is the one sold by Rogers. This version offers a minimum bulk, minimum weight and wearing comfort. The straps are nylon and incorporate Velcro adjustments that allow the rig to be fitted to any size wearer. The over-the-shoulder straps are leather, as is the holster body. A Velcro-fastened safety strap is used, allowing for a fumble-free release of the gun. This holster system carries the butt down for maximum concealment and ease in drawing. Two pouches under the opposite arm allow for up to two cylinders full of spare ammo to be carried. The lightweight carrying comfort of this rig has made this Rogers Double Agent holster a well deserved favorite with a great many people.

When selecting any holster, inspect it carefully for workmanship. Sewn seams have an affinity for coming undone after limited use if the workmanship is poor. Also, be sure to try on the holster with your gun and its normally used grips. Often what appears to be a compact holster turns out to be just the opposite because of the angle at which it carries the gun. And when in doubt, ask an old-time plainclothes cop what he uses. Chances are the years have shown him what rigs are the most comfortable while offering the security and concealment needed.

ARCHERY

PART IV

SELECTING A BOW 27

Archery is the oldest surviving form of a shooting sport. The bow and arrow traces its origins to ancient times. But the bows used by today's target shooters and hunters have very little in common with their ancestors. Modern lamination of highly efficient woods, metals, epoxies and similar materials enable bow-makers to fabricate bow limbs that are extremely efficient in storing and releasing energy. This results in a high arrow velocity for a given weight of pull. Thus, today's archer using a 50-pound bow will have a greater range capability than the bow hunter of even twenty years ago using a similar bow weight.

The weight of pull, or draw weight (the amount of energy required to draw the bow to a comfortable shooting position), has long been the limiting factor in a bow's range. Most shooters can draw a bow comfortably if the weight of pull falls between 45 and 75 pounds. But even within this range, few archers can perform very well with a bow that has a draw weight of 60 pounds or more. It's one thing to bring a bow to full draw and then quickly release the arrow. It's quite another thing to draw the bow and then hold it at full draw for some period of time while the sight is aligned and the archer concentrates on all the fine points of release and so on. While modern recurve bows are efficient, the physical abilities of most shooters have prevented them from using heavier bows to gain flatter arrow trajectories and the resulting increase in range.

But the ingenious compound bow has now all but replaced the recurve bow. Compound bows use a system of two, four or six pulleys and a flexible steel cable to create a unique draw and let-off process. With a recurve bow, the effort to draw the string rearward begins at a low level. As the string is brought back, the weight of pull increases gradually until the arrow has been drawn about 24 inches. Then, for each additional inch the arrow is drawn, the weight of pull increases notably—about 2 pounds for each inch of draw. Thus, the greatest effort is required when holding the bow at its full draw position in order to aim the arrow. This is not the case with a compound bow.

As a compound bow is drawn, it reaches its maximum draw weight when the arrow is drawn about halfway. Then, as the arrow is drawn farther to the rear, a let-off in draw weight occurs. That is, the effort required to pull the bow suddenly reduces, so that at full draw the effort required to hold the bow may be as much as 50 percent less than its maximum draw weight. The exact amount

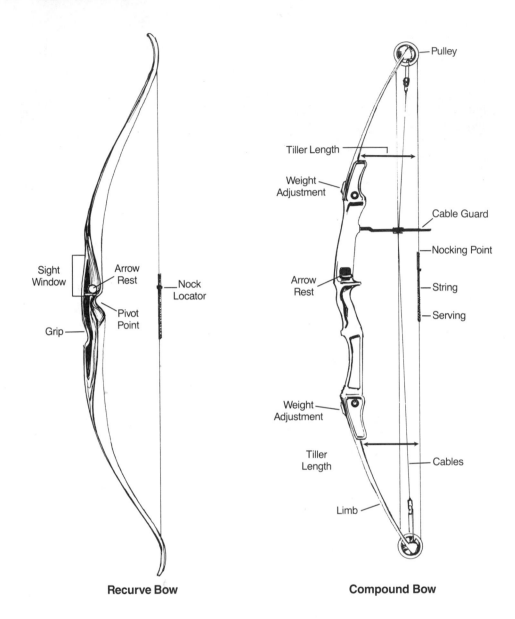

Recurve Bow

Compound Bow

The traditional recurve bow, although accurate, imposes limitations on the archer as the draw weight increases. Great strength is required to hold a recurve bow with a draw weight of 60 pounds or more at full draw. With the compound bow, however, the system of pulleys decreases the draw weight as the archer reaches full draw, so that the effort to hold the bow may be as much as 50 percent less than its maximum draw weight.

of let-off is dependent upon the design of the bow, but the usual range is a 30 to 50 percent decrease in weight of pull when held at full draw.

Advantages of Compound Bows

The advantage of this system is that it allows a shooter to achieve accuracy with a bow that has a very heavy draw weight. Suppose a shooter finds that the heaviest draw weight he can hold when using a recurve bow is 50 pounds. If this shooter were to select a compound bow with even a 65-pound draw weight, with a 30 percent let-off, he would actually have to hold only 45½ pounds when at full draw. This is a gain of 15 pounds in peak draw weight but a decrease of almost 5 pounds in holding weight. Thus, the shooter selecting such a bow would find that he must work harder to get the bow to full draw, but once the let-off occurs, he will be holding a more comfortable weight. Aiming, sighting and, when needed, waiting while at full draw will be accomplished more readily because of the reduced strain on the shooter's muscles. The increased arrow velocity supplied by the higher draw weight will also offer flatter trajectory, making it easier to hit the target. In sum, because of a compound bow's mechanical advantage, most shooters will become better archers.

So long as you can handle the peak draw weight of a compound bow well enough to get the arrow drawn past it, you can elect to use the maximum weight of pull you desire. Then, by selecting a compound that allows a let-off that will provide a comfortable holding weight for your capabilities, you will be able to draw, hold, aim and release without any accuracy-destroying muscle strain. Where a 50–55-pound pull was common with recurve bows, today's compound bow users frequently select draw weights of 60 to 75 pounds, yet need only to hold against pulls as little as 30 to 40 pounds when at full draw. Quite an advantage indeed.

Draw Weights

Bow selection must be geared to the intended purpose but, more importantly, must also be geared to the physical requirements of the shooter. If the draw weight is too much, the shooter will be unable to obtain any real accuracy. Equally, if the draw weight is excessively light, it will be difficult to obtain sufficient accuracy with the bow.

For most archers, too light means a holding weight of less than 25 pounds. Recurve bows with a peak draw weight of less than 35 pounds are seldom used by adults. Even a 50-pound compound bow with a 50 percent let-off will have a holding weight of 25 pounds. Therefore, bows that will prove too light are seldom encountered. The one possible exception is a compound bow with a draw weight of less than 50 pounds and a 50 percent let-off—or, in fact, any compound bow weight that, when combined with the specific let-off of the bow, would provide a holding weight of less than 25 pounds. My wife's Browning Cobra bow is an example of this type of problem. The bow has a peak draw weight of 35 pounds, so that with its 50 percent let-off the holding weight is only 17½ pounds. For her, this holding weight is borderline light, yet the draw weight is about all she can handle. She must exercise constant care to obtain a good

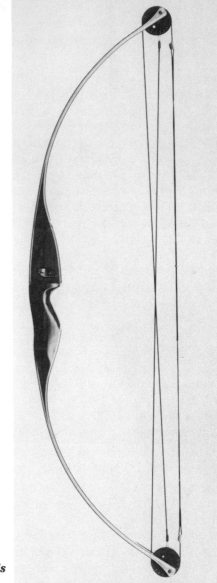

The Cobra compound bow is rugged and simple.

release. If her 35-pound bow had a 30-percent let-off, the holding weight would be 24½ pounds and prove, I'm sure, much more satisfactory.

The maximum draw weight on a recurve bow selected by a shooter should be that weight the archer can hold *comfortably* at full draw for at least twelve seconds. Many shooters, perhaps because of some macho image problem, select a bow weight that is too heavy. It is true that with constant practice one can learn to handle additional weight, but the initial struggle with a bow that is too heavy will also result in "learning" some very poor shooting habits that will prove extremely difficult to break. For a recurve bow, the maximum weight that can be drawn and held quite comfortably for at least twelve seconds at the store is the one to purchase and bring home.

If the archer can practice with his bow often enough and develop his shooting muscles to the point of being able to handle a heavier bow, then a second bow can be purchased. The lighter one can then be used each year when the archer first begins his practice, and as his muscles come back into tune, he can switch to the heavier bow.

A typical situation might be an archer who finds that when using a conventional recurve bow he can hold perhaps 45 pounds comfortably for fifteen seconds or so before his muscles begin to tremble or before his drawing hand starts to move involuntarily forward to lessen strain. Yet, this same archer may be able to flex a bow of 55 pounds readily, even though he cannot hold it for more than a second or two at full draw. By selecting a compound bow of 55 pounds, the archer will need only to overcome the resistance of the 55-pound peak draw weight for a fraction of a second. The bow reaches its peak weight before it has been fully drawn. The peak weight then quickly falls off to the holding weight as the bow reaches its maximum draw length. Depending upon the exact amount of mechanical gain built into the compound bow, the holding weight of a 55-pound bow might fall off to somewhere between 38½ pounds (30 percent let-off) and 27½ pounds (50 percent let-off).

Thus, the archer who was comfortable with no more than a 45-pound recurve bow can use a 55-pound compound bow and enjoy a holding weight notably lighter than his maximum capability. This will result in the archer being able to shoot an arrow at a higher velocity and, hence, flatter trajectory. The hunting archer will find it easier to hit with a bow that delivers flat trajectory combined with a comfortable holding weight—therefore, compound bows are without doubt the preferred bow type for hunting.

Because compound bows are usually built shorter than recurve bows, the archer will note an increase in finger pinch at full draw because of the tighter angle formed by the upper and lower half of the string. This additional finger pinch can become uncomfortable and interfere with accuracy on the heavier draw weights if the bow is excessively short. Therefore, select compound bows of moderate or long lengths rather than those that are extremely short.

Target archers who shoot a great many arrows in a single day often still prefer a long recurve bow over a compound. The reasons include: less finger pinch than a shorter compound bow, smoother draw and release and minimum recoil (bow jump). For the target archer, the extra arrow speed supplied by a compound offers little advantage. Accuracy and arrow speed are certainly not synonymous. But a smooth draw and release coupled with a minimum of bow jump can help obtain the slight increase in accuracy that could make the difference between winning a match and simply making a good showing. None of this is to say that a good target-grade compound cannot prove effective in competition.

Bows of Adjustable Weight   Adjustable-weight bows are becoming more common. Compound bows frequently offer such adjustments, and a few recurve bows are also available with this feature. The advantage to adjustable draw weight is that the shooter can begin at a light weight and, as muscle tone increases, can continue to use the same bow simply by turning the adjusting screws to a heavier weight. The cost of an adjustable bow is frequently considerably less than the price of two fixed-weight bows.

There is, however, some care required when adjusting peak draw weight. Adjustments are made by turning a screw that holds the limb to the handle. If these screws are not carefully turned exactly the same amount for each limb, however, the bow can become seriously out of tune, making top accuracy nearly impossible. On some bows, a set of reference graduations is placed on the handle riser, giving a reference to the weight of adjustment for which the bow is set. However, the calibrations are often crude and line up with nothing more specific than an unspecified point on the limb. It's easy to not know the weight of pull for which the bow has been set once the factory setting has been altered. To make matters worse, the reference marks placed on adjustable bows are often nothing more than decals, which quickly fall off when the bow is put into service. Bows such as the Bear Brown Bear eliminate this problem by casting in the reference mark on a plastic table and using the edge of the handle to align the reference marks.

If you purchase an adjustable bow that does not have adequate reference marks, place several indelible marks on each limb that will line up limb and riser at the factory adjustment. Then, when you have lost track of the bow adjustment, you can return the bow to its original setting and begin anew. The instructions packaged with a bow will usually indicate how many pounds of pull a single turn of the adjusting screws will produce, thus enabling you always to reference from the factory setting if it is well marked and if you have a record of the weight of pull for the factory adjustment.

Some adjustable bows require very careful tuning if the best accuracy is to be obtained. Improper tuning can overstress one limb, resulting in premature failure of that limb. Adjustable bows are best suited to the archer who is willing to learn the proper methods of adjustment and tuning and who will, when making any adjustments, proceed meticulously. For the archer who would rather not bother with all this, a fixed-weight-pull bow will prove more satisfactory.

If an adjustable-weight bow is to be selected, pick one that offers the heaviest weight range that includes your preferred peak draw weight. For instance, suppose you want a 55-pound peak draw weight, and in the model you like there are two offerings—one bow is adjustable from 45 to 60 pounds, the other from 55 to 70 pounds. By selecting the 55–70-pound bow for use at 55 pounds, you will be using the bow when the limbs are set for minimum stress. By using the 45–60-pound bow set at 55 pounds, you would be working it at near maximum stress. The bow working at the reduced stress level will provide longer life and prove less finicky to tune.

If you decide upon a compound bow, keep in mind that many such bows are often deliberately designed to stress materials to the maximum, because of the manufacturer's desire to obtain maximum velocity. Because of this, some compound bows have a very short useful life, often considerably less than 5,000 shots.

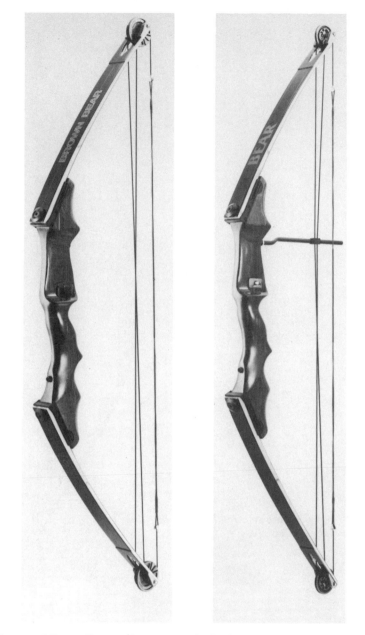

Brown Bear and Super Brown Bear are typical adjustable-weight bows. With these bows the archer can increase draw weight as he grows stronger.

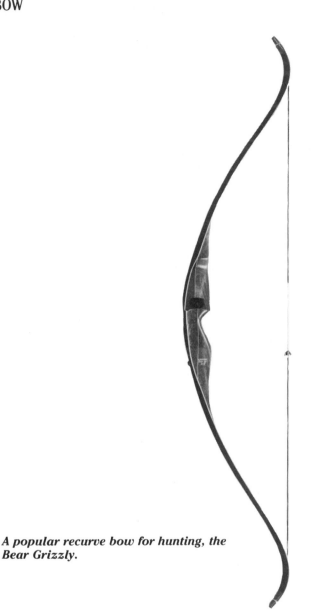

A popular recurve bow for hunting, the Bear Grizzly.

Selecting Arrows   The beginning archer is seldom in the position to know exactly what arrow length he will be using until he finds the anchor point that is best for him. The anchor point is that place at which the drawing hand is held for each shot. Usually, it is at some point along the chin bone, at least for beginning archers. Some archers may vary this anchor point considerably, starting with a 29-inch arrow and using arrows of 30, 31 and even 32 inches before the anchor point has been finalized. Recurve bows will accommodate all four arrow lengths, but most compound bows will handle only a 2-inch change in arrow length, because of their complex design. Thus, the purchaser of a compound bow must be certain of his draw length, or at least know it within an inch or so.

A good recurve bow is often desirable for the beginning archer. This is because most good recurves allow for a very wide range of arrow lengths to be used. It is possible on most recurve bows to use an arrow from 24 to 32 inches long.

Those who wish to start with a compound bow despite their lack of experience and, hence, uncertainty of their final draw length, would perhaps be wise to look to the experience of other archers. A beginning archer's muscle tone and style usually mean a limited draw length. As muscles become accustomed to bow shooting, almost all archers will find that their draw length has increased. Often they buy longer arrows (and perhaps a new compound to match their new draw length), then almost immediately discover that a different anchor point helps improve their accuracy. This usually means a still longer draw length. The lesson is that it pays to select a compound bow whose minimum draw length begins with the equivalent of what you suppose as a beginner to be your arrow length. This will allow some room to accommodate a longer draw length at a later date.

Of course, this suggestion must be modified if you use an anchor point that results in an obviously long length of pull. A shooter who begins with an anchor that places the bowstring on the tip of his nose will most likely never find an anchor point that results in a shorter draw length. At the other extreme would be the shooter who uses the top of the jawbone as an anchor point. Such a shooter is unlikely ever to relocate his anchor point to any position that would require a longer draw length.

Much can be gained by listening to experienced archers or salespersons who are open-minded and have no specific ax to grind. The selection of a bow to fit the specific physical requirements of the individual shooter rules out the possibility of many general statements on what length bow, what length pull, what peak weight (and let-off percentage) as well as what mass weight would be most suitable for any given shooter.

There are some basics that nevertheless do apply to all shooters. A bow that is too short will cause excessive finger pinch when held at full draw. A bow that is too long will be difficult to maneuver in heavy hunting cover. Compound bows with axle-to-axle lengths between 42 and 52 inches seem well suited to most archers. Recurve bows are best when they have a length from 57 to 71 inches. Too much peak weight will result in fatigue for the archer and thus a falling off in his accuracy. Too much holding weight will prove equally disastrous to accuracy. Excessive bow mass can be tiring during a long hunt. Heavy-mass target bows, however, will minimize recoil and vibrations and thus aid accuracy. New-model bows are best left to the experts or those who can afford to tinker with a number of bows. Established models often are the easiest for which to determine potential bow life, quality and accuracy. Long recurve bows offer the smoothest draw and release, hence are easy to shoot accurately. A highly stressed compound bow will provide maximum arrow speed but the shortest bow life. Center-shot bows are usually the least finicky about arrow spine weight. Bow hunters who forget that they may have to hold an arrow at full draw for twenty to sixty seconds before the best shot presents itself often purchase a bow that is too heavy. Target shooters have no great need for high-velocity arrows—high velocity does not mean accuracy.

These are truisms, but not all will apply to any specific archer. The most important step in selecting a bow is to get one that you can comfortably bring to a full draw and that you can easily hold at full draw for at least twelve seconds. The ability to hold the bow at full draw easily for a period greater than twelve seconds (up to a full sixty seconds) is far more beneficial than a few extra pounds of peak draw weight.

TUNING A BOW FOR ACCURACY 28

No bow, regardless of how well designed and built, can shoot well unless it is properly adjusted. If the brace height, nocking point, arrow rest, plunger adjustment, tiller adjustment and eccentric balance are not all in the best tune, then peak accuracy will be impossible.

Parts Needing Adjustment

Not every bow lends itself to each of the mentioned adjustments. Standard recurve bows, of course, allow no adjustment for tiller and eccentric cam balance—these are features of compound bows. Often, conventional bows are not equipped with plungers, hence no adjustment is possible. In that compound bows often incorporate almost all of the mentioned adjustments, the proper tuning of a bow will be discussed as it applies to the compound. The reader then can apply the pertaining points to a recurve bow.

Brace Height   On compound bows, the brace height—the distance from back edge of grip to nocking point—where applicable, is dependent upon the adjustment of bow weight, draw length and length of bowstring. On traditional recurve bows, the brace height is dependent upon length of bowstring alone. For all practical purposes, this adjustable distance is ignored on compound bows. Tiller adjustment, to be discussed later in this chapter, will give the proper brace height. On recurve bows, the brace height can be adjusted by twisting the bowstring before bracing the bow. Too much brace height will result in a loss of cast, while too little brace height will cause inaccuracy and excessive bow vibration and make it difficult to nock an arrow with long fletching. Always adjust brace height to the manufacturer's suggested length.

Nocking Point   The proper positioning of the nocking point is essential to accuracy; placing it is the first step in tuning a bow. Using a bow square, locate a point on the bowstring ⅜ inch above a straight line drawn from the arrow rest. This is done by attaching the bow square to the string and laying the bottom edge of its horizontal bar on the rest. Set the indicator at ⅜ inch and make a mark on the bowstring at the spot shown by the indicator. Then, with the bow

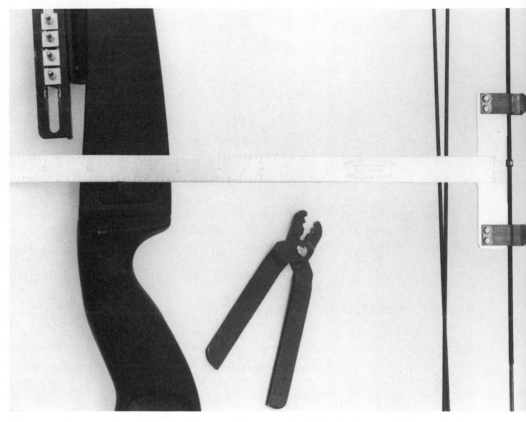

You can place a clamp-on nocking point precisely ³/₈ inch above right angles to the bowstring with the aid of a bow square and nocking-point pliers.

square removed, install an arrow with the nock centered over the mark. With the arrow nock so centered and the arrow shaft laying on the arrow rest, position a nocking point on the bowstring so that it just touches the top of the arrow nock. Do not move the arrow while securing the nocking point into place. Later, when testing the bow, the nocking point may require a slight adjustment upward or downward. However, in general, the arrow nock should never be more than ¼ inch above a point that is level with the arrow rest. Some shooters will place the nock exactly level with the arrow rest in the beginning. Knowing that this adjustment should never be any lower, they then have to concern themselves only with a possible upward adjustment not to exceed ¼ inch. On some bows, the nocking point is preset at the factory. The distance from the center of the pulley to the nocking point should be measured on such bows, to facilitate its duplication when it's time to replace the bowstring.

Arrow-Rest Plunger   An adjustable arrow-rest plunger is required for best handling of the next step in bow tuning, as it will be necessary to move the vertical support position of the arrow rest to the left or right. Of course, the careful shooter can adjust a fixed rest by placing shims between the bow and the rest to accomplish movement to the left (for right-handed bows). And he can reduce the thickness of the handle, creating a deeper sight window, to move the arrow rest to the right. However, such an undertaking can result in bow damage if the shooter does not proceed with caution. Bows that are predrilled allow easy installation of adjustable plungers. (Some bows come equipped with such a plunger as original equipment.) For bows that are not predrilled, I suggest that only a highly qualified person attempt the necessary drilling for plunger installation.

Frequently, the factory-supplied plungers are made of a polyester material that wears rather rapidly, requiring the rest to be adjusted frequently. It is best to replace these units with a more durable plunger, such as a Berger Button. Some hunters prefer not to use a plunger, finding them too fragile or too easily moved for hunting under rugged conditions.

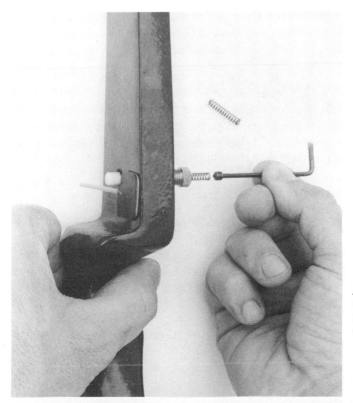

A cushion plunger arrow plate is spring-loaded to yield as an arrow leaves the bow. Spring loading is adjustable with the turn of an Allen wrench.

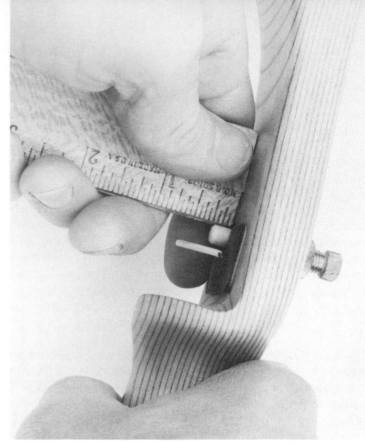

For best shooting results, the cush-ion plunger button should be set about ¼ inch away from the bow.

Making the Adjustments

Using Bare Arrows   To make necessary adjustments to the arrow rest and nocking point, the shooter will need a number of arrows from which all fletching has been removed. At least four arrows will be required; five would be ideal. A straw bale is needed for a backstop. Tightly woven targets may be less than ideal for this bare-shaft testing, since the "grain" built into such woven targets may affect the path of the arrow by causing it to follow the grain.

Using arrows of the correct length and spine, and with the target at the same level as your arrow, fire four or five shafts into the target from a distance of 6 feet. When the bow is properly tuned, the arrows will enter the target straight, with no tipping of the rear of the arrow either up or down, left or right. The accompanying drawings will clearly show what is meant. Since there are variations in bows, arrows and shooting styles, it is highly unlikely that your first shots will enter the target straight.

Because of the critical nature of the bare-arrow adjustments, it is vital that the target bale of straw be level and square with the arrow held at its full draw position. It is also essential, when inspecting the arrow's relative angle in the bale, that your eye level be the same height at which the arrow was released.

Arrows in the target that show the nock higher than the front end of the shaft indicate a need to lower the nocking point. And, of course, arrows that have the nocks lower than the front end of the shaft indicate a need to raise the nocking point. Arrows with nocks to the left of the front end of the shaft will require that the plunger to be moved to the left, while arrows with the nocks to the right require the plunger to be moved right. In other words, the nocking point should be moved in the direction in which you wish to move the nock. The plunger should be moved in the direction opposite to that you wish to move the nock. When the arrows are entering the target with the nocks level, both horizontally and vertically, the nocking point and plunger are properly adjusted.

Perfect form must be used when shooting bare-arrow tests. Poor releases, lack of follow-through and other errors will affect how the arrow strikes the target. Firing four or five arrows for each test will help eliminate false readings caused by faulty shooting. If four of five arrows are tipped in a specific direction, and the fifth indicates a different angle, you can safely eliminate the nonconforming arrow from your reading of the bow's need for adjustment. Random positioning of the nocks will indicate the need for extensive improvement in shooting form. Should this occur, delay fine tuning until your style has improved.

Using Fletched Arrows   After adjusting the bow for bare arrows, you must then test with fletched arrows. Shooting at the same 6-foot distance, and using the same level and square straw bale, fire four or five arrows into the

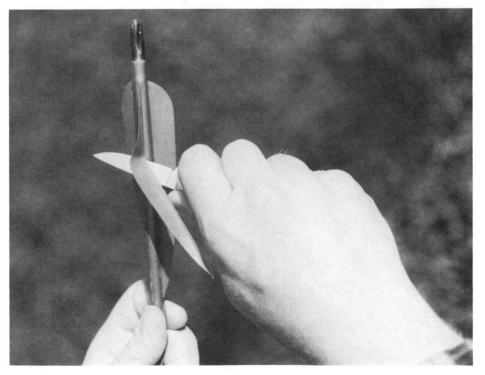

To tune a bow, you should first strip the fletching from one of your arrows to create a bare, tuning-sensitive shaft.

From a distance of 6 to 10 feet, shoot a bare shaft at a target to determine how it enters the bale.

Tail high—move nocking point down.

Tail left—move arrow-rest plate to left.

*A perfect bare-shaft entry—
the bow is now properly tuned.*

target. If any deflection is noted (very minor deflections can now be ignored), it indicates that the fletching is hitting either the cables or the bow handle. To determine the cause of interference, apply a coating of soft, greasy lipstick to the fletching and shoot four or five more arrows. (You need not coat the cock feather, as it cannot possibly contact the bow or cables.) Either the cables or bow handle will then have a smear of lipstick at the point(s) of interference after shooting.

The correction of this problem of cable or bow contact has several solutions. The first to be tried should be rotating the nocking point of the arrow to position the fletching so as to avoid contact with bow or cable. If contact with the cable is still made, a cable guard may eliminate the problem. Smaller fletching may, however, be the only solution.

If a reduction in fletching size results in insufficient arrow spin and the associated arrow planing when shooting over normal ranges, it may be necessary to use a four- rather than a three-vane fletch. A four-vane fletch will allow for a substantial reduction in vane size while affording sufficient total vane surface to ensure adequate arrow rotation.

Use fletching with the minimum amount of spiral required to prevent arrow planing. Excessive spiral will result in increased arrow spin, which will reduce velocity. The use of no more spiral than necessary to ensure true flight will result in the highest possible arrow velocity.

Other Adjustments   Please keep in mind that any tiller adjustment or any adjustment to draw weight will cause a change in bare-arrow performance. Increasing the bow's draw weight will cause the nocks to be positioned to the left, while decreasing the draw weight will cause nocks to be positioned to the right. Often, a substantial increase in a bow's draw weight, perhaps 7 to 10 pounds, will require a change in arrow spine to provide optimum accuracy. And, of course, a change in arrow spine will cause a change in bare-arrow test results.

If you are unable to adjust the plunger to provide satisfactory bare-arrow test results, with an adjustable bow you can resort to a bow-weight adjustment to provide a well-tuned bow. If you wish to use the bow at a specific draw weight, you may need to use a different arrow spine if the bare-arrow test results cannot be adjusted to perfection. Shooters whose bows are not equipped with a plunger often use draw-weight adjustments to correct for left and right deflection during bare-arrow testing.

Increasing Your Range   Once you are obtaining perfect results at 6 feet, move back to 25 feet and repeat your test with fletched arrows. Some slight additional adjustment of plunger and nocking point may be required. After the proper nocking point has been accurately established, use a bow square to determine its exact location; record this information. The exact plunger location can be measured from the vertical surface of the bow to the end of the plunger's face with a vernier. Record this measurement also. Thereafter, so long as string length, tiller adjustment (or brace height on recurve bows) and bow draw weight

Shot at a distance of 25 feet, these feathered arrows exhibit no tip in any direction and are evidence of a properly tuned bow.

remain unchanged, and assuming you use the same type of arrow rest, these adjustments will remain constant. Thus, when changing bowstrings, you will know exactly where to locate the nocking point, and as the arrow-rest plunger wears, you will know to what length it needs to be adjusted.

The arrow-rest plunger may wear with a groove being cut into its face. This groove should be flattened with a file from time to time, and the plunger readjusted to the proper length. Also, arrow rests can wear down. When any deterioration in accuracy is noted, replace the arrow rest, being careful to locate the new one exactly in the same place as the original.

Always repeat the bare-arrow test when replacing or adjusting nocking points, arrow rests or plungers. Then double-check with fletched arrows at 6-foot and 25-foot ranges.

If you make any draw-weight or draw-length adjustments to a bow, follow the manufacturer's instructions exactly. It is wise to mark, with chalk or crayon, the starting point before actually turning any bolts or screws. In that it is easy to lose track of adjustments, proceed with the utmost care. Make careful notes of each adjustment relating to your "zero" reference marks.

Tiller Adjustment   Usually, most bow-tiller adjustments are precisely set by the manufacturer. Therefore, these factory adjustments should be carefully recorded before attempting any change in draw weight or replacement of cable or string. To ensure that this information is recorded accurately, it is best to measure the tiller adjustment prior to putting a new bow to its first use. Wear and tear on limbs, cables and strings can cause a change in tiller adjustment. Also, even the most carefully executed draw-weight adjustment may cause a change in tiller adjustment. Therefore, whenever anything has occurred that may have resulted in a tiller-adjustment change, measure the tiller on both limbs and adjust according to your records of the original factory adjustment.

Tiller length is measured from the face of the bow at the junction of the handle and limb to the bowstring. In that a change in the profile of the measuring instrument could cause a false reading, it makes sense to keep a single measuring instrument with your archery tackle, thus ensuring the accuracy of all future measurements.

It is important that the eccentric cams of all compound bows be carefully balanced. The top and bottom pulleys must roll over precisely at the same time. While this adjustment is factory set, any relocation of the nocking point or variation in the shooter's method of holding the string may make some additional adjustment necessary. If the cams do not roll over evenly, the shooter will often feel a rocking motion in the limbs. Uneven adjustment can severely strain one or both limbs and result in premature bow failure. Accuracy will also suffer if the pulleys do not roll over simultaneously.

After making any adjustments to the rollers (according to the manufacturer's instructions), you will need to double-check the tiller adjustment. As a general rule, the lower limb of a bow should have a tiller adjustment from ⅛ inch less to exactly the same as the upper limb.

Some compound bows have the capacity to alter the amount of let-off occurring at full draw. This usually involves a change in pulleys or the use of alternate pulley axle holes and requires that the bow be completely relaxed. Hence, weight of draw, tiller adjustment and fine tuning of bow must be made after any such change. Such drastic bow adjustment and preliminary tuning should be attempted only by highly experienced persons. But the actual shooter must accomplish the final tuning of the bow.

Shooting a bow that has no provisions for tuning other than the nocking point location can be likened to the use of a lever-action rifle. Accuracy can range from rather poor to quite acceptable. But regardless of the degree of accuracy, the shooter will be unable to effect any noticeable improvement. The use of an adjustable bow is similar to the use of a bolt-action rifle. The adjustable bow, like the bolt-action rifle, enables the shooter to accomplish all the necessary tuning adjustments required to obtain the best possible accuracy within the capabilities of the bow and arrows used.

SELECTING ARROWS 29

When an archer begins shooting, he will normally purchase arrows of the correct spine for the bow to be used. This is relatively easy to do, since arrow packages are generally marked with the peak bow weight for which they are best suited. However, the length of the arrow first chosen is often somewhat shorter than the archer eventually finds is best. For this reason, the beginning archer is well advised not to purchase any more arrows than are absolutely needed for his immediate shooting.

Additionally, a specific bow, when combined with a specific shooting style, may not be best served with arrows matched to the peak draw weight of the bow. An arrow spine somewhat lighter or notably heavier may well provide the best accuracy. A shooter capable of grouping six arrows consistently into 6 inches at 40 yards or more, can quickly tell if a particular arrow spine is unsatisfactory. When groups of 8 to 10 inches are the best he can obtain, it will be obvious that something is wrong. Then it is simply a matter of trying heavier-spined arrows. If accuracy improves, the archer knows he now has the right arrow spine for his bow and shooting style. If accuracy decreases even further, a lighter-spined arrow must be tried.

Proper Length of Arrows   Selection of arrow length is vital. Excessive length means excessive weight, hence a comparatively poorer trajectory. Excessive shortness results in poor accuracy, as the shooter strives to use an anchor point that is less than ideal. Also too short a length with hunting arrows can result in the blade of the arrow severely cutting the archer's knuckles when the bow is brought to full draw.

When the archer has his bow at full draw, there should be ¾ to 1 inch of space between the hunting head and his hand, as measured at the shortest distance from head to fingers. Anything less and, sooner or later, a nasty wound will be self-inflicted.

Target arrows can be shorter. Some shooters choose to use an arrow length that brings the rearmost edge of the target point to within ⅛ inch of the bow when the arrow is fully drawn. If the same bow is used for hunting and target, it is best to use the same length of shaft for both types of shooting. When the hunting head and the target point weigh nearly the same, and the shafts used

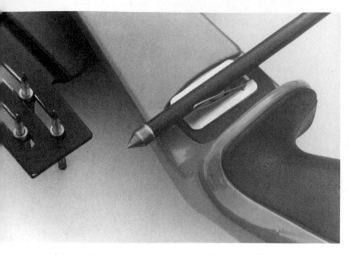

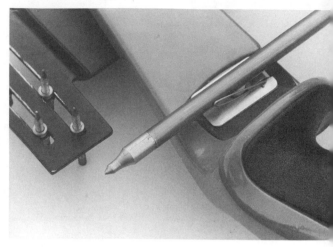

A target arrow is the proper length when the end of the shaft is flush with the edge of the bow.

A field arrow is the proper length when about ¾ inch of the arrow extends past the edge.

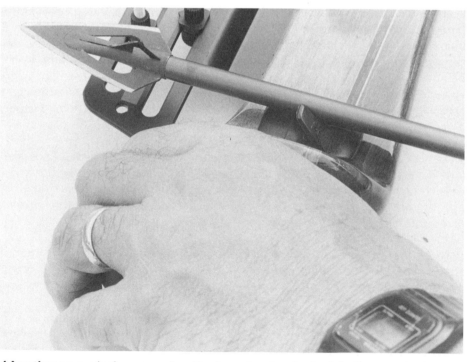

A hunting arrow is the proper length when about an inch of shaft protrudes beyond the edge of the bow, leaving ample room so bow or hand can't contact the broadhead.

are identical, the trajectory of both target and hunting arrow will be identical. Thus, the archer will become quite familiar with his hunting arrow performance during practice sessions. This will also allow for the same sight settings to be used for target and hunting.

Arrow Spines   Arrows to be used with compound bows frequently need to be spined differently than arrows used with conventional recurve bows. The amount of let-off built into the compound bow's pulley system can be a notable factor in the spine requirement of the arrow. Also, the actual length of the arrow affects the stiffness required. The longer an arrow, the more stiffness required for a given peak draw weight.

The accompanying table shows the comparative bow weight ranges for recurves, compounds with 30 percent let-off and compounds with 50 percent let-off, matched to the spine weight as normally expressed on the arrow packages as "for use with bows of x pounds to x pounds." If the arrow packaging clearly states "for use with compound bows of x pounds to x pounds," then select the spine matched to your compound bow weight, assuming a 50 percent let-off.

By using the table, you will be selecting the lightest possible arrow that is likely to perform well. By using the lightest possible arrow, you will attain the highest arrow velocity and, hence, the flattest trajectory. If the arrow spine shown does not shoot well when combined with your bow and shooting style, invariably the next heavier spine will be correct.

Package markings always take into consideration the length of the arrow. Thus, 28-inch arrows marked for 50- to 60-pound bows will have a lighter spine than 31-inch arrows marked for 50- to 60-pound bows. Be concerned only with selecting the right arrow length and then matching the spine weight indicated to your bow, according to the weights shown in the accompanying spine chart.

The exception to all the foregoing is when extremely heavy hunting heads are used. In this case, it is suggested that the arrows' spine stiffness be increased slightly.

Fletching   Two additional factors to be considered when selecting arrows are the size of the fletching and the material of which the arrows are made. Overly small fletching will not impart the necessary spin to stabilize the arrow, while fletching that is too large will create excessive drag that will rapidly slow down an arrow in flight, giving it poor trajectory.

In general, light arrows can be used with fletching of a minimum size. Target arrows with their light points require less fletching than hunting arrows with their heavy and often wide heads. Be careful when using compound bows, since larger fletching could strike the cable when the arrow is released, causing inaccuracy. For this reason, some archers prefer to use an arrow with four smaller fletches rather than three larger ones.

The nock on the arrow should fit the serving on the bowstring closely. It should take only a minimum amount of effort to snap the nock on or off the serving. Too loose or too tight a fit can reduce accuracy.

A good way to determine the length of arrow that may best suit you, assuming

Depending on weight and use, arrows are fletched in different sizes.

you anchor your thumb under your jawbone and rest the string on the tip of your nose, is as follows: Determine your height in inches, then divide this figure by 2.42. Round the result to the nearest full inch. This measurement will be the correct arrow length in inches (from bottom of nock groove to the back edge of the point). Some minor change will be called for, depending upon your exact style of shooting, but this arrow length will be a good starting point. The math of this system has been done in the accompanying table. Allow an extra ¾ to 1 inch of length for hunting arrows.

Different Materials Used for Arrows   The material used for the construction of arrows may be wood (Port Orford cedar), fiberglass, fiberglass and graphite combined or aluminum. Good aluminum arrows will outlast and outshoot all others, but poor aluminum arrows will not be as good a buy as the very best wooden arrows. It pays to purchase the very finest arrows unless you know beforehand that they will see only limited use.

The very best aluminum arrows are made using Easton X-7 shafts. The next grade down is the Easton XX75 shaft, which will prove satisfactory if arrows will not see extensive use. There is a difference between X-7 target shafts and X-7 hunting shafts. The target-grade shafts receive an extra straightening step in production and, therefore, will prove slightly more accurate from a technical standpoint. However, the X-7 hunting shafts are fully capable of being made into arrows that will group into 6 inches at 50 yards and are somewhat less expensive than the target grade. I continue to find the Bear Metric Magnum and Bear Easton X-7 to be among the finest hunting and target arrows available to the archer.

Turkey feathers have been the traditional material for fletching, but plastic vanes are a great improvement. Although turkey feathers will spin an arrow somewhat easier than the plastic vanes, the latter are more durable, do not require constant steaming and work when wet. Any target shooter or hunter who has ever attempted a shot in the rain knows how useless turkey feathers can be when they are wet. Plastic vanes may require slightly more surface area to get the job done, but in every other way they are superior to turkey feathers.

Thus the best and, in the long run, the least expensive arrow is one of the correct length made with Easton X-7 or XX75 shafts and having plastic vanes. Ideally, a snap-on nock with a raised rib will be used so that the arrow can be nocked properly without looking at it.

No rifle, shotgun or handgun shooter would deliberately select inferior ammunition except for the most unimportant shooting. So it should be with the archer. Good arrows are a must for good accuracy.

SPINE CHART
(Weights shown are peak draw weights)

Recurve Bows Draw wt. at length of pull	Compound Bows		Arrow spine required*
	With 30% let-off	With 50% let-off	
35-39 lbs.	41-46 lbs.	47-52 lbs.	35-39 lbs. or 30-40 lbs.
40-44 lbs.	47-52 lbs.	53-59 lbs.	40-44 lbs. or 40-50 lbs.
45-49 lbs.	53-58 lbs.	60-66 lbs.	45-49 lbs. or 40-50 lbs.
50-54 lbs.	59-64 lbs.	67-72 lbs.	50-54 lbs. or 50-60 lbs.
55-59 lbs.	65-70 lbs.	73-79 lbs.	55-59 lbs. or 50-60 lbs.
60-64 lbs.	71-76 lbs.	80-86 lbs.	60-64 lbs. or 60-70 lbs.
65-70 lbs.	77-82 lbs.	87-93 lbs.	65-70 lbs. or 60-70 lbs.

*First listing is ideal weight.

ARROW LENGTH TABLE

Shooter height (in inches)	Approx. Correct Arrow Length (in inches)	Shooter height (in inches)	Approx. Correct Arrow Length (in inches)
60	25	69	29
61	25	70	29
62	26	71	29
63	26	72	30
64	26	73	30
65	27	74	31
66	27	75	31
67	28	76	31
68	28	77	32

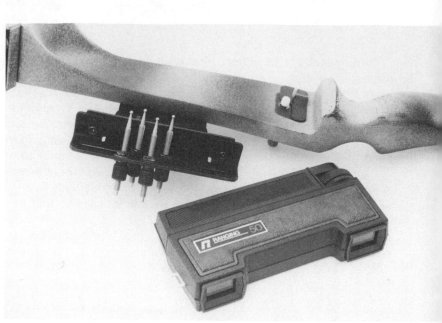

A bowsight plus a good-quality archery rangefinder combine to make a deadly accurate shooting setup.

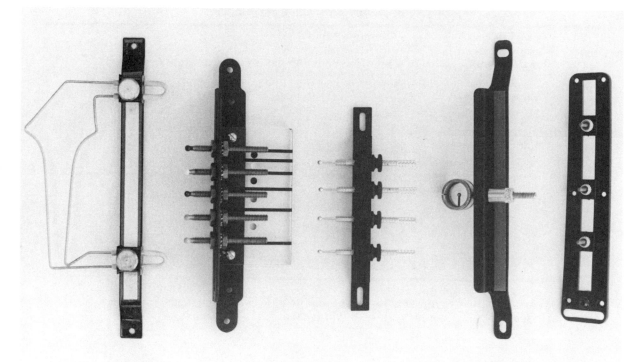

Various kinds of bowsights are available today. A few of the more popular types are (left to right): a two-wire rangefinder sight meant to bracket a broadside deer; a five-pin sight with depth-of-body rangefinding bars for deer hunting; a simple four-pin sight; a single-pin sight that slides for various distances; and a three-pin model which insets in the face of the bow.

IMPORTANT ARCHERY ACCESSORIES

30

A bow and some arrows are basics for the archer. However, in order to attain any notable degree of proficiency, the shooter needs a number of other accessories—some would be better termed essentials. The day of the instinctive shooter equipped only with a bare bow and a back quiver has passed.

Sights

Just as the rifle or pistol hunter requires sights, so does the archer. No longer can one justify instinctive shooting in which no sights of any type are used. Yes, a few very fine instinctive archers have gained world fame. But these gentlemen were and are exceptional individuals, and their performance with bare bows cannot be equated to the likely performance of most archers. Also, these people gained their reputations in days when a good bow sight was nonexistent. When these shooters were excelling with their instinctive methods, bow sights were not much more than a strip of heavy tape holding some hatpins to the bow.

A few of the most notable instinctive archers continue their careers even today. I suspect, however, that today's archers, who are beginning their careers with good-quality bow sights, will equal and surpass the accomplishments of the old masters and that today's equipment will result in a great many highly skilled shooters, as opposed to the limited few from the old bare-bow school.

These old shooters aimed by aligning the arrow tip (front sight) with the eye (rear sight) and placing the arrow tip at some point well below to well above the target, depending upon the range. Target shooters using a bare-bow technique often would place a stake in the ground at some distance in front of the target in order to have a positive reference point with which to align the arrow tip. Hunters, of course, did not have this option. Today's shooters need not resort to such crude methods. Modern sights are available to fit almost any bow.

Using Pins   The modern bow sight is a series of sturdy pins adjustable for both windage and elevation. The tips of the pins are the front beads of the sighting system. The eye is the rear sight, much as in shotgun shooting. To align a bow sight properly, the pin is brought into horizontal alignment with the bowstring in reference to the aiming eye. The pin is then held on the target for precise aiming. Because of the different aiming points required to compensate for the arrow's rather curved trajectory, a series of pins is generally used, with four or five pins being the number most often encountered. One pin might be adjusted for 20 yards, while each succeeding pin might be adjusted for 25, 30, 35 and 40 yards.

Bow sights are, in my opinion, the most essential of all archery accessories. One cannot hope to attain a high level of skill with a sightless bow any more

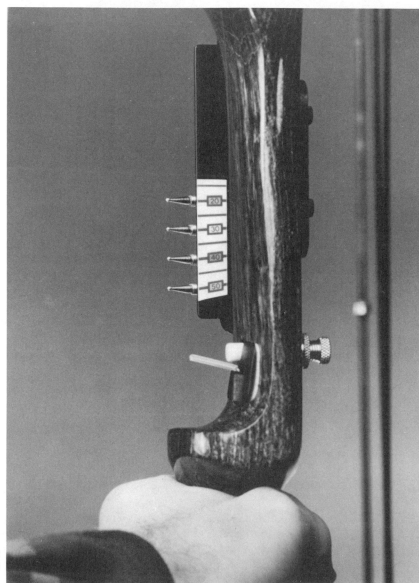

The pins on a bowsight are usually set for even ranges like 20, 30, 40, and 50 yards.

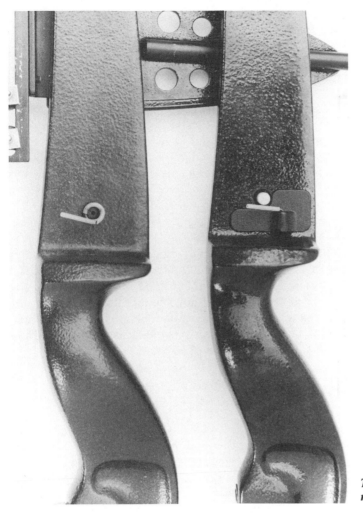

Two popular arrow rests are the springy rest (left) and plunger/flipper combo.

than one would expect a rifleman to do well with a sightless rifle. When selecting a bow sight, it is important to purchase a unit that is rugged. It is equally important to have a sight that offers sufficient pins to cover all likely ranges. In that a change of 5 yards in range can drastically alter the point of impact of an arrow, a sight that offers enough pins to cover each 5-yard increment from 20 to 40 yards is in order. That means five pins. The exceptional archer who can group his arrows into a 6-inch circle at greater ranges may require an additional pin for 45 and perhaps even 50 yards.

Too many pins can, however, become confusing. I use a maximum of five pins even when shots to 50 yards will be taken. I simply set the first pin for 22 yards and each additional pin for another 7 yards of range. I thus wind up with pin selectors for 22, 29, 36, 43 and 50 yards.

Pins should be easily adjusted for elevation without disturbing the windage setting and vice versa. Additionally, sights that incorporate a toothed or threaded track allow easier adjustments, since the original elevation setting will not be easily lost as the lock is loosened.

Some sights incorporate a shield to prevent damage to the pins should the bow be dropped. However, in that such a shield protects the pins from only one direction, its value is much more limited than one might first assume.

Range Finders   Some sights include built-in or accessory range finders color coded to the sight pins. These range finders have a lot of initial appeal, since it is quite easy to misjudge the distance of a deer or other animal by 4 to 10 yards. Knowing that a range estimate error of only 5 to 7 yards can create a miss, hunting archers are quick to purchase range finders.

Regrettably, most range finders invariably base their distance estimates on an assumed deer belly-to-back height of 18 inches. The likelihood of encountering such an exact specimen in the field would be pure chance. Because deer bodies vary in size, most being notably smaller than 18 inches, the error in range estimation when using most range finders is as great, if not greater, than the judgment of most shooters. However, optical range finders that use a focusing screen are quite accurate. But these are not bow mounted and therefore seldom prove practical for the bow hunter, who usually has at least one hand if not both busy with bow holding, arrow nocking and so on.

Other Accessories

Carrying Cases   A means to carry arrows safely is the next most important archery requirement. For target shooting, any good belt or back quiver will prove useful. The belt quiver is the easiest to use and by far the most popular with target shooters. But the hunter will need a good bow quiver capable of holding four to six arrows. Larger capacity may be desired on extended wilderness hunts.

A bow quiver must be designed with sufficient spacing between arrows to prevent them from bumping into one another as the bow is shot. Additionally, selection should be limited to those models that completely cover the hunting tip. Exposed heads can result in serious self-inflicted injury. And the razor-sharp hunting heads can become quickly dulled if exposed to contact with brush and other obstacles.

Back quivers, popular years ago, should never be used with hunting arrows. They are noisy when arrows move against one another, hard to use without spooking game and *dangerous*. Sometime back I wrote about an accident that I witnessed when a friend, drawing a hunting arrow from his back quiver, pulled along a second arrow when the head of the first hung up on the other's blades. The second arrow fell free as it cleared the quiver, inflicting a serious wound in my friend's calf. That particular writeup has resulted in a half-dozen archers telling me of similar incidents that occurred to them. Obviously, such accidents are not rare.

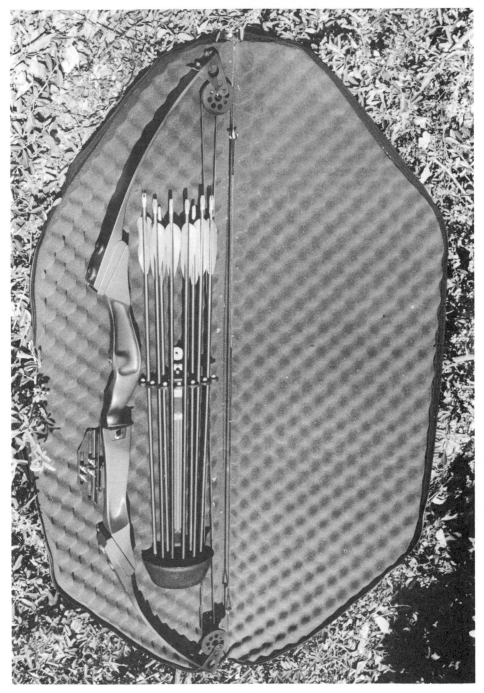

A foam-padded case protects a bow from impact, moisture, and heat.

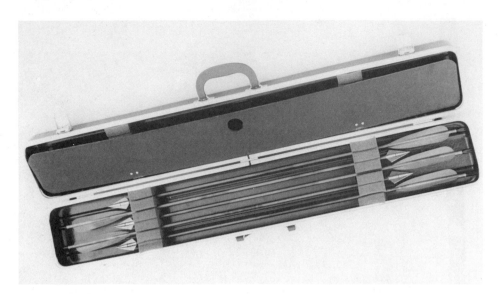

Commercial arrow cases keep shafts in tip-top shooting condition.

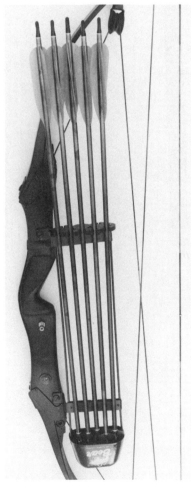

A bow quiver holds arrows snugly and compactly within easy reach for quick shots.

A hip quiver is popular because it leaves a bow light and maneuverable.

Old-style shoulder quivers are still the choice of some tradition-minded archers.

Bow quivers such as those made by Bear and Browning work well, are easy to use, are quiet and completely shield the arrowheads from any accidental contact with brush or flesh. These quivers will fit most bows equipped with accessory bushings. They often include a great deal of extra hardware, allowing the unit to be mounted to almost any bow.

Arm Guards and Gloves

Of course, a good arm guard and archer's glove are required. The plastic ones, so common, are poor choices because they quickly wear out, crack or otherwise deteriorate. Select the thickest leather units you can find. They cost a bit more than plastic, but they will last a long, long time.

Spare Parts

The archer will need to include a number of items in his kit to keep his bow and his arrows performing well. Bowstrings can wear rapidly, and fletching has a way of falling off. Arrow nocks and tips are frequently damaged. In addition, arrow rests and plungers are noted for quitting at just the wrong moment. Therefore, extra strings, fletching, fletching cement, arrow nocks, nock cement, arrow rests, a plunger and a few spare nocking points should be included in the archer's maintenance kit.

Miscellaneous Extras

Depending upon the types of bow shooting the archer participates in, other accessories will be required or prove useful as time goes on. For instance, a bow square can be very beneficial in helping to place the nocking point on the string exactly. Or a compound bow user may find that a bow relaxer is required to change a string or to do maintenance work on certain makes and models of bows. Recurve bow users who frequently string and unstring their bows will find a bow stringer essential to prevent twisted bow limbs.

The shooter should be aware, however, that some of the accessories sold do nothing more than take advantage of wishful thinking. There are, for instance, bowstring silencers that do no more than add weight to the bowstring. And I have yet to find a cable silencer that produced any kind of results without wearing out so quickly as to be a real challenge to keep up with replacements.

While not necessary, some accessories, such as a bow sling, can be beneficial to the target shooter and hunter alike. And mechanical releases can help shooter accuracy greatly. I have never understood why some states outlaw their use for hunting. I should think that enhancing accuracy and preventing cripples would be the indirect goal of all lawmaking efforts.

Finally, a lot of fun can be had with a fishing arrow and reel. Where legal, the hunting of carp or other nongame species with a bow can provide some real "fishing" thrills. A 20-pound carp pulling on the bow line is not easily bested. Bow, shooter and carp can wind up equally wet. And ridding a stream of lamprey eels will surely improve both your shooting and the fishing in general.

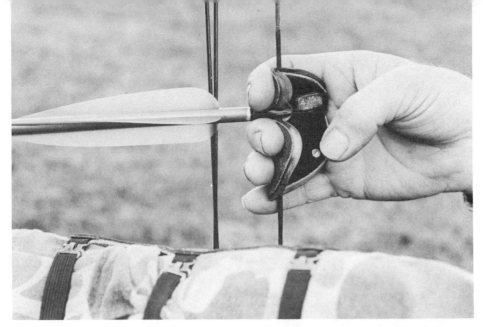

A finger tab is popular with both hunters and target buffs because it adequately protects the fingers and also yields a very smooth bowstring release.

An armguard protects the forearm from painful string slap and also holds down a baggy shirtsleeve for better accuracy.

Mechanical bowstring releases are incredibly accurate and enjoy widespread popularity among both hunters and target enthusiasts.

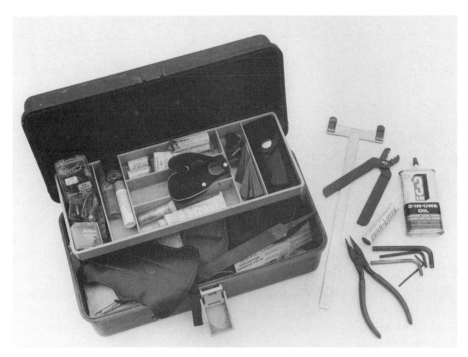

A medium-sized fishing-tackle box is an idea place to store various bow-shooting accessories.

A bow-fishing reel and arrow for taking non-game species such as carp.

31 TARGET SHOOTING

Preliminary Checks

Before the first arrow is released, each shooting session with a bow should begin with a safety check. A bow that fractures or relaxes because of a broken string or cable, or an arrow that fractures, can inflict painful wounds on the shooter. Therefore, a safety check makes good sense and should be performed routinely.

The Bow and Its Components The bow itself should be inspected first. Look for worn, loose, broken or otherwise deteriorated hardware and fittings. These include string, cables, pulleys, axles, snap rings, teardrop hooks and cams. Do not use any bow until all parts have been restored to A-1 condition, if any prove less than so during the inspection. Next, inspect the limbs and the handle riser for fractures, cracks, splits, lamination separations and so on. All set screws must be tight. When checking set screws, be sure not to apply undue torque, thereby stripping the threads of aluminum or plastic pulleys and fittings.

When checking bow cables, start at the junction of string and cable and carefully follow the cable into the pulley and out the other side. Also, flex the bow so as to bring into view portions of cable that might otherwise go unnoticed. Be sure to follow the cable for its entire length, from string juncture to anchor point.

The bowstring should receive close scrutiny, as it is the portion of the bow that most easily deteriorates. Replace the bowstring as soon as any fraying is noted, certainly no later than discovering the first broken thread.

Draw the bow several times, and try to note any limb rocking, squeaks, twisting, wobble in the cams and so on. Take any corrective measures required.

Of course, the bow should be completely relaxed before you attempt any kind of maintenance. The exception is the replacement of bowstrings on bows equipped with dual teardrop hooks at the cable ends. With these, a replacement bowstring can be installed by slightly flexing the bow, using the old string and having an assistant slip a new bowstring over the empty hooks on each end. Then relax the bow and again flex it, this time using the new string. Have an assistant remove the old string.

A bowstring that breaks when the bow is being used can cause limbs to shatter and/or serious personal injury. Therefore, it makes good sense to replace any bowstring as soon as it begins to show the first signs of wear.

The Arrows   Finally, you should inspect each arrow. Look for cracked, broken or loose nocks. A nock that fails at the moment of release can cause bow damage, because if the arrow is not properly sent on its way, you will in effect be dry-firing the bow. Also, look for any damaged or loose fletching. Check all tips for damage or looseness. Each shaft should be carefully inspected for cracks, nicks, splits, fractures, bends or dents. Any one of these conditions could result in an arrow that ruptures upon release. The potential of serious injury to a shooter or a bystander is indeed great when an arrow disintegrates into two or more pieces as it is released.

Shooting

Proper Stance   Having completed the safety inspection, the shooter will be ready to begin. First, proper stance must be assumed. The target is "addressed" by placing the feet at right angles to the target with a comfortable and easy spacing. Body weight should be equally distributed between both feet. A line drawn across the tips of the toes should, if extended, come to rest on the target center.

Holding the bow horizontally, with it facing the target, lay an arrow across the arrow rest and nock it just below the nocking point, sliding it up against that point. The center of the index finger's first joint should be placed on the string just above the arrow nock. The middle and fourth finger should be placed below the arrow nock, with the string running across the first joint. The cock feather should be positioned away from the bow to prevent fletching from striking cable or bow.

The shooting fingers should be protected by a well-fitting archer's glove made of good leather. If the fingers are properly placed on the bow, the string will turn slightly as the bow is drawn, so that the right side moves toward the shooter, preventing any tendency of the arrow to walk off the arrow rest. If the arrow tends to come off the rest, it is an indication that too much finger is wrapped around the bowstring, causing the right side of the string to twist toward the front of the bow as it is drawn. Left-handed shooters will twist the string in the opposite direction.

Applying an inch or so of draw, swing the bow into a vertical position, with the left arm pointed directly at the target. Your head will be turned to face the target. As the left arm is extended, begin to draw the arrow. The left arm should be extended so that any flexing of the elbow would create a horizontal movement of the forearm. If the elbow is turned so that a natural flex would result in vertical movement of the forearm, the bowstring will hit the upper forearm, resulting in poor accuracy (not to mention rapid wear of the arm guard or a painful bruise).

Maintaining Proper Technique   As the bow is brought to a full draw and held there, a number of things become important. One is that the drawing

TARGET SHOOTING

1. Address the target by placing the feet at right angles to it, comfortably spread, weight equally distributed between both feet.

2. Hold the bow horizontally, facing the target, and lay an arrow across the arrow rest. Nock it just below the nocking point and slide it against the point.

3. Drawing the bow an inch or so, swing it into the vertical position. As the left arm is extended, begin to draw the arrow.

4. Bring the bow to full draw and hold it there. This photo shows one kind of anchor point, with the bowstring at the side of the nose and the tip of the index finger in the corner of the mouth.

5. Holding the bow at full draw, visually place the tip of the front sight on the target. The proper sight picture is to see the bead either to the left or to the right of the string.

6. The proper grip should be extremely relaxed, the bow supported by pressure against the web of the hand and the base of the thumb. The index finger should be curved around the bow and pressed lightly against the thumbtip.

7. Holding before the release. With the bow held at full draw, no strain must be exerted to hold it in position, otherwise the sight cannot be kept in alignment.

8. Release the arrow by relaxing the fingers of the drawing hand and allowing the tension of the bow to uncurl them completely. At the same time, maintain the bow in position with the left arm. Keep that position—that is, follow through—until the arrow strikes the target.

hand must be anchored into the same position for each shot. If it is not, the relationship of the eye and the sight will vary, causing the point of arrow impact to change with each change in anchor position. The anchor spot may be altered as the shooter gains experience.

If you are not satisfied with the results of a specific anchor point, do a bit of experimenting. The anchor that I find best suited to both target and hunting is to lock the inside of the thumb joint on the corner of the jawbone. This position allows most shooters to use two double checks as they hold the bow at full draw. The first check is the bowstring resting firmly on the tip (never on the side) of the nose; the second is the placement of the tip of index finger into the corner of the mouth. If the fingertip cannot be "tasted" in the corner of the mouth at any point during aiming, the shooter will know that he has allowed his shooting hand to creep forward. When this happens, a poor shot will always result.

With the bow at full draw, the sights must be aligned properly. As in shotgun shooting, the shooting eye is the rear sight. Thus, it is essential that the bow be supported, positioned and held identically for each shot. Obviously, the head also must be turned and the anchor placed identically for each shot. An anchor that offers some extra checks, such as the one described, is preferred.

Aim   Proper aiming calls for the placement of the front-sight tip (bead) on the target. The proper sight picture is to see the bead either to the left or to the right of the string.

The holding of the bow at full draw, while the sight is aligned and held steadily on the target, must be accomplished without any movement of the bow arm. If you allow the arm to move backward, even slightly, from its normal position, inaccuracy will result. Ditto with the drawing hand. If it moves, even just a tad, the shot will not produce the desired results.

Grip   The grip on the bow is really not a grip at all. The bow is properly supported by the pressure of its pushing against the web of the hand and the base of the thumb where it approaches the wrist. The index finger should merely be curved around the bow and pressed lightly against the tip of the thumb. The remaining fingers do nothing to grip the bow. Bows that are held by the fingers simply will not produce the desired accuracy.

The proper bow "grip" is so relaxed that on occasion a good tournament archer's bow will fall to the ground when the shot is made, unless the bow is attached to the wrist with a sling. This occurs when the archer forgets to keep the index fingertip against the tip of the thumb. A great many less-than-good archers are guilty of trying to strangle the bow within their grip. Less is always best with respect to bow grip.

With the bow properly held at full draw, and the sight aligned on the target, the successful archer places no undue strain on the muscles used to hold the bow in position. Any strain will make it extremely difficult to keep the sight in alignment. Those who choose a bow with a holding weight beyond their capability will rapidly become aware of this problem.

Release and Follow-Through   Everything being done properly and with the sight steady on the bull's-eye, the archer must now execute a perfect release. This is accomplished by relaxing the drawing hand's fingers and allowing the tension of the bow to uncurl them quickly, thus releasing the string from the shooter's grip. While doing this, you must maintain the bow arm position and the pulling arm's tension. If one arm or the other stops working, even slightly, the shot will be a poor one. The release must be executed smoothly.

As the arrow is released, it is essential that the archer follow through properly. Correct follow-through demands that the bow arm maintain its position. Do not allow it to drop as the arrow is released. The drawing hand, because of the tension of holding the string at draw length, will move rearward to some extent upon the release. Try to keep this movement to a minimum without placing undue emphasis on your control. The follow-through should be held until the arrow strikes its target. This will prevent premature movement. Your eye should remain on the target and lose sight of the arrow completely.

Practice   That's all there is to it. A lot of practice will reduce each movement to rote. But do continue to think each shot through. If you nock, draw, aim, release and follow through as described, superb accuracy will come with sufficient practice that allows for ample muscle development and mental coordination. Make no mistake about it, even light target bows demand that muscles be kept in tune. Until the bow can be held at full draw comfortably with the sight rock-steady on the bull's-eye, you will be unable to shoot in the best possible fashion.

Although in actual field situations, the hunter usually has to hold his bow at full draw for 3 to 10 seconds, he should practice holding longer and checking on his anchor points. Here the author's anchor places the bowstring against the tip of the nose and the tip of the index finger in the corner of the mouth. His thumb is locked on the end of his jawbone.

A bowhunter must wait for his quarry to step into the clear. There must be no brush between them that could deflect an arrow.

SHOOTING THE HUNTING BOW

32

Problems and Challenges

The shooting of a hunting bow demands that the archer put into practice all the basics of target shooting plus some additional skills. Because the hunting bow often has a peak or holding weight considerably heavier than does a target bow, the stamina and muscle tone of the archer must be more fully developed. This means extensive practice.

Hold and Trajectory   The hunting archer usually has to hold the bow at full draw for 3 to 10 seconds. He frequently (and wisely) may choose to wait until his quarry looks away before releasing the arrow. This will prevent the target from literally sidestepping the arrow, a task easily accomplished if the archer is more than 20 yards away.

The shooter also must carefully consider the likely trajectory path of the arrow between him and the target. There can be no interfering brush. If the arrow strikes even a tiny branch at the top of its trajectory, it will surely never hit the intended mark. These calculations should be made prior to the draw.

Estimating Ranges   Another problem facing the hunting archer is the ability to judge ranges. As experienced shooters know, a mistake of 2 to 3 yards in range estimation can result in an arrow passing harmlessly under or over a deer. The archer needs to be able to judge distances from 20 to 50 yards very exactingly. To gain the level of proficiency required takes a heap of practice. One needs to take the time to go out into the fields and woods and pick out spots where a target might be standing and then estimate the range. Then pace it off and compare the actual distance to your estimate.

Do not select such objects as trees, large boulders, bushes and so on when trying to estimate distance. Look at a spot on the ground, perhaps a small pebble or a small patch of dirt, on which your imaginary quarry has placed a foot. Game animals are considerably smaller than bushes, trees or boulders. Learning to estimate distance to small spots will allow you to develop the necessary accuracy without requiring the proximity of a large landmark.

When you can estimate ranges fairly accurately, take along your bow and a half-dozen arrows with field tips on a practice walk through the woods. As you make your estimates, select the appropriate sight and try to hit a small mark on the ground at that range. When you first attempt this, a new problem will occur. You will find that often you do not have a sight pin set for the exact range. If so, pick an imaginary spot between pins to hold on the target.

When taking these random-distance shots, you will also be forced to find a way to get your arrow from the bow to the target without hitting any intervening brush. If you add a mental game of now-the-deer-is-looking-at-me-and-now-it's-looking-away, you can even practice holding the draw for 3 to 10 seconds.

Walking the archery course at a local club that uses 3D or printed deer targets is superb practice, until you commit to memory the distance from each shooting station to each target. Then the value of this practice will be diminished somewhat, though it will always be worthwhile.

Poor Light Conditions   Bow hunters are frequently faced with the opportunity for a shot during the early light of morning. Unless you practice under such conditions, you will, in all probability, make a gross mistake in range

Practice-shooting from awkward positions helps an archer prepare for actual hunting situations.

Shooting downward invariably results in a higher-than-normal point of impact. Archers should practice such shooting to learn how to adjust.

estimation. Also, you will find that because the sight pin is difficult to see, you will invariably hold it a good deal to the side of the bowstring.

There is not much you can do to overcome the darkness. Keep in mind, however, that in poor light things tend to look much farther away than they actually are. For the sake of good sportsmanship, never attempt shots in poor light unless you have practiced under similar light conditions and have established your capability to accomplish the task.

Awkward Positions   The hunting archer must learn to shoot uphill and downhill from uneven footing and sometimes from awkward positions. Thus, the hunter must practice shooting from a great many stances. Do learn to shoot from a kneeling position. Often this is the only way an arrow can be delivered to a target without hitting intervening limbs. If you hunt from tree stands, then practice shooting from a garage or porch roof. Do everything possible to duplicate actual field shots. And don't forget to include a few practice sessions in the rain and/or snow, since it may be appropriate to the season during which you will be hunting.

Applying Proper Technique in the Field   Finally, learn to draw and release an arrow with the absolute minimum of motion. Ditto for silently removing an arrow from the bow quiver and nocking it into place. If you practice as though the target on your hay bale were indeed a deer, you may well find that your actual hunting shot can be, after all, an easy one. And that's the way it should be.

Shoot your hunting bow with all of your hunting accessories in place. Camouflage tape, slip-on camouflage covers, bow quiver full of arrows, string silencers (if any) and range finder (if used) should all be in place. And it's not a bad idea to wear the same clothes, arm guards and archer's glove that will be used in actual hunting. Doing so will point up clothing that interferes with the bowstring or cables or that proves restricting when attempting to shoot from different positions.

Practice

No shooter can gain sufficient experience by limiting his shooting to actual hunting shots. It takes 3,000 to 5,000 practice arrows each year, under widely varying conditions, to produce even a fair shot with a hunting bow. Even more practice, considerably more, is necessary to become a highly skilled archer.

The best thing about constant practice is that you will become aware of your own capabilities and limitations. Thus, you will know if a lung shot is possible when it is presented in the field. And having the knowledge of what you can accomplish will make it much easier to pass up shots that would in all likelihood result in a wounded animal that escapes to suffer for some period of time.

Too many archers believe that almost any hit will allow their quarry to bleed to death in a short while. This just isn't so. Unless you effect severe hemorrhage, the bleeding will eventually stop, and a lost and perhaps crippled animal will be your only memory of the hunt. An extremely sharp arrow placed into a vital organ is the only acceptable level of performance for the true sportsman. Anyone who hunts with a bow and takes shots beyond his ability is not worthy of the name hunter.

Shooting the hunting bow demands that the archer use only razor-sharp heads. If you are unable to sharpen heads to a very fine edge, you should replace the heads after each shot. The best marksman will fail to get the job done if the arrowhead is not sharp enough to cause violent hemorrhage. A dull blade will

The smart bowhunter spends pre-season time practicing in the field in full regalia.

often simply push veins and arteries to the side or fail to penetrate to the vitals.

Hunting with a bow can be an immense source of pleasure. But if you fail to perform well, the memories of the hunt may be quite unpleasant. Constant practice and attention to detail will ensure that things go as planned.

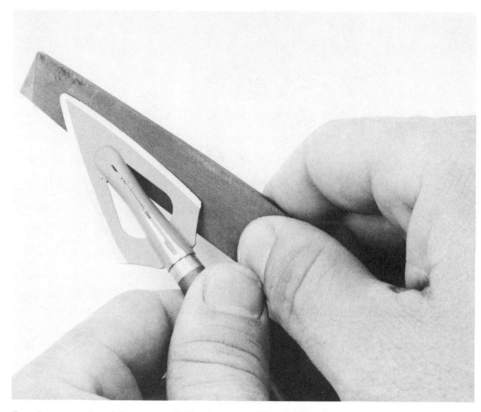

Bowhunters should use carefully sharpened broadheads to ensure quick, humane kills. A small file makes a good sharpening stone.

MUZZLELOADING FIREARMS

PART V

SELECTING A MUZZLELOADER

33

There is a wide range of safe-to-shoot, muzzleloading firearms manufactured today. Available to the interested shooter are small pocket guns, full-size pistols and revolvers, rifles, shotguns and even double-barreled rifles. And many of the offerings are available both as finished firearms or in kits that the purchaser assembles and finishes.

Caliber

However, not all of the muzzleloading firearms available offer the serious shooter all of the accuracy and reliability needed for hunting or competitive target shooting. Careful selection is important if the shooter is to be completely satisfied. The most important consideration is always, of course, caliber. It makes little sense to select a muzzleloader suitable to small-game hunting if your intent is to hunt big game. Nor should you select a large-caliber gun if what you want is a small-game rifle.

Legal Restrictions   Additionally, if the chosen muzzleloader is to be used for hunting during the primitive-weapons season, then you must determine exactly what kind of muzzleloading weapons are legal in the jurisdiction in which you intend to hunt. Some governing agencies have specified smoothbore only, no cartridge-to-muzzleloading conversions, no breechloading guns, no guns using modern primers for ignition and so on. Additionally, you may be required by law to use a gun of certain caliber or gauge, and in some localities it is mandated that only round balls be used to the exclusion of any bullet-shaped projectiles. A few areas require that only flintlocks be used for hunting during primitive season. Of course, target shooters may select any gun or guns that appeal to them.

Guns for Hunting   Big-game hunters should select rifles of .50 to .58 caliber to ensure sufficient energy to accomplish their goals. It has been my experience that it is easiest to blend a high-level of accuracy and energy with a .50-caliber rifle. The larger-caliber guns may, however, be somewhat more effective with round balls at short ranges.

The use of .45-caliber guns, in my opinion, is marginal for big game. Those who wish to hunt both small game and big game with one gun sometimes favor the .45 caliber. However, this diameter is too large for small game and really too small for big game. The .45-caliber muzzleloader equates to a 30-30 rifle cartridge: too much energy for small animals and not enough energy for big game. The .50-caliber muzzleloading rifle equates well to the 30-06 cartridge, being ideal for most big-game applications. However, do not let my comments lead you to believe that muzzleloading guns possess the power of modern smokeless cartridges. They do not.

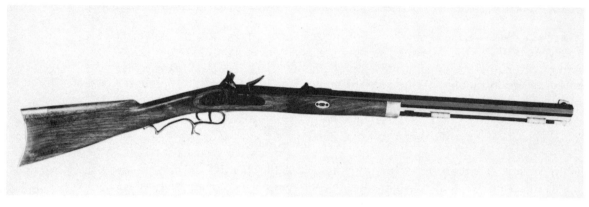

Navy Arms flintlock Hawken rifle.

Navy Arms left-handed percussion Hawken rifle.

Navy Arms Civil War replica 58 caliber rifle.

CVA percussion Hawken rifle.

CVA percussion Hawken rifle kit for the do-it-yourself muzzleloader.

Thompson Center Hawken rifle.

The small-game hunter is usually best served with a rifle of .32 to .36 caliber or a shotgun, preferably 12 gauge. Obviously, the bird hunter will, by necessity, require a shotgun.

Southpaw shooters have a muzzleloader made especially for them. It is Navy Arms' Hawken .50 caliber percussion rifle. The CVA double-barreled shotgun will work equally well for left- or right-handed shooters.

Handguns

Muzzleloading handguns are offered in a wide range of calibers, but the .44 or .45 caliber pistols and revolvers will prove most useful to the average shooter. Handguns in these diameters are accurate and supply sufficient power for small-game hunting at short range.

The serious shooter who desires a muzzleloading or, better stated, front-of-the-cylinder-loading revolver would do best to select one of the Remington or Rogers and Spencer type revolvers. These guns offer a solid frame and a rear sight that is part of the solid frame. Both of these features contribute greatly to accuracy. The Colt-type revolvers have detachable barrels and no frame top strap, and the rear sight is a notch in the hammer, all of which add up to less than the maximum in accuracy. The nostalgia buff, enamored with the Colt heritage, may wish a Colt lookalike, but he should realize that a handicap in accuracy will come as part of his choice.

Muzzleloading oddities such as gambler pistols, derringers, duckfoots, pepper boxes and double-barreled pistols do carry a certain appeal. But such guns are at best poor shooters. If shooting performance is important, selection of the more standard types will better serve the shooter's needs.

Manufacturers

Navy Arms Co., Connecticut Valley Arms and Thompson/Center Arms are the major suppliers of muzzleloading guns today. Navy Arms offers the broadest selection, while Thompson/Center offers a very high level of quality in workmanship. Muzzleloaders from any of these three firms should, in general, prove satisfactory so long as the shooter selects a type appropriate to his intended purpose.

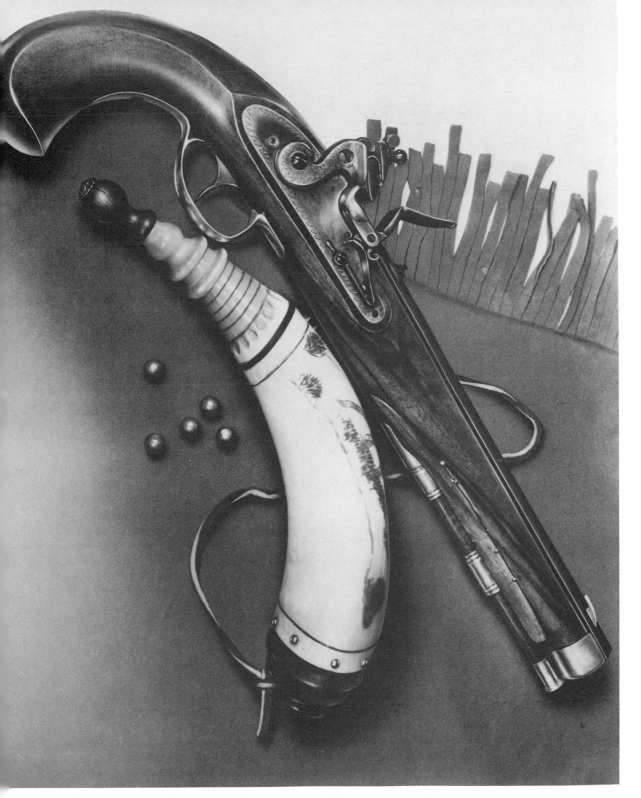

Navy Arms replica flintlock pistol.

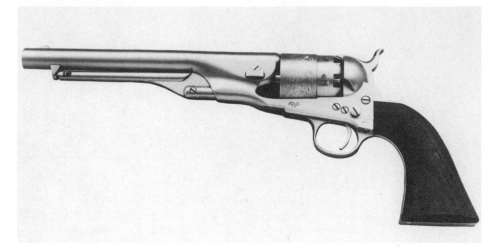

CVA Colt 1861 Navy replica.

A Remington (look-alike) Army revolver. Solid frame and adjustable sights make this revolver a fine choice for the serious shooter.

It is recommended that original antique muzzleloading firearms not be used for shooting. Because these older guns may have been subjected to abuse or may have deteriorated internally, they might present a real hazard to the user if they are shot. Additionally, such guns will lose much of their value as antiques if subjected to the rigors of continued shooting. Modern-made muzzleloaders are often stronger, more accurate and certainly more dependable than the originals. Therefore, they will provide greater shooter satisfaction at considerably less expense than original firearms.

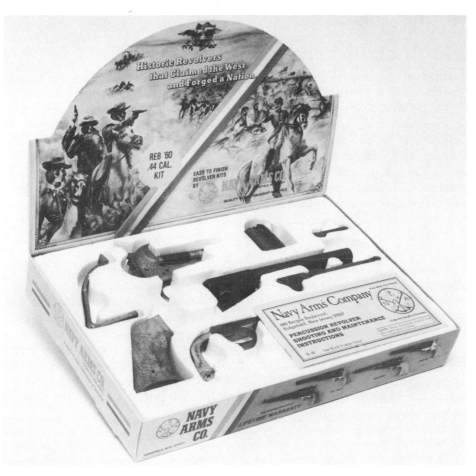

CVA percussion revolver kit.

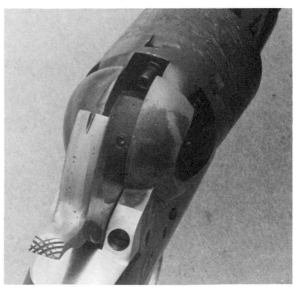

Revolvers with the rear sight nothing more than a notch in the hammer may be nostalgic but offer little in the way of a truly useful sight.

Flintlock or Percussion?

Having arrived at a decision on which caliber or gauge is required, the shooter then is faced with deciding upon a flintlock or percussion gun. If the flintlock is not mandated by law for hunting, most shooters will be far more satisfied with a percussion gun. Flintlocks are considerably more difficult to shoot accurately. The flash of the pan in front of the shooter's face frequently leads to an accuracy-destroying flinch. Additionally, a flintlock supplies only semireliable ignition, at best. It is not uncommon for the pan powder to fail to ignite or to ignite and then fail to fire the powder charge in the barrel. The reasons for such problems are many and will be discussed in following chapters.

Percussion guns, on the other hand, offer reliable ignition even in damp weather. And such guns are more dependable, being less prone to the parts failures common to flint mechanisms.

The accompanying table lists a number of muzzleloading firearms for specific applications. The selection suggestions are based on the author's personal experience and preference. In all cases, if the muzzleloader is to be used for hunting, check local regulations and restrictions before purchasing a gun.

A point not to be overlooked when selecting any muzzleloader for competitive target shooting as well as hunting is the adjustability of the sights. Many of today's replica firearms have "primitive"-style sights. These are fixed sights that are extremely difficult to adjust, if indeed they can be adjusted at all. Fully adjustable sights are essential if you wish the point of impact and the point of aim to coincide.

The best possible muzzleloading rifle sight is this Williams Foolproof aperture sight. It's easy to adjust and locks positively in place.

MUZZLELOADING SELECTION CHART

Application	Brand and model	Caliber or gauge	Comments
Target & plinking	CVA Frontier rifle & pistol	.50	Available with flint or percussion lock
	CVA Kentucky rifle & pistol	.45	Available with flint or percussion lock
	CVA Mountain pistol	.50	Fixed "primitive"-style sights
	Thompson/Center Seneca	.45	Percussion "New England"-style rifle
	Thompson/Center Renegade	.54	Flint or percussion "carbine"
	Navy Mississippi 1841	.58	Historic Civil War-type percussion rifle
	Navy Enfield	.58	Barrels of 24″, 33″ and 39″; percussion rifle
	Navy Springfield 1863	.58	Historic Civil War-type percussion rifle
Small game	CVA Squirrel rifle	.32	Available with flint or percussion lock
	CVA shotgun	12	Double barrel, percussion
	CVA 1858 Remington Target model	.44	Solid frame revolver with adjustable sights
	Thompson/Center Seneca	.36	Percussion "New England"-style rifle
	Ruger Old Army	.44	Percussion revolver with adjustable sights
	Navy Rogers and Spencer	.44	Six-shot solid-frame revolver
	Navy Classic side by side	12	Double-barrel percussion
Big game	CVA Pennsylvania long rifle	.50	Flint or percussion with set triggers
	CVA Mountain rifle	.50	Flint or percussion with set triggers
	CVA Hawken or Frontier rifle	.50	Flint or percussion with adjustable sights
	Thompson/Center Hawken rifle	.50	Flint or percussion with excellent sights
	Thompson/Center Renegade	.50	Lower cost version of T/C
	Thompson/Center Renegade smoothbore	.56	For use where smoothbores are required by law
	Navy Kentucky rifle	.50	"Primitive"-style sights, flint or percussion
	Navy Hawken Mark I rifle	.50	Percussion
	Navy Ithaca Hawken	.50	Traditional-style sights; percussion or flint

34 LOADING THE MUZZLELOADER

Each shooter who uses a muzzleloading firearm must become expert at loading his chosen gun. Accurate and careful loading of all muzzleloading guns is essential if the shooter is to be able to hit his target. Careless or sloppy loading will always result in poor accuracy, while only the most precise loading will result in maximum accuracy.

Each basic type of muzzleloading firearm requires a specific loading procedure. However, there are similarities. A single-shot percussion rifle is loaded exactly the same as is a single-shot percussion pistol, and a flintlock rifle is loaded like a flintlock pistol. Percussion revolvers require a specific technique, as do percussion shotguns.

For the purposes of this chapter, I will describe the loading process for flintlocks using a CVA Hawken rifle as an example. Whatever model flintlock or pistol you use, the procedure will be the same. Also, to prevent redundancy, our loading of the flintlock will be with the use of a patched ball. The procedure for a Minié or Maxi bullet is covered fully under percussion rifle loading.

For percussion loading instructions, a Thompson/Center Hawken rifle and Maxi ball-type bullets will be used. Those wishing to use a patched ball can obtain instructions for such use from the flintlock loading procedure. Percussion pistol loading will, of course, duplicate the rifle procedure.

For percussion revolver loading, a CVA 1861 Colt Navy replica is used. The procedure is identical whether a ball or bullet is used. No cloth patching is employed when loading balls in a revolver.

Smoothbore percussion or flint muskets are loaded the same as are rifled models, when balls or bullets are used. Shot loading is also explained in detail.

Of course, the proper size of ball and patch or bullet must be employed when loading any percussion or flintlock firearm. The best way to be certain of using the right size is to follow the manufacturer's suggestions. To attempt to do otherwise could result in a damaged firearm and/or poor accuracy.

Loading the Flintlock

Removing All Oil from the Barrel   The first step in loading is to ensure that all traces of oil are removed from the barrel's interior. If any oil is left in the barrel, especially in the breech area, the powder charge will become contaminated and either fail to ignite or produce erratic ballistics. The best way to accomplish oil removal is first to run a few dry patches up and down the barrel. Then prime the flash pan. Do not overfill the pan; simply fill the recess. Then close the pan, cock the hammer and, with the barrel pointed safely, "flash" the powder in the pan. Repeat this process three or four times. Some of the flash will enter the flash hole and burn off oil remaining in the breech area. Should you forget to remove all oil from the bore by swabbing and by "flashing" several pans of powder, you may find it necessary to remove the ball from the gun with a "worm" and then pour out the contaminated powder.

After removing any residual oil from the bore, the actual loading process can begin. For succeeding shots, obviously, the loading procedure will begin at this point.

Be sure the pan is open and the hammer is in the fired position. If any of the pan flashes used to dry oil from the barrel failed to fire, now is the time to reposition the flint or replace it as need be.

Pouring in the Powder   Rest the butt of the rifle on top of the left foot (assuming a right-handed shooter). Carefully pour an accurately metered powder charge into the barrel. (Keep the barrel pointed away from any portion of your body during the entire loading procedure.)

It is important that each powder charge poured into the barrel be identical to the last charge if accuracy is to be at an acceptable level. The most exacting shooters will carefully weigh out powder charges beforehand, storing them in plastic or glass vials for later use. Powder poured from a bulk container into a measuring unit at the time of loading will also prove satisfactory if the operation is performed carefully. The actual pouring of powder into the barrel must be done meticulously to prevent any spilling. Charge weights that are not uniform will cause poor accuracy.

Of course, the right grade of powder and the correct charge weight must be used. Refer to the manufacturer's literature or a black-powder data source for specific loads. In general, FFFg powder is used for all guns of .40 caliber or smaller. FFg is the proper selection for .41 to .54 caliber, and for .55 caliber or larger Fg powder is appropriate.

Settling the Charge   After carefully pouring the correct weight and type of powder into the bore, raise the rifle from your foot, keeping the muzzle vertical, and strike the breech area with several blows of your palm against the stock. This will help ensure proper settling of the powder charge. Return the butt of the rifle to its position atop your left foot.

Inserting the Ball   Next, carefully place a precut, lubricated patch (or strip of lubricated patching material) centrally over the bore. Place a ball on

LOADING A FLINTLOCK

1. To begin loading the flintlock, swab the bore with several dry patches to remove excess oil and then prime the flash pan.

2. After closing the frizzen, "flash" the powder in the pan. Repeat this procedure several times to burn off any residual oil left in the flash hole or breech end of the barrel.

3. Start with the gun resting on top of your foot and with the muzzle pointed away from your body.

4. Pour a measured powder charge into the barrel, taking care not to spill any powder.

5. *Raise the gun off your foot and strike the breech area several times to settle the powder.*

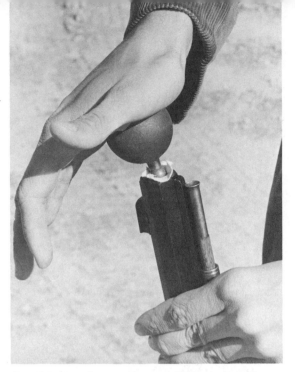

6. *With a pre-cut patch centered over the bore, place a ball over the patch, pressing it into the bore with thumb pressure.*

7. *With the short starter and the palm of your hand, press the patch and ball as far into the muzzle as possible with the starter's shortest protrusion.*

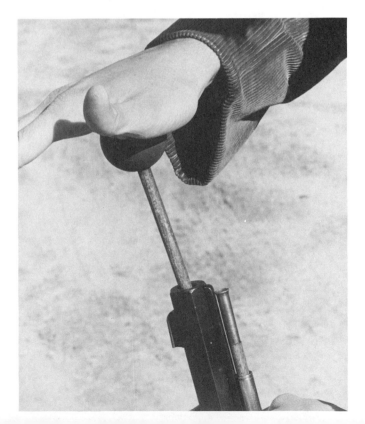

8. *Repeat the process with the longest protrusion of the short starter.*

9. *Then, using the ramrod, seat the patch and ball firmly on top of the powder.*

10. *Prime the pan and then carefully close the frizzen, avoiding spillage of any of the "prime."*

the patch, with the sprue facing up and centrally located. Then take the short starter and place its shortest extension over the ball. Press the starter downward with the palm of the hand, pushing the ball into the barrel.

At this point, the uppermost portion of the ball will be flush with the muzzle. If a patch strip was used, cut the patch flush with the muzzle, using a sharp patch knife. If a precut patch was used, this step can be eliminated. It has been my experience that the use of precut patches usually results in better accuracy, most likely because of better uniformity of the patching material.

Next, using the longer section of the short starter, push the ball into the barrel as far as possible. Some shooters skip the use of a short starter and, as a result, never attain a high degree of accuracy. Proper use of the short starter demands that only palm pressure be applied. Any attempt to bang on the ball will distort it and cause inaccuracy.

Using the Ramrod   After pressing the patch and ball into the barrel as far as possible with the short starter, seat them fully onto the powder charge by using the ramrod. Again, care must be taken not to deform the ball. Steady, uniform pressure on the ramrod will prevent any damage. On succeeding shots, the ball will become harder to seat. In order to avoid the need to use undue force, the barrel should be scrubbed to remove accumulated fouling. A final pressure of about 80 pounds is ideal for seating the ball on the powder charge.

To gain a feeling for what 80 pounds of pressure is like, stand your rifle on a bathroom scale while applying ramrod pressure on a load. After doing this a few times, you should be able to duplicate the same pressure without the use of a scale.

Caution: Never fire any muzzleloading firearm without the ball, bullet or shot charge fully seated on the powder. To do so could result in extensive damage to the gun as well as serious personal injury. If for any reason the projectile cannot be fully seated, it should be removed and corrective steps taken to eliminate the difficulty.

It is wise to mark your ramrod at a point that is flush with the muzzle when it rests on a fully seated projectile and an appropriate powder charge. In this way, the ramrod will serve as a visual check on the gun's readiness to be shot. If the rod goes too deeply into the barrel, the reference mark will not be visible, and the shooter will know immediately either that the powder or the projectile is missing or, perhaps, that insufficient powder was used. If the rod mark protrudes above its normal flush position, the shooter will know that something is wrong. It may be a double charge of powder or projectile or a projectile not fully seated on the powder charge. All of these problems will require that the gun not be fired until it has been properly loaded. A piece of white tape works well for marking the ramrod. When you change your powder charge weight or projectile style, the tape can be replaced at a new location as required by the total volume of the new load.

Keep in mind that poor projectile fit may cause a bullet or ball to move forward away from the powder charge, because of the normal jostling received by the gun during a day's hunt. It therefore pays to check the position of the projectile with a marked ramrod from time to time.

Priming the Pan   With the powder charge and projectile properly loaded, the pan must then be primed. The only powder that is 100-percent acceptable for this purpose is FFFFg black powder. However, FFFg can be used if 4F is unavailable. The use of 3F, however, will result in some failures of the propellant charge to ignite when the pan powder is flashed.

Many shooters tend to overcharge the pan in an attempt to guarantee positive ignition. The fact remains that the pan's recess should be filled flush and no further. Excess powder will not help ignition and, moreover, often results in poor accuracy when increased pan flash and smoke causes the shooter to flinch.

To prime the pan, draw the hammer back to the half-cock position and pour the proper amount of FFFFg powder into the pan. Then close the frizzen carefully, being sure not to spill any of the priming charge. To fire the flintlock, all that remains to be done is to draw the hammer to full cock and pull the trigger.

Loading the Percussion Gun

The warning never to discharge a muzzleloading weapon unless the projectile is fully seated on the powder charge, as described in the instructions for loading the flintlock, applies equally to all percussion guns.

Cleaning the Barrel   To load the percussion rifle, begin by firing three or four caps on the nipple, with the barrel pointed in a safe direction. This will clean the breech area of the barrel of any oil that might contaminate the powder charge. If there is excess oil in the bore, it will be best to swab the bore with several dry patches before firing the caps. Make sure there is no cap on the nipple, and gently lower the hammer.

Settling the Charge and Bullet   Having assured a dry bore, place the butt of the rifle on your left foot. (Left-handed persons should use the right foot.) Be certain that you do not point the barrel at any portion of your body during the loading procedure. Carefully pour a measured powder charge into the bore, making certain not to spill any of it. Settle the powder by striking the breech area of the gun several times with the palm of your hand. Then place a properly lubricated bullet squarely into the muzzle as far as possible with the fingers. Next, using the smallest protrusion of the short starter, push the bullet into the barrel as far as possible. Take care not to cock the bullet, driving it as squarely as possible into the bore. Then switch to the longer extension of the short starter and, again with care, press the bullet farther into the bore until the short starter comes to rest on the muzzle. The use of the short starter will help ensure that the bullet is driven into the barrel without tipping, thereby preventing inaccuracy that could otherwise occur.

LOADING THE PERCUSSION GUN

1. *After swabbing the bore with dry patches, snap several caps on the nipple to burn off any oil in the nipple or remaining in the breech area.*

2. *Place the gun on your foot and pointed safely away from your body.*

3. *Carefully pour in the correct powder charge.*

5. Start a lubricated bullet into the bore with the fingers, being careful to keep it correctly aligned without tipping.

4. Settle the powder with several bows of the palm to the breech area.

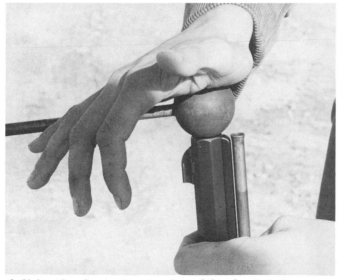

6. Using the shortest protrusion of the short starter, press the lubricated bullet into the bore as far as possible.

7. Repeat the procedure with the longer portion of the starter.

8. *With the ramrod firmly seat the bullet onto the powder charge.*

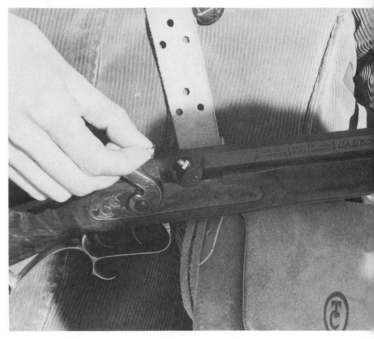

9. *Place a snug fitting cap on the nipple.*

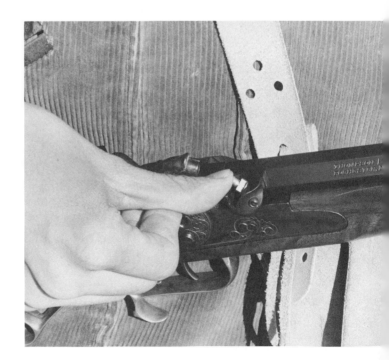

10. *To fire, cock the hammer and pull the trigger.*

Using the Ramrod   With the ramrod, fully seat the bullet on the powder charge. Use firm pressure, but avoid any excess or pounding that could deform the soft lead projectile. As with the flintlock, a final rod pressure of about 80 pounds is the optimum.

Your ramrod should be marked, as described under flintlock loading, to ensure that the bullet has been fully seated over a correct powder charge. From time to time while hunting, use the marked ramrod to check that a poorly fitting bullet has not moved away from the powder charge.

After loading powder and projectile, draw the hammer to full cock and place a well-fitting cap on the rifle's nipple. Next, lower the hammer to the half-cock "safety" notch. The gun is now ready to fire, requiring only that the hammer be brought to the full-cock position and the trigger squeezed.

Loading the Percussion Revolver

Unlike other muzzleloaders, the percussion revolver is not loaded from the muzzle of the barrel. Powder and ball are placed directly into the cylinder chambers from the front end of the cylinder.

Cleaning the Barrel   To start, place a cap on each nipple; then, with the revolver pointed in a safe direction, fire all the caps. Repeat this process three or four times to ensure that any oil in the nipples or cylinder has been burned off completely. Place the revolver hammer into the loading notch, and remove all fired caps and any pieces of them that may be present.

Seating the Powder and Bullet   Carefully charge a cylinder with a measured amount of powder, press a bullet or ball into the front end of the cylinder and rotate the cylinder to bring the partially seated projectile under the rammer. Then swing the ram lever fully downward, fully seating the projectile. Repeat this process until all chambers but one have been loaded.

Make no attempt to charge each cylinder with powder prior to seating bullets. It may be faster to do so, but it often leads to spilled powder and inaccuracy. When all cylinders but one have been properly charged, the space in front of the projectile must be filled with a thick lubricant. This substance will ensure that the barrel fouling, which occurs when shooting, will remain soft. Without lubricant, the accuracy of the revolver will deteriorate drastically before a half-dozen shots have been fired. Equally important, the lubricant will prevent the flash of burning powders from entering the front of another chamber and possibly igniting it. This is a real risk, since bullets and balls do not create a positive seal. Shooters who forget to lube the front end of cylinders can experience chain fires in which multiple chambers are discharged almost simultaneously. If even only one extra chamber fires, the shooter and bystanders will be exposed to severe danger, and the revolver may be ruined.

Capping the Chambers   Cap each nipple, except on the unloaded chamber. After capping, cover all caps with lubricant to prevent flash-over, causing a chain ignition of other chambers.

When all chambers but one have been capped, lower the hammer on the empty chamber for safe carrying. Removing the nipple of one chamber will prevent any possible confusion when loading and capping and ensure that the hammer is carried down on the correct chamber. The gun may now be fired simply by cocking the hammer and pulling the trigger.

LOADING A REVOLVER

1. After thoroughly removing all oil from the bore and cylinder, snap several caps on each nipple to be sure that there is no oil left in them.

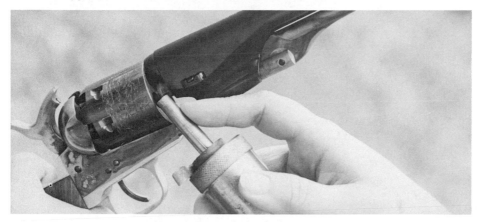

2. Carefully pour a measured charge of powder into a chamber.

3. Start a ball into the cylinder with thumb pressure.

4. Rotate the cylinder (hammer must be in the loading notch position) to place the ball directly under the rammer.

5. With the rammer, seat the ball into the cylinder and onto the powder charge with firm pressure.

6. *After all but one chamber has been loaded, completely seal the front end of each chamber. Force in grease, filling chambers flush with cylinder face.*

7. *Place a cap on each nipple and then apply a generous coating of grease over the nipple area, and finally lower the hammer onto the unloaded chamber for safe carrying.*

8. *You need now only cock the hammer and pull the trigger to fire the revolver. The fog is smoke from an earlier shot.*

Use only black powder or Pyrodex powder in any muzzleloading firearm.

Loading the Muzzleloading Shotgun

Loading a shotgun is quite similar to the loading of other muzzleloaders. Begin by snapping three or four caps on the nipple(s) while the gun is pointed in a safe direction. This will clean the nipple(s) and chamber area(s) of any residual oil. Then clean the nipple(s) of any cap residue and lower the hammer(s) fully. Place the butt on top of your left foot. Keeping the muzzle pointed away from all parts of your body, carefully pour a measured amount of powder into the barrel. Settle the powder by striking the breech area of the gun several times with the palm of your hand. Then start a wad of the proper diameter into the muzzle. Lubricated wads at least ⅜ inch thick are suggested, and ½ inch is better. Press the wad into the barrel until it is flush with the muzzle. Now use a ramrod to seat the wad firmly on the powder with about 80 pounds of pressure.

At this point, carefully pour in a measured amount of shot. Then place a ¼-inch-thick wad into the muzzle, carefully seating it with the ramrod. This wad is all that will hold the shot in place during the hunt (and during recoil when a double-barreled gun is used). Therefore, it must fit quite snugly.

The use of a marked ramrod (as discussed under loading the flintlock) will help determine when the shotgun has been properly loaded and if the top wad has worked forward during the course of a hunt.

After loading one barrel, duplicate the process for the second barrel, if appropriate. Then place the hammer(s) at full cock and carefully cap the nipple(s) with a cap of the proper size. Finally, lower the hammer(s) to half-cock safety.

It is important to avoid distractions when loading a double-barreled shotgun. Many a shooter has loaded a second powder charge into a fully loaded barrel, realizing the error only after seating the wad.

Important Considerations

Proper Powder Always be certain to use the correct granulation of black or Pyrodex powder in any muzzleloader. (Only these powders are safe to use in muzzleloading weapons.) For specific charge-weight recommendations, always follow the firearm manufacturer's instructions. All reliable manufacturers will supply this type of information for their guns.

Proper Fit The proper fit of patch and ball or the correct bullet is essential. It is imperative that the shooter follow the manufacturer's guidelines when selecting projectiles, patches, shot charges or wads.

The fit of cap to nipple is vital. On revolvers, it is essential that caps fit properly so as to prevent interference between the cap and revolver frame. Any excess protrusion could cause ignition as the cylinder turns, thus creating serious hazards. Additionally, the cap should fit snuggly on the nipple to help prevent flash-over.

Caps should not be pinched in an effort to obtain a snug fit. Pinching will invariably leave gaps between cap and nipple. Nor should an undersized cap be forced onto a nipple; the cap might split. Overly long caps should not be used on short nipples. Positive ignition will not always occur with poor fit. Take time to ensure that a well-fitting cap is used. When a cap is found that fits well, it is wise to purchase a large supply, since cap availability by brand and size tends to be quite erratic.

Nipples should be replaced as soon as they show any visible damage. Always keep nipples tight, and be sure that flash holes are clear before beginning to load. It is good practice to push a well-fitting nipple pick through the flash hole before commencing to load.

Dealing with Misfires Should there be a misfire, keep the gun pointed in a safe direction for at least thirty seconds. Delayed firing is not uncommon with muzzleloaders. A damp or oil-contaminated powder charge could have a glow in it that will eventually cause ignition.

Years ago, in my youth, I was using a .58 caliber original Civil War musket. I had fired only one cap on the nipple prior to loading the powder charge and Minié ball. When I attempted to fire, the cap snapped, but no ignition occurred. I tried two more caps with no success. Laying the gun down on the grass, I turned to get a worm in order to remove the bullet. Suddenly, the gun went off and slid past me on the grass. Such lengthy delays in firing are not common but obviously can occur. Wait at least thirty seconds after flashing a pan or firing a cap before trying to find out what went wrong. And even after that, keep the muzzle pointed in a safe direction at all times.

Misfires can be caused by contaminated powder charges, plugged flash holes or nipples, weak caps, particles of previously fired caps preventing the hammer from delivering a full blow, ill-fitting caps, soft frizzens, poor flints and a host of other causes. Any misfire is always a reason to proceed with extreme caution.

Sooner or later, all but the most meticulous loader will load without powder. It may then be necessary to pull a ball or bullet from the barrel using a ramrod with a screwlike unit placed into its end. When doing so with any revolver or multibarrel weapon, make absolutely sure that all the chambers or the remaining barrel have been fired. Only then is it safe to attempt to pull the projectile.

Sometimes, it may not be necessary to pull the ball or bullet. Removing the nipple on a percussion gun will often allow sufficient powder to be worked into the breech end of the barrel or into a cylinder chamber to effect a firing. Follow the manufacturer's instructions when attempting to use this procedure, and be certain the projectile is fully seated on the powder before firing.

If the shooter is conscientious and careful about the loading of his muzzleloader, no difficulties will be encountered. However, a moment's distraction or inattention can cause all kinds of problems. Should you ever be guilty of a goof, take great care to avoid harm to yourself or the gun. When in doubt, or if you cannot correct the problem without the use of force, seek the help of a gunsmith or an experienced individual. A great many muzzleloading guns have been ruined by impatient shooters who resort to force in an attempt to correct a problem.

35 SHOOTING THE MUZZLELOADER

The muzzleloading shooter would be well advised to incorporate the shooting techniques used with more modern weapons. Thus, all of the information contained in the sections on rifle, shotgun and handgun shooting pertains fully to the use of the corresponding types of muzzleloading guns. Of course, the nature of muzzleloading means that some additional knowledge must be employed to ensure maximum accuracy and performance.

Problems

Flintlock shooting can be extremely difficult even when all the correct procedures are followed. Utter frustration is often the result of attempts to use a flintlock when the shooter does not take the time to learn special techniques.

Moisture Moisture in the powder pan is the biggest problem associated with a flintlock gun. If the pan powder becomes damp from rain, snow, oil contamination or any other cause, almost assuredly the results will be no flash when the trigger is pulled. The shooter must take great pains to keep his powder dry. This presents no overwhelming problem for the target shooter, but the hunter's difficulties can at times be nearly insurmountable. All sorts of devices have been tried to keep the powder in the pan dry. Some hunters completely wrap the lock area with waterproof material, such as a light plastic food wrap. Leather "cow legs" are also used for the same purpose. Even when cleverly done, these water-proofing techniques present problems when it comes time to cock the hammer and fire. Some shooters use soft waxes to make a seal around the frizzen. This seems to work reasonably well.

Whatever method chosen to keep the powder dry, moisture has a great way of winning out. If water gets into the pan or flash hole, a misfire will result. Do your best to prevent such occurrences, but be ready to deal with the inevitable.

Percussion guns do not present a problem with moisture at the breech. A tight cap-to-nipple fit will usually be sufficient to avoid problems. To prevent the possibility of a cap coming loose and exposing the nipple to moisture migration, some shooters employ varying means of added security. A bit of heavy grease seems to help somewhat, but good fit of cap to nipple remains paramount.

Plastic (or leather) wrapped locks can help keep the flintlock's pan powder dry when you hunt in rainy weather, but such systems are not foolproof.

After placing a cap on a nipple, always check its fit by attempting to slide it off. If you decide on any extra precaution, be sure that it does not interfere with the hammer fall or positive ignition of the cap.

Regardless of the type of muzzleloading gun used, when you're hunting in inclement weather, take steps to prevent water from gaining access to the powder charge from the muzzle. A small rubber balloon pulled tightly over the muzzle works quite well.

The balloon can be removed easily and replaced whenever you decide to check the position of the projectile with the ramrod. Always remove the cap or pan powder when checking the position of the projectile. If you ever find that the ball or bullet has moved forward from the powder charge, reseat it carefully. Then consider the fact that your chosen patch-and-ball combination or bullet is indeed a poor fit for your barrel. Take the necessary steps to increase the friction of your projectile within the bore. An increase in patch thickness, ball

A balloon stretched over the muzzle and taped into place will keep moisture from entering the powder charge from the front end.

diameter or bullet diameter is obviously called for. This is not always easy to accomplish. On occasion, a custom-diameter ball or bullet mold may be required.

Maintaining Position
Flintlock shooters need to develop nerves of steel. When the pan powder is ignited by sparks from the flint striking the frizzen, the resulting flash and puff of smoke occur immediately in front of the shooter's face. Yet, he must maintain his sight alignment as this happens, since it is the flash from the pan entering the flash hole that causes ignition of the propelling charge. The time delay between pan and propellant ignition is not long. But it is of sufficient duration that if the shooter flinches, loses sight alignment or fails to follow through, the result will be a missed target.

Maintaining Follow-through
Because of the relatively low velocities generated by black powder or Pyrodex, muzzleloading projectiles have a relatively long in-barrel time. Therefore, as with rimfire cartridges or most handgun cartridges, the shooter must strive to maintain a rather long follow-through. Muzzleloading guns actually begin their recoil movement before the projectile leaves the gun. For this reason, the shooter's follow-through should last until the gun is well into its recoil movement. The importance of this with respect to accuracy cannot be overstressed.

Proper Ignition
Also important in shooting any muzzleloader is uniform ignition. Poor flints will cause misfires, but poor caps may go unnoticed except for the resultant poor accuracy. Choose caps that give positive uniform ignition. If you note any variation in time delay between hammer fall and ignition, chances

are the caps being used are not "hot" enough or do not have uniform priming charges. A change in brand may well be advised.

Safety   All shooters should always wear protective glasses when firing their guns, but this is especially true for percussion and flintlock gun users. Sparks and flashes from a flintlock pan can cause serious eye damage. Bits of the percussion cap can on occasion fly off the cap when it is detonated and cause serious eye injury. A lifetime of regret can be avoided by wearing glasses.

A light leather glove worn on the trigger hand can also protect the shooter from bits of percussion caps. Hand cuts caused by flying bits of cap can be completely eliminated by this safety step.

The flash and smoke of a flintlock pan firing can bring on an involuntary flinch unless the shooter concentrates on following through until the shot is discharged.

Attaining Accuracy

Proper Powder Charge   The most important step in obtaining accuracy with a muzzleloader is to become a meticulous loader. The importance of using a precisely measured powder charge cannot be overstressed. The best shooters invariably use charges that are carefully weighed on a good powder scale at home and stored in glass or plastic vials for later use.

Careful inspection of fired patches is required to determine if the patch is standing up to the powder charge. Patches that burn through are inadequate. An increase in thickness and/or change in material may be required, or the powder charge being used may simply be too heavy and need to be reduced.

Proper Ball and Patch   To obtain a preliminary estimate of the required ball diameter and patch thickness, one must select a ball that is somewhat smaller than the bore diameter to allow for patch thickness. Ideally, the patch should fill the grooves to prevent excessive blow-by. Thus, if a barrel has a bore (land) diameter of .440 inches and a groove diameter of .448 inches, the patch thickness should ideally be .008 inches (the difference between bore diameter and groove diameter). If the patch material can be reasonably compressed to .004 inches, then a ball diameter of .432 inches would be indicated. This allows for .004 inch patch around the ball, or a total of .008 inches.

Actually, ball and patch size must often be a compromise. Molds are not available in .001-inch increments, and neither is patch material. Also, the patch lubricant used will affect the amount of patch compression. Seldom do the first ball and patch tried prove to be the very best combination. Range trials of various combinations in conjunction with different powder charges are always an essential part of obtaining the best accuracy. Some manufacturers eliminate much of the guesswork by testing various combinations and suggesting the use of those that perform the best.

Bullet selection also requires range experimentation. Will a Minié-type projectile (hollow-base bullet) shoot better than the so-called Maxi ball (a solid-base bullet)? Only actual shooting tests can supply the correct answer.

Generally speaking, I start with a ball diameter of approximately .010 inches under the land diameter and use as thick a patch as I can load without distorting the ball. I clean the bore with a bronze brush after every four shots, as doing so allows me to use a patch considerably thicker than I could if I brushed the bore only every half-dozen shots.

When using a ball and patch for .45-caliber guns, a charge weight range of 60 to 90 grains of FFg will cover minimum and maximum loads. With .50-caliber loads, add 5 grains to the lower and upper levels of powder charge. Fifty-five caliber rifles seem to be well-served with a range of 70 to 100 grains. I suggest shooting four-shot groups at each 10-grain level. When the best charge has been selected, try it again along with charges of 5 more and 5 less grains. There is little to be gained by varying charge weights at finer increments. When using Maxi-style bullets, use the same upper charge limits but increase the minimum charge by 5 grains.

A stiff wire cleaning brush and a jag for patches are essentials.

Commercial patch lubricants are far superior to the old "spit" patch.

Today a number of manufacturers offer swaged lead balls that often are more uniform than the home-cast kind.

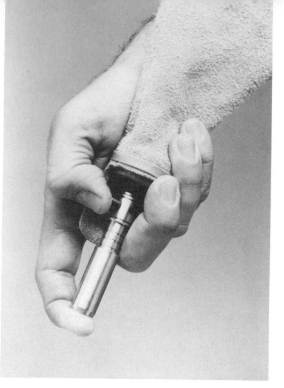

Some shooters meter powder (and shot) directly from various types of powder and shot containers such as this leather pouch.

"Possibles" kits are available with all the accessories a muzzleloader needs. The CVA kit contains a powder measure, short starter, patches, balls, grease, loading instructions, caps and capper.

MAINTAINING EQUIPMENT, SKILLS AND SAFETY

PART VI

The infrequent shooter can get everything he needs for gun cleaning in a kit such as this Outers Kit.

MAINTAINING ACCURACY 36

The accuracy of many a fine firearm deteriorates simply through lack of maintenance. And perhaps an equal number of firearms have had their accuracy destroyed by overzealous but misguided maintenance and cleaning efforts. To maintain accuracy, centerfire rifles should be cleaned after every twenty to thirty rounds of use. For the ultimate in accuracy, clean after every 10 shots. Rimfire rifles should be cleaned every 50 rounds to preserve accuracy.

Cleaning is necessary to remove accumulations of powder residue, copper fouling from jacketed bullets and lead fouling from cast or swaged bullets, along with the residue of priming mixtures. All of these residues are detrimental to fine accuracy. The longer fouling is left in the bore, the harder it is to remove. It is a rather simple chore to remove the fouling or leading generated by ten or twenty rounds of ammunition. It is another thing to remove the by-products of fifty to 100 rounds of shooting.

Most shooters should clean their guns after each shooting session. Only those who shoot less than a box of cartridges each season can skip routine cleaning. On the other hand, as mentioned, overzealous cleaning can be ruinous to a firearm.

Damage to the crown of the muzzle is frequently noted when a shooter has insisted upon cleaning his barrel from the muzzle end. Cleaning-rod handles and pointed patch jags run against the muzzle will take their toll.

When cleaning from the breech end, one also needs to exercise care. A moment's inattention can lead to a slip that results in a cleaning rod being jammed into a scope lens. Using care and having scope caps in place before cleaning can prevent such expensive errors. Some shooters go to great lengths to protect their rifles, using rod guides that replace the firearm's bolt. These prevent possible chamber damage that might otherwise occur in a negligent moment.

The first step to damage-free, effective gun cleaning starts with the purchase of cleaning rods, brushes, patches, etc. Such a purchase can be geared to an inexpensive cleaning kit. Typically, such kits offer an aluminum cleaning rod of the appropriate diameter, a bronze wire brush, several patch jags for the rod, patches, solvent and oil. Kits offer the casual shooter everything he needs to get the job done.

For frequent cleaning, aluminum or brass rods will prove less than durable—

399

purchasing a stainless steel rod makes good sense. Belding & Mull and Rig both offer excellent one- and multiple-piece stainless steel rods, as do other manufacturers. For revolver cleaning, which must be done from the muzzle end, the Rig rod has a nice feature that protects the muzzle crown from damage. It is a nylon buffer that fits over the rod and prevents damage if the handle section is inadvertently bumped against the muzzle. This rod comes complete with all attachments and brushes for .22 to .45 caliber.

Brushes for bore cleaning are available from a large number of suppliers including Hoppes and Outers, to mention just two. Nylon brushes serve little purpose; the shooter should purchase bronze wire brushes only. For heavy-duty cleaning, you might want to consider the premium-quality Bruno Benchrest brushes, which offer a very precise fit and are long lasting. Because of their exacting fit, the Bruno brushes will quickly remove fouling without danger of damage to the bore.

The solvent used in bore cleaning can be any one of the name brands. But if you do a good deal of shooting, you might well wish to purchase Shooter's Choice. This solvent will quickly remove copper fouling that is stubborn or heavily deposited. It will get amazing amounts of copper fouling out of barrels that were previously "cleaned" with less effective solvents. Unlike some bore cleaners, Shooter's Choice is nonabrasive. But its potency demands that you use care not to get any on your stock finish, as it will, given a chance, remove it also.

To clean a rifle or shotgun bore properly, proceed as follows: Always work from the breech end whenever possible, even if it requires disassembly of the firearm. When you must work from the muzzle, do so with extreme care. Do not allow the crown to be damaged by careless insertion of the rod or the jamming of a rod handle against it.

After selecting a rod of the proper diameter, place a patch over the end of the patch jag. A pointed patch jag is far preferable to a slotted one, as it assures complete patch-to-bore contact. The patch should be thoroughly soaked in a good bore cleaner, then pushed through the bore to remove any loose fouling or residue. Push the patch through the bore in one direction only, allowing it to fall free at the end of its passage. It is ruinous to pull the gritty patch back through the bore. Don't pump the rod; this serves only to scrape the bore with the gritty patch. Repeat with a second patch. Follow this with a thoroughly soaked bronze brush. Push the brush the full length of the barrel, and allow it to exit. Then bring it back through the bore, allowing it to exit at the original insertion end.

Use this pumping-type stroke for a total of perhaps twelve in-and-out passes through the bore. Then let the barrel sit for about twenty minutes. After this soaking period, run a patch soaked in solvent through the bore (in one direction only). Repeat this for a total of three wet patches. Again allow the bore to soak for about twenty minutes. Then pass a dry patch through the bore to remove the fouling that has been raised from the pores of the metal. Copper fouling will appear as a green stain on the patch. The entire process should then be repeated to ensure that all this fouling has been removed. So long as a green stain appears

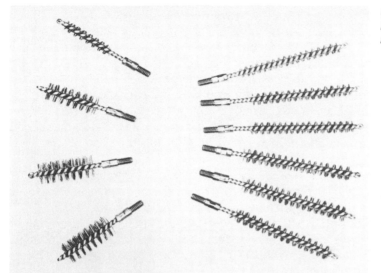

Good quality cleaning brushes, such as these from Bruno, are essential to proper maintenance of a firearm.

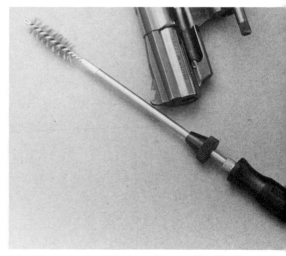

The Rig pistol rod has a slip-on "buffer" to help prevent damage to revolver muzzles.

Cleaning inside frame surfaces and cylinders of revolvers will require the use of a brush to remove accumulated leading.

on the first dry patch, you will know that your bore is not yet truly clean. Black stains are carbon fouling, and it is unlikely that you will be able to remove all of the carbon from the steel's pores. But you should clean out all of the copper fouling. If there are still signs of copper presence after the second effort, you may wish to allow the gun to soak for a longer period. If your bore cleaner allows for continuous chemical reaction, you may want to allow an overnight soaking. Some bore cleaners stop working after fifteen or twenty minutes, so that nothing can be gained by longer soaks. Cleaners such as the aforementioned Shooter's Choice will continue to work so long as the bore is still wet with solvent.

The same process applies to bores that have been used with lead shot or lead bullets. The leading will be removed as small silver flakes on your patch. Heavy leading will require extensive brushing with a good-fitting bronze brush.

Shotgun ammo that utilizes a plastic sleeve around the shot will not cause leading, but it will leave a plastic residue that should be removed. Additionally, shotgun chambers should be scrubbed to remove any plastic residue. Outers offers a fine bronze chamber brush and rod for this purpose.

After thoroughly cleaning the bore, leave a very thin film of light, high-quality oil in the bore to help prevent fouling buildup when the gun is next used. This should be applied by a dampened patch followed by a dry patch. Do not leave any excess oil in the barrel, however, as to do so can cause serious barrel damage if the gun is fired.

If you use Marksmans Choice bore cleaner, you will not need to apply any oil to condition your bore for its next use because this solvent contains an oil of a very high grade.

After cleaning your bore, you should of course clean all the action surfaces. This can be done with a toothbrush soaked in solvent. Revolvers require special care if they have been used with lead bullets. Such use results in a buildup of lead on the face of the cylinder and on the inside frame surface adjacent to the barrel cylinder gap. The use of an inexpensive bronze brush is usually required to remove this leading. It is pointless to use a good brush, as this kind of cleaning will quickly destroy any brush, regardless of quality.

Follow the manufacturer's instructions for any detailed disassembly and cleaning required. It is a good idea to keep the original instructions supplied with your gun for a refresher course on what should or should not be cleaned.

If you will be using your rifle in very cold temperatures, remove all the oil before use. However, in more moderate temperatures, a small amount of oil will prevent excessive wear of moving parts.

Gas-operated shotguns need special cleaning care. The gas systems of such guns must be wiped free of all solvent, and no oil should be applied. The important point is to follow the shotgun manufacturer's instructions exactly. Many gas-operated shotguns are brought to gunsmiths each year with complaints of malfunctions, when all that is wrong is that the gun needs to be disassembled and thoroughly cleaned.

Proper firearm maintenance also means tight screws. This especially applies to action screws and those that retain scope mount bases and scope rings. A loose scope ring or base will play havoc with accuracy. However, one should not attempt to tighten gun screws with a carpenter's screwdriver. To do so will result in burred and unsightly screwheads that will seriously detract from the gun's value. Use only quality gunsmithing screwdrivers such as those offered by Bonanza and others. And be sure the chosen screwdriver fits the slot of the screw exactly. Oversized or undersized screwdriver blades will result in damage to screwheads or surrounding surfaces. All gunsmithing screwdrivers have hollow-ground blades.

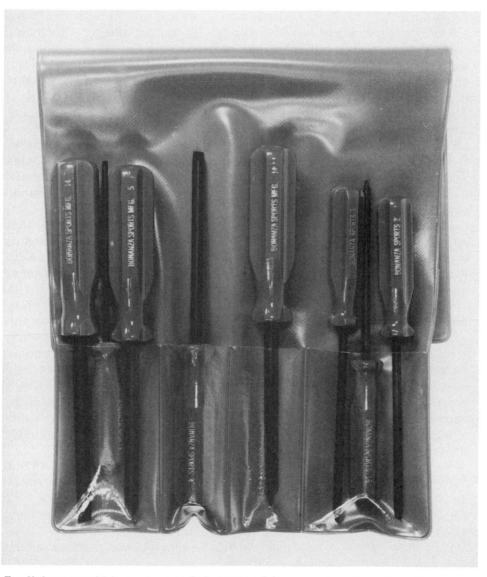

For light gunsmithing, properly fitting screwdrivers, such as these from Bonanza Sports, will prevent damage to screw slots.

Periodically inspect the bore of unused firearms. A cleaning every three or four months can prevent a bore from being ruined by rust. Also, wiping down the outside of the gun with a silicone cloth once each month or after each handling will keep the gun free of rust and looking new.

Cleaning a Muzzleloader   Proper cleaning of a muzzleloader is vital to preventing rapid corrosion and the resulting poor accuracy. Guns fired with black powder should be cleaned as soon as possible after use, and no later than twenty-four hours after last being fired.

Black-powder fouling quickly absorbs moisture and induces rapid rusting and pitting. Therefore, it must be removed promptly, but not with the solvents you use to clean modern cartridge firearms. Hot, soapy water is the best solvent for dissolving and removing black-powder fouling. The proper procedure for cleaning is enhanced by a hooked breech, which allows rapid and simple removal of the barrel from the action and stock.

To clean your muzzleloading rifle, musket or shotgun, place a pail of very hot, soapy water on the floor in front of you and insert the breech end of the barrel into the pail. Soak a snug-fitting patch in the water and place it on your ramrod. Push the patch into the muzzle and all the way through the barrel until it stops against the breech plug. Then slowly pull the patch forward until it reaches the muzzle. This will cause the hot, soapy water drawn into the barrel through the nipple or flash hole to fill the barrel behind the patch.

Do not allow the patch to come free at the muzzle, or the water will drain out. Pump the patch up and down your barrel fifteen or twenty times. The water in the pail will become blackened during this procedure as all the powder fouling is dissolved. Then remove the patch from the barrel, and allow the water to drain from the barrel into the pail.

After rinsing the pail, fill it three-quarters full with *very* hot water—no soap this time. Then repeat the wet-patch-and-pumping routine until the barrel is very warm to the touch. Drain all the water from the barrel, and set it aside to dry. The heat introduced by the very hot water will cause the moisture in and on the barrel to evaporate, and it will dry very rapidly. After the barrel has dried, soak a patch in oil and pump it up and down the bore a dozen times. This will prevent the bore from rusting between use. Then wipe off the outside of the barrel with an oily rag. Also wipe down the outside of the lock and stock with a heavily oiled rag to remove any powder or cap residue. Finally, reassemble the gun.

The cleaning of a black-powder gun after each use is a must to prevent rapid and irrevocable damage. Such cleaning is looked upon by some as a smelly chore. Perhaps this is a fair appraisal; nonetheless, if you do not complete the chore promptly, your gun will soon become a worthless pile of scrap metal and wood.

For revolver cleaning, the cylinder should be removed and given the bucket-of-hot-soapy-water treatment. The barrel of a revolver should be cleaned with hot, soapy patches followed by plain-water patches without any immersion, to prevent water getting into the action.

Muzzleloading weapons are best cleaned with hot, soapy water.

Some shooters who live in apartments have used a bathtub instead of a bucket for cleaning their muzzleloaders. This works OK, but you had best be living with a very understanding family before giving this method a try. Black-powder residue gives off a horrible stench when being dissolved, and the stain left on the tub is very difficult to remove.

Several brands of commercial black-powder solvent are offered to those who are unable to use hot, soapy water. I have tried a number of these, including the Hodgdon and Outers brands. They work well enough if the directions are followed carefully. But nothing will clean up black-powder residue as quickly and as effectively as hot water and soap.

General firearms' maintenance is a must to ensure the years of accurate shooting designed into the gun by the manufacturer. It doesn't make sense to purchase a fine gun and then provide anything less than the ideal in maintenance.

A good rifle/shotgun holding vise will help make the cleaning chore easier and prevent accidental damage to your firearm. I use the Decker vise and have found it to be an essential part of firearms' maintenance equipment. This or a similar unit can prevent a lot of dings and nicks that frequently happen when a gun is not adequately supported during the cleaning process. Such a vise can also be used for stock inletting, scope mounting and other repair chores. For a $35 bill, a Decker vise offers fine long-term insurance against damage to your expensive firearms.

A gun-cleaning stand such as this Decker Vise will help you to avoid nicking and scratching your rifle when cleaning it or performing minor maintenance chores.

PRACTICE MEANS RELOADING 37

Cost Factors   Shooting is not unlike other athletic endeavors. Becoming proficient requires a considerable amount of practice. However, the necessary shooting practice can be extremely costly if undertaken with factory-loaded ammunition. Today, a single factory-loaded 30-06 cartridge sells for more than seventy-five cents, and a 12-gauge target load sells for almost thirty-five cents. The cost of a day at the range can become prohibitive at these prices. Yet, if you are to maintain proficiency at your chosen shooting sport, you will need to spend many days at the range every year.

Reloading can reduce the cost of 30-06 ammunition from seventy-five cents to about twelve cents each. And 12-gauge target loads can be assembled for approximately fourteen cents each. The actual amount you save will depend on the exact load you assemble, but typical savings range from 60–75 percent or more. This means that for a given expenditure, you can shoot more than three reloads for each factory load you might purchase for an equivalent amount of money.

Safety Considerations   Many shooters recognize the savings but feel that a potential danger is associated with the use of handloaded ammunition. Yet, through knowledgeable and safe handling, they have overcome the potential hazards associated with firearms. Therefore, there is no reason to assume that the potential dangers of reloading are insurmountable. Using common sense, one can easily load ammunition that is every bit as safe as factory loads.

To prove this point, consider that the ammunition industry (Remington, Federal, Winchester, et al) will load approximately 475 million centerfire cartridges and 1.2 billion shotshells during 1985. During this same time period, 4 million reloaders will assemble approximately 1.1 billion centerfire and 936 million shotshells. The combined output of reloaders will exceed the combined output of the major ammunition manufacturers by 361 million rounds. The sheer volume of reloads assembled each year should convince you that reloading is a safe practice. If it were not, reloading would not be as popular as it is.

Reloading Metallic Cartridges

Equipment and Supplies   A small investment in equipment is required to enjoy the additional shooting that reloading savings will allow. The shooter wishing to reload will need to purchase a suitable press, dies, shell holder, powder scale, powder funnel, loading block, vernier, case trimmer and deburring tool in order to get started. Later, you may add a number of convenience items such as a powder measure, remote priming tool and other handy accessories. But the first purchase should always be a good book that will provide sufficient knowledge to assemble safe and accurate ammunition.

You can expect to spend between $150 and $250 on your initial equipment, depending upon the tools you purchase and your ability to shop well. This is a relatively small amount to amortize over a lifetime of shooting. To get a good start, select items that will last for a great many years. Equipment that becomes obsolete as you learn what reloading is all about represents a poor investment. I would suggest the following as being suitable for both the beginner and experienced metallic cartridge reloader. The listed equipment will load in excess of 50,000 rounds of ammo without replacement if it receives proper care.

RCBS RS2 reloading press
RCBS 1010 powder scale
RCBS die set for appropriate caliber
RCBS shell holder for appropriate caliber
Loading block in wood or plastic
RCBS or Wilson case trimmer with deburring tool
Dial indicating vernier of high quality
Powder funnel
Handbook of Metallic Cartridge Reloading

These basics will allow you to completely reprocess fired cases into safe and accurate ammunition. You will have everything you need to resize your brass; to remove the old primer and seat a new one; to trim cases back to the required length and remove burrs from the brass; to weigh out and put the correct charge of powder into the case; and finally, to seat the bullet properly. Please keep in mind that you must first obtain an in-depth understanding of handloading. This cannot be gained from a single book chapter, and therefore the purchase of a thorough handbook is essential.

As time goes on, you may want to purchase additional die sets and shell holders to allow you to load several calibers. Keep in mind that certain families of cartridges all use the same shell holder. For instance, the 22-250 Remington, 243 Winchester, 6mm Remington, 250-3000, 25-06 Remington, 270 Winchester, 280 Remington, 300 Savage, 308 Winchester, 30-06 Springfield and the 358 Winchester all use the same shell holder. You may also wish to add a powder measure to your equipment to speed up the loading process, along with a good powder trickler and a set of scoops to make weighing powder charges a quick and simple task.

Step-by-Step Handloading   The most important aspect of handloading is to double-check every step. The second most important aspect is to know what needs to be done and why.

Basically, metallic cartridge reloading requires that you follow these steps:

STEP 1   Inspect your brass cases for any sign of weakening such as cracked mouths, body splits, gas leakage around the primer or of body separation.

STEP 2   After inspection, apply a high-quality case sizing lubricant to prevent the case from becoming hopelessly jammed in the sizing die. A lubricating pad can prove useful for this operation, or you can simply anoint your fingers with lubricant and then run them over the case.

STEP 3   Place the fired case into the shell holder, and operate the press handle to run the case completely into the sizing die. This will return the fired case to its original dimensions and remove the fired primer from the case.

STEP 4   After resizing the brass, carefully measure its length with a quality vernier. Cases must fall between a minimum and maximum length. When they reach maximum length, they should be trimmed back to the minimum length. On the first loading, all brass, whether once-fired or new, should be trimmed to the minimum length. This will assure a square case mouth, which is essential for accuracy, and will also guarantee that all cases are of a uniform length.

RELOADING A CARTRIDGE

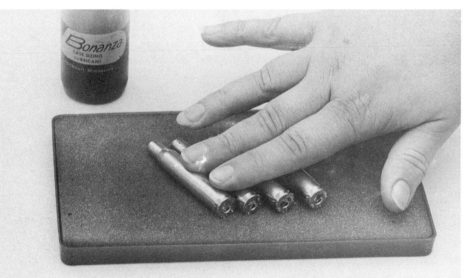

1. After inspecting fired cases for flaws or damage, carefully lubricate each case by rolling it on a lubricant pad.

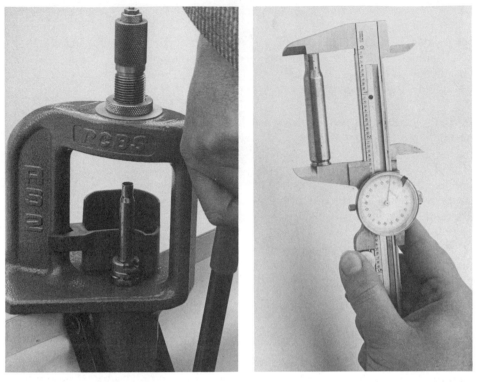

2. *Place the lubricated case into the shell holder and lower the press handle, forcing the case into the sizing die and removing the fired primer.*

3. *After sizing, carefully measure the case to insure that it falls between the minimum and maximum case length.*

4. *Trim all cases that reach or exceed maximum length and all new brass to square-up the case mouth. Trimmers should be adjusted to produce a case length equal to the minimum (trim-to) length.*

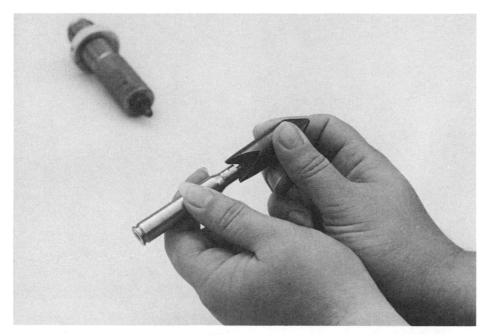

5. After trimming, deburr case mouths on the outside as well as the inside.

6. With the priming unit screwed into place and properly adjusted, place a primer into the priming punch.

7. Slip the case into the shell holder and fully seat the primer.

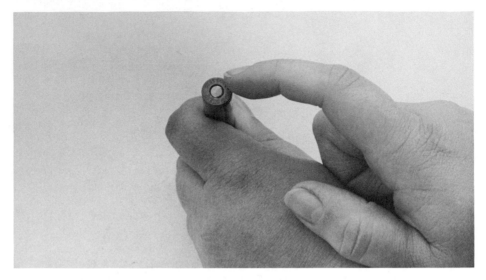

8. Check to insure that the primer is seated slightly below flush by sliding your finger over the base of the case.

9. Carefully weigh out a powder charge using a trickler to add the last few kernals of powder.

10. *When the pointer lines up with the index mark, the charge is correct.*

11. *Pour the powder into the case using a powder funnel.*

12. Next place the charged case into the shell holder and hold a bullet in place over the case. Lower the press handle to seat the bullet.

STEP 5   Carefully trim cases to a minimum length before the first loading and whenever they reach the maximum allowable length.

STEP 6   Remove the burrs created by case trimming with a deburring tool. Be sure to chamfer both the outside and inside of the case. If the inside edge of the case mouth is not slightly chamfered, bullet seating can be difficult.

STEP 7   Carefully seat a new primer. Be sure the primer is bottomed in the primer pocket. A properly seated primer will be from .003 inches to .008 inches below flush with the case head. A primer that is seated too deeply may be crushed, and the priming pellet cracked. This condition will result in a misfire. A primer that is not seated deeply enough can also cause a misfire. Primers that protrude above the case are potential hazards because they could be fired during the feeding cycle of the firearm. Primers must be handled with clean, dry hands. Any contamination of the primer might cause its deterioration, resulting in poor ignition of the powder or a misfire.

STEP 8 After priming, run your finger over each primer to ensure that it does not protrude and that it is indeed seated below flush. You can quickly learn the "feel" for this procedure.

STEP 9 Carefully weigh the powder charge and pour it into the case. Check the scale poise before weighing each charge to ensure that it was not inadvertently moved when the previous charge was removed from the scale.

STEP 10 Seat the bullet to the correct depth. Crimping, when required, is accomplished during bullet seating. All ammunition to be used in tubular magazines or semiautomatic rifles should have the bullet crimped firmly into place to prevent it from being driven into the case during recoil (in a tubular magazine) or during the violent feeding of semiautomatics.

Selecting Powder, Primer and Bullets
That's all there is to it. Reloading metallic cartridges is that easy. Of course, you must select the proper powder, primer and bullets. And you must use the correct powder charge with the appropriate bullet weight. The details of component selection and use can be obtained from any good reloading manual.

In order to help you select a suitable powder and bullet for varmint, deer, target or heavy game, a chart has been included showing those powders and bullets that I have used and found to be excellent performers in a great many rifles.

A similar chart has been included for handgun cartridges. This chart shows the ideal powders for target loads and for hunting loads. A specific bullet recommendation is made for each purpose. For home defense, the hunting bullets will prove to be the ideal selection.

No attempt has been made to list specific powder charges. These should be obtained from a reliable handbook or from the powder manufacturers' data. Never attempt to use any specific powder charge until you are thoroughly familiar with starting charges, maximum charges and pressure indications.

Properly assembled reloads can often provide better ballistic uniformity than mass-produced factory ammunition. In the case of metallic cartridges, this increased uniformity will mean a greater degree of accuracy. In fact, in benchrest shooting, where the absolute ultimate in accuracy is required, the competitors use handloads 100 percent of the time. Factory ammunition simply isn't accurate enough for this kind of competition.

Reloading Shot Shells
The shotshell reloader has it somewhat easier than the metallic reloader. This is because a shotshell tool is, for the most part, a complete and self-contained unit.

Equipment and Supplies
The shooter who decides he wants to reload shotshells need only purchase a good reloading tool of the appropriate gauge,

On tools such as the Versamec shown, the reloader can produce 100 to 125 rounds in an hour without haste or waste.

a powder scale, a few spare powder bushings and perhaps a few shot bars for different charge weights. I most often use the Mec 700 Versamec tool. It is easy to use, adjusts simply and will load 100 to 125 shells per hour. It will serve the novice or the experienced reloader equally well and will last a great many years, loading thousands of shells annually.

Step-by-Step Handloading
The loading of shotshells is quickly and easily accomplished. After having ascertained that the tool to be used is indeed throwing the correct charges of shot and powder, you need only perform the following eight simple steps.

STEP 1   Inspect your cases, eliminating any that show signs of undue wear or fatigue such as slit mouths or bodies or gas leakage around the primer.

STEP 2   Place your shell on the first station of the press, and by operating the press handle, completely resize it and remove the old primer. Both operations are accomplished simultaneously.

STEP 3   Place a primer into the priming station. Place the case over it and operate the press handle, seating the primer until its rim bears firmly against the shell head.

STEP 4   Placing the primed case beneath the drop tube, meter a powder charge into the case.

STEP 5   Put a wad into the wad guide and seat it with approximately 40 pounds of pressure. The wad pressure may require adjustment (between 20 to 100 pounds in 10-pound increments) to ensure the proper forming of the crimp.

STEP 6   Meter a charge of shot into the case.

STEP 7   Start the crimp. The case should close between one-third and two-thirds of the way during this crimp-starting operation.

STEP 8   Form the final crimp. Some reloaders like to have a bevel on the case. The Mec 700 will do this automatically if the die is properly adjusted.

RELOADING A SHOTSHELL

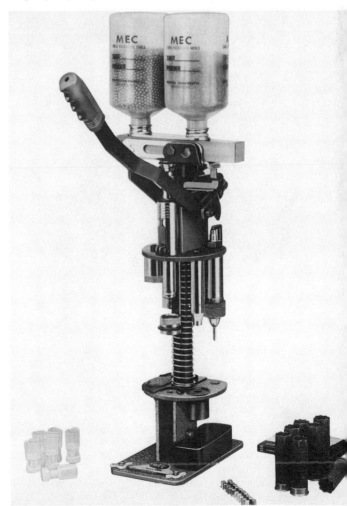

1. A shotshell press ready to load.

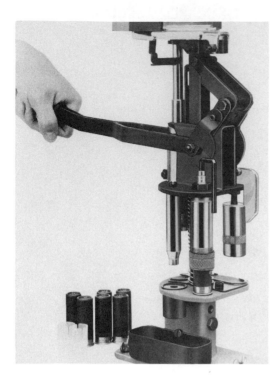

2. First full-length resize and deprime the shotshell case by placing it on station one and pushing down on the press handle.

3. Place a primer in the priming station.

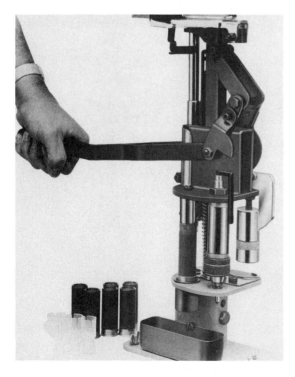

4. Then place a case on the priming station and seat the primer by pulling down on the press handle.

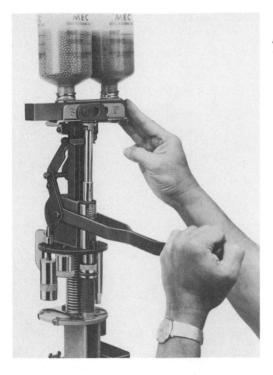

5. *Place the primer case under the charge tube, pull down the press handle and meter a powder charge by pushing in on the powder bar.*

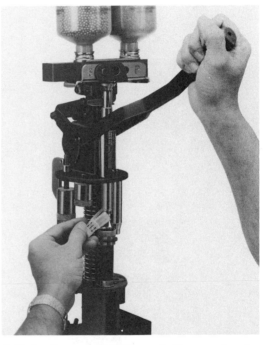

6. *Raise the press handle and slip a wad onto the charge tube.*

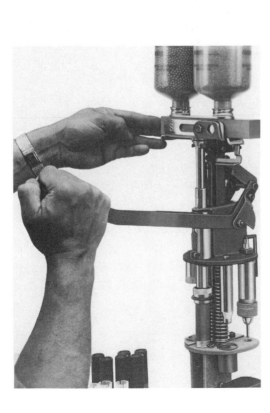

7. *Pull down on the handle to seat the wad and push in the shot bar to meter a charge of shot.*

8. *Place the case on the crimp start station to form the first step of the crimp.*

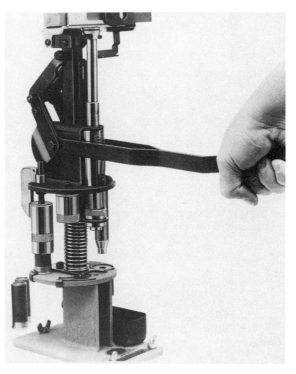

9. *With the shell on the final station pull down the handle to complete the crimp.*

10. *Remove the finished shell from the press.*

With the appropriate powder bushings and shot bar, one can assemble loads suitable for tiny rail birds, a day of clay-target shooting, waterfowl hunting or even turkey hunting. Any factory load can be duplicated with the one exception of slug loads.

It has also been my experience that it is nearly impossible to duplicate the accuracy of factory slugs with reloads. At one point, I spent six months of lab time trying to work up accurate slug loads for the 12, 16 and 20 gauges. I could have put the time to far better use, since all my efforts resulted in only mediocre slug performance. The state of the art is such that all slug shooting is best done with factory ammunition. This is the single exception to good handloads providing performance superior to factory loads.

The shotshell reloader should keep in mind that every difference in case construction requires different data. A 12-gauge Remington SP case is ballistically different from a 12-gauge Remington RXP case or any other 12-gauge case. Shotshells must be carefully segregated into different lots, and the appropriate loading data must be used for each lot.

Also, shotshell primers and wads are each ballistically different from another. Never attempt to substitute any shotshell case, primer or wad for another. Use only data that specifically lists the exact components, and use the data exactly, with no deviations. Doing so will help ensure that your shotshell reloads will perform as you expect.

Reloading is a means of increasing the amount of shooting you can enjoy. As such, it is a vital factor in your being able to practice sufficiently to become proficient with your chosen firearms.

SUGGESTED POWDERS FOR VARIOUS SHOTSHELL LOADS

Gauge	Shell Length (in inches)	Load Type	Shot Wt. (in ounces)	Powder
12	3	Magnum	1⅝	Hercules Blue Dot
12	2¾	Magnum	1½	Winchester 571
12	2¾	High Velocity	1¼	Du Pont SR 4756
12	2¾	Standard Velocity	1¼	Hercules Unique
12	2¾	Target	1⅛	Hercules Red Dot
12	2¾	Light Target	1	Hercules Red Dot
16	2¾	Magnum	1¼	Hercules Blue Dot
16	2¾	High Velocity	1⅛	Hercules Herco
16	2¾	Standard Velocity	1	Hercules Red Dot
20	3	Magnum	1¼	Winchester 571
20	2¾	Magnum	1⅛	Winchester 571
20	2¾	High Velocity	1	Du Pont SR 4756
20	2¾	Standard Velocity	1	Du Pont SR 4756
20	2¾	Target	⅞	Hercules Unique

Assumes the use of Winchester compression-formed cases, although the suggested powder will often work well in other types of cases.

SUGGESTED POWDER AND BULLET SELECTIONS FOR THE NOVICE RIFLE CARTRIDGE RELOADER

Caliber	Powder	Varmint bullet
22 Hornet	Du Pont IMR 4227	45-gr. Nosler SB
222 Remington	Hodgdon H335	50-gr. Nosler Expander
223 Remington	Hodgdon H335	55-gr. Speer Spitzer
222 Remington Mag.	Hercules Reloder 7	55-gr. Speer Spitzer
22-250 Remington	Du Pont IMR 4064	55-gr. Speer Spitzer
220 Swift	Du Pont IMR 4064	55-gr. Nosler SB
243 Winchester	Du Pont IMR 4350	75-gr. Sierra HP
6mm Remington	Du Pont IMR 4350	85-gr. Sierra Spitzer
250-3000 Savage	Du Pont IMR 3031	87-gr. Sierra Spitzer
257 Roberts	Du Pont IMR 4350	100-gr. Speer HP
25-06 Remington	Du Pont IMR 4350	100-gr. Speer HP
264 Winchester Mag.	Du Pont IMR 4831	100-gr. Speer HP
270 Winchester	Du Pont IMR 4350	90-gr. Sierra HP
7mm Mauser	Du Pont IMR 4350	115-gr. Speer HP
7mm-08 Remington	Winchester 760	115-gr. Speer HP
280 Remington	Du Pont IMR 4350	115-gr. Speer HP
7mm Remington Mag.	Du Pont IMR 4831	115-gr. Speer HP
30-30 Win.	Du Pont IMR 4064	—
300 Savage	Du Pont IMR 4064	110-gr. Sierra HP
307 Winchester	Du Pont IMR 4064	—
308 Winchester	Du Pont IMR 4064	125-gr. Sierra HP
30-06 Springfield	Du Pont IMR 4350	125-gr. Sierra HP
300 H & H Magnum	Du Pont IMR 4350	—
300 Winchester Mag.	Du Pont IMR 4831	—
32 Winchester Special	Winchester 748	—
8mm Remington Mag.	Du Pont IMR 4831	—
338 Winchester Mag.	Du Pont IMR 4350	—
356 Winchester	Du Pont IMR 4064	—
358 Winchester	Hercules Reloder 7	—
375 Winchester	Hercules Reloder 7	—
375 H & H Magnum	Du Pont IMR 4064	—
44 Remington Mag.	Winchester 296	—
444 Marlin	Hercules Reloder 7	—
45-70 Government	Du Pont IMR 3031	—
458 Winchester Mag.	Hercules Reloder 7	—

SB = solid base
HP = hollow point
gr. = grain
FP = flat point
RN = round nose
SP = soft point

Deer bullet	Target bullet	Heavy big-game bullet (over 400 lbs)
—	45-gr. Nosler SB	—
—	50-gr. Nosler Match	—
—	53-gr. Sierra HP	—
—	53-gr. Sierra HP	—
—	53-gr. Sierra HP	—
—	53-gr. Sierra HP	—
100-gr. Nosler Partition	100-gr. Sierra Spitzer	—
100-gr. Nosler Partition	100-gr. Sierra Spitzer	—
100-gr. Nosler Partition	100-gr. Speer HP	—
120-gr. Nosler Partition	100-gr. Speer HP	—
120-gr. Nosler Partition	100-gr. Speer HP	—
125-gr. Nosler Partition	100-gr. Speer HP	140-gr. Nosler Partition
130-gr. Speer Spitzer	150-gr. Speer Spitzer	130-gr. Nosler Partition
140-gr. Sierra Spitzer	160-gr. Speer Spitzer	140-gr. Nosler Partition
140-gr. Sierra Spitzer	140-gr. Sierra Spitzer	140-gr. Nosler Partition
140-gr. Sierra Spitzer	140-gr. Sierra Spitzer	160-gr. Nosler Partition
140-gr. Sierra Spitzer	175-gr. Hornady Spire	175-gr. Nosler Partition
170-gr. Speer FP	—	—
150-gr. Speer Spitzer	125-gr. Sierra Spitzer	—
170-gr. Speer FP	—	—
150-gr. Speer Spitzer	168-gr. Speer Gold Medal	180-gr. Nosler Partition
150-gr. Speer Spitzer	168-gr. Speer Gold Medal	180-gr. Nosler Partition
165-gr. Nosler SB	168-gr. Speer Gold Medal	180-gr. Nosler Partition
165-gr. Nosler SB	168-gr. Speer Gold Medal	180-gr. Nosler Partition
170-gr. Hornady FP	—	—
220-gr. Hornady Spire	220-gr. Hornady Spire	200-gr. Nosler Partition
200-gr. Speer Spitzer	275-gr. Speer Semi-Spitzer	210-gr. Nosler Partition
200-gr. Hornady RN	—	—
250-gr. Speer Spitzer	—	250-gr. Speer Spitzer
220-gr. Hornady FP	—	—
235-gr. Speer Semi-Spitzer	235-gr. Speer Semi-Spitzer	285-gr. Speer Grand Slam
240-gr. Speer HP	—	—
240-gr. Speer HP	—	—
400-gr. Speer SP	—	—
400-gr. Speer SP	—	510-gr. Winchester SP

SUGGESTED POWDER AND BULLET SELECTIONS FOR THE NOVICE HANDGUN CARTRIDGE RELOADER

Caliber	Target Loads		Hunting Loads	
	Powder	Bullet	Powder	Bullet
221 Remington	Du Pont IMR 4227	52-gr. Speer Gold Mat.	Du Pont IMR 4227	45-gr. Speer Hornet
32 S & W Long	Winchester 231	98-gr. Cast Lead WC	—	—
32 Auto	Winchester 231	71-gr. FMC	—	—
380 Auto	Hercules Bullseye	90-gr. Sierra JHP		
9mm Luger	Hercules Bullseye	100-gr. Speer JHP	Winchester 231	100-gr. Speer JHP
38 Special	Hercules Bullseye	148-gr. Speer LHBWC	Winchester 231	110-gr. Sierra JHP-PP
357 Magnum	Hercules Bullseye	148-gr. Speer LHBWC	Winchester 231	140-gr. Sierra JHP-PP
357 Maximum	Hercules Bullseye	148-gr. Speer LHBWC	Winchester 296	158-gr. Sierra JHP-PP
41 Remington Mag.	Winchester 231	210-gr. Cast Lead WC	Hercules 2400	210-gr. Sierra JHP-PP
44 Special	Hercules Bullseye	240-gr. Speer LSWC	Hercules Unique	200-gr. Speer Mag. HP
44 Remington Mag.	Hercules Bullseye	240-gr. Speer LSWC	Hercules 2400	240-gr. Speer Mag. HP
45 Auto	Hercules Bullseye	200-gr. Speer LSWC	Hercules Unique	200-gr. Speer JHP
45 Colt	Hercules Bullseye	200-gr. Speer SWC	Hercules Herco	200-gr. Speer JHP

Gold Mat. = gold match

WC = wadcutter

FMC = full metal case

JHP = jacketed hollow point

JHP-PP = jacketed hollow point with power point

LHBWC = lead hollow base wadcutter

LSWC = lead semiwadcutter

HP = hollow point

SWC = semiwadcutter

EXERCISES TO INCREASE SHOOTING SKILLS

38

The best way to keep in practice for any sport is to participate frequently. But few of us shooters are fortunate enough to be able to shoot as often as we care to or, for that matter, often enough to maintain physical and mental capabilities sufficient to assure a high degree of shooting competence. For most enthusiasts in this modern world, it is almost impossible to get near a place to shoot during the course of a given work week. Weekends are frequently devoted to many do-it-yourself chores designed to save money for the annual hunting trip. And there is the family, to which a great deal of time must be devoted. All this often reduces our actual shooting practice to far too few occasions.

Yet, there are steps that the individual can take to help maintain shooting skills. Seemingly insignificant daily exercises can add greatly to your ability to hold a rifle or handgun steady, to swing a shotgun smoothly or to hold a bow at full draw without wobble.

Building Stamina Stamina plays an important part in shooting capability. The hunter must be able to traverse his range without fatigue. No one can shoot well when tired or out of breath from climbing a hill or walking a long distance. Target shooters also need stamina to maintain their capability during a given course of fire. The rifle shooter may fire 100 rounds during a practice session, and a handgun shooter will often fire considerably more. Skeet and trap enthusiasts frequently shoot 100 rounds in a few hours. Bow shooters also can shoot a great deal in a practice session. And a long muzzleloading rifle can get pretty heavy around the twentieth shot.

Thus, anything the shooter can do to increase stamina will help him with his actual shooting. One exercise in which we can all participate is walking. Simple as it may seem, even a half-hour a day can pay dividends. Of course, more time is preferred. But not everyone can devote an hour or an hour and a half every day to exercise.

Yet, in your ordinary daily activities, you can get in more walking than you might first imagine. Instead of using the phone to talk to a coworker at the other end of the building, walk down to his or her office or work station. And remain standing as you discuss your business. Don't drive the half to three-quarters of a mile for that milk or bread from the corner store; walk instead. Need to talk to a neighbor? Instead of calling, walk over to discuss the matter. Want to say something to the kids? Don't call them to your chair, get up and go to them.

In short, stop doing things as a lazy person—do them as an energetic and enthusiastic person. Skip the shopping cart and carry those two bags to the car. And make an effort to walk briskly for at least thirty minutes each day. This amount of walking time can be squeezed into even the busiest routine, if you are serious about it. If you're convinced that you can't spare the time, think about the days, months or perhaps even years that a vigorous walk each day might add to your lifespan. You will get back a great deal more time than you put into the effort. Kind of like getting compound interest on your savings in the bank of good health.

Walking vigorously for one hour a day is entirely adequate to put you into reasonably good condition for most hunting and other kinds of shooting. But do check with your doctor before undertaking these walks. And when covering ground at a fast pace, it's best to vary the terrain—uphill, downhill, level, easy and rough.

After a bit of daily practice, you'll find that you won't be yelling, "Hey, honey, when you come downstairs, please bring my ...". Instead, you'll be getting up and going to fetch it yourself.

Gun Mounting   Another exercise that should be routine each day is a five-minute session of gun mounting and sight alignment. Simply stand holding the gun as you would in the field, then bring it to your shoulder smoothly and align the sights, reticule or bead on a spot on the other side of the room. Strive not for speed but, rather, for smooth and effortless control that results in positive sight alignment as the butt touches your shoulder. Speed will come without conscious effort as your actions are repeated time after time, day after day. Handgun shooters should add getting the proper grip on the gun before swinging it up to align the sights. Holding a shotgun, rifle, handgun or bow requires development of specific muscles. By actually bringing the gun into the shooting position repeatedly each day, these muscles can be developed. Five or ten minutes daily is all that it takes.

Some may want to practice when their gun or bow is not available, such as at the office, when first getting up or just going to bed. A half-gallon plastic milk container and some sand can be kept handy and provides excellent exercise.

Fill the container with sand until it weights twice as much as your loaded long gun or bow. Then, using your left hand (for right-handed shooters), bring the container from a position at your side through a smooth arc to a position at arm's length and shoulder height. Then simply hold it there until you tire. Do not lower it until you actually begin to feel some strain, but equally important, do not fight to maintain the jug in position once the strain is felt. Repeat this exercise three or four times with sufficient pauses to allow a rest period in between.

Handgun and Bow Techniques   Handgunners will naturally hold the jug in the hand with which they normally hold their gun. It takes only five minutes a day to develop the power required to support your gun or bow at arm's length without tremors or wobbles of any notable degree.

Bow shooters have no easy substitutes for developing the finger, wrist, arm and back muscles used when bringing the bow to full draw. So slide an old bow under the couch or stand it in the corner. And frequently as you pass by, pick it up, bring it to full draw and hold that draw for as long as possible up to a full minute. Then slowly, very slowly, relax the bow. This reverse tension will add a great deal of benefit to the exercise. Ideally, the bow used for this kind of exercise should have a holding or draw weight 5 pounds heavier than the bow used for actual shooting.

Body Movement   To help with swinging from the waist, you can perform a simple exercise. Simply stand erect with knees and hips locked into position. The feet should be in the normal shooting position. With the arms extended straight out to each side, twist the entire upper torso from waist to head as a unit, first as far to the right as possible, then as far to the left as possible. Do not move any portion of the legs. This may sound easy, but if you try it, you will find that it is extremely difficult to move the upper torso more than a small amount without twisting from the knees or hips. Limit your upper-torso swing to however much you can accomplish without moving from below the waist. You will, in time, be able to execute a 30- to 40-degree twist. If you swing more than this, chances are you are moving below the waist. To check for below-the-waist movement, have someone hold your hips.

To develop complete gun-turret flexibility, you can also bend forward and rearward with the arms extended as above. Again, be certain that all motion occurs from the waist.

In both the twisting and bending exercises, it will take considerable concentration to ensure that your neck and head remain motionless and move only with your torso.

You can also practice gun mounting with an imaginary gun. Assume the correct shooting stance and bring your imaginary gun to the shoulder using your arms and hands. Concentrate on keeping your supporting arm's elbow directly below the gun barrel while placing the trigger-hand elbow above the horizon as the "gun" is mounted. Remember to swing the "gun" outward far enough from your clothing not to hang it up, and remember to pull the butt against your shoulder.

Your spouse and kids may feel you have gone off the deep end when they see you mounting an imaginary gun. But you will gain a good deal of smooth gun-mounting technique that will allow you to get gun to shoulder in minimum time.

It doesn't take much in fanciness or in time to help keep your body in tune for shooting. But it does take a dedication to wanting to stay in shape. A half- to a full hour's walking daily and perhaps another ten or fifteen minutes of the described exercises can make a big difference. It may not seem like much in the beginning, but the results of dedication will become obvious in your shooting in as little as thirty days of daily effort.

39 SAFETY WITH FIREARMS AND AMMUNITION

Safety at Home

Firearms safety should be foremost in the minds of all those who use guns. Safety with firearms begins, quite naturally, in the home. Obviously, the ownership and use of firearms should be undertaken only by persons capable of mature thinking. Such persons will find the five basic parameters of home firearms safety easy to follow. The observance of these basic rules can result in a positive atmosphere that will keep your home free of the tragedy of a firearms-related accident.

Unload Guns After Use First and most important, all firearms brought into the home must be unloaded. An unloaded gun can cause no bodily harm. A gun kept for self-protection should be kept secure from both inquisitive hands as well as intruders. A bureau drawer or the night table are the first places an intruder will look. Even the most well-behaved child will occasionally go on a house hunt, taking in many places normally thought secure. As mentioned in Chapter 21, I feel the best way to keep a loaded handgun for protection is in a "Gunsafe." This metal case will keep the handgun locked away from unauthorized persons, yet allow easy access to those who know the right combination. All other guns kept in the home should be unloaded.

Check Guns Before Handling Most gun owners enjoy handling their rifles, shotguns and handguns. They also take pride in showing them to others. Thus, the second basic rule of home firearms safety is never to handle any firearm until first carefully determining that it is indeed unloaded. Take no one's word for the fact. Do not accept a gun as unloaded because someone else has just examined it and found it to be empty. Countless examples could be cited in which "unloaded" guns have gone off, sometimes with tragic results. Parents have killed or maimed children in a careless moment, and children have caused similar tragedies.

Live cartridges left in magazines through neglect, poor gun design or malfunction can wind up as chambered rounds at the most inopportune times. Every gun should always be considered loaded and so treated until you personally have established that it is indeed empty. Proper gun safety demands that each

428

Make sure a gun is unloaded before bringing it into the house.

A child on a house hunt can spell disaster if he or she finds gun and ammo. Don't let this happen.

Firearms are best kept under lock and key and separated from ammunition.

Gunsafe can prevent unauthorized hands from obtaining access to firearms.

person handling a gun determine that it is unloaded and therefore safe to be handled.

Keep Guns Locked Up   Third, all stored guns should be kept under lock and key. Even firearms stored in a gun rack should be locked securely in place. Such locks may or may not provide security from theft, but they will keep guns from being handled needlessly by unauthorized persons. (The firearms owner who locks his guns from sight has taken a giant step in preventing his guns from being stolen and perhaps later being used in a crime of violence.)

Store Ammunition Carefully   The fourth rule concerns ammunition. As with firearms, ammunition should always be kept under lock but in a place removed from firearms. Should unauthorized persons gain accidental or deliberate access to either ammo or firearms, having the other in a remote place may prevent a tragedy.

Be Careful Where the Gun Is Pointing   Finally, the fifth home safety rule is always to keep the muzzle pointed in a safe direction when handling a firearm. Even if all other rules go unheeded, this one can still prevent tragedy. A safe direction is not necessarily a wall, ceiling or floor. What's on the other side of that wall, ceiling or floor? A high-powered rifle or even a modern handgun cartridge is capable of penetrating quite a bit of home construction and still inflicting serious harm. A gun pointed at a window can cause injury or death to a neighbor or distant person. Up may not be a safe direction if there is someone upstairs, on the roof or in the attic. In other words, one needs to think about where the muzzle is pointing and what represents a safe direction. The junction of an outside wall and the floor often is a safe direction.

Safety for Handloaders

Shooters who reload need to observe additional safety measures in the home. For example, one cannot store unlimited quantities of powder and primers in a home reloading workshop without adding undue risk in the event of fire.

Storage Limits   Powder consumed in a fire will, under most circumstances, simply burn with intense heat. Keeping powder inventories at reasonable levels will ensure that the flame and heat caused by burning powder will not add measurably to the danger created by the original fire. To store powder properly, it should always be kept in its original container and away from any source of flame or sparks. Because powder will deteriorate if stored under adverse conditions, hot attics and damp cellars should not be chosen for storage areas.

It would be extremely difficult to justify the storage of more than 20 pounds of powder in any residence. Ideally, powder should be stored in a nonconfining wooden cabinet. Storage in any tightly sealed space could amount to the storage container becoming a bomb. Always allow ample room for venting and expansion of the gases of burning powder.

Because primers are designed to explode, care must be taken in handling them. Primers should never be stored in bulk. Primers that are kept in their original containers present no explosion hazard. However, pour primers into a glass jar and you have built a potentially lethal device. Keeping primers at a reasonable level will keep any hazard at a minimum. Surely, 1,000 of each size is enough to satisfy the demands of the most active reloader. Thus, with two rifle primer sizes, two pistol primer sizes and two shotgun primer sizes, even the most ardent reloader should be well stocked with a total of 6,000 primers. Even if variations in primer sizes are used, a stock of 10,000 or less primers should be more than sufficient. The National Fire Prevention Association suggests that a maximum of 20 pounds of powder and a maximum of 10,000 primers not be exceeded in any home.

Safety Information   Every reloader should obtain copies of *Sporting Ammunition Primers* and *Properties and Storage of Smokeless Powder.* These pamphlets are available in single copies by sending a request and a stamped, self-addressed envelope to: Sporting Arms and Ammunition Manufacturer's Institute Inc., P.O. Box 218, Wallingford, CT 06492. These brochures list the rules for storage and handling of powders and primers in detail. Other pertinent information, such as how to check for powder deterioration, is also included. Available from the same source is *Properties of Sporting Ammunition and Recommendations for Its Storage and Handling.* This pamphlet also contains worthwhile information.

Storage of black powder should be handled with extreme care. Black powder is a Class A explosive, usually subject to strict legal controls and fire-prevention regulations. Be sure to observe any local, county or state laws. Sometimes, home-protection insurance policies may be invalidated by the storage of even very small quantities of black powder. Any such powder kept on hand should be limited to a maximum of 1 pound of each type required for use in personal firearms, never to exceed 4 pounds.

Improper storage of ammunition and components has taken the life of more than one individual. All shooters should make the effort to learn exactly how to store ammunition and components safely. Detailed storage information for reloading materials is available from: The National Fire Prevention Association, 60 Batterymarch St., Boston, MA 02110, by requesting NFPA booklet No. 495, which is available for $1.50 per copy.

Safety in the Field

Firearms safety on the range or in the field is far more complex than in the home because the firearms are now being handled in a loaded condition. The following rules of safety are an absolute minimum:

1. Don't rely on a gun's safety. Treat every gun as if it were loaded and ready to fire.

2. Never cross a fence, climb a tree, jump a ditch or attempt to negotiate any other obstacle with a loaded gun. Unload before attempting any movement that cannot be classified as a normal walk.
3. Never load a gun or carry a loaded gun unless you are ready to use it. Equally, never set aside a loaded gun. Firearms should be loaded only while actually shooting or hunting. If you take a break, unload your gun.
4. Keep your muzzle pointed in a safe direction—always. There can be no excuse for pointing a firearm at anything that you would not deliberately shoot.
5. Keep guns and ammo secured during transportation. Do not leave guns or ammo where unauthorized persons may gain ready access.
6. Never shoot at anything until you have established the positive identity of your target and what lies beyond it.
7. Keep in mind the great range of modern ammunition. A misdirected shot can travel great distances and still inflict deadly harm.
8. Always wear eye protection whenever shooting. Ear protection is also a must, except perhaps for hunting where only a few shots are to be fired.
9. Never fire any gun when there is anything in the barrel, and always be certain to use the correct ammunition.

A number of safety pamphlets have been published by the National Shooting Sports Foundation, P.O. Box 1075, Riverside, CT 06878. Make it a point to obtain copies and read them carefully.

One could easily fill a volume with tragic stories of unforeseen and freak accidents involving firearms. Only with continued effort and diligence can each firearm owner ensure that he or she will not become a victim or the cause of a firearm accident. There is no such thing as too much caution. Treat every gun as though it were about to fire, and you will be on the right road to firearms safety. And don't hesitate to remind the "other guy" of any breach of these rules.

Index

Accessories. *See* Archery
  accessories; Handgun
  accessories; Rifle
  accessories; Shotgun
  accessories
Accuracy
  double-action handguns, 266, 274
  firearm maintenance and, 399–406
  handgun ballistics and, 234
  handgun tuning for, 228–232
  muzzleloaders and, 364, 368, 394
  revolver/semiautomatic pistol
    compared, 205, 207
  rifle tuning and, 89
  single-action handguns, 254
Adjustable sights, 221–224, 228, 230
Adjustable weight bows, 313–314
Aiming. *See* Sighting
Ammunition
  handgun ballistics, 235–236
  handgun cleaning, 234–235
  reloading and, 407–424
  revolver cylinder adjustment and,
    231
  revolver/semiautomatic pistols
    compared, 214–215
  storage of, 431
  22 rimfire silhouette shooting, 284
  See also Ballistics; Cartridges
Antique muzzleloaders, 366
Aperture sights
  adjustment of, 8
  description of, 10–14
  scopes compared, 14
  shotgun selection, 141, 144
  See also Bow sights; Handgun
    sights; Rifle sights; Shotgun
    sights
Archery. *See entries under* Arrow;
  Bow
Archery accessories, 335–345
  arm guards and gloves, 342
  carrying cases, 338, 342
  field hunting and, 356
  miscellaneous, 342
  range finders, 338
  sights, 335–338
  spare parts, 342
Arm guards (archery), 342
Arrow
  bow tuning techniques and,
    322–326
  inspection of, 347
Arrowhead, 356, 358
Arrow selection, 316–318, 329–333
  fletching, 331–332
  length in, 329, 331, 333
  material considerations in, 332–333
  spines, 331, 333

Ballistics

cartridge and bullet weight table,
    121–122
  moving targets and, 48
  muzzleloaders, 394
  small-bore target shooting, 51–53
  See also Ammunition; Cartridges;
    entries under types of guns
Barrels
  handgun accessories, 251
  rifle tuning, 90, 92
  shotgun accessories, 181
Bedding, 90
Benchrest target shooting, 63–70
  accessories for, 105, 106
  See also Rifle target shooting
Big-bore target shooting. *See* Large-
    bore target shooting
Bipods, 102–104
Bird shooting. *See entries under*
  Shotgun
Body movements
  exercises for, 427
  rifle shooting and, 44
  shotgun hunting and, 163
  skeet shooting, 153
  trap shooting, 173–174
Bolt-action rifles
  selection of, 78-79
  See also entries under Rifle
Bow hunting, 353–358
  exercise for, 426–427
  field techniques, 356
  hold and trajectory, 353
  light conditions and, 354–355
  position and, 355–356
  practice in, 356, 358
  quivers for, 338
  range estimation in, 353–354
Bow selection, 309–318
  adjustable weight bows, 313–314
  arrow selection and, 316–318
  compound bow advantages, 311
  draw weights and, 311–313
  types of bows, 309
Bow sights selection, 335–338
Bow target shooting, 346–351
  aim, 350
  arrow inspection, 347
  arrow selection, 329
  bow inspection, 346–347
  bow selection, 313
  exercises for, 426–427
  grip and, 350
  practice in, 351
  quivers and, 338
  release and follow-through, 351
  stance for, 347
  technique in, 347, 350
Bow tuning, 319–328
  arrow-rest plunger adjustment, 321
  bare arrow technique in, 322–323
  brace height adjustment in, 319
  fletched arrow technique in,
    323–326

interactions in, 326
  nocking point adjustment in,
    319–321
  range improvement, 326–328
  tiller adjustment in, 328
Brace height adjustment, 319
Breath control
  shooting technique, 25–26
  single-action handgun shooting,
    263
  trigger control and, 43–44
Bullet shape, 115–117. *See also*
  Ammunition; Ballistics

Cartridges
  benchrest target shooting, 70
  handgun ballistics, 237–240
  handgun selection, 215–218
  reloading of, 407–424
  revolver/semiautomatic pistol
    compared, 214–215
  shooting techniques and, 28
  22 rimfire rifles, 73
Centerfire handguns, 288–291
Centerfire rifles
  hunting with, 36
  selection suggestions for, 87
  sight adjustment, 5, 8
  silhouette target shooting, 56, 59
  See also entries under Rifle
Chokes
  adjustable chokes, 183–184
  crazy quail and, 176–177
  hunter's clays and, 178
  screw-in chokes, 181–183
  shotgun accessories, 181
  shotgun selection, 135–137
  skeet shooting, 145
  trap shooting, 168, 174
Cleaning
  accuracy and, 399–406
  equipment for, 399–400
  handgun ballistics and, 234–235
  handgun tuning and, 232
  muzzleloaders, 370–371, 377,
    404–406
  screw tightning and, 402–403
  techniques in , 400, 401–402
Cleaning kit (shotgun accessory), 186
Cobra-type slings, 99. *See also* Slings
Cocking
  double-action handgun, 265, 266
  single-action handgun, 257,
    260–261
Combat-style grips
  double-action handguns, 269, 272
  handgun accessories, 248
Compound bow
  action of, 309
  advantages of, 311
  arrow selection and, 331
  See also entries under Arrow; Bow
Crazy quail, 176–178
  technique in, 176–178

variations on, 178
See also Skeet shooting; Trap shooting
Customized handguns, 232

Double-action handgun shooting. *See* Handgun shooting (double-action)
Double-set trigger, 104
Double shotguns, 138–139
skeet shooting, 147
See also entries under Shotgun
Dram-equivalent system, 187–190
Draw weights, 311–313

Exercise. *See* Physical condition
Eyeglasses, 8
Eyesight
handgun sight alignment, 224, 226
rifle sight alignment, 4

Firepower, 207, 213
Fire prevention, 431–432. *See also* safety
Fixed sights
handguns, 219–221
See also entries under types of guns
Fletching, 331–332
Flintlock muzzleloaders, 368
loading of, 370–377
see also entries under Muzzleloader
Follow-through
bow target shooting, 351
muzzleloaders, 392
rifle shooting, 163
single-action handguns, 262
Foot placement
shotgun hunting, 160–161, 163
skeet shooting, 148, 149, 153
see also Stance
Free-floating barrels, 90, 92. *See also* Barrels

Glass bedding, 92–93
Glasses. *See* Eyeglasses
Gloves (archery), 342
Gordon, Skip, 63
Grips
double-action handguns, 269–270
handgun accessories, 248
handgun tuning, 228
single-action handguns, 254–257
Gun cases
handguns, 251
selection of, 106–107
shotgun accessories, 186
Gun locks, 252–253

Hammer cocking. *See* Cocking
Handedness
bolt-action rifle, 79
handgun safeties, 248
muzzleloader loading, 371
muzzleloader selection, 364

rifle shooting technique, 44
Handgun accessories, 245–253
barrels, 251
cases and holsters, 251
combat grips, 248
gun locks, 252–253
magazines, 251
safeties, 248
speed loaders, 251
tangs, 248, 251
target hammers, 247
target stocks, 248
target triggers, 245–247
Handgun ballistics, 234–244
ammunition variations, 235–236
cartridge selection, 237–240
double-action shooting, 266–267
gun variations, 234–235
hunting and, 295, 297
long-range, 244
performance standards, 234
power index rating (PIR), 241–244
revolver cylinder alignment and, 231
single-action shooting, 254–255
Handgun exercises, 426–427
Handgun holsters. *See* Holsters
Handgun hunting, 292–298
ballistics in, 295, 297
holsters for, 299–304
position for, 295, 297
selection of gun for, 292, 295
Handgun muzzleloaders, 364
Handgun selection, 205–218
brand names in, 218
caliber and, 215–218
double-action shooting, 266–269
hunting, 292, 295
revolvers and semiautomatics compared, 205–215
suggestions for, 206
22 rimfire silhouette shooting, 277–282
Handgun shooting (double-action), 265–274
advantages of, 265–266
disadvantages of, 266
grips, 269–270
gun selection, 266–269
practice in, 273–274
trigger squeeze, 270–272
Handgun shooting (single-action), 254–264
breath control, 263
grip, 254–257
hammer cocking, 257, 260–261
practice in, 263–264
regripping, 257
sight alignment, 262
stance for, 262–263
trigger finger placement, 261–262
trigger squeeze, 262
Handgun sights, 219–227
adjustable sights, 221–224

alignment of, 224, 226–227
customizing, 232
double-action shooting, 273
fixed sights, 219–221
hunting, 297
screw adjustment tuning, 228, 230
selection of, 227
single-action shooting, 262
telescopic sights, 224, 227
Handgun silhouette shooting, 275–291
centerfire guns, 288–291
gun selection, 215, 216, 217–218
22 rimfires in, 275–288
Handgun target shooting
ballistics, 238
sights, 227
telescopic sights, 224
triggers, 245–247
Handgun tuning, 228–232
adjustable sight screw, 228, 230
cleaning, 232
customizing, 232
cylinder alignment, 230–232
grip fitting, 228
trigger pulls, 232
Hasty-sling position, 98, 99, 102
Holsters, 299–306
concealed-type, 304–306
handguns, 251
hunting-type, 299–304
magazine-release button and, 303–304
Hunters' clays, 178–179
Hunting rifles. *See* Rifle hunting

Injured games. *See* Wounded game
International Handgun Metallic Silhouette Association (IHMSA), 276, 277, 286

Kilbourn, Lysle, 115
Kneeling position, 33–34

Large-bore target shooting, 54–55, 106
Lead bullets
handgun cleaning and, 234–235
revolver cylinder allignment and, 231
Leading
ballistics and, 200
game type and, 122–123
shotgun hunting, 159–160
techniques in, 46–48
trap shooting, 172–174
See also Moving targets
Left handedness. *See* Handedness
Lever-action rifles
selection of, 76–78
semiautomatic rifles compared, 74
See also entries under Rifle
Lighting, 354–355

Magazines
   handgun accessories, 251
   holsters and, 303–304
   semiautomatic pistols, 214
Magnum-type ballistics, 109–111
Military-sling position, 98, 102
Mounting. *See* Gun mount
Moving targets
   ballistics and, 48
   crazy quail, 176–178
   game speed and, 49
   leading, 46–48
   shooting position and, 48–49
   shotgun hunting, 159–160, 163, 166
   skeet shooting, 154–155
   trap shooting, 170–174
   See also Leading
Muzzleloader cleaning, 404–406
Muzzleloader loading, 370–389
   fit and, 388
   flintlocks, 370–377
   misfires, 388–389
   percussion guns, 377–382
   percussion revolver, 382
   powder type in, 388
   shotgun, 387–388
Muzzleloader selection, 361–369
   chart for, 369
   flintlock versus percussion, 368
   handguns, 364
   hunting guns, 361–364
   legal restrictions and, 361
   manufacturers and, 364, 366
Muzzleloader shooting, 390–396
   accuracy and, 394
   follow-through, 392
   ignition, 392–393
   moisture and, 390–392
   position and, 392
   safety and, 393
Muzzleloader sights, 368

National Rifle Association (NRA),
   54, 276
National Shooting Sports
   Foundation, 434
Nocking point adjustment, 319–321
Noise, 28

Offhand position
   described, 34–35
   foot positioning and, 40
   handgun hunting, 297
   moving targets and, 48–49
   silhouette target shooting, 58
   trigger control, 43
Open sights
   description of, 8–10
   shotgun selection, 141
   See also entries under *types of guns*

Peep sights. *See* Aperture sights
Percussion muzzleloaders, 368
   loading of, 377–382

See also entries under
   Muzzleloader
Physical condition
   exercises for, 425–427
   shooting technique and, 25–26
Pistols. *See* Semiautomatic pistols;
   entries under Handgun
Power index rating (PIR)
   double-action handgun, 267
   handgun ballistics, 241–244
Prone position
   described, 31–32
   handgun hunting, 295
Pump-action rifles, 78
Pump-action shotguns, 138, 147

Quivers, 338, 342

Ramrod, 376–377, 381–382
Range finders, 338
Rear sights, 223
Recoil
   benchrest target shooting, 68
   big-bore target shooting, 54–55
   double-action handgun, 266, 272
   handgun selection, 216
   revolver/semiautomatic
      compared, 207
   semiautomatic rifles, 74
   shooting techniques and, 28
   shotgun selection and, 135, 138
   single-action handgun shooting,
      254–255, 257
   skeet shooting, 148
   stock fit and, 93
   trap shooting, 175
Recoil lug, 91–93
Recoil pads, 105
   importance of, 97–98
   shotgun accessories, 186
Recurve bow
   action of, 309
   arrow selection and, 331
   See also entries under *Arrow; Bow*
Reloading, 407–424
   cost factors in, 407
   handgun cartridge reloader
      chart, 422
   metallic cartridges, 408–415
   rifle cartridge reloader chart,
      423–424
   safety considerations in, 407,
      431–432
   shot shells, 415–421
Reticule
   alignment of, 23–24
   description of 21–22
Revolvers
   accuracy of, 205, 207
   ammunition for, 214–215
   cylinder alignment, 230–232
   double-action shooting, 267
   experience with, 213–214
   firepower of, 207, 213
   hammer cocking, 257

muzzleloaders, 382
   recoil of, 207
   reliability of, 213
   safety removal, 214
   semiautomatic pistol compared,
      205–215
   single–action, 254
   speed loaders, 251
   target hammers, 247
   22 rimfire silhouette shooting,
      278, 282
   wear and, 232
   See also entries under *Handgun*
Rifle accessories, 97–107
   bipods and unipods, 102–104
   essential, 104–105
   gun cases, 106–107
   recoil pads, 97–98
   set triggers, 104
   slings, 98–102
   target shooting, 105, 106
Rifle ballistics, 109–127
   average velocities/energies table,
      126–127
   bullet shape and, 115–117
   comparative trajectory table,
      124–125
   comparisons in, 111–112
   game types and, 114–115
   magnums, 109–111
   table use, 117–119
   uniform performance and, 112–114
   wind draft table, 120
Rifle hunting, 36–49
   accuracy and, 37–38
   body movements, 44
   gun mount, 41–43
   moving targets, 44–49
   practice in, 38–39
   rifle configurations and, 36
   stance in, 40–41
   supporting rifle, 39–40
   trigger control, 43–44
Rifle selection, 71–88
   bolt-action rifles, 78–79
   centerfire rifles, 87
   factors in, 83
   features in, 83–84
   level-action rifles, 76–78
   pump-action rifles, 78
   rimfire rifles, 86
   semiautomatic rifles, 74–76
   silhouette target shooting, 59
   22 rimfire rifles, 71–73
   weight and length factors, 84–86
Rifle shooting positions, 31–35
   benchrest target shooting, 70
   big-bore target shooting, 54–55
   foot position, 40–41
   kneeling position, 33–34
   mounting the rifle, 41–43
   moving targets and, 48–49
   offhand shooting, 34–35
   prone position, 31–32
   rifle support and, 39–40

silhouette target shooting, 58
sitting position, 32–33
small-bore target shooting and, 51, 53
Rifle shooting technique, 25–30
  accuracy and, 37–38
  ballistics and, 48
  benchrest target shooting, 68, 70
  body movements and, 44
  breath control and, 25–26
  follow-through in, 28
  foot position and, 40–41
  leads, 46–48
  mounting the rifle, 41–43
  moving targets, 44–50
  position and, 48–49
  practice in, 38–39
  rifle support and, 39–40
  sight alignment and, 25
  silhouette target shooting, 62
  trigger control, 43–44
  trigger squeeze, 26–28
Rifle sights, 3–24
  adjustment of, 4–8
  alignment of, 3
  aperture sights, 10–14
  open sights, 8–10
  reticules, 21–22
  rifle tuning, 94–95
  rimfire rifles, 22–24
  small-bore target shooting, 53–54
  telescopic sights, 14–24
  variable-power telescopic sights, 18–20
  See also Telescopic sights
Rifle target shooting, 51–70
  accessories for, 105, 106
  benchrest shooting, 63–70
  big-bore shooting, 54–55
  gun selection and, 84
  silhouette shooting, 54, 56–63
  small-bore shooting, 51–54
Rifle tuning, 89–95
  accuracy and, 89
  action to stock fitting, 92–93
  bedding, 90
  free-floating barrels, 90, 92
  sights and, 94–95
  stock fit, 93–94
  trigger pull, 94
Right handedness. See Handedness
Rimfire rifles
  hunting with, 36
  selection suggestions for, 86
  sight adjustment, 8
  silhouette target shooting, 56
  small-bore target shooting, 51–54
  telescopic sights for, 22–24
  22 rimfire rifles, 71–73
  See also entries under Rifle
Riverside skeet, 179–180

Safeties
  handgun accessories, 248

revolver/semiautomatic pistol compared, 214
Safety considerations, 428–434
  ammunition storage, 431
  archery, 338, 346–347
  double-action handguns, 266
  field situation, 432–434
  handling guns, generally, 428, 431
  handloaders, 431–432
  muzzleloaders, 366, 393
  pointing guns, 431
  reloading and, 407
  security precautions, 431
  semiautomatic rifles and, 74, 76
  single-action handguns, 257
  target triggers and, 245, 247
  trigger pull adjustment and, 94
  unloading, 428
Scopes. See Telescopic sights
Screw tightning, 402–403
Semiautomatic pistols
  accuracy, 205, 207
  accuracy barrel bushing for, 232
  ammunition for, 214–215
  barrels, 251
  experience with, 213–214
  firepower of, 207, 213
  magazines of, 214, 251
  recoil of, 207
  regripping and, 257
  reliability of, 213
  revolvers compared, 205–215
  safety removal, 214
  single-action, 254
  tangs, 248, 251
  22 rimfire silhouette shooting, 276
  wear and, 232
  See also entries under Handgun
Semiautomatic rifles
  bolt-action rifles compared, 79
  lever-action rifles compared, 76
  selection of, 74–76
  See also entries under Rifle
Semiautomatic shotguns, 138
  cleaning of, 186
  skeet shooting, 145, 147
  See also entries under Shotgun
Set triggers, 104, 105
Shilen, Ed, 63
Shooting positions. See Rifle shooting positions; entries under names of specific positions
Shooting rests, 102–104, 105
Shotgun. See Crazy quail; Hunters' clays; Skeet shooting; Trap shooting
Shotgun accessories, 181–186
  adjustable chokes, 183–184
  barrels, 181
  cleaning kit, 186
  gun cases, 186
  recoil pads, 186
  screw-in chokes, 181–183
  slings, 184–185
  vent rib, 185–186

Shotgun ballistics, 187–202
  dram equivalent, 187–190
  lead shooting and, 160
  skeet shooting and, 148
  trap shooting and, 174–175
  velocity comparisons, 190–202
Shotgun hunting, 159–167
  aiming, 163
  coordination in, 166
  gun fit, 161–162
  leads in, 159–160
  mounting the gun, 161
  practice in, 166–167
  skeet shooting practice for, 159
  slug barrel for, 181
  stance for, 160–161
  swing and follow-through in, 163
Shotgun muzzleloaders, 387–388
Shotgun selection, 131–144
  actions and, 138–139
  barrel length and, 137–138
  choke considerations, 135–137
  gauge considerations, 131–135
  sights, 139, 141, 142–143
  skeet shooting, 145–148
  stocks, 139, 141
  trap shooting, 168–170
  weight and length considerations, 131
Shotgun sights
  shotgun selection and, 139, 141, 142–143
  skeet shooting, 147
Sight alignment, 25
Sighting
  adjustable chokes and, 183–184
  bow target shooting, 350
  shotgun hunting, 163, 166
  trap shooting, 172–174
Sighting-in, 284–287
Sights. See entries under types of guns; Telescopic sights
Silhouette target shooting, 54, 56–63
  accessories for, 105
  See also Handgun silhouette shooting
Single-action handgun shooting. See Handgun shooting (single-action)
Single-set triggers, 104
Sitting position, 32–33
Skeet shooting, 145–158
  body swing, 153
  eight stations in, 155–157
  foot position, 148, 149, 153
  game description, 153–154
  guns for, 145–148
  hunting practice, 159
  lead and follow-through, 154–155
  mounting, 149
  practice in, 157–158
  shot selection, 148
  slug barrel for, 181
  stance in, 149, 153
  trap shooting compared, 168, 174
  See also Trap shooting

Slings, 105
  positions of, 99, 102
  rifle bedding and, 90
  selection of, 98–99
  shooting position and, 31–32
  shooting technique and, 39
  shotgun accessories, 184–185
Slug barrel, 181
Small-bore target shooting, 51–54
  accessories for, 105, 106
Speed. See Leading; Moving targets
Speed loaders, 251
Stamina, 425–426. See also Physical
  condition
Stance
  body movements and, 44
  bow target shooting, 347
  double-action handguns, 273
  shooting techniques and, 40–41
  shotgun hunting, 160–161, 163
  single-action handguns, 262–263
  skeet shooting, 149, 153
Stock fit (rifle tuning), 93–94

Tangs, 248, 251
Target hammers, handguns
  cocking of, 257, 260–261
  handgun accessories, 247
Target stocks, handguns, 248
Target triggers, handguns, 245–247
Telescopic sights
  alignment of, 23–24
  benchrest target shooting, 67, 70

cleaning damage to, 399
description of, 14–24
handguns, 224, 227
power-selection guide for, 22
reticules, 21–22
rifle selection and, 85–86
shotgun selection, 142, 144
sight adjustment, 8
silhouette target shooting, 59, 62
variable-power, 18–20
See also entries under types of guns
38 caliber handguns, 216
38 Special cartridge, 216
Tiller adjustment, 328
Trajectory tables, 124–125
Trap shooting, 168–175
  aim and leads in, 172–173
  angle gauging in, 170–172
  game in, 168
  loads for, 174–175
  practice in, 174
  shot guns for, 168–170
  skeet shooting compared, 168, 174
  speed and swing in, 173-174
  See also Skeet shooting
Trap stocks, 147
Trigger
  bolt-action rifles, 79
  handgun accessories, 245–247
  rifle tuning, 94
  set triggers, 104
  shotgun selection, 139

stock fit and, 93–94
Trigger control
  benchrest target shooting, 68
  shooting techniques, 43–44
Trigger finger placement, 261–262
Trigger pull
  adjustment of, 232
  handguns and, 265, 266
Trigger squeeze
  double-action handguns, 270–272
  rifle shooting technique, 26–28
  single-action handguns, 262
22 rimfire cartridge, 216
22 rimfire handgun, 275–288
22 rimfire rifle, 71–73

Unipods, 102–104

Variable-power telescopic sights,
  18–20

Wind, 65, 67
Windage adjustment
  aperture sights, 12
  bow sights, 335
  handgun sights, 221, 224
Windage screws, 8, 10
Wind drift table, 120
Wounded game
  moving targets and, 45, 49
  shooting accuracy and, 37–38
  silhouette target shooting and, 63